YARDS AND GATES

Gender in Harvard and Radcliffe History

Edited by
Laurel Thatcher Ulrich

palgrave
macmillan

Frontispiece: "The Gate of Opportunity." Poster designed for the Radcliffe Endowment Fund by C. Howard Walker, 1922. From *Make a Record for Radcliffe* 2, no. 1 (Jan. 5 [1922]). Courtesy Radcliffe College Archives.

YARDS AND GATES

Copyright © Laurel Thatcher Ulrich, 2004.

All rights reserved. No part of this book may be used or reproduced in any manner whatsoever without written permission except in the case of brief quotations embodied in critical articles or reviews.

First published 2004 by PALGRAVE MACMILLAN™
175 Fifth Avenue, New York, N.Y. 10010 and
Houndmills, Basingstoke, Hampshire, England RG21 6XS.
Companies and representatives throughout the world.

PALGRAVE MACMILLAN is the global academic imprint of the Palgrave Macmillan division of St. Martin's Press, LLC and of Palgrave Macmillan Ltd. Macmillan® is a registered trademark in the United States, United Kingdom and other countries. Palgrave is a registered trademark in the European Union and other countries.

ISBN 1-4039-6098-4 hardback

Library of Congress Cataloging-in-Publication Data
Yards and gates : gender in Harvard and Radcliffe history / edited by Laurel Thatcher Ulrich.
    p. cm.
Includes bibliographical references and index
ISBN 1-4039-6098-4 (cloth)
1. Harvard College (1780-)—Students-History. 2. Radcliffe College—Students—History.
3. Women college students—Massachusetts-Cambridge—History. 4. Discrimination in education—Massachusetts—Cambridge-History. 5. Women—Education—Massachusetts—Cambridge-History. 6. Women—United States—Intellectual life. I. Ulrich, Laurel.

LD2160.Y37 2004
378.744'4 -dc22   2003058245

A catalogue record for this book is available from the British Library.

Design by planettheo.com

First edition: April 2004
10 9 8 7 6 5 4 3 2 1

Printed in the United States of America.

Contents

Snapshots: Women Working at Harvard

V. COEDUCATION BY DEGREES, 1941–2001

Snapshots: Midcentury Memories

Snapshots: Memories of Change

Preface

In the fall of 1997, Harvard College dedicated a new gate on the north side of the fenced-in "yard" that marks the oldest part of the university. On one side they mounted a plaque commemorating the moment, 25 years before, when female students began living in the freshmen dormitories in the Yard. On the other side of the new gate they attached a plaque with a sentence from the autobiography of the seventeenth-century Puritan poet Anne Bradstreet: "My heart rose up when I beheld a new country with new manners."

By planting Bradstreet's words on one side of the gate and the 1972 anniversary on the other, the College symbolically linked centuries of female achievement with a presumed landmark in Harvard's history. But in beginning women's history at Harvard in 1972, they also obliterated the history of Radcliffe, its ostensible sister college. That fact was not lost on the Radcliffe alumnae who bitterly objected to the supposed "Twenty-Fifth Anniversary of Coresidency." In their view the new gate fortified old fences.

The argument over the Bradstreet gate was one of several public controversies over relations between Harvard and Radcliffe in the years before the final merger of the two institutions. This anthology grew out of a joint effort by Harvard's Charles Warren Center for the Study of American History and Radcliffe's Schlesinger Library for Women's History to elevate historical discourse during that troubled period. Together, the Warren Center and the Schlesinger Library sponsored summer grants for senior thesis writers, organized two well-attended conferences on gender in Harvard and Radcliffe history, and supported the creation of a women's history tour of Harvard and Radcliffe Yards. This anthology is a final step in our collaboration.

Like the conferences that preceded it, this book brings together scholarly essays, "snapshots" from the archives, and memoirs. It includes work by professional historians and by the gifted undergraduates who were recipients of Warren Center-Pforzheimer grants for summer research. We began this project in the hope that serious history might improve communication within the Harvard-Radcliffe community, but our larger objective was to demonstrate new ways of writing history.

Although I am responsible for the final editing of the book, many others contributed to its completion. Mary Dunn, then director of the Schlesinger

Library, helped launch the larger project. Jane Knowles, Radcliffe archivist and later acting director of the Schlesinger Library, was co-conspirator from the beginning. Susan Hunt, then administrator of the Charles Warren Center, and Sylvia McDowell of the Schlesinger Library offered wonderful support in the early stages. Later, Elizabeth Nichols gathered and edited essays. Odette Binder assumed the many administrative tasks necessary to a project of this scope, and also compiled the index. Patricia Denault, associate director of the Warren Center, skillfully accomplished the final editing. I am grateful to Helen Horowitz and Ruth Feldstein for reviewing an early version of the manuscript, and to the many Harvard and Radcliffe alumni/ae—students, faculty, and staff—who shared their stories, insights, and frustrations. Most of all, I thank the authors who generously contributed their time and energy to this volume.

Laurel Thatcher Ulrich
Cambridge, Massachusetts
August 2003

List of Illustrations

INTRODUCTION: REWRITING HARVARD'S HISTORY

Laurel Thatcher Ulrich

In the opening pages of *A Room of One's Own,* Virginia Woolf imagines her fictional self walking across the grass at a college she calls Oxbridge when a stern beadle in a cutaway coat intercepts her. His outraged face reminds her that only the fellows and scholars are allowed on the grass. A few minutes later, inspired by her reverie on a passage from Milton, she ascends the steps to the library. "Instantly there issued, like a guardian angel barring the way with a flutter of black gown instead of white wings, a deprecating, silvery, kindly gentleman, who regretted in a low voice as he waved me back that ladies are only admitted to the library if accompanied by a Fellow of the College or furnished with a letter of introduction."[1]

I thought of these passages when late on a summer day in 1997 I walked into the newly renovated Barker Center for the Humanities at Harvard University. There was no living person to be seen in the grand public rooms, but everywhere I turned, the eyes of long-dead men looked down at me from their portraits. "What are you doing here?" they seemed to be saying. "Have you a letter of introduction?" There was no room on these walls for ladies. Nine eminences, bewhiskered and stiff collared, asserted the power of Harvard past.

At the gala dedication a few weeks later, the ghosts were less formidable. There were as many women as men in the crowd, and some of them were faculty. Professor Helen Vendler gave a graceful dedicatory reading that

An earlier version of this essay appeared in *Harvard Magazine* as "Harvard's Womanless History: Completing the University's Self-Portrait" (Nov.-Dec. 1999).

included lines from Elizabeth Bishop and Adrienne Rich, as well as from Lord Tennyson and Seamus Heaney. Dean Jeremy Knowles said how pleased he was that both the chief architect and the project director for the new Barker Center were women. The tone was light, but both speakers knew that something in the room needed exorcising.

I should have been reconciled, but as I started to leave the building, I felt a tug of something like responsibility. I was going to lecture on *A Room of One's Own* the following week, and I wanted to make sure I had come to terms with my own disquiet on my first visit to the Barker Center. Seeing two young women with "Staff" badges near the entrance, I asked if there was someone who might be able to answer a question about the portraits. They pointed to a woman standing in a nearby doorway.

I approached her awkwardly, concerned about raising what might be perceived as a negative question on a day designed for celebration. The renovation was lovely, I told her, but I was puzzled by the portraits. Had the absence of women been discussed?

"Of course, it was discussed," she said briskly. "This is Harvard. Everything gets discussed."

Was she annoyed at me? At the question? Or at a situation that forced her to explain a decision she did not control?

I pushed on. If the issue had been discussed, what was said? She told me there had been so much controversy about turning the old Freshman Union into the Barker Center that some people thought it was a good idea to keep some things just as they had been before.

"Besides," she continued, "Harvard doesn't have any portraits of women."

I was stunned. "No portraits of women! Not even at Radcliffe?"

"No," she said firmly. "Nothing we could use."

As she walked away, she turned and said firmly, over her shoulder, "You can't rewrite history."

Maybe *you* can't, I thought, but that is my job description.

I thank the woman in the Barker Center for this book. If I hadn't been preparing to teach *A Room of One's Own,* I might not have been so attuned to the subtle discriminations around me. If the woman in the Barker Center hadn't tossed off her quip about history, I wouldn't have been provoked into learning more about Harvard's past.

Most people assume that history is what happened in the long ago. Historians know that history is an account of what happened based on surviving evidence, and that it is shaped by the interests, inclinations, and skills of those who write it. Historians constantly rewrite history not only because we discover new sources of information but also because changing circumstances invite us to bring new questions to old documents. History is limited not only by what we *can* know about the past but also by what we *care* to know.

When I came to Harvard in 1995, I naïvely assumed that female students had been fully integrated into the university. I soon discovered ivy-covered partitions that divided the imaginative as well as the administrative life of the institution. My encounter with the woman in the Barker Center epitomized the problem. Obviously, if Harvard had no portraits of women, it couldn't integrate women into a vision of a past that required portraits. But the woman's allusion to history told me that the real problem was not missing artifacts but a curiously constricted sense of what belonged to Harvard's past. In the weeks that followed, I found the same narrow vision everywhere I turned.

The standard assumption was that female students were recent arrivals. Yet, by any historical standard, that notion is absurd. Women were studying with Harvard faculty at the Harvard Annex in 1879, 20 years before Henry Lee Higginson donated the money for the Freshman Union. Radcliffe College, chartered in 1894, is older than the House system, the tutorial system, and most of the departments now resident in the Barker Center. Its faculty—and sometimes its presidents—were members of the Harvard faculty. Radcliffe's history always has been an essential part of Harvard's history, yet few of Harvard's custodians of the past have acknowledged that.

Womanless history has been a Harvard specialty. The glossy booklet handed to guests at the Barker Center dedication was a particularly egregious example. This short history of the humanities at the university had nothing at all to say about Radcliffe's many distinguished graduates. All the featured artists and scholars were male. If the author had wanted to write a history that was not only more gracious and inclusive but also more accurate, he had plenty of source material to draw upon.[2] That he did not suggests that at some fundamental level the wall between Radcliffe and Harvard was impenetrable.

The brochure might have mentioned Gertrude Stein, A.B. 1898, as well as Henry Wadsworth Longfellow, LL.D. 1859. It could have pictured Pulitzer Prize–winning poet Maxine Kumin, A.B. 1946, as well as Pulitzer Prize–winning composer Walter Piston. And it could have included the fact that Henry Lee Higginson, the man whose portrait by John Singer Sargent commands the central foyer of the Barker Center, was not only the founder of the Boston Symphony Orchestra and the donor of the old Freshman Union, but a champion of women's education and the first treasurer of Radcliffe College.

Women staff of the Harvard College Observatory, 1920 (Harvard College Observatory).
See the essay by Jane Knowles, "Four Portraits," pp. 187-190.

Harvard may not be the world's greatest university, but it is certainly the nation's oldest, and no one who enters a dormitory, walks through the Yard, or sits in the library is allowed to forget it. But what the university chooses to celebrate about its past has been highly selective.

Part of the problem is that the history of women at Harvard is both extraordinarily long and exasperatingly complex. Does the history of undergraduate women begin with the Woman's Education Association in 1872, the establishment of the Harvard Annex in 1879, the chartering of Radcliffe College in 1894, the merging of classroom instruction in 1943, the awarding of Harvard degrees to Radcliffe students in 1963, or some time earlier or later?

The complexity of this history helps explain the anger of Radcliffe alumnae over the gala event at Harvard in the fall of 1997 commemorating the twenty-fifth anniversary of the integration of freshmen dormitories in the Yard. The College organized seminars for undergraduates, published an expensive picture book honoring recent alumnae, students, and faculty, and in a moving ceremony dedicated one of the Yard's many gates to women. Yet where was Radcliffe, some wondered, in this celebration of Harvard's past?

The inscriptions on the new gate added to the puzzlement. To the right was a cryptic quotation from the Puritan poet Anne Bradstreet, who died in 1672; to the left, a statement, beautifully engraved in gold, explaining that the gate "was dedicated twenty-five years after women students first moved into Harvard Yard in September of 1972." Intentionally or not, the organizers left a gaping hole between Bradstreet's death and the integration of Harvard dormitories 300 years later.

Walking into the Yard the Monday after the dedication of the gate, I saw two first-year women looking at the plaques. One of them had attended the dedication and was very excited about the day, but when I asked her what had happened in 1972, she said, "That was the year female students were first admitted to Harvard!" She was not alone in her confusion. Before the dedication of the gate, I attended a luncheon where a female faculty member who should have known better announced that the college was about to celebrate the "twenty-fifth anniversary of coeducation at Harvard." A few days later, a professor in my department used the same newly invented anniversary to comfort me on the absence of women in the Barker Center brochure. "After all, coeducation at Harvard is only 25 years old," he reasoned. Ironically, the very effort to add women to Harvard's public history erased a full century of their presence.

There was no conspiracy here, just collective complacency and an ignorance compounded by separatism. Writers and publicists at Harvard had never considered Radcliffe their responsibility. Radcliffe had been too busy negotiating its own status to promote its history.

Some departments within Harvard were, of course, aware of Radcliffe history. When the Afro-American Studies Department moved into new quarters on the second floor of the Barker Center, they embellished one wall of their main office with a roster of student photographs from the late nineteenth century to 1920. "I wanted our current students to know who came before them," Professor Henry Louis Gates explained. By including Radcliffe as well as Harvard students, Gates acknowledged the joint histories of the two institutions. He also offered an instructive history in interlocking discrimination. Not only are there fewer female than male students in the gallery; there are also more blank ovals where their photographs should be.

Fortunately, the intense discussion over relations between Harvard and Radcliffe encouraged other groups within the university to begin thinking more creatively about the university's history. In the introduction to a 1998 exhibit at the Harvard University Archives, archivists Patrice Donaghue, Robin McElheny, and Brian Sullivan took an expansive view:

Q: Since when have there been women at Harvard?
A: From the establishment of the "College at Newtowne" in 1636 to the present, the Harvard community has included women.
Q: Then where can we find them?

A: Everywhere—from the Yard dormitories, where they swept the halls and made the beds, to the library, where they cataloged the books and dusted the shelves—and nowhere, their documentary traces hidden between the entries in directories that include only faculty and officers, or missing from the folders of correspondence that they typed and filed.[3]

Despite the obvious problem with sources, the archivists were astonished at how much they could document once they put their minds to it. "From our initial fear that an exhibition on women at Harvard would barely fill one display case, we found that we could amass enough evidence to fill twice as many cases as we have at our disposal."

"The history of men's opposition to women's emancipation is more interesting perhaps than the story of that emancipation itself," Virginia Woolf wrote, adding that perhaps someday a student at one of the new women's colleges at Oxbridge might "collect examples and deduce a theory—but she would need thick gloves on her hands, and bars to protect her of solid gold."[4] Why did Harvard persist for so long in its curious system of apartheid? Shall we attribute it to tradition? Testosterone? Or the fabled prudery of proper Boston?

In studying historical attitudes toward women, some historians find the concept of gender useful. In academic usage, the word *gender* is neither a euphemism for sex nor a synonym for women. It is a convenient term for describing the varied and continually changing ways people define maleness and femaleness. In sociological terms, gender is a system of ordering social relationships based on perceived differences between the sexes. Put in more ordinary language, we could say that sex makes babies; gender manufactures pink and blue booties. Hence, gender is present even when women are not, perhaps especially so.

Gender is also, as historian Joan Scott has written, "a primary way of signifying relations of power."[5] In certain settings—fishing boats, construction sites, and elite colleges come to mind—men establish their own identities precisely in the exclusion of women from their work. It is probably no accident that the period in which Harvard achieved its ascendancy was also a period of rigid gender separation. In 1899, when Henry Lee Higginson donated $150,000 for the new Freshman Union, the men of Harvard and the women of Radcliffe dined, studied, and listened to lectures in different spaces. One could argue that Radcliffe was founded not so much to promote the education of women—which could have been accomplished through coeducation—as to protect new notions of maleness at Harvard. In the Freshman Union, the rugged virtues of Harvard men were symbolized in the masterful portraits of Theodore Roosevelt and Higginson, in the inscribed names over the central doorway of the 11 Harvard men who died in the Spanish-American War, and in the antler chandelier that still hangs in the Barker Center. Gender made demands on men as well as on women.

Gender norms also invited women to participate in male domination. Virginia Woolf was surely thinking of such arrangements when she wrote, "Women have served all these centuries as looking-glasses possessing the magic and delicious power of reflecting the figure of man at twice its natural size."[6] Our campuses are filled with such mirrors, from the Radcliffe gate on Garden Street given by Anna Lyman Gray "in Memory of her Husband, John Chipman Gray Teacher at Harvard Law School for 44 Years, Member of the Council of Radcliffe College from its Incoporation in 1894 until his death in 1915," to the greatest mirror of them all, Widener Library, offered to the university by a mother in memory of her son. In such a system, women enlarged their own status by caring for the reputations of men.

Today's undergraduates have a hard time understanding that hundreds of bright women lived happy and productive lives despite such assumptions. Some, of course, did not. In her famous fantasy about Shakespeare's sister, Woolf explored the costs of gender discrimination. Judith Shakespeare, born like her brother with a great gift, ran away from home, became pregnant by a London actor, and died in despair.[7]

Harvard history offers equally grim examples of unfulfilled genius. The Barker Center brochure described Henry Adams, A.B. 1838, as "a pioneering figure in the serious study of American history." What it didn't tell us was that his brilliant wife Clover (born Marian Hooper) was for years an unacknowledged assistant in his research (it was her language skills, not his, that got him into Spanish archives). Clover Adams killed herself on December 6, 1885, "by swallowing the potassium cyanide she had used in developing photographs." She probably suffered from what we would today think of as clinical depression, but at least one factor in her growing despair, biographer Eugenia Kaledin concludes, was an "education that exposed her to so much— but did not want her to take any of it seriously." She belonged to what Alice James, the thwarted sister of another of the pictured luminaries in the Barker Center brochure, the great psychologist William James, called "hemmed in humanity."[8]

Such a history could be narrated at every gate of the College, beginning with the west wall that commemorates the godly ministers who in the 1630s

Harvard scrubwomen seated outside Widener Library, date unknown (Harvard University Archives). See the essay by Linzy Brekke, "Fair Harvard?" pp. 159-172.

assured the survival of a learned ministry in Massachusetts by establishing Harvard College and by banishing the brilliant and recalcitrant Anne Hutchinson, a person who ultimately preferred the growing voice of God within to the authority of clerics. That is not, of course, the kind of history a donor would want to see printed in a glossy brochure.

But then neither would one want to include Henry Adams's own comment on Harvard education:

> Our men . . . cram themselves with second-hand facts and theories till they bust, and then they lecture at Harvard College and think they are the aristocracy of intellect and are doing true heroic work by exploding themselves all over a young generation, and forcing up a new set of simple-minded, honest prigs as like to themselves as two dried peas in a bladder.[9]

Virginia Woolf put the same idea more crisply as she contemplated the shut door of Oxbridge's library: "I thought how unpleasant it is to be locked out; and I thought how it is worse perhaps to be locked in."[10]

Ironically, the most powerful tribute to the value of a Harvard education is in the stories of those who struggled for so many years to achieve it. If I were to choose an unsung hero whose story ought to be preserved for future generations, I would pick Abby Leach of Brockton, Massachusetts, who came to Cambridge in 1878 to ask three Harvard professors for instruction in Greek, Latin, and English. Her brilliance and enthusiasm changed their ideas about female education. Thirty years later, Leach, then head of the Greek Department at Vassar College, spoke at Radcliffe's graduation. Radcliffe president Le Baron R. Briggs exaggerated only slightly when he said, "No one can speak more fitly at a Radcliffe Commencement than she who was the Commencement of Radcliffe."[11] John Harvard contributed books. Anne Radcliffe gave money. But Abbie Leach offered Harvard the best gift of all—a passion for learning.

In that spirit, a group of faculty, alumni/ae, students, and friends of Harvard and Radcliffe have joined together to begin "rewriting" Harvard's history.

The essays and memoirs offered here look at selected moments in the long history of gender relations at Harvard and Radcliffe. Five overarching arguments unite the individual pieces.

1. *There have always been women at Harvard.* Although colonial Harvard treasured its character as a "scholastic family of boys," there were women in the scullery and sometimes in students' beds. Nor were women entirely excluded from the scholarly life of eighteenth- and early nineteenth-century Harvard. Frances Lord's exploration of the scientific investigations of Hannah Winthrop, who in the 1760s acted as an assistant to her scientist husband, and Sally Schwager's discussion of the "Harvard women" who helped to create Radcliffe College show female intellectual communities operating in the background of a male institution. Margot Minardi's essay on two eighteenth-century slave women connected to Harvard and Linzy Brekke's story about early twentieth-century scrubwomen further document the ways in which women were present in an institution that ostensibly excluded them. The memoir by Phyllis Keller on nonfaculty administrators and the portrait essay by Jane Knowles on invisible faculty further extend the story.

2. *Arguments for and against female education have been an ongoing part of Harvard's history.* From Hannah Winthrop's plaintive letters to Mercy Otis Warren in the 1770s to Mary Bunting's exploration of coeducation in the 1960s, educated women have struggled to expand opportunities for women in an environment that often excluded them. Brian Sullivan's

research reminds us that even in the 1860s, an age of presumed "separate spheres," male students, too, fantasized about coeducation. Essays by Sally Schwager and Helen Horowitz on Radcliffe's founding and by Marcia Synnott, Marie Hicks, and Andrew Mandel on the mid-twentieth century show how changing social norms shaped an ongoing debate. In one generation a separate female institution seemed a stepping stone to eventual integration; in another it became a desirable end in itself, as women learned to combine "feminism and femininity in equal parts." These debates, though different in different eras, show why a simplistic narrative of gradual progress from discrimination to inclusion falsifies the past and prevents intellectual engagement with gender issues in the present.

3. *Radcliffe has a rich and compelling history that is related to but separate from Harvard's.* Radcliffe was never merely an extension of Harvard, as thousands of its graduates can testify. Karen Lepri and Gloria Bruce show how the development of all-female theatricals and sports provided expanded notions of what it meant to be female at the turn of the twentieth century. Jo Anne Preston traces the career paths of Radcliffe's graduates, showing how the initial optimism of early graduates gave way to the realities of a Depression-era economy and the difficulties of negotiating marriage, motherhood, and career. Marie Hicks explains why Oxford's female dons and Radcliffe's wary alumnae predicted disaster if male institutions opened their doors to women without first addressing fundamental inequities in their treatment, and Jennifer Stetzer shows how Radcliffe students who engaged in antiwar demonstrations in 1969 came to understand the value of female-focused political action. Memoirs by Radcliffe alumnae show how separatism alternately nurtured and inhibited individual development.

4. *Gender is present even when women are not.* Because gender is a relational category, one cannot talk about "femaleness" or "maleness" without implying its opposite. Conrad Wright's and Kristin Hoganson's essays look specifically at ideas about manliness at Harvard in different centuries, Wright emphasizing the attempt to turn young boys into "gentlemen" in the eighteenth century, and Hoganson stressing the concern 100 years later that too much studiousness would transform healthy males into "dudes." In every century, moralists pondered the impact of women on the development of boys. Student misbehavior in the early

nineteenth century led some men to propose the admission of girls, thinking the "softer sex" might civilize the young hellions. More commonly, Harvard officials considered young women both a temptation and a distraction. Until 1955, for example, the few women who attended services in Harvard's Memorial Church were forced to sit behind a screen. As late as 1966 Harvard student leaders still argued for the exclusion of women from Lamont Library, claiming that "Girls in Lamont would inevitably be a distraction."[12]

5. *Attitudes toward women intersected with attitudes toward others who seemed marginal to Harvard's mission.* In the 1770s, when Harvard undergraduates were debating "the legality of enslaving the Africans," a Boston slave, Phillis Wheatley, was astounding the Atlantic world with her poetry. As Margo Minardi explains, 14 of the 18 men who underwrote Wheatley's poems were Harvard alumni. Since the seventeenth century when English benefactors offered scholarships to Christian Indians, Harvard has prided itself on its liberality. Yet, as Marcia Synnott shows, well into the twentieth century written and unwritten quotas reduced the numbers of African Americans and Jews at the College. Through much of its history Radcliffe had a slightly better record of enrolling minorities, but it too had unspoken quotas and segregated housing. Synnott explains that it was a larger concern for civil rights in a period of competitive admissions that finally led to the end of quotas for women.

Taken together, the essays and memoirs in this volume argue for the centrality of gender in Harvard's history and for the importance of Radcliffe's history to Harvard's history.

There are still few portraits of women in Harvard buildings. For those who are interested, however, the University Information Center offers a self-guided women's history tour of Harvard and Radcliffe Yards.[13] This tour, created by Harvard graduate student Linzy Brekke with the guidance of Radcliffe archivist Jane Knowles, helps us to see that rewriting history often means simply noticing what has always been there.

Pausing in front of John Harvard's statue, visitors can now learn about his counterpart, Ann Radcliffe, "whose bequest of 100 pounds sterling in 1643 established the first scholarship fund" at Harvard College. Passing through the Yard, they will learn that H. H. Richardson's masterpiece, Sever Hall, "a turning point in American architecture," was the gift of another woman, Anne Sever. The tour not only highlights women's contributions to Harvard; it acknowledges the ironies of the College's exclusions. Long before Harvard admitted women to its classes, women were sustaining Harvard.

At Warren House near the Harvard Faculty Club, visitors learn about the bathtub that inspired Carolyn Heilbrun's mystery novel *Death in a Tenured Position,* a witty and trenchant attack on male privilege. Passing through Johnson Gate onto Cambridge Common, they will pass Anne Whitney's sculpture of the Civil War senator Charles Sumner. Whitney won a design competition in 1875 but, when the committee discovered that she was a woman, they rescinded her commission. Twenty-five years later, the statue was finally erected.

In Radcliffe Yard, they will see what women created for themselves and how that work in turn nourished Harvard. In the theatre in Agassiz House, for example, Radcliffe's Idler Club built a tradition of collegiate drama that paved the way for Harvard's famous "Workshop 47," a landmark playwriting and producing workshop. The histories of women and of men wind in and out of both Yards, inviting us to consider them together. Today, Fay House, once the administrative center of Radcliffe College, is the home of Harvard's new Radcliffe Institute for Advanced Study.

The Radcliffe Institute was born on October 1, 1999, when Harvard and Radcliffe formally merged. Some Radcliffe alumnae were dismayed at the seeming disappearance of their alma mater. As *Boston Globe* columnist Ellen Goodman wrote, "We wonder when a merger is a submerger, when we have been welcomed on our own terms and when we've been taken over."[14] Others saw the merger as the fulfillment of Radcliffe's original mission. Trustee Susan S. Wallach argued that the concept of the merger "was actually embedded in the wording of the 1882 Massachusetts Act by which the College was incorporated," and since Harvard had already assumed almost all responsibility for undergraduate instruction and housing, "the establishment of the Radcliffe Institute for Advanced Study was the act of getting our letterhead to catch up with what we actually were."[15]

In this volume's final essay, originally a speech to the entering class of 2005, Drew Gilpin Faust, dean of the Radcliffe Institute, summarizes the complex history of women and men at Harvard. Today's students, she explains, are the heirs of multiple traditions, some more noble than others: "If men and women are to be truly equal at Harvard, all traditions cannot be viewed as equal." In her view—and ours—a more inclusive Harvard demands a more inclusive history. This volume is one step in that direction.

Notes

1. Virginia Woolf, *A Room of One's Own* (New York: Harcourt Brace Jovanovich, 1929; 1981), 6.
2. He could, for example, have consulted Dorothy Elia Howells, *A Century To Celebrate: Radcliffe College, 1879-1979* (Cambridge, Mass.: Radcliffe College, 1978), a readable and still-useful survey.
3. Exhibit text, "Gender at the Gates: New Perspectives on Harvard and Radcliffe History," Harvard University Archives, Nov. 1998.
4. Woolf, *A Room of One's Own*, 55.
5. Joan Wallach Scott, *Gender and the Politics of History* (New York: Columbia University Press, 1988), 42.
6. Woolf, *A Room of One's Own*, 35.
7. Ibid., 46-50.
8. Eugenia Kaledin, *The Education of Mrs. Henry Adams* (Philadelphia: Temple University Press, 1981), 222, 229, 118.
9. Henry Adams to Robert Cunliffe, Aug. 31, 1875, quoted in Kaledin, *The Education of Mrs. Henry Adams*, 139-40.
10. Woolf, *A Room of One's Own*, 24.
11. Howells, *A Century To Celebrate*, 1.
12. Letter from the Harvard Undergraduate Council to Merle Fainsod, director of the University Library, Jan. 3, 1966, quoted in *Women in Lamont* (May 1999).
13. Linzy Brekke, *A Self-Guided Walking Tour of Harvard Women's History* (Cambridge, Mass.: Harvard Events and Information Center, 2000). Quotations following are taken from this pamphlet.
14. Ellen Goodman, "Something Gained, Something Lost," *Boston Sunday Globe*, April 25, 1999.
15. Susan S. Wallach, "A Radcliffe Trustee Looks Back: A Girl's Guide to the Merger," *Radcliffe Quarterly* (Spring 2000), also available on-line at http://www.radcliffe.edu/quarterly/200002/merger.html.

I.

BEFORE RADCLIFFE
1760–1860

CREATING A FELLOWSHIP OF EDUCATED MEN

Forming Gentlemen at Pre-Revolutionary Harvard

Conrad Edick Wright

Boys. They were everywhere. On the bed. By the doors to both small studies. Leaning against the faded, grimy, whitewashed walls. In the deepening shadows at one corner of the room. In the soft, golden, late-afternoon sunlight that still streamed through a large window illuminating the center of the wide-planked wooden floor. Occupying almost every patch of space in the sparsely furnished room 20 feet square. The date was July 14, 1767. The place was the dormitory chamber of Stephen Peabody, a Harvard junior.[1]

The boys were in Cambridge for a reason—to be set apart from the rest of New England society. Four years at Harvard College in a highly structured, almost entirely male community would transform their lives, they believed, turning them into educated men. At the start of this journey they were callow and unformed; by its end they hoped to leave college as gentlemen.

Samuel Moody, the master of Dummer Academy in Byfield, had prepared a bumper crop of candidates for the Harvard class of 1771, 13 of them. Between school and college, though, there was a hurdle—the admissions examination. Harvard's College Laws specified the process and standards for entrance. Each candidate faced an oral examination in the classics. Every boy had to be able to translate "the Greek and Latin authors in common use." He had to demonstrate his knowledge of grammar and his ability to write proper Latin. And he had to appear to be of good character.[2]

By custom, in mid-July at commencement time, when much of Massachusetts descended on Cambridge to enjoy the annual festivities that accompanied Harvard's graduation, New England's teachers brought in the boys they were offering for consideration. Thus Moody had herded his flock of students the 40 miles from Byfield to Harvard Yard to meet with Edward Holyoke, the College's elderly president, and whichever other faculty members happened to be available. Thanks to the large number of candidates on July 14, the process had taken so long that Moody had turned to Peabody, a former student of his at Dummer Academy, for a place to stay the night with his boys before setting out for home the next day.

As formidable as the admissions requirements now sound, the entrance examination did not pose much of a challenge for Moody's candidates—or for anyone else who had received decent classical preparation. To be sure, the prospect of a grilling by members of the College faculty was enough to intimidate nearly anyone; according to one of the boys, to "be weighed in the Scails" was a "fiery Tryal."[3] Nevertheless, the students and their teachers knew the school's expectations in advance, and in most cases the outcome was foreordained. Harvard accepted all 13 of Dummer Academy's candidates in 1767; between July 14 and July 20, the faculty examined 58 students, of whom it immediately admitted 49. Of the remaining 9, 2 were to return for re-examination after a few more weeks of review. The other 7 had to wait for another year.[4] Eventually, the class grew to 64, Harvard's largest up to that time.[5]

As entering freshman, they were about to begin a new phase of life. For most of them, college marked their first time away from home and family. Mother Harvard would try her best to keep an eye on her adopted children—to be a real alma mater for them—but college was a family in a certain sense only and there were limits to this oversight. Not yet on their own, the boys were nevertheless taking their first steps toward maturity.

The freshmen who began their studies at Harvard College in 1767 entered a community within a community.[6] The wider of the two was Cambridge, a town of 1,600 residents on the northern bank of the Charles River, a shade more than two miles west of the peninsula that Boston occupied. Cambridge had been settled in 1630 at the same time as Boston, and within half a dozen years it had become the educational center of the Massachusetts Bay Colony. During the late 1630s, the village had been a tiny cluster of perhaps 50 houses, most of them occupied by families who farmed at least part of the time, huddled on a flat, open meadow at the apex of the V-shaped plain eight miles long allotted to the town.[7] By 1767, the town's acreage had grown, then had shrunk, as tracts had been added to the original grant and later were subtracted whenever new settlements had broken away from it to become townships in their own right.[8] In the late 1760s, Cambridge retained its original village core, still complemented by some outlying agricultural districts.

Samuel Moody and his charges had traveled to Harvard from Byfield along a network of roads that passed through the farming and commercial towns of coastal Essex County, through Middlesex County, and into Cambridge from the northeast. Other boys came from the northwest through Cambridge's agricultural Menotomy precinct; from western farming communities through Watertown; and from Boston and points south by the long bridge that spanned the Charles River, then along a causeway made of dirt, stone, and gravel through the flats along the northern river bank to Wood Street, which led up a gentle incline a quarter of a mile, past a couple of dozen small houses, shops, and taverns to the College.[9]

Harvard College was located on the north side of Cambridge's main village. It was within a few yards of the boxy, spired meeting house, its façade of vertical planks painted white, and of the lemon-yellow county courthouse with a big red front door and an octagonal cupola that shared the traditional center of town.[10] About half of Cambridge's population lived here in modest two- and three-story wooden structures. The rest resided in the outlying districts, most of them on farms, but several dozen of them in elegant country homes belonging to members of Boston's merchant elite.[11]

Over the course of 130 years the village had grown up beside the College. In the late 1760s, the majority of its inhabitants lived along three long dirt roads that traveled up from the river roughly southwest to northeast and four shorter crossing roads. Tavern keepers, stable owners, carpenters, masons, glaziers (who replaced the windows the boys broke), tailors, cobblers—all had settled here to serve the needs of the College and its students.[12]

Harvard itself made up the smaller, inner community, the scholastic family the boys would come to know. The first sight of the College must have been impressive to almost any New Englander.[13] Unlike most of the structures of rural New England—squat, irregular, and made of wood[14]—Harvard's principal buildings were tall, imposing, Enlightenment statements about order: symmetrical Georgian brick piles with white-painted wood trim, aligned in two adjacent open quadrangles. The larger, southern square consisted of three edifices—Massachusetts Hall, Stoughton College, and Harvard Hall. Harvard Hall also served as one edge of the second quadrangle, together with Hollis Hall and Holden Chapel.

At any given time in the late 1760s and early 1770s, the College community numbered a little more than 200 souls, including faculty members, administrators, resident graduates, undergraduates, and employees both full- and part-time. Unlike the wider society, the College was almost entirely a male preserve. The handful of women, with but one exception, were marginal figures, easily overlooked. Aside from Elizabeth Hastings, the wife of Harvard's steward (or business manager) and the person in charge of the College commons, the only other women regularly present were several sweepers, who cleaned the dormitories in return for gratuities from the residents, and possibly a few cooks.[15] Even faculty families and their domestics seem to have been largely outside the undergraduates' ambit. The school was not quite a cloistered monastery and its students were not quite novice monks; beyond the formal demands of the College day, girls and women still had important places in the boys' lives. The prospect of socializing with the opposite sex made vacations, visits to the shops of Cambridge, and possibly even the morning and afternoon church services every Sunday worth anticipating. Nevertheless, to a remarkable extent the students spent their four years in college in the company of other boys and men.

In theory, Harvard was a rigidly hierarchical society, a relic of the medieval great chain of being, although student fractiousness meant that in reality the situation was otherwise. The school's formal, adult façade masked an informal, adolescent culture.

At the pinnacle of the formal structure was the president, the patriarch of this scholastic family. Then in descending order of honor and authority came the College's three professors, four tutors plus the librarian (who ranked with the tutors), a couple of degree holders serving Harvard as petty administrators, perhaps a dozen recent graduates who were preparing for the ministry, 170 or more undergraduates, and everyone else—cooks (at least some of whom were African Americans),[16] cleaning ladies, carpenters, masons, blacksmiths, and so on. Further status refinements differentiated the undergraduates. Each graduation year had priority over the succeeding ones, and a ranking system determined by the faculty established an individual hierarchy within each class, not of personal accomplishment but of family standing. (It was abandoned with the class of 1773.)[17] Hierarchical considerations carried over into required forms of address: in College exercises undergraduates went by their surnames, recipients of the bachelor's degree added the honorific "Sir," and masters of arts merited "Mr."[18]

Both by tradition and by College law, respect and deference were the due of the men at the top of the hierarchy. From a requirement that the undergraduates doff their caps whenever the president or a member of one of Harvard's two governing bodies (the Board of Overseers and the Corporation) was in the College Yard, to a regulation allowing any member of the faculty to draft a student to help him maintain order, to a set of sumptuary laws preventing undergraduates from wearing clothing that was elaborate beyond their station, the written statutes of the school established the authority of the boards, the president, the professors, and the tutors.[19]

Near the bottom of the ladder, above only the hired help, the entering freshmen endured a probationary year of submission, subservience, and initiation. One evening each year, shortly after the start of the fall term, the sophomore class instructed the freshmen to remain after chapel to learn the unofficial but longstanding codes, more than 20 of them, that also governed the College. "No freshman shall ware his hat in the College yeard except it rains, snows, or hails," the customs began. "No fresman [*sic*] shall talk saucily to his senior or speak to him with his hat on." Worst of all, the freshmen had to serve everyone above them in the college hierarchy. To avoid constant imposition, many freshmen took an individual senior as a patron and protector; in exchange for exclusive service, his senior would shield him from the demands of others.[20] With the end of classes in 1767, Stephen Peabody noted, the relieved first-year students "rejoic'd very much when their Freshmanship was up."[21]

The rules and customs that governed colonial Harvard established an invisible line between it and its Cambridge neighbors, making it a society in its own right. Of course, town and gown were not entirely isolated from one another. The wider world of women and men beckoned only a few steps from the entryways to the dormitories. Cambridge furnished Harvard with most of the domestics and tradesmen who maintained its facilities and fed its students. The undergraduates patronized the shops and taverns of the village. A small number of boys, most of them freshmen, boarded in town where they lived with local families, each of them overseen by the lady of the house. When Sunday came, the students went to church with the people of Cambridge. And frequent vacations offered opportunities to escape the Harvard cocoon. But the low wooden wall that enclosed the College grounds expressed the division between the wider and narrower communities. The freshman year was a boy's time of passage, of separation from his family, of entry into a structured, male world set off from that of his childhood, his introduction to a new, homosocial culture. When the College's tutors recommended a candidate to the president, they were doing more than allowing him to take a few courses. They were setting him apart from most of the rest of New England. Once he joined the College community, he began a new existence.

The new life was a never-ending commitment to personal improvement and social order. At the same time that many boys their age were undergoing an apprenticeship in a craft, Harvard students were novices of a different sort. Before the Revolutionary War, Harvard had a clear and important civic role. It was to define and nurture colonial New England's elite. Much as modern medical schools teach their charges to think like doctors and law schools mold their students into lawyers, pre-Revolutionary Harvard transformed its students into refined and educated gentlemen. A diploma from the College was the surest entrée into polite society.

Harvard and the other colleges established in the American colonies before independence were not simply finishing schools, though, at least not in the sense later generations have used the term, implying an alternative to academic rigor. Instead, academic and social objectives, classroom instruction and extracurricular cultivation complemented each other. Learning was a mark of a true gentleman. The nine American colleges stood at the pinnacle of formal education in the colonies.[22] At the same time, they provided an avenue into the honorable and genteel world of the upper reaches of colonial American society. Not only was Harvard the oldest of these institutions; it was the largest, the wealthiest, the most prestigious, the most demanding.

Lecture and recitation rooms were the site of formal instruction at Harvard. Professors at colonial Harvard devoted their classroom hours to lecturing. Public talks, for which faculty were paid with endowment income, were introductory and open to the entire student body. Private lessons, for which students in the upper classes paid additional fees, provided advanced instruction.[23] For the most part, the professors stood apart from the daily affairs of the undergraduates, as removed from their concerns as it was possible to be in a community of about two hundred members.

The tutors, far less remote from the undergraduates than the professors, bore the brunt of the responsibility of instruction day-to-day through the recitations they led. They also oversaw the students' conduct and morals. By College law they had to be unmarried: "If any Tutor shall enter into the Marriage State, his Place shall be *ipso facto* void," the institution's statutes read.[24] Without other family responsibilities, they would be surrogate uncles or older brothers to the undergraduates. Each tutor was assigned to a room in a dormitory, where he oversaw his obstreperous charges all day, every day when school was in session.

In class, the tutors conducted recitations in all the principal subjects of the College curriculum—Greek, Latin, logic (including ethics and metaphysics), and natural philosophy (mathematics and the sciences)—as well as offering less frequent instruction in such supplements as theology, geography, oratory, English composition, and belles-lettres.[25] Memorization was the key to success in most subjects. Monday through Thursday each week the tutors drilled their students on the basic topics within the college curriculum. Friday and Saturday were given over to the supplementary areas, of which elocution was of the greatest interest and practical importance. The ability to speak articulately to an audience was indispensable to a gentleman in an aural society such as colonial New England,[26] and in 1756 Harvard began to require each student to declaim publicly.[27] In the late 1760s and early 1770s, as the public arena filled with talk of the imperial crisis, the students wrestled with the same issue in their elocution classes: "Their declamations and forensic disputes breathe the spirit of liberty," one member of the Corporation remarked to a friend, ". . . but they have . . . been wrought up to such a pitch of enthusiasm, that it has been difficult for their tutors to keep them within due bounds."[28]

At the end of the year, when a class advanced so did its tutor, who remained with the same students as long as they stayed in school and he continued on the faculty.[29] Forced to deal with each other every day for years, a class and its tutor might come to loathe one another. It was almost inevitable that a tutor, as a drillmaster and monitor, would come into conflict with many of the students he supervised. But under the best of circumstances, a permanent bond developed between the teacher and his pupils, and at graduation a grateful class ordinarily gave its tutor a commemorative silver bowl or flagon.[30]

It is hard to imagine making a career of such a demanding office; indeed, each tutor's appointment was for only three years, although the position might be renewed repeatedly for additional three-year terms. Most tutors were recent graduates, men in their mid-20s—not much older than most of their students and often younger than a few of them—who served as instructors while they prepared themselves for the ministry.[31] Beginning at the end of the seventeenth century, though, the College was blessed—or cursed—with a number of tutors, who came and—it seemed—would never leave. Henry Flynt, a 1693 graduate, held the record for service. First appointed in 1699, he endured the adolescent horseplay of the undergraduates until 1754, when he was 79. Belcher Hancock, class of 1727, another long-serving tutor, left a week after commencement in July 1767 at the age of 58; he had spent a quarter of a century on the faculty minding College boys.[32]

With Hancock's resignation, the last of the career tutors was gone. The members of the class of 1771 thus encountered a young and energetic corps of instructors when they arrived in Cambridge. In 1767-1768, the average age of the four tutors was about 25. Each had graduated from Harvard within the past five years and most in this Congregationalist enclave were at least considering a life in the ministry once the classroom tour was over.

The tutors would need all the energy they could muster. Their days began early with morning prayers in the chapel at 6:00 A.M. and lasted until bedtime at 9:00 P.M. Breakfast was in the College commons. Each boy brought his own knife and fork; when he was done, he wiped the dirty utensils on the tablecloth. Recitations and lectures began at 8:00 A.M. and ran until the noon meal of beef and Indian pudding back in the commons. Then it was time for afternoon recreation, supper, and evening prayers. Harvard kept the undergraduates busy from early morning until bedtime and the tutors kept them under control.[33] And whenever a student transgressed one of the many College laws, the tutors met with the rest of the faculty to consider the crime, determine guilt, and decide on a sentence.

The College authorities sometimes referred to their students as "scholars," but the term carried none of its modern meanings connoting academic research. There was another purpose behind the memorization and drilling that occupied so many days of school. Boys attending Harvard in the late 1760s and early 1770s had "improvement,"[34] not the increase of knowledge, on their minds.

Self-cultivation took two forms, mental training and social refinement. Like a muscle, so the accepted theory went, the mind could be strengthened with exercise. Not every subject challenged the mental faculties: "The study of history cannot be considered as a severe application of the mind," one member of the class of 1774 advised an entering student two decades later. But "the habit of thinking closely" that certain other disciplines like mathematics and logic required could enhance the mental faculties.[35]

If some subjects were of at best limited use in strenuously training the mind, then there had to be a different reason for them to belong in the College's curriculum. Pre-Revolutionary Harvard was not a vocational school devoted to indoctrinating would-be doctors, lawyers, ministers, or merchants, so the reason was not preprofessional. Harvard undergraduates studied the classics, English literature, oratory, geography, and, for extra fees, French and dancing because every real gentleman needed to be acquainted with them. As one alumnus told an incoming student: "The Roman and Grecian writers of established reputation will assist you in thinking, writing, and speaking well. In their works you will find the most liberal and elegant sentiments. Many of their productions may be considered as finished models of good sense, and good language."[36] Meanwhile, an acquaintance with the French language introduced the student "to the politest people on earth."[37] The College licensed a local instructor, a Mr. Peter Curtis, to teach the undergraduates French, although it did not grant him a regular faculty appointment.

Curtis also taught dancing, a subject that included etiquette, though he offered this instruction across the river in Boston without the official approval of the College government. Dancing class provided the students with an opportunity, which they savored, to meet girls of their own age. Twice a week between 1771 and 1774 boys and girls from Boston's finest families, together with a representation of Harvard undergraduates, gathered at Curtis's school on Queen Street to learn how gentlemen and ladies carried themselves in polite society. From courtly forms of address to the steps of reels, cotillions, and gavottes, dancing masters like Curtis showed their students the conventions of public intercourse in eighteenth-century Anglo-America's most refined circles. Of these, instruction in the minuet was perhaps the most important because of the risk the dance presented for public humiliation. In the most elevated social circles, every assembly began with a minuet. Each couple danced it alone in turn before the critical eyes of the rest of the company. A man who could not perform a creditable minuet, Harvard students knew, instantly and publicly revealed himself to be no gentleman.[38]

Ambitious boys often knew better than their parents that the ability to dance was a social necessity. Sammy Phillips, a member of the class of 1771, was from rural Andover, something of a cultural backwater in the late 1760s and early 1770s, and his parents did not appreciate the importance of an elegant line at an assembly. During the fall of his junior year, Sammy asked his parents for permission to attend dancing classes. His father was not happy with this prospect, afraid "that it will Engross too much of your Mind and Time now, and will in Time be a great Temptation to Attend Balls and

Assemblies, to lead you into Company and to be abroad at unseasonable hours." But Sammy would not be deterred, and Samuel, Sr., relented: "I shall not Object to your Attending one quarter of a year," he concluded, "the Tutors consent being first obtain."[39]

Four years of instruction in the classics, logic, natural philosophy, theology, oratory, English composition, and belles-lettres, as well as in French and dance, did not ordinarily produce creative scholars. Even after years of study, this learning was often superficial and ornamental.[40] If Harvard did not spawn many intellectuals of the first order, though, no one was particularly concerned. Harvard undergraduates were ambitious, but their aims had little to do with the life of the mind. The College's purpose was to provide New England with a polished elite—with gentlemen. No one gave the possibility of an intelligentsia even a thought.

On May 12, 1770, the president, professors, and tutors of the College voted to rusticate Winthrop Sargent, a senior two months shy of graduation. Short of expulsion, rustication was Harvard's most severe penalty for students who were failing to meet expectations. Fourteen of the 204 members of the classes of 1771-1774 were rusticated at some point during their College careers.[41] Reprimands, fines, and degradation—reducing a student from his natural place in the class order to a lower position[42]—served when transgressions were minor, but Sargent, age 17 and no gentleman, had become a pus-filled boil on the College's face, a wine-red stain on its good name. Nothing less than rustication—suspension for a year in an isolated town under the supervision of a trusted rural minister—would do. Someone who had been cast out could have no interaction with the College or its students until he had completed his sentence, on pain of further punishment for himself and anyone whom he contacted. For a year, as far as the members of the College community were concerned, he was a nonperson, an outcast. And if the second most-severe sanction were not enough, then there was always expulsion.

Sargent had run riot during the course of the spring. College life with its genteel aspirations had become too confining for him. By the time the faculty voted to excise him from the body collegiate, it had compiled a lengthy bill of particulars. Toward the end of March, Sargent had entertained two prostitutes overnight in his dormitory room. On May 3 and again on May 8 he had taken a pistol outside and fired it wildly, endangering the citizens of Cambridge. When the faculty had called him in to discuss these actions, his response had been "insulting and Contemptuous." Sargent had then joined two school-mates in assaulting Captain William Angier, a Cambridge resident who had reported on his earlier misdeeds to the College authorities. All three boys had been "for a great while in their general Conduct, idle vicious, and disorderly persons disturbing of the peace of the College and of the town of Cambridge and a common Nuisance to both."[43]

Vandalism, petty thefts, rowdiness, and consorting with prostitutes were recurring problems for the College authorities. In June 1771, a sophomore and a junior torched the College outhouse late one night after unsuccessfully attempting to force a cow into Holden Chapel. A year and a half later, after his readmission, one of the two was also apparently suspected of breaking into a student's chest and stealing a small sum of money. An affluent member of the class of 1773 even kept a prostitute for several weeks in a house near the Yard.[44]

Rustication was a public humiliation no less than confinement in a New England town's pillory had been during the seventeenth century. Harvard reserved the punishment for acts that violated basic community values. The boys who burned down the outhouse in 1771 received this sentence.[45] The president imposed it in the center aisle of the chapel before the entire community except the paid help.

Most boys accepted this punishment sullenly or angrily but without overt protest. Not Winthrop Sargent. He and his confederates "all exclaimed with a loud voice the Sentence is unjust and then threw themselves out of the Chapel."[46] Sargent would not be back for 12 months when, after a humble public apology in the chapel before the community that had exiled him, he would contritely take his place with the class of 1771, which had entered a year after he had.

Winthrop Sargent led a more tumultuous college life than most under-graduates, but the central lesson of his experience had broad application. Social realities rarely conform in all respects to social theory, and in fact Harvard was not the "deliberately, elaborately, smotheringly paternalistic" hierarchy to which its government aspired.[47] The boys who made up most of the College community had their own ideas about its objectives and values. Less visible than the formal hierarchy of the administration and the faculty was a second—more fluid and voluntary—structure. Out of sight except when misconduct or rebellion brought it into view, there was an adolescent society, a boys' culture.

Early each fall, at about the same time the sophomores instructed the freshmen in the College customs, the two classes observed a distinctively masculine ritual, a wrestling tournament that went on for several days. The sophomores, a year older and a year more experienced, usually prevailed, thus confirming their social dominance. But no matter what the outcome, one lesson for the newcomers in this particular custom was that there was room at Harvard for battlers as well as conformists.

After prayers one evening during the second week of the school year, the sophomores arranged the members of the two lowest classes in a large ragged circle on the playing field behind Holden Chapel. In 1767, the first day of wrestling was Thursday, August 20. When everyone was in place, one of the sophomores swaggered to the center of the makeshift arena, challenged the newcomers' manhood, and dared them to send out their best. At first, there were dozens of matched jousts. Puny freshmen fought puny sophomores; burly members of each class wrestled with one another. From his vantage point as a junior, Stephen Peabody could watch the proceedings with detachment: "there are some smart Fellows in the Freshman class," he concluded after a day of grappling. Eventually, after several more sessions of combat following evening prayers, only one boy remained standing. The winner was Daniel Tyler, a freshman from Canterbury, Connecticut, who whipped two sophomores on the final evening: "& so," Peabody concluded, "the Freshman Class have concur'd [conquered] the Sophomores in Wrestling."[48]

Pre-Revolutionary Harvard was no meritocracy. College honors often went to the wealthy and well connected. Within the school, though, there was a space, an informal culture of adolescents largely beyond the reach of the faculty, for undergraduates to prove themselves no matter where they stood in the formal class list. Boys could pick their own friends and associates. Whenever they did, they established their own hierarchies—of insiders and outsiders, of students who held the respect of their peers and those who did not, of scholars and slackers, of leaders and followers.

Over the course of an academic year, students came together in a variety of combinations. Sometimes they organized to stage plays for each other; classical themes were popular.[49] Sports occupied some of the boys at all times of year; during the warmer months, in addition to wrestling, the students played at quoits and cricket, and they challenged each other to foot races across the College playing field. Fisher Ames, of the class of 1774, liked to go hunting, and during the winter he and friends sometimes traveled a mile to Fresh Pond to skate.[50] As part of his freshman year of initiation in 1768, Clement Weeks chipped in to buy bats, balls, and other athletic equipment for the undergraduates.[51] Swimming with schoolmates in the river during hot weather in 1773 cost John Paddock, a freshman, his life when he could not escape an undertow.[52] Stephen Peabody often liked to join in group sings in a dormitory room during the evening after prayers.[53] And toward the close of their senior year, ten of the more stylish members of the class of 1772 took a day off for an excursion to the ocean at Point Shirley in what is now the town of Winthrop.[54]

Student clubs and societies, almost all of them kept secret from the faculty and other nonmembers, also occupied the attention of many under-graduates. Prayer societies, with which the College administration would certainly have had no reservations, dated back at least to 1707. Most Saturday evenings in the late 1760s, a small group of undergraduates still met in a dormitory room for a "private meeting" to pray together.[55] Another group of undergraduates, concerned about a rash of profanity, gambling, and irrever-ence at the College, organized an association in 1767 for the suppression of vice.[56] And social clubs for promoting cultural interests and genteel conduct, the most desirable of goals to the minds of the faculty and administration, dated from at least as early as the formation in 1728 of the Philomusarian Club for discussion and poetry reading.[57]

In the early 1770s at least five undergraduate clubs, four of them secret societies, were active at Harvard. The Speaking Club, the Mercurian Society (which merged with the Speaking Club 18 months after establishment in September 1771), and the Clitonian Society all promoted social polish through oratory, discourse, and literature. As the political temperature in the American colonies started to rise in the early 1770s, current events were often on the clubs' agendas.[58] Surviving membership rosters indicate that these clubs drew impartially from most sectors of the student population, with one exception—almost all the members lived in College housing, where upper-classmen predominated. In the fall of 1771, of the 49 club members in College, 46 lived in a Harvard dormitory.[59]

Secrecy ensured the members' privacy from prying eyes, although it seems that most of the fraternities were really interested in their own independence and had no disorderly behavior to hide. In fact, far from engaging in subversion, clubs with cultural objectives reinforced the class-room lessons of the College. The only student organization that did have a reason to conceal its activities, the Spunke Club, made up of aspiring physicians, apparently plotted to rob graves to provide bodies for anatomical investigations.[60] Only the Martimercurian Company, an undergraduate militia with more than 60 members, established in 1769 or 1770, acted in the open. Wearing dashing uniforms of long blue coats faced in white, nankeen breeches, white stockings, black gaiters, and three-cornered hats, and carrying muskets supplied by the province, the members of the company drilled in public, then passed around buckets of rum toddy.[61]

Away from home, in many cases for the first time, the students learned to rely upon themselves and one another. Although grownups were around, they were less of a presence for these boys than in any previous situation they had encountered. Not yet independent of adult supervision, nevertheless they were beginning to strike out on their own.

Collectively the undergraduates had more power over the affairs of the College than either they or the authorities acknowledged. In a College community of slightly more than 200 at any one time, the undergraduates numbered at least 170 and sometimes as many as 180, or nearly 90 percent of the whole. When the students believed that they had a grievance, they were so numerous that Harvard's administration had to pay attention to them.

During the late 1760s, a series of student actions shook the College. In the spring of 1768 the most serious of these upheavals, a student strike, crippled the school for weeks and caused the entire senior class to petition for permission to transfer to Yale.

At the root of the disturbance was concern among the tutors about the laxity of some students in class. By custom, pupils who had failed to prepare for recitation could excuse themselves by answering "nolo"—"I don't wish to"—when called upon to recite. To force the undergraduates to study, the tutors announced on March 21 that henceforth they would accept only excuses presented in advance. Only the seniors, whose College careers were nearly at an end, were exempt. The lower three classes revolted immediately. The new policy was "so rediculous that it is really sickish," junior Stephen Peabody angrily entered in his diary.[62]

Tensions swelled between March 21 and April 4. Most of the underclassmen indignantly refused to comply with the new regulation, and at night the tutors had to dodge the brickbats that exploded through their windows. One tutor's room was ransacked and another found his door covered with manure. Rumors flew that one tutor had imprisoned a freshman for most of a day to try to compel him to inform on the ringleaders of the uprising.

The undergraduates' trump card was to quit school, leaving it a broken shell. On April 4, more than 100 underclassmen resigned their rooms, and the seniors, who had tried to avoid becoming involved in the argument, petitioned President Holyoke for permission to transfer to the college in New Haven. The prospect for Harvard was a catastrophic reduction in the student body to about 40.

By resigning their chambers and returning home, however, the students inadvertently sabotaged their own cause. No longer in regular contact with one another, they were prey to the maneuverings of the faculty, who gradually persuaded individual strikers to apologize, abandon their cause, and return to school. By early May, all but a few agitators had come back to Cambridge. One ringleader transferred to Rhode Island College rather than apologize for his role in the upheaval. By early July, though, the rest were back in class after offering humbling statements of repentance.[63]

Harvard had never seen anything like the disturbances of the 1760s. Student misbehavior was nothing new, but the concerted actions of angry undergraduates were a concern. It was hard to imagine what else might go wrong.

"If any man wishes to be humbled and mortified, let him become President of Harvard College," Edward Holyoke declared on his deathbed in 1769.[64] By the end of his tenure, after more than 30 years in office, the frustrations of dealing with fractious students finally became too much for the father of the College community. If Holyoke had known about the fate of his successor, though, he would have felt grateful to escape to his grave with his reputation intact. For all the problems due to student disobedience in the pre-Revolutionary years, the source of Harvard's greatest embarrassment was its twelfth president, Samuel Locke.

The search for a new president took half a year. In advance, no one could have guessed the surprising candidate it yielded, the short, stout, handsome, and thoroughly obscure minister of the Congregational Church in Sherborn, Massachusetts.[65] Locke, who had graduated from the College in 1755, was only 37 years old at his inauguration, the youngest man ever to hold Harvard's presidency, 42 years younger than Holyoke had been at the time of his death. The new president had never served on the faculty in any capacity, although between taking his two degrees he had spent some time in the late 1750s at the College as a petty administrator. Over slightly more than a decade between his ordination in November 1759 and the invitation to succeed Holyoke, he had come to the public attention only once, in 1762, when he preached the annual sermon before the Ancient and Honorable Artillery Company in Boston.

As observers thought about Locke's selection, though, it began to make sense to some of them. John Adams, a classmate of Locke, was full of praise for the appointment: "no Man was better qualified."[66] And Andrew Eliot, a member of the Corporation, saw at least half a dozen arguments in Locke's favor: "He has fine talents, is a close thinker, had at College the character of a first rate scholar; he is possessed of an excellent spirit, has generous, catholic sentiments, is a friend to liberty." Locke was "universally acceptable so far as I have heard."[67]

Personable and approachable to a degree that Holyoke had never been, Locke quickly set about to win the favor of members of the governing boards, faculty, and students alike. His most lasting legacy was the decision a few months later to abandon class ranking based on family dignity in favor of alphabetical order.[68] The Corporation responded at the July 1773 commencement by awarding him an honorary doctorate. By now, though, Locke was already sowing the seeds of his own downfall. When his wife's housekeeper became pregnant during the summer of 1773, President Locke tried to bribe her to disappear. She refused, and Locke, humiliated and under pressure from the College's Corporation, quietly resigned his office on December 1.[69]

What kind of moral leadership could an adulterer provide the young boys under his direction? Decency and propriety may have distinguished Locke's induction into office; his departure was characterized by nothing of the sort.

Commencement arrived four years, almost to the day, for most boys from their first, heart-gripping interviews with the tutors and the president. The college years were over. It was time to celebrate.

During the eighteenth century, Harvard commencement was the great summer festival in eastern Massachusetts, an excuse not only for the graduates and their families but also for men and women who had nothing to do with the College to drop their work for a day and carouse. Graduation took place each year on the third Wednesday of July. In 1771 that day fell on July 17. Inside the Yard, and in the meeting house of the First Parish, where the College conducted the formal morning and afternoon exercises, the atmosphere was dignified and decorous, for the most part. To the north of the Yard, however, in instructive counterpoint to the mood at the College ceremonies, the ambience was anything but seemly. If the goal of college was to prepare young men for genteel and honorable lives, then the activities off the College grounds were an unmistakable reminder of another path.

The members of the class of 1771 performed during the morning exercises, offering addresses, dialogues, and disputations. It was a high honor to be asked to speak at graduation, but the student commencement parts were also the most unpredictable and potentially controversial pieces on the program.[70] One irreverent speech in 1771, on "Quackery in all Professions," caused such hilarity at the expense of the dignity of the careers that many of the graduates planned to pursue that a Boston minister angrily published a pamphlet deploring "the satyrical drollery at Cambridge last Commencement Day."[71]

During the afternoon, following a recess for dinner, the master's degree candidates took their turn, offering disputes and an English oration. After the degrees were conferred, the ceremonies concluded with a Latin oration. According to the notice that the College placed in the Boston newspapers, "The whole was conducted with Elegance and Propriety much to the Credit of the College and to the Satisfaction of the Audience."[72]

The graduates and their families had been preparing for the festival for weeks, laying in stores and securing rooms to entertain guests.[73] In the interval between the morning and the afternoon exercises, Colonel John Murray celebrated the graduation of his son Daniel in 1771 with a lavish commencement spread attended by "A Large Company, the Governour, Councill and too many to Enumerate."[74] The following year, George Inman's graduation party at his family's Cambridge home boasted a guest list of 347, 210 of whom dined at a single long table.[75]

Even at their most raucous, though, the parties of the graduates and their families were staid in comparison with what was going on to the north of the College grounds. A more rowdy swirl of activities ebbed and flowed outside the Yard and the meeting house. Commencement was carnival time, complete with jugglers, caged animals, paupers, pickpockets, games of skill, and games of chance. In one corner, archers tested their marksmanship. In another, wrestlers grappled with each other. Fat dripping from grilling meats caused smoky cooking fires to leap and dance. If the College exercises attracted dignitaries, the parents of graduates, and alumni, the festivities outside the Yard drew a considerably less genteel audience—sailors, farm laborers, journeymen mechanics, apprentices. Row upon row of large cream-colored tents appeared almost overnight, the work and property of opportunistic petty entrepreneurs. Each tent held tables and chairs as well as a crude counter to serve as a bar. For the rugged men and women who came to Cambridge each year to have fun, not to observe a collegiate rite of passage, commencement was a time for drinking, gambling, and cavorting.

Dusk came late to Cambridge in mid-July. The festivities were winding down. By sunset, many of the revelers, gentle folk and common folk alike, were beginning to wend their way home to Lynn or Dedham or Waltham. For many of those who had spent the day in Cambridge, the night would be short enough to sleep off the glow before the morrow came. And for the proud graduates, it was now time to think about the future.[76]

Notes

This essay is adapted from the author's forthcoming book, *Revolutionary Generation: Harvard Men and the Consequences of Independence* (Amherst: University of Massachusetts Press).

1. Stephen Peabody, Diary, July 14, 1767, Massachusetts Historical Society, Boston.
2. "The Laws of Harvard College [1767]," *Publications of the Colonial Society of Massachusetts* 31 (1935): 347.
3. Samuel Phillips, Jr., to Samuel and Elizabeth Phillips, June 15, 1767, Phillips Papers, Phillips Academy, Andover, Mass.
4. Peabody, Diary, July 18, 20, 1767.
5. *Sibley's Harvard Graduates* 17:466-67.
6. Although it takes a different approach than I have, the most valuable study of the relationship between Harvard and Cambridge is John D. Burton, "Puritan Town and Gown: Harvard College and Cambridge, Massachusetts, 1636-1800" (Ph.D. diss., College of William and Mary, 1996).
7. For a map of Cambridge in 1638, see Samuel Eliot Morison, *The Founding of Harvard College* (Cambridge, Mass.: Harvard University Press, 1935), between pp. 192-93.
8. Lucius R. Paige, *History of Cambridge, Massachusetts, 1630 to 1877* (Boston: H. O. Houghton, 1877), 3.
9. Rupert Ballou Lillie, *Cambridge in 1775* (Salem, Mass.: Newcomb and Gauss, 1949), 7 and map.
10. Lillie, *Cambridge in 1775*, 11-13; Bainbridge Bunting and Robert H. Nylander, *Survey of Architectural History in Cambridge: Report Four: Old Cambridge* (Cambridge, Mass.: MIT Press, 1973), 33; *An Historic Guide to Cambridge* (Cambridge, Mass.: Daughters of the American Revolution, 1907), facing p. 14.
11. Burton, "Puritan Town and Gown," 18-20.
12. On the economic relationship between Harvard and Cambridge, see Burton, "Puritan Town and Gown," chap. 6; see esp. pp. 182-86 for a discussion of Harvard as an employer.
13. Winfred E. A. Bernhard, *Fisher Ames, Federalist and Statesman, 1758-1808* (Chapel Hill: University of North Carolina Press, 1965), 20.
14. Richard L. Bushman, *The Refinement of America: Persons, Houses, Cities* (New York: Alfred A. Knopf, 1992), 110-17.
15. Information on the cooks is very difficult to discover. Extensive searching has resulted in no firm information on either their number or their sex.
16. Samuel Phillips, Jr., to Samuel and Elizabeth Phillips, Dec. 1, 1767, Phillips Papers.
17. Clifford K. Shipton, "Ye Mystery of Ye Ages Solved, or, How Placing Worked at Colonial Harvard & Yale," *Harvard Alumni Bulletin* (Dec. 11, 1954), 258-59, 262-63. Yale followed a similar practice until 1766, when it opted for the alphabet instead. See Brooks Mather Kelley, *Yale: A History* (New Haven, Conn.: Yale University Press, 1974), 75-78. Harvard's decision to reorder the class of 1771 came after a complaint over rankings by Samuel Phillips, Sr., who understood that it had the potential for causing discontent and jealousy.

As Samuel, Sr., wrote to Samuel, Jr.: "You are now in the most Difficult Scituation, the Eyes of all Above and below you will be upon you, and I wish if it might be that you could be at home till the talk about the Change was a little over, but this dont Expect. Every word, action & even your Countenance will be watchd perticularly by those who Envy you, and perhaps by those who do not; Therefore keep as much retired as possible, wave all Conversation about it, dont let it appear that you are in the least degree Affected wth the Change. If any difficulties should arise with your any of your Classmates, that now fall below you, treat them with all possible tenderness" (Aug. 29, 1769, Phillips Papers). At about the same time that Harvard and Yale gave up their traditional ranking system, many New England towns abandoned a similar practice—assigning seats in their meeting houses based on personal dignity. See David Hackett Fischer, *Growing Old in America* (1976; rev. ed., New York: Oxford University Press, 1978), 78-79.

18. These terms were also used at other American colleges; see Melvin Yazawa, *From Colonies to Commonwealth: Familial Ideology and the Beginnings of the American Republic* (Baltimore, Md.: Johns Hopkins University Press, 1985), 66.

19. "Laws of Harvard College," 350, 355, 359.

20. "College Customs Anno 1734/4," *Publications of the Colonial Society of Massachusetts* 31 (1935): 383-84; Sidney Willard, *Memories of Youth and Manhood,* 2 vols. (Cambridge, Mass.: J. Bartlett, 1855), 1:258-59.

21. Peabody, Diary, July 14, 1767.

22. The other eight, in order of founding, were: William & Mary (1693), Yale (1701), Princeton (1746), Columbia (1754), Pennsylvania (1755) , Rhode Island College—soon renamed Brown (1764)—Rutgers (1766), and Dartmouth (1769).

23. Seymour E. Harris, *Economics of Harvard* (New York: McGraw-Hill, 1970), 39, 139; Thomas Jay Siegel, "Governance and Curriculum at Harvard College in the 18th Century" (Ph.D. diss, Harvard University, 1990), 237, 238, 251-52; Samuel Eliot Morison, *Three Centuries of Harvard, 1636-1936* (Cambridge, Mass.: Harvard University Press, 1936), 80n.

24. "Laws of Harvard College," 377.

25. Harvard's curriculum was quite similar to what one found at the other colonial colleges: see, for example, Kelley, *Yale: A History,* 78-83; Mark A. Noll, *Princeton and the Republic, 1768-1822* (Princeton, N.J.: Princeton University Press, 1989), 20-21.

26. Oratorical training led to periodic public exhibitions and, ultimately, to public addresses at commencement. Declamations took two forms: syllogistic, in which an individual speaker logically analyzed a proposition, and forensic, in which two students debated a point at issue. At the same time that Harvard was placing increasing emphasis on public speaking, the same reform was taking place at other American colleges, including Yale and Princeton. See Christopher Grasso, *A Speaking Aristocracy: Transforming Public Discourse in Eighteenth-Century Connecticut* (Chapel Hill: University of North Carolina Press, 1999); Siegel, "Governance and Curriculum at Harvard College," 265-66; Josiah Quincy, *The History of Harvard University,* 2 vols. (1840; Boston: Crosby, Nichols, Lee, 1860), 2:124ff.; Louis Leonard Tucker, *Puritan Protagonist: President Thomas Clap of Yale College* (Chapel Hill: University of North Carolina Press, 1962), 77; Noll, *Princeton and the Republic,* 35.

27. Burton, "Puritan Town and Gown," 44; Morison, *Three Centuries of Harvard,* 89-90.

28. Quincy, *History of Harvard University,* 2:163.

29. Until 1767, each tutor was responsible for his class's instruction in each College subject. A reform introduced that year assigned each tutor to one of the four major academic subjects—Greek, Latin, logic, and natural philosophy. In addition to his special subject, though, each tutor continued to have charge of a graduating class, which he instructed in all the minor subjects until either he left or the class did. Morison, *Three Centuries of Harvard,* 90.

30. For a late example of this silver, see Kathryn C. Buhler, *American Silver, 1655-1825, in the Museum of Fine Arts, Boston,* 2 vols. (Greenwich, Conn.: New York Graphic Society, 1972), 1:365-67. Buhler also lists three other donations of tutorial silver from this era.

31. Between 1767-1768 and 1773-1774, the average age of the tutors ranged from 24 3/4 to 30; the average age of the professors was 40 in 1767-1768; all three professors were still in place six years later in 1773-1774.

32. *Sibley's Harvard Graduates* 4:162-67; 8:137-40. Also see Daniel Munro Wilson, "Tutor Henry Flynt, New England's Earliest Humorist," *New England Magazine* 23 (1900): 284-93.

33. Sheldon S. Cohen, "Harvard College on the Eve of the American Revolution," *Publications of the Colonial Society of Massachusetts* 59 (1982): 175; "The Harvard Diary of Pitt Clarke, 1786-1791," transcribed and ed. by Ernest John Knapton, ibid., 238; Willard, *Memories,* 313; *Sibley's Harvard Graduates* 15:448-49.

34. William Gallison to Col. John Gallison, Oct. 27, 1773, C. E. French Papers, 18: 427-28, Massachusetts Historical Society.

35. John Clarke, *Letters to a Student in the University of Cambridge, Massachusetts* (Boston: Samuel Hall, 1796), 72, 80-92, 97.

36. Clarke, *Letters to a Student,* 47-48.

37. Ibid., 76.

38. Corporation Records, 2:260, 322, 327, 338, Harvard University Archives; Clement Weeks, Diary, 1768-1796, July 27, 1772, New Hampshire Historical Society, Concord; Barbara Lambert, "Music Masters in Colonial Boston," *Publications of the Colonial Society of Massachusetts* (1980) 54:1110-12. On the social role of the minuet, see Cathleene B. Hellier, "Dance in the Virginia Gentry Household: A Tutor's-Eye View in the 1770s," unpublished paper, Research Department, Colonial Williamsburg Foundation, Williamsburg, Va., esp. 6-7, 12, and Hellier, "'These Rules and Customs': Gender, Power, and the Rules of Assemblies in Two Novels by Fanny Burney," unpublished paper, Research Department, Colonial Williamsburg Foundation, Williamsburg, Va., esp. 12-14.

39. Samuel Phillips, Sr., to Samuel Phillips, Jr., Nov. 20, 1769, Phillips Papers. In the same collection, see also Samuel Phillips, Sr., to Samuel Phillips, Jr., Nov. 5, 1769.

40. Bernard Bailyn, *The Ideological Origins of the American Revolution* (Cambridge, Mass.: Harvard University Press, 1967), 23-24.

41. Faculty Records, 2:468-69, 504; 3:37, 83, 131-32, 155, 183, 193, 195, 212-13, Harvard University Archives.

42. Fourteen members of the classes of 1771 through 1774 were degraded at some point during their college careers. Only one student in these classes, John Barnard Swett, suffered both degradation and rustication. Twenty-seven of 204 students (13 percent) incurred rustication, degradation, or both. Faculty Records, 3:67, 132, 162-63, 183-84, 195, 198, 201, 209-10.

43. Ibid., 152-53.

44. Ibid., 193, 194, 195, 201, 208; Sarah E. Mulkern, ed., "Harvard on the Eve of the Revolution," *Harvard Graduates' Magazine* 10 (1902): 377-78.

45. Faculty Records, 3:194-95.

46. Ibid., 152-54.

47. Bernard Bailyn, et al., *Glimpses of the Harvard Past* (Cambridge, Mass.: Harvard University Press, 1986), 25.

48. Willard, *Memories,* 260-61; Peabody, Diary, Aug. 20-24, 1767; Morison, *Three Centuries of Harvard,* 130.

49. *The Nation* 98 (1914): 295; Morison, *Three Centuries of Harvard,* 91-92.

50. Willard, *Memories,* 315-17; Bernhard, *Fisher Ames,* 25.

51. Weeks, Diary, Aug. 1768.

52. Mulkern, "Harvard on the Eve of the Revolution," 529-30.

53. Peabody, Diary, Aug. 21, 26, 1767.

54. Weeks, Diary, June 9, 1772.

55. Siegel, "Governance and Curriculum at Harvard College," 301; William C. Lane, "A Religious Society at Harvard College, 1719," *Proceedings of the Colonial Society of Massachusetts* 24 (1923): 309-13; Albert Matthews, "A Society at Harvard College, 1721-

1723," *Publications of the Colonial Society of Massachusetts* (1923) 24:156-59; Morison, *Three Centuries of Harvard,* 61-63; Peabody, Diary, passim.

56. Articles of an Association for the Suppression of Vice, April 7, 1767, Harvard University Archives.

57. Philomusarian Club, Articles, 1728, Harvard University Archives. A group of resident graduates formed an even earlier society, the Spy Club, for discussing philosophical topics in 1719. Siegel, "Governance and Curriculum at Harvard College," 302-3.

58. Speaking Club, Minutes and Other Records, Harvard University Archives; Bernhard, *Fisher Ames,* 28.

59. Speaking Club, Minutes and Other Records, Harvard University Archives; Clitonian Society, Diploma, 1773, Massachusetts Historical Society [photostat]; "A List of the Officers of the Martimercurian Company at College 1771," *Publications of the Colonial Society of Massachusetts* 24 (1923): 161-65; Faculty Records, Original, 1771-1772, [n.p.], Harvard University Archives.

60. The full membership of the Spunke Club is now impossible to reconstruct through a few cryptic surviving mentions.

61. Morison, *Three Centuries of Harvard,* 141; "Officers of the Martimercurian Company, 1771," 161-65. Harvard was not alone in sponsoring a student militia company. Yale, Brown, and Columbia also had them. See Kelley, *Yale: A History,* 84; John F. Roche, *The Colonial Colleges in the War for American Independence* (Millwood, N.Y.: Associated Faculty Press, 1986), 61-63.

62. For a full account of this event, see Sheldon S. Cohen, "The Turkish Tyranny," *New England Quarterly* 47 (1974): 564-83; Peabody, Diary, March 22, 1768.

63. Administrative Records of College Disorders, April 1768, Harvard University Archives.

64. Quoted in Morison, *Three Centuries of Harvard,* 99.

65. Corporation Records, Dec. 18, 1769, 3:322.

66. L. H. Butterfield, et al., *Diary and Autobiography of John Adams,* 4 vols. (Cambridge, Mass.: Harvard University Press, 1961), 3:260.

67. Andrew Eliot to Thomas Hollis, Dec. 25, 1769, *Collections of the Massachusetts Historical Society,* 4th ser., 4:447-48.

68. *Sibley's Harvard Graduates* 13:624; Faculty Records, 3:168-69.

69. Morison, *Three Centuries of Harvard,* 100.

70. In September, near the start of their final year, the members of the senior class gathered to hold elections. They voted for two commencement orators and four thesis collectors, who drafted the graduation program. These six men were, in effect, the officers of the graduating class. Morison, *Three Centuries of Harvard,* 119; Siegel, "Governance and Curriculum at Harvard College," 325-26.

71. Andrew Croswell, *Brief Remarks on the Satyrical Drollery at Cambridge, Last Commencement Day* (Boston: Ezekiel Russell, 1771). For a rejoinder accusing Croswell of being too stuffy, probably by Rev. Thomas Prentice, the minister of the Congregational church in Charlestown and a member of the Board of Overseers, see Simon, the Tanner, *A Letter to the Reverend Andrew Croswell* (Boston: Ezekiel Russell, 1771).

72. *Boston Post-Boy,* July 22, 1771.

73. Peabody, Diary, July 3, 4, 1767.

74. John Rowe, Diary, July 17, 1771, Massachusetts Historical Society.

75. Elizabeth [Murray] Inman to Lady Don, fall 1773 (filed 1774), J. M. Robbins Papers, Massachusetts Historical Society. A published account of this party appears in the *Boston Gazette,* July 20, 1772. For these citations I am grateful to Patricia Cleary.

76. For an account of Harvard commencement in the late colonial period, see Morison, *Three Centuries of Harvard,* 123-31.

Harvard Once Removed

The "Favorable Situation" of Hannah Winthrop and Mercy Otis Warren

Frances Herman Lord

"Dr. Price thinks Thousands of Boyles Clarks and Newtons have probably been lost to the world, and lived and died in Ignorance and meanness, mearly for want of being Placed in favourable Situations, and Injoying Proper Advantage," Jane Franklin Mecom wrote to her self-made brother, Benjamin Franklin, in 1786.[1] The wife of an unsuccessful Boston tradesman and mother of 12 children, Mecom was repeating the sentiments of her minister, which expressed the constraints facing eighteenth-century women without the advantages of education and leisure. Conscious of her own struggles caused by poverty, middle-aged widowhood, and the premature death of almost all of her children, the 74-year-old Mecom continued, "Very few we know is able to beat thro all Impediments and Arive to any Grat Degre of superiority in Understanding." Mecom possessed extraordinary pluck, common sense, and resourcefulness, but she could not translate those qualities into the advantages enjoyed by women fortunate enough to occupy "favourable Situations."

The lives of two of Mecom's Boston-area contemporaries, Mercy Warren and Hannah Winthrop, in contrast, illustrate what could be achieved by women of privilege in the mid- to late eighteenth century. Although responsible for child rearing and household management, Warren and Winthrop were members of a class that had the opportunity for both education and leisure. What set the two women apart from other women of advantage, however, was their close and profitable association with Harvard-educated men—an extraordinary advantage that shaped their intellectual endeavors.[2]

Warren and Winthrop were daughters of men of substance who were leaders in the intellectual and political circles of colonial and Revolutionary-era Boston. The two childhood friends could advance beyond the informal education that introduced young children throughout New England, male and female, rural and urban, to the rudiments of reading, writing, and ciphering. Post–dame school education for "young misses" such as Winthrop, Warren, and their social peers could comprise several terms at a fashionable needlework school or attendance at urban dance or painting classes. There, aside from a smattering of French, geography, and history, the emphasis was on moral instruction rather than on what was viewed as "rational" instruction, that is, instruction "agreeable to reason"[3] and commensurate with higher academic learning.

Meanwhile their brothers would be privately tutored or would attend male-only Latin school. In both settings, schoolboys would be drilled in speaking and reading Latin and Greek and would be introduced to higher mathematics as the prerequisite for entrance to college. In colonial colleges such as Harvard, they would recite the writings of classical authors in their original language and also study the mathematics and experimental science of Boyle, Newton, and Clarke. The study of Newtonian natural philosophy (astronomy, physics, and optics) was required of all juniors and seniors at Harvard.[4] Introduced to the curriculum in the late 1720s by Isaac Greenwood, the first Hollis Professor of Natural Philosophy and Mathematics, its study was firmly entrenched by John Winthrop, who succeeded Greenwood in 1738 at the age of 24. By midcentury Winthrop was recognized as the foremost member of New England's scientific community.[5]

Young women of means, impeded by their sex rather than by their social circumstances, were ineligible for college because they lacked the necessary classical preparation. True, their schooling would impart the social skills and deportment necessary for genteel living as well as the elevated sentiments and expressions of polite, rather than ordinary, discourse. But they would not learn the rational thought imbued in traditionally male subjects, whether mathematics and science or philosophy and logic. Thus all women, not only those in Mecom's straitened circumstances, faced a seemingly insurmountable impediment—rooted in gender rather than intellectual capability—to achieving a "Grat Degre of superiority in Understanding" comparable to that of men. Although this obstacle was strengthened by cultural attitudes and unconsciously internalized, occasionally there did exist circumstances that placed certain women in situations that favored a breach of the barriers.

Hannah Winthrop's unique position as the wife of John Winthrop, the renowned professor of natural philosophy and mathematics at Harvard, offered the potential for such a situation. The family desk, so Hannah Winthrop reminded Warren, was "generally adornd with a Variety of Authors" whose works covered history, literature, theology, and natural philosophy.[6] Hannah's reading indicates the scope of the intellectual life she shared with her husband, for John Winthrop was, in fact as well as in name, Hannah's "Dear Preceptor" and "Philosopher." Professor Winthrop was his wife's teacher and intellectual guide to the world of rational ideas in general and of natural philosophy in particular.

Hannah Winthrop's intimate friendship with Mercy Warren contributed another dimension to this "favourable Situation." Like Winthrop, Warren was the wife and sister of Harvard graduates and, like Winthrop, she profited from this association: first, as an attendant at her brother's tutorial preparation for entrance to Harvard, and second, as the intellectual as well as domestic partner of her husband, James Warren.[7] Aware, as Warren once expostulated, that an apparent "Deficiency . . . of Female Intellects" was the result of "the different Education bestow'd on the Sexes," the two women reveled in the "Cultivation of the Mind" afforded by sharing their husbands' interests.[8]

Although preoccupied in her rural Massachusetts home with her five sons and the Whig politics of her husband, Mrs. Warren was a keen observer of the Revolutionary War and, through her poetry and plays, an acute commentator on politics.[9] As evident in their private correspondence, both she and Hannah Winthrop fiercely supported their husbands' active advocacy of the colonies' overthrow of English rule. Following the outbreak of hostilities, James Warren, then speaker of the Massachusetts House, served as a member of the Navy Board for the eastern department; John Winthrop's age and frail health, if not his position at Harvard, precluded his active involvement in military affairs. Mercy Warren's admiration of Professor Winthrop as "a distinguished genius of our time," however, was no less fervent than Hannah Winthrop's admiration of Colonel Warren as a political and military leader.[10] Moreover, as we shall see, the correspondence between the two friends provided a sounding board that reinforced their engagement in their husbands' endeavors. Spanning nearly 20 years, their "conversing by letter," instigated at Mercy Warren's "kind invitation" in 1768, marked the decades and the reflections of their mature years and continued until at least 1786.[11]

Early in 1777, upon considering the firsthand news from the military and diplomatic fronts that entered their Cambridge home by way of familial and political connections, Hannah Winthrop cleared a space for her pen, paper, and inkwell among the books on the family desk. She industriously applied pen to paper—any news of the war, now in its second year, would be welcome to Warren who, residing in the town of Plymouth, south of Boston, was "remove[d] from the scene of action."[12] After a sally deprecating General's Howe's latest boast to conquer America, Mrs. Winthrop paused in her writing: Would her "dear Friend," she wondered, charge her "with an Affectation of dabbling in Astronomy" if she revealed her participation as "an humble Attendant" in her husband's recent scientific project, the observation of a lunar eclipse of the sun. Despite her doubts, Winthrop proceeded with an elegantly refined description "of Cynthia in Eclipsing that glorious Luminary that rules the Day." Drawing a practical and moral conclusion, she remarked that the eclipse and other celestial phenomena are "great Points to an astronomer, tho the greater part of Mankind are . . . inattentive to these Glorious works of an almighty Creator. . . ." With a nod to the conventions of polite discourse, she concluded, "Now [if] I have incurrd your Censure pray pass Sentence."[13]

Hannah Winthrop's attendance upon her husband's observation of the eclipse and her subsequent remarks to Mercy Warren reveal the benefits conferred by her association with Harvard College, albeit an acquaintance once removed from the academic classroom. For both women the College represented the center of New England's intellectual life, the "Seat of Science [i.e., learning] and Polite Literature," as they termed it. In Warren's opinion, Winthrop's access through her husband to the academic world insured that she was "surrounded with advantage," as Winthrop had acknowledged to Warren early in their correspondence. Indeed, Hannah felt that Warren's "good opinion" of her "situation" formed Mercy's "expectation" of the intellectual content of their exchanges. For her part, however, she used Warren's envy of her proximity to Harvard and its educational advantages as the bait in urging her friend to visit more often.[14]

Among those advantages was one that Hannah Winthrop especially cherished: the use of John Winthrop's own astronomical instruments as well as a number from the College collection. As the Hollis Professor of Natural

Philosophy and Mathematics, Winthrop had the privilege of borrowing various instruments from the College—a practical arrangement that allowed him to conduct experiments and observations at his house in the days before Harvard had either science laboratories or an observatory. An inventory of the College apparatus in their home taken shortly after John Winthrop's death lists some 11 instruments, including astronomical telescopes and quadrants.[15] That Professor Winthrop was able to conduct various experiments at home also illustrates the lack of professional barriers between workplace and home in the mid-eighteenth century. His home work and the instruments he employed became a source of enjoyment for Hannah and contributed to her informal science education.

These opportunities set Hannah apart from most of her contemporaries. The approved place of women as well as their lack of proper education acted together to suppress their actual practice of science.[16] Although lecturers sought women's attendance at public science demonstrations and booksellers sought their business, both groups tacitly acknowledged women's (and most men's) lack of science education. This is evident in newspaper advertisements that touted "fashionable" demonstrations of electricity and pneumatics and also introductory texts made "plain and evident" for the benefit of those "who have not made Philosophy a previous study."[17] The passage in which Winthrop relates her experience makes clear that Newtonian astronomy exerted a special appeal for her and also provided a special opportunity. From her remarks, it is apparent that her participation in scientific activity was motivated not by fashion's dictates but rather by rational and religious concerns.

As her husband's "humble Attendant," Hannah Winthrop had access to the apparatus and the knowledge necessary for the practice of astronomy. Her brief description of the eclipse, while deliberately couched with "sentimental elegance and dignity" in the language of polite discourse, hints at what her astronomical activities may have included.[18] "The Sky at the beginning of the Eclipse," she reported to Mercy Warren, "was unkindly overspread with Clouds but soon Cleard off, and gave so good a View as to be able to judge with Precision the Quantity and duration of the Moon's path over the Sun. He has also this fall taken a trip with little Mercury across the Sun similar to the Transit of Venus. I think it a beautiful Sight."[19]

With this description Winthrop relates the atmospheric conditions at the time of the sighting, alludes to the precise scientific measurements involved, suggests her familiarity with a recent transit of the sun by the moon and Mercury, and compares the latter to the transits of Venus that had occurred in 1761 and 1769. Winthrop does not specify what measurements she assisted in taking. Nonetheless, her remark that they concerned the "Quantity and Duration of the Moon's path across the sun" leads to the conclusion that she may have had the knowledge to make sightings and readings that required a telescope, an astronomical quadrant, and a clock. For these observations, Winthrop and her husband probably used the family clock, a standing quadrant borrowed from the Harvard apparatus collection, and telescopes belonging to her husband and to the Harvard collection.[20] Although Hannah's letter contained only a verbal description of the eclipse, a diagram with calculations made by Professor Winthrop of a much earlier lunar eclipse of the sun (1747) serves to indicate the close attention and precise readings required by an "Attendant" at such astronomical observations: five sightings taken over the course of 12 hours were necessary to plot the path of the moon and the angle of its course, from the moment of ingress to the moment of egress across the face of the sun.[21]

In the manner of ministers and poets, Hannah Winthrop "improvd" the incident by "expiating" on its meaning. Her defense of astronomical practice rested on its teleological message. "I assure you," she emphasized, "these are great Points to an astronomer, tho the greater part of Mankind are so inattentive to these Glorious works of an almighty Creator that they rise and shine and perform their amazing Circuits without any other observation than its being sometimes a fine sunshine day, or a fine Starlight Evening."[22] Acquired through the guidance of her husband, Winthrop's knowledge of astronomy, no matter how rudimentary, provided her with a heightened awareness that allowed her to appreciate the glories of the universe manifested in its daily, not just extraordinary, operations. Moreover, this was privileged knowledge, because it drew Hannah into a sphere of learning set apart from the "greater part of Mankind" and defined not by gender but, as Jane Mecom phrased it, by a "superiority in Understanding."

Yet astronomy had an even more poignant, personal appeal. By turning her gaze to the celestial world, Winthrop found escape from the very real uncertainties that surrounded her: the disorder, dislocation, and depredations brought on by the "Horrors of the Civil War" now in its second year.[23] In referring to the celestial world, she marveled, "However enwrapt in incertainty the events in which we of this Terrestrial ball are interested a perfect regularity reigns there. No intervening accident can prevent the Completion of their appointed route." Thus the "appointed" order and constancy—what natural philosophers spoke of as the "design" of the natural world—evident even in extraordinary celestial phenomena offered solace that could be found nowhere else in the disordered times brought on by the "unnatural" condition of war conducted by England, the "mother country," against her colonial subjects. Winthrop reinforced this idea in the closing sentence of this passage, when she proffered the hope that "the inhabitants of those States [i.e., the planets and stars] are better employd than in spreading devastation and death among their Loyal Subjects and brethren."[24] Winthrop's report of the eclipse reflected her own synthesis of astronomy, religion, and politics. Her "improvement" upon it validates her modest claim to "dabbling" in astronomy while it also elucidates the ingeniousness of her disclaimer, "Now I have incurrd your Censure pray pass Sentence."

One of the bonds that enriched the friendship between Warren and Winthrop was that each regarded the other's husband with equal affection and respect. More important than respect born of external achievements was affection engendered by their mutual awareness that, as Mercy Warren once remarked, "We are both happily united to such companions as think we are capable of taking part in whatever affects themselves." Mercy, therefore, felt confident in asserting her political views, frankly telling Hannah, "Nor shall I make an apology for touching on a subject a little out of the line of female attention."[25] Winthrop, writing sometime later in a similar vein to her "sister Heart," praised their spouses for allowing them a role beyond mere "domestick use":

> Dear Mrs. Warren I often contemplate Your & my happy Lot in the kind disposition of Providence in our dear Consorts formd with disinterested enlargd minds, not only pursuing the happiness of Mankind in general, but making happy Domestic life, not keeping that awful distance some persons imagine Heaven designd between the Social Tye, who look upon Wives only fit for domestick use. I am sure we may Bless our selves in Consorts who delight in forming our Ideas & in Communicating Intellectual Pleasure.[26]

Conversation with her husband enlarged Hannah's sphere, creating a *mutual* "Domestic life" wherein she could engage in the practice of science.

For Winthrop the practice of science fell within the realm of "rational" rather than "polite" pursuits. Indeed, as Hannah told Warren, she was "unacquainted with Polite Life, the encreasing dissipation, the round of Elegant amusements which are becoming the work of every Evening." Warren, too, prided herself on her ability to transcend the superficiality often ascribed to female pursuits. Despite her avowal of "retired life," Warren was far from being secluded. Through her literary endeavors and her personal association and correspondence with political activists, she negotiated what has been termed "an associative, public sphere," a sort of middle sphere of "social, discursive, and cultural production."[27] Like Winthrop, she attributed her good fortune to a supportive husband. Concluding a long letter to Winthrop on the infringement of despotic rulers on the natural rights of those whom they governed, she protested, "As for that part of mankind who think every rational pursuit lies beyond the reach of a sex too generally devoted to folly, their censure or applause is equally indifferent to your sincere friend."[28]

Moreover, for Warren any "rational pursuit," including science, was inextricably tied to the pursuit of moral goodness, as she made clear in a letter to Winthrop prompted by the government crisis of 1773. Without moral goodness and knowledge, she maintained, the "path of Rectitude" would be beset by "Anarchy & darkness," especially now when the "enemies of America" were "sacrificing the rights of Posterity to . . . Ambition & Avarice." She advised Hannah,

> Let us turn our eyes to the more rational satisfaction of the good man who exerts his talents for the good of society. . . . [who]
>> Tracing the depth of Nature's hidden Laws
>> With Godlike Newton, mounts beyond the stars,
>> And ranging o'er the vast etherial plain
>> Surveys each System of the wide domain.

She coyly concluded, "If you know a person who answers to this Character, I hope you will not fail to make my respectful regard acceptable to him."[29] Warren knew her friend would pass the compliment on to her husband, John Winthrop.

Following John Winthrop's death in May 1779, Warren expressed her condolences to Hannah in the form of a poetic eulogy. She not only eulogized her friend's husband but also exhibited her own awareness of Newtonian philosophy in verses adorned with scientific allusions, perhaps gained from her once-removed association with Harvard and its professor of natural philosophy. Warren's litany of philosophic sages extended from the ancients to the moderns: from Socrates and Plato to Newton, Boyle, and Locke, Huygens and 'sGravesande.[30] Yet, she regarded their truths as a poor substitute for the "reveal'd" truths of "Christian faith and hope," which she identified as

. . . the perfect code,
Seal'd by a messenger divine,
The sacred son of God.[31]

Warren's elegy celebrated Winthrop as the perfect "guide to Harvard's youth," among whom were her own sons.[32] For, in her view, he successfully combined the rational truths of philosophy with the revealed truths of Christianity. Indeed, in a letter to Hannah, Warren had commented that Professor Winthrop "has often in the silence of midnight observed the rotation of the stars & with holy rapture adored the divine architect who constructed the stupendous fabric, & set the wheels in motion."[33] What Warren here identifies as a felicitous blend of religion and natural philosophy on the professor's part mirrored her own accommodation of piety and science, which was rooted in her Puritan religious heritage.[34]

The gift of Warren's poem was balm to Hannah Winthrop, whose loneliness was heightened by the loss of the intellectual stimulation her husband had always provided: "That fatal fall from the Sublime pleasures of the most engaging Converse to the trifling," as she confided in a letter to Mercy.[35] Her response to Warren's "Consoling animating ingenious poetic piece" was to share it with her minister. He in turn saw that it was published (on the front page of the *Independent Chronicle* for October 21, 1779) so that, as Hannah reported to Mercy, "others might enjoy the Pleasure likewise."[36]

The consolation Mercy Warren afforded Hannah Winthrop was short-lived; within the next five months Hannah's loss of her husband was compounded by the loss of the scientific instruments she had shared with him. In April 1780, after she was required to surrender the apparatus kept in their home, she poured out her wounded feelings to Warren. Hannah's polite diction cannot conceal her anguish: "Could you have thought," she asked her friend,

that after being bereft of my most essential Portion, I should be [so] deeply affected with being derob'd of those emblems, those badges of office that mark[t] the Astronomer, that gave such pleasing amazement to my dear departed Philosopher[?] ah! My poor wounded heart was most exquisitely touchd by a requisition of those enlightening Tubes [i.e., telescopes] thro which He often led me to View the wonders of creating power, but a Successor must enjoy all those advantages.[37]

With the removal of the instruments by the Harvard officials, Hannah suffered a multiplicity of losses: the overt losses of her husband himself and of the astronomical activities they formerly shared, and the more subtle losses associated with her husband's prestige and his power to evoke the immediacy of creation and hence Hannah's own comprehension of the "creating power" of God. Without the assistance of her husband or the possession of his instruments, Hannah was powerless to pursue even casual astronomical observations.

Most important, widowhood deepened Hannah Winthrop's cognizance of her dependence on her husband for "forming ideas" just as it deprived her of the "intellectual Pleasure" of conversational exchange. Marriage had invested her, "with all those pleasures the rational soul could possibly desire," she wrote to Mercy Warren in April 1780. The divesture of those pleasures was especially painful on this occasion only a few days after what would have been her twenty-fourth wedding anniversary—the first of 11 anniversaries she would spend alone before her own death in May 1790. Her husband's death had "dissolved the endeared Connection" that bound her to the world of ideas just as certainly—and just as strongly—as it had bound her to her husband.[38]

Perhaps Winthrop's heightened awareness of the extent that her intellectual development had depended on the role of a supportive husband precipitated her reevaluation of women's prescribed role in even the most enlightened marriage. Only two years later, her correspondence with Mercy Warren upon the occasion of the annual installation ceremonies at "Alma Mater" (as she now familiarly referred to Harvard) suggests that she had become a champion for women's higher education. "Learning," she observed in the early years of the new republic, had become "suitable"—that is, appropriate to a wider audience than those young men served by Harvard. "Why should not the Capital [Boston] be Philosophied," she queried, "& the Fair ones of the present day, be taught to square the Circle, & the important knowledge of the laws of Attraction, & Cohesion."[39]

In academic circles "to square the Circle" and to know "the laws of Attraction, & Cohesion" were shorthand references to advanced mathematics and to Newtonian natural philosophy—"rational" subjects that symbolized and were exclusive to advanced, male instruction. Thus, Winthrop advocated that young women, "the Fair ones of the present day," acquire an education equal to the rational education of young men. From the vantage of her widowhood, she realized that only such instruction would enable them to fulfill the "prevailing thirst for <u>acquirement</u>"—a thirst not satisfied by the once-removed position of "the Professor's wife" but by the "favourable Situation" of young women as students in their own right.[40]

Notes

I would like to acknowledge my twentieth-century preceptors—Jan Golinski, for introducing me to the history of science; Laurel Thatcher Ulrich, for introducing me to women's history; and I. Bernard Cohen, for his aid in unraveling the intricacies of Newtonian science as a member of my dissertation committee—and to thank my colleague Beth Nichols, for her critical reading of this essay in its embryonic form.

1. Quoted in Anne Firor Scott, "Self Portraits: Three Women," in *Uprooted Americans: Essays to Honor Oscar Handlin,* ed. Richard L. Bushman et al. (Boston: Little, Brown and Company, 1979), 55. For a biography, see Carl Van Doren, *Jane Mecom, the Favorite Sister of Benjamin Franklin: Her Life Here First Fully Narrated from Their Entire Surviving Correspondence* (New York: Viking Press, 1950). Mecom refers to Isaac Newton (1742-1727) and Robert Boyle (1627-1691), whose late seventeenth- and early eighteenth-century scientific discoveries ushered in the era of the "new"—i.e., experimental—science, and to the English clergyman Samuel Clarke (1675-1729), whose writings popularized Newtonian science in the defense of Christianity.

2. Hannah Fayerweather Tolman Winthrop (1726-1790) was the daughter of Thomas and Hannah Waldo Fayerweather of Boston, and sister to Samuel Fayerweather (Harvard, 1743). The childless widow of Farr Tolman, she married Professor John Winthrop in 1756. Winthrop's first wife Rebecca Townsend, whom he married in 1746, died in 1753, leaving four sons whose care Hannah assumed. *Sibley's Harvard Graduates* 10:246-48. Mercy Otis Warren (1728-1814) was the daughter of James and Mary Allyne Otis of Barnstable and sister of James Otis (Harvard, 1743); in 1754 she married James Warren (Harvard, 1745) with whom she had five sons. Jeffrey H. Richards, *Mercy Otis Warren* (New York: Twayne Publishers, 1995), 5. Mercy Warren's brother and husband were both students of John Winthrop, as was Hannah Winthrop's brother. For James Warren, who attained the rank of general in the colonial forces, see *Sibley's Harvard Graduates* 11:584-606.

3. Samuel Johnson, *A Dictionary of the English Language in which the Words are Deduced from Their Originals . . .* (London, 1755).

4. In the eighteenth century, the term "natural philosophy" comprised mathematics and the physical sciences; it was a distinct branch of "science," a term used synonymously with "knowledge." The modern use of the term "science" was not introduced until the 1830s. For the general curriculum at Harvard, see Samuel Eliot Morison, *Three Centuries of Harvard, 1636-1936* (Cambridge, Mass.: Harvard University Press, 1936); for the science curriculum, see I. Bernard Cohen, *Some Early Tools of American Science: An Account of the Early Scientific Instruments and Mineralogical and Biological Collections in Harvard University* (1950; rpt., New York: Russell & Russell, 1967).

5. Winthrop (1714-1779) was known for his astronomical observations, correspondence with members of the international science community, and contributions to the *Philosophical Transactions* of the Royal Society of London; he was awarded an honorary doctorate by the University of Edinburgh and in 1765 was elected a Fellow of the Royal Society. See Raymond Phineas Stears, *Science in the British Colonies of America* (Urbana: University of Illinois Press, 1970), 742-70.

6. Hannah Winthrop to Mercy Otis Warren, Jan. 9, 1778, Warren-Winthrop Papers (1758-1789?), Massachusetts Historical Society, Boston [hereafter, W-W Papers]. Winthrop mentions books on these topics in various letters to Warren. The Warren-Winthrop Papers include 49 letters (46 from Winthrop, 3 from Warren) that survive from their correspon-

dence extending from late 1768 to at least March 23, 1786. The letters deal with intimate family news as well as contemporary political and military events; some are reproduced in whole or part in "Warren-Adams Letters, Being Chiefly a Correspondence among John Adams, Samuel Adams, and James Warren," vol. 1, "1743-1777," *Collections of the Massachusetts Historical Society* 72 (1917), and vol. 2, "1778-1814," ibid. 73 (1925) [hereafter, "W-A Letters"].

7. For Mercy Otis Warren's education, see Rosemarie Zagarri, *A Woman's Dilemma: Mercy Otis Warren and the American Revolution* (Wheeling, Ill.: Harlan Davidson, 1995).

8. Warren's comments regarding female education, made in response to a young woman seeking advice, are quoted in Alice Brown, *Mercy Warren* (New York: Charles Scribner's Sons, 1896), 241-42.

9. For Warren's poems and plays, see *The Plays and Poems of Mercy Otis Warren,* comp. and intro. Benjamin Franklin V (Delmar, N.Y.: Scholars' Facsimiles & Reprints, 1980).

10. Professor Winthrop was elected to the Massachusetts Provincial Congress in 1774 and 1775, but he declined re-election in 1777, citing ill health and his professorial duties. *Sibley's Harvard Graduates* 10:258-60. Quotation, Warren to Winthrop, June 3, 1775, Mercy Warren Letterbook, Mercy Warren Papers (microfilm), Massachusetts Historical Society [hereafter, MW Letterbook], 76. See also, Warren to Winthrop, April [?], 1773, ibid., 63; Winthrop to Warren, Jan. 4 and April 12, 1773, W-W Papers; "W-A Letters," 1:16-17.

11. Quotations, Winthrop to Warren, Oct. 6, 1768, W-W Papers (in response to a letter from Warren, Sept. 23, 1768). Winthrop also wrote of her delight at the "renewal of former friendship . . . the many happy hours we spent together in our youth"; ibid.

12. Winthrop to Warren, Jan. 3, 1775, W-W Papers.

13. Winthrop to Warren, Jan. 14, 1777, W-W Papers; "W-A Letters," 1:283-84.

14. Winthrop to Warren, Nov. 10, 1773, W-W Papers.

15. See the catalog of instruments taken May 20, 1779, *"At the House of Mrs.* WINTHROP" following Professor Winthrop's death. The catalog was added to a separate inventory of the College apparatus and is published in Cohen, *Early Tools of American Science,* appendix II.

16. Only one woman in the northern colonies, Caroline Colden Farquher (1726-1766), daughter of Lt. Gov. Cadwallader Colden of New York, has been recognized by historians of science and social historians as a "scientist." Introduced to botany by her father, Colden (as she is known to historians) collected specimens and corresponded through him with European natural historians; Joan Hoff Wilson, "Dancing Dogs of the Colonial Period: Women Scientists," *Early American Literature* 7 (1973): 225-27. Colden abandoned her botanical pursuits after her marriage in 1759; Margaret W. Rossiter, *Women Scientists in America: Struggle and Strategies to 1940* (Baltimore, Md.: Johns Hopkins University Press, 1982), 2-3. Applying a twentieth-century concept of "scientist" (i.e, one who publishes or teaches), Rossiter regards Colden as "America's pioneer (and only) woman scientist for almost ninety years" (p. 3), whereas Wilson, using a more inclusive approach, lists nine colonial women "scientists" active in agronomy, horticulture, and botany; "Dancing Dogs," 225-351, esp. 232n3. For her scientific work, see Jane Colden, *Botanic Manuscript,* ed. H. W. Rickett (New York: Chanticleer Press, 1963). For Southern women scientists and their books, see Kevin J. Hayes, *A Colonial Woman's Bookshelf* (Knoxville: University of Tennessee Press, 1996), chap. 6.

17. See, for example, the advertisement for "Two LECTURES on PNEUMATICS," *Boston News-Letter,* June 21 and 28, 1770. For science lectures and demonstrations in Boston, see Frances H. Lord, "Piety, Politeness, and Power: Formation of a Newtonian Culture in New England, 1727-1779" (Ph.D. diss., University of New Hampshire, 2000), chap. 4; for their appeal to women, see ibid., esp. 173-77 and 191-210.

18. Winthrop uses this phrase to describe her own writing, Winthrop to Warren, Nov. 10, 1773, W-W Papers. Winthrop's style was an extreme example of conversational politeness whose object was to achieve "verbal agreeableness" through the "dextrous management

of words"; Lawrence Klein, *Shaftesbury and the Culture of Politeness: Moral Discourse and Cultural Politics in Early Eighteenth-Century England* (New York: Cambridge University Press, 1994), 4.

19. Winthrop to Warren, Jan. 14, 1777, W-W Papers; "W-A Letters," I: 284.

20. Among the entries in the 1779 inventory of College instruments in the Winthrop home were "A standing Quadrant of 2 feet Radius," "An ac[h]romatic Telescope . . . ," and "A large reflecting Telescope"; Cohen, *Early Tools of American Science,* appendix II.

21. John Winthrop's diagram and calculations of the 1747 lunar eclipse are reproduced in Cohen, *Early Tools of American Science.*

22. Winthrop used these terms in a letter to Warren, Nov. 10, 1773, in which she described the "beauties of creation" viewed on a trip from Portsmouth to Dover, N.H., stating that if she had the "poetic Genius" of Warren, she "might have improvd the happy opportunity of expatiating on the beauteous scene"; W-W Papers. Four years later, Warren herself improved Winthrop's description with a poem, entitled "To Honoria, on her Journey to Dover, 1777." Moving from a description that "trace[s] the scene" described by Winthrop, Warren contemplates the "august design" marked out by heaven for the "happy land." Here, where truth and genius rule, "other Boyles or Newtons yet may rise, / And trace the wonders of the western skies." *Poems, Dramatic and Miscellaneous,* 216-17 [hereafter, *Misc. Poems*], in Franklin, ed., *Plays and Poems of Mercy Otis Warren.*

23. Winthrop to Warren, Sept 27, 1774, W-W Papers; "W-A Letters," 33. Hannah Winthrop's description of the evacuation of Boston following the Battle of Bunker Hill is one of the most vivid eyewitness accounts of the war; see Winthrop to Warren [April or May] 1775, W-W Papers; "W-A Letters" 2:409-11.

24. Winthrop evidently subscribed to the belief that the planets were inhabited, a belief common in the eighteenth century.

25. Warren to Winthrop, [?] 1774, MW Letterbook. Winthrop expresses a similar willingness to contravene "the sphere of female life" that precludes being "any way active in the manoeuvres of state" by making "observations" on the patriotic activities of fellow Bostonians; Winthrop to Warren, June 14, 1774, W-W Papers.

26. Winthrop to Warren, June 23, 1775, W-W Papers. Winthrop's awareness here is remarkably akin to Klein's description of reason as a "habit actuated in the practice of conversation"; unspoken in Winthrop's letter is also an attitude similar to Klein's observation of participants as "agents [who] resisted the passivity of mere listening"; Klein, *Shaftesbury,* 98.

27. Lawrence Klein, "Gender and the Public/Private Distinction in the Eighteenth Century: Some Questions about Evidence and Analytic Procedure," *Eighteenth-Century Studies* 29, no. 1 (1994): 97-109. For an insightful analysis of Warren's correspondence, see Richards, *Warren,* chap .2.

28. Warren to Winthrop, [?] 1774, MW Letterbook, 71.

29. Warren to Winthrop, Feb. [?], 1773, MW Letterbook. See also Warren to Winthrop, April [?], 1773, MW Letterbook, 63.

30. John Locke (1632-1704), English political philosopher; Christian Huygens (1629-95), Dutch astronomer, mathematician, and physicist; Willem 'sGravesande (1688-1742), Dutch mathematician and physicist, whose work explicating Isaac Newton's major work, *Mathematical Principles of Natural Philosophy,* was among the most popular Newtonian texts in New England.

31. "On the Death of the Hon. John Winthrop . . . ," *Misc. Poems,* 237.

32. At least three of the four Warren sons would have studied under Professor Winthrop. Several also boarded in the Winthrop home. See Winthrop to Warren, Aug. 14, 1772, Oct. 12, 1779, and Jan. 16, 1782, W-W Papers.

33. Warren to Winthrop, June 3, 1775, MW Letterbook, 76.

34. Cheryl W. Oreovicz, "Mercy Warren and 'Freedom's Genius'," *University of Mississippi Studies in English,* n.s. 5 (1984-1987): 218.

35. Winthrop to Warren, Oct. 12, 1779, W-W Papers.

36. Ibid. The elegiac poem apparently became a favorite of Harvard students, for it was included on the reading list of the Harvard Speaking Club which met biweekly from Sept. 11, 1770, until at least 1781; Albert Goodhue, Jr., "The Reading of Harvard Students, 1770-1781, As Shown by Records of the Speaking Club," *Essex Institute Historical Collections* 73 (April 1937): appendix A. Warren's elegy was published later in her *Poems, Dramatic and Miscellaneous* (Boston, 1790).

37. Winthrop to Warren, April 20, 1780, W-W Papers. Because John Winthrop would have posted a bond securing the College instruments in his possession, return of the instruments and discharge of the bond were required to settle his estate; I. Bernard Cohen, conversation with author, Aug. 19, 2000. For the source of the inventory of instruments in Hannah Winthrop's possession upon her husband's death, see n. 15 above. After Winthrop's death, his family donated two of his own telescopes to the Harvard apparatus collection; David P. Wheatland, *The Apparatus of Science at Harvard, 1765-1800* (Cambridge, Mass.: Harvard University Press, 1968), 13.

38. Winthrop to Warren, April 20, 1780, W-W Papers.

39. Winthrop to Warren, Jan. 16, 1782, W-W Papers.

40. Ibid. Not until science entered the curriculum of female seminaries was the systematic study of science available to women; Rossiter, *Women Scientists in America*, 3-8. For specific curricula developed to meet the popular enthusiasm for science in the mid-nineteenth century, see Deborah Jean Warner, "Science Education for Women in Antebellum America," *Isis* 69 (1979): 58-67. Ironically, Hannah Winthrop spent her last days in Harvard College. At some point after John Winthrop's death, Hannah moved from their house on Boylston Street to a room in one of the residential halls. On Monday, May 10, 1786, Pitt Clarke (class of 1790) noted in his undergraduate diary that he attended the funeral of "Mrs. Winthrop" and two days later he recorded, "Moved my abode for study down to the room lately occupied by Madam Winthrop deceased." "The Harvard Diary of Pitt Clarke, 1786-1791," transcribed and ed. Ernest John Knapton, *Publications of the Colonial Society of Massachusetts* 59 (1982): 305.

THE POET
AND THE PETITIONER

Two Black Women in
Harvard's Early History

Margot Minardi

On the eve of the American Revolution, Harvard College was a tumultuous place. The widespread social and political unrest of the Revolutionary era fused with students' youthful exuberance and indignation, resulting in a strange combination of principled protest and sheer silliness. In 1768, amid colonial clashes with the British over the crown's taxes on imported goods, seniors in the College voted to stop drinking tea, while others insisted on using American-made paper.[1] A few years later, still another group of independent-minded Harvardians boycotted tutor Stephen Hall's Greek classes on the lofty grounds that "wee don't chuse to spend any more of our time in the study of Greek then wee should be willing to throw away."[2]

Given such antics, Harvard's young men were in need of a stern lecture on the perils of moral dissipation. In 1773, they got their due in the form of 30 verse lines directed "To the University of Cambridge, in New-England."* The poem cautioned students to focus their school years on bettering themselves that they might attain salvation:

---

* The entire poem may be found on pp. 59 of this volume.

> Improve your privileges while they stay,
> Ye pupils, and each hour redeem, that bears
> Or good or bad report of you to heav'n.
> Let sin, that baneful evil to the soul,
> By you be shun'd, . . .[3]

Ever since the Puritan migration to Massachusetts 150 years earlier, exhortations like this one had frequently come forth from the pulpits and presses of the Bay Colony. But this version was unique in that its author was neither William Bradford nor John Winthrop, neither Increase Mather nor Jonathan Edwards. Instead, these lines came from the pen of someone who was young, female, and a slave: the African-born poet Phillis Wheatley.

For most of her brief life, Wheatley was an acknowledged rarity in the world she inhabited. In 1761, when John and Susanna Wheatley selected their servant girl from the cargo of the slave ship *Phillis,* recently arrived in Boston harbor, there were close to 5,000 blacks already living in Massachusetts, most of them slaves. Though people of African descent never amounted to more than 2.2 percent of the Bay Colony's population, slavery as an institution was significant enough and the size of the black population large enough to have attracted the concern of the commonwealth's most noted leaders.[4] Among the first was the Reverend Cotton Mather, Harvard class of 1678, New England's archetypal Puritan cleric. In his 1706 pamphlet *The Negro Christianized,* Mather urged masters to teach their slaves scripture and guide them in worship. He also appealed to slaveowners' pragmatism by claiming that Christianization made slaves more obedient. To aid masters in fulfilling their moral duty to educate their slaves in religion, Mather provided a version of the Lord's Prayer specially paraphrased for blacks so that it could "be brought down unto some of their Capacities." He also published two catechisms, a three-question one "for the Negroes of a Smaller Capacity" and a lengthier one "for the Negroes of a bigger Capacity."[5]

The small, sickly 7- or 8-year-old girl whom John Wheatley purchased as a personal servant for his aging wife turned out to be "of a bigger Capacity" than Cotton Mather—or most colonial Anglo-Americans—had imagined an African could be. As her earliest biographer tells it, when Phillis was still young enough to be losing her baby teeth, she was "frequently seen endeavoring to make letters upon the wall with a piece of chalk or charcoal."[6] Heartened by such precociousness, the Wheatleys' 18-year-old daughter Mary soon started to teach the child how to read and write. Years later, Phillis's master proudly recounted how quick a learner the girl had been:

> Without any Assistance from School Education, and by only what she was taught in the Family, she, in sixteen Months Time from her Arrival, attained the English Language, to which she was an utter Stranger before, to such a Degree, as to read any, the most difficult Parts of the Sacred Writings, to the great Astonishment of all who heard her.[7]

A great astonishment, indeed. Phillis read not only the Bible but also contemporary English poets (Alexander Pope was a favorite). A keen interest in the classics led her to study Latin in order to better understand the ancient bards. The slave girl's immersion in poetry prompted her to try her hand at it herself, starting when she was as young as 12. Phillis Wheatley wrote the first draft of "To the University of Cambridge" when she was no older than 14.[8]

By any measure, the course of Wheatley's education was unusual. Still, literate girls in colonial New England often learned to read and write with little or no "Assistance from School Education." Just what kind of education was proper for young ladies was a subject of much debate in eighteenth-century Anglo-America, for it was widely believed that learning made women dangerously and distastefully masculine.[9] "You need not be told how much female Education is neglected, nor how fashionable it has been to ridicule Female learning," future first lady Abigail Adams lamented to her husband John in 1778.[10] Most of the concern about female education in early America centered around white girls, especially those from well-to-do families, as has the subsequent historical scholarship on the subject.[11] Opportunities for blacks to secure formal education were rare in the eighteenth century, although a few missionary-run schools—including a short-lived one headed by Cotton Mather—did exist.[12] Mather's propagandizing notwithstanding, a primary barrier to the education of slaves was their owners' fear that literacy would lead to disobedience. One knowledge-hungry Boston slave woman named Chloe Spear (a contemporary of Phillis Wheatley) hired a local schoolmistress to give her reading lessons. But Spear's clandestine schooling ended when her master discovered her with a book and beat her on the grounds that "it made negroes saucy to know how to read."[13]

In spite of the cultural taboos against educating women and blacks, Phillis Wheatley did not simply learn how to read; she also became conversant in the underpinnings of eighteenth-century Anglo-American culture, including classical history and mythology, republican political ideology, and, most important, evangelical religion. Susanna Wheatley, a woman of deep personal piety and active involvement in church and mission work, devoted herself to introducing her young charge to Christianity. "To the

University of Cambridge" shows how well Phillis learned those lessons. In the eight middle lines of the poem, she elegantly summarized the Passion story that grounded Christian belief, imploring her readers to visualize Christ's crucifixion. Beyond inspiring theological subjects for her slave girl's poems, Susanna's religiosity brought Phillis into a network of reform-minded evangelicals on both sides of the Atlantic. Several wealthy and well-connected members of that circle helped launch Phillis's brief literary career, which would climax in 1773.[14]

In the summer of that year, with the publication of several poems in English and American periodicals already behind her, Phillis Wheatley crossed the Atlantic to meet her patrons and look into putting together a book. While the 20-year-old poet was in England garnering the admiration of everyone from the Earl of Dartmouth to Benjamin Franklin, commencement exercises were underway at Harvard College. The festivities that year included a "forensic dispute" between Theodore Parsons and Eliphalet Pearson (both A.B. 1773, A.M. 1776) on the question of "the legality of enslaving the Africans." Taking the abolitionist side, Pearson noted that "stupidity is by no means the natural characteristic of these people."[15] As if to corroborate that cautious statement in support of African intellectual prowess, later that summer Phillis Wheatley's *Poems on Various Subjects, Religious and Moral,* including "To the University of Cambridge, in New-England," came off the London presses. At the front of the book was a note "to the Publick," assuring readers that the accompanying poems had indeed been written by "a young Negro Girl," born an "uncultivated Barbarian" but currently "under the Disadvantage of serving as a Slave." "She has been examined by some of the best Judges, and thought qualified to write [the poems]," the statement proclaimed, lest readers worry they were buying into a literary sham. The signatories to this preface were 18 respected men of Massachusetts, including the colonial governor, his lieutenant governor, a future state governor, seven ministers, and John Hancock, one of the most famous signers of the Declaration of Independence. Fourteen of those 18 powerful men were graduates of Harvard.[16]

This, then, was Phillis Wheatley's world. In it, relationships of dependence and patriarchy—endorsed in literature like Mather's *Negro Christianized*—linked slaves to masters, women to men, and children to adults. Formal educational institutions were closed to those who happened to be female or black. And the men whose voices mattered most were by and large men who had attended Harvard College. Not, perhaps, the most receptive environment for a young black slave woman to tell white male college students how to lead their lives. Phillis Wheatley simply could not help herself: "WHILE an intrinsic ardor prompts to write, / The muses promise to assist my pen," she admitted at the beginning of her poem. Then she turned quickly to her own story:

> 'Twas not long since I left my native shore
> The land of errors, and *Egyptain* [*sic*] gloom:
> Father of mercy, 'twas thy gracious hand
> Brought me in safety from those dark abodes.

Lines like these cause some modern readers to cringe and others to look for ways to explain away Wheatley's apparent complacency toward her kidnapping and dismissiveness toward the land of her birth.[17] One response is to read this passage not as literal autobiography but as a metaphor for the conversion experience.[18] Still, a simple conflation of the voyage from Africa to America with the journey from paganism to Christianity conceals the violence at the core of slavery and the slave trade. A more nuanced reading requires close attention to the dynamics between speaker and audience.

The transplantation-as-conversion reading of the poem is compelling because it acknowledges Wheatley's religious faith as genuine and profound, not simply the by-product of pressure to "assimilate."[19] Wheatley's primary intent in the poem was to draw contrasts between sin and redemption. She launched that theological effort in the opening autobiographical lines, with a few bold strokes ("Father of mercy," "thy gracious hand") drawing attention to her own experience of God's saving power in the face of human suffering. The second section of the poem continued to highlight Christianity's stark and nearly paradoxical contrasts. One line asked readers to "See [Jesus] with hands out-stretcht upon the cross"; in the next, Wheatley turned abruptly from the pain and sorrow of the crucifixion to Christ's transcendent and "Immense compassion." A few lines later, she juxtaposed the indignity of Jesus's suffering with the glory of humanity's consequent salvation: "He deign'd to die that they might rise again."

Wheatley's insertion of autobiographical detail into the poem's theological substance set up a different kind of contrast, calling attention to the distinct circumstances of her own life and those of the young men to whom she directed her verse. Wheatley made no attempt to conceal her identity from her Harvard audience. She presented herself as a native of Africa and a slave, shrouded in the "*Egyptain* gloom" that contrasted sharply with the light that filled the students' minds:[20]

> Students, to you 'tis giv'n to scan the heights
> Above, to traverse ethereal space,
> And mark the systems of revolving worlds.
> Still more, ye sons of science ye receive
> The blissful news by messengers from heav'n,
> How *Jesus'* blood for your redemption flows.

Twelve years before this poem's publication, while an earlier class of Harvard boys was metaphorically traversing that marvelous "ethereal space," the girl who would become Phillis Wheatley was traveling the nightmarish yet all too real Middle Passage. While this poem's juxtaposition of Wheatley's past with her audience's privilege includes nary a note of self-pity, it is hard to miss an envious tinge in the longings of a bright young woman denied the formal opportunity "to scan the heights Above."

The sole consolation for Wheatley the believer was that the two sets of contrasts her poem invoked—sinner and saved, black woman and white man—were not analogous. The blood of Christ flowed not only for privileged young men at Cambridge but also for her; redemption was available not only to those with the best education that the colonies could offer but also to those who had to rely on their own wits and resources to make their way in a hostile world. If by all outward considerations Phillis Wheatley was inferior to the people she addressed, in the eyes of God she was their equal. As such, she was entitled to end her poem with one last exhortation:

> Suppress the deadly serpent in its egg.
> Ye blooming plants of human race divine,
> An *Ethiop* tells you 'tis your greatest foe;
> Its transient sweetness turns to endless pain,
> And in immense perdition sinks the soul.

The students whom Wheatley called "blooming plants" were barely younger than she, if not older. Ever intent on drawing attention to the unusual relationship between speaker and audience, she was careful to identify herself as an African again in the final lines. Surely the gory solemnity of her "*Ethiop*"'s warnings about pain and perdition rivaled the gloomiest sermons of New England's greatest fire-and-brimstone preachers. Yet as frightening as the "deadly serpent" is, these lines evoke another, more subtle but no less powerful image: an African woman addressing a captivated white male audience, using *their* language and belief system to express *her* own sense of self and rightness.

To the University of Cambridge, in New-England

Phillis Wheatley

WHILE an intrinsic ardor prompts to write,
The muses promise to assist my pen;
'Twas not long since I left my native shore
The land of errors, and *Egyptian* gloom:
Father of mercy, 'twas thy gracious hand
Brought me in safety from those dark abodes.

Students, to you 'tis giv'n to scan the heights
Above, to traverse the ethereal space,
And mark the systems of revolving worlds.
Still more, ye sons of science ye receive
The blissful news by messengers from heav'n,
How *Jesus'* blood for your redemption flows.
See him with hands out-stretcht upon the cross;
Immense compassion in his bosom glows;
He hears revilers, nor resents their scorn:
What matchless mercy in the Son of God!
When the whole human race by sin had fall'n,
He deign'd to die that they might rise again,
And share with him in the sublimest skies,
Life without death, and glory without end.

Improve your privileges while they stay,
Ye pupils, and each hour redeem, that bears
Or good or bad report of you to heav'n.
Let sin, that baneful evil to the soul,
By you be shun'd, nor once remit your guard;
Suppress the deadly serpent in its egg.
Ye blooming plants of human race divine,
An *Ethiop* tells you 'tis your greatest foe;
Its transient sweetness turns to endless pain,
And in immense perdition sinks the soul.

Phillis Wheatley, "To the University of Cambridge, in New-England," in *Poems on Various Subjects, Religious and Moral* (London, 1773), 15-16.

Singular as that image may seem, it emerges again only a few years later in the history of Massachusetts. On February 15, 1783, the state legislature (known as the General Court) received a petition on behalf of a 70-year-old woman called "Belinda, an Afffican." Before elaborating Belinda's request, the petition narrated her life story. It described an idyllic childhood on a verdant West African riverbank, cut short by the horrors of the slave trade. Life in Africa "would have yielded [young Belinda] the most compleat felicity, had not her mind received early impressions of the cruelty of men, whose faces were like the moon, and whose Bows and Arrows were like the thunder and the lightning of the Clouds." When Belinda was only about 11, those men "ravished [her] from the bosom of her Country, from the arms of her friends,—while the advanced age of her Parents, rendering them unfit for servitude, cruelly seperated [sic] her from them forever!" More nightmares awaited: the "excruciating torments" of the slave ship's long journey, ending in a land where Belinda discovered that "her doom was Slavery, from which death alone was to emancipate her." There she toiled 50 years in "ignoble servitude" until the colonies rebelled and her master, a Tory, fled to England. Finally, with the war drawing to a close, her master dead, and a lifetime of unpaid work behind her, Belinda was left with scant means of financial support. Poverty motivated her to turn to the General Court. Her master's property having been confiscated by Massachusetts when he went into political exile, Belinda wanted the legislators to grant her money from his estate so that she could provide for herself and her sickly daughter. The legislators quickly acceded, ordering that an annual allowance of £15 12s be set aside for Belinda from the estate of her former owner.[21]

Despite the superficial similarities they share—African-born women brought to eighteenth-century Massachusetts as slaves—Belinda and Phillis Wheatley apparently form a study in contrasts. Scholars today can go to Harvard's Houghton Library to view an autographed first edition of Wheatley's compositions and to decipher the words of one poem written in her own hand. Visitors to the Massachusetts Archives, however, will find that an "X" scratched at the bottom of Belinda's petition is the only writing certainly attributable to her. That mark in place of a signature indicates that Belinda could not write; chances are she did not know how to read either. Whoever transcribed the petition for her likely had a hand in composing it as well, for the florid and sentimentalized prose must have come from someone well versed in eighteenth-century literary forms. Of these two women who came to Massachusetts as slaves, one was a prodigy, the other illiterate, yet their two documents, the poem and the petition, served similar purposes. They got the men of Harvard College and the General Court—two of the oldest and most important secular institutions in Massachusetts—to pay attention, if only for a few minutes, to the thoughts and experiences of black women.

By laying claim to a portion of her master's Massachusetts estate and by seeking recourse through the government, Belinda proved that she had a stake in America. In a roundabout way, she had a stake, too, in Harvard. Belinda had been a slave to Isaac Royall, Jr., the heir to an Antiguan sugar fortune and a long-time resident of a lavish estate in Medford, Massachusetts. Throughout the eighteenth century, the Royalls were Medford's richest family, owning more slaves than any other household in town.[22] Though Isaac Royall and his immediate family fled the colonies shortly after the Battle of Lexington in 1775, his fondness for his old haunts—Medford, Charlestown, Cambridge—persisted even in exile. When Royall died in 1781, he left a number of bequests to friends back in Massachusetts, as well as gifts to support Medford's church and school. One of his most generous bequests was to Harvard. Though Royall himself was not an alumnus, prior to the Revolution he had served the College as an Overseer, and he had contributed money for the restoration of the library and laboratory following the Harvard Hall fire of 1764.[23] In his will, Royall left over 2,000 acres of land in the towns of Granby and Royalston "to be appropriated toward the endowing of a Professor of Laws in said College, or a Professor of Physick and Anatomy, whichever the said overseers and corporation shall judge best for the benefit of said College."[24]

Harvard's governing boards decided in favor of creating a chair in law, though it was not until 1815 that the Royall professorship actually came into being.[25] Isaac Parker, the first Royall Professor (1815-1827), was also Harvard's first professor of law. Once it was established in 1817, the Law School borrowed for its official seal the image of three sheaves of wheat from the Royall family coat of arms.[26] That gesture was a nod to the fact that Harvard Law School's very existence stemmed from Isaac Royall's generosity with his American lands. But the same will that created the Harvard professorship featured other allocations as well. To his "beloved son-in-law" Royall left "my Negro Boy Joseph and my Negro Girl Priscilla," while a "Negro Girl Barsheba and her Sister Nanny" were to go to Royall's daughter and "her heirs forever." Then Royall added, "I do also give unto my said daughter my Negro Woman Belinda in case she does not choose her freedom; if she does choose her freedom, [she is] to have it, provided she get security that she shall not be a charge to the town of Medford."[27]

Royall's will left Belinda something that was not really his to give, save for the fact that he had denied it to her for so long. All evidence suggests that

Belinda opted for freedom rather than continued bondage to a Royall heir, but her decision posed a dilemma that modern-day observers can easily overlook.[28] However meager their status, slaves in eighteenth-century New England could at least claim a recognized social position. The relationship between master and slave (like those between husband and wife and parent and child) was hierarchical, to be sure, and could turn coercive and even violent. But New England society acknowledged certain obligations that masters had to fulfill on behalf of their servants and slaves.[29] Chief among these was basic material support. Once freed, a former slave was expected to be financially independent, which was difficult in the rocky postwar economy, even for a white person who did not have to worry about race prejudice.[30] When she petitioned the legislature in 1783, two years after Royall's death and eight years after his flight to England, perhaps the economic uncertainties of freedom had taken their toll on Belinda. Or maybe by that point she simply felt ready to claim what she saw as her due.

Were it not for Belinda and her petition, it might be possible to separate the two strands of Isaac Royall's will and the two sides of the man himself. On the one hand, he was a magnanimous benefactor who transcended political differences to support the New England institutions he loved; on the other, he was a slaveowner who held on to his human chattel even as black and white New Englanders were intensifying their demands for freedom. Belinda's petition draws attention to the fact that the money Royall donated to Harvard was money he had not paid the people whose labor had helped amass his wealth from the beginning. The point is not that Harvard was built by slave labor. Such an extrapolation from Belinda's story alone would overstate both Royall's importance to Harvard and one woman's role in a complex economic system—though a fuller accounting of Harvard's connections to slavery and the slave trade would indeed be revealing. What Belinda does confirm is the inextricability of Harvard's long history from the political currents, economic institutions, and social structures of the world surrounding it. Her petition is a reminder that abundance and opportunity do not necessarily translate to equity and justice: "What did it avail her," the petition asked rhetorically, "that the walls of her Lord [i.e., her master] were hung with splendor . . . while she, by the Laws of the Land, is denied the enjoyment of one morsel of that immense wealth, apart whereof hath been accumulated by her own industry, and the whole augmented by her servitude." Some two centuries later, how to distribute nearly immeasurable resources in an equitable way remains the primary challenge facing both Harvard and the country whose history is so often mirrored in the university's own.

The institution that attracted Wheatley's poetry and Royall's philanthropy would go on to become arguably the most renowned university in the world. In contrast, the lives of Belinda and Phillis Wheatley ended at best obscurely and at worst tragically. Despite her triumph before the Massachusetts legislature in 1783, within a few years Belinda had stopped receiving her allowance. In 1787, she complained to the General Court, which promised to resume its annual payment to her from Isaac Royall's estate. The state finally sold the Royall property in 1805, by which time Belinda had most likely died.[31] If more is known about Wheatley's final years, the tale is hardly more satisfying. Freed shortly after the publication of her first book, in 1778 she wed John Peters, a free black man variously described as a respectable Bostonian and a dissolute businessman. In any case, Peters developed financial problems in the later years of the war, and his wife's abortive writing career could not support the family. Though she circulated a proposal for a second book of poetry (under the name Phillis Peters), the Revolution had ruptured Wheatley's Anglo-American network of supporters. While she continued to publish individual poems in local periodicals, she never found a printer for the new collection. Always in precarious health, Phillis Wheatley Peters followed her last surviving child to the grave in December 1784. She was 31.[32]

What place do people like Phillis Wheatley and Belinda have in Harvard's history? Efforts to "diversify" history sometimes search out dark-skinned and female faces to position among the scores of white male portraits that illustrate the College's centuries-old narrative. But there is something jarring about that image—not simply because we are unaccustomed to seeing women and people of color on the walls of the Faculty Club or University Hall, but because the contributions Wheatley and Belinda made to Harvard's history are so far outside the roles played by the distinguished faculty, alumni, and administrators whose images have long graced the university's most sacred spaces. Writing these two women into the school's history is not really a matter of inclusion, because in their time both were categorically excluded from Harvard as well as from the social space that Harvard students and alumni occupied. Instead, comprehending Phillis Wheatley and Belinda as part of Harvard's history requires careful consideration of the relationship between Harvard and the world around it. On the one hand, Phillis Wheatley's poem "To the University of Cambridge" invoked a Harvard that existed apart from the world, the kind of place worthy of a poet's loftiest religious and moral exhortations. By inserting herself into the poem, Wheatley reminded her readers that such an idealized space did not exist, at least not for everyone. From within

Harvard's gates, Wheatley's poem and biography prompt us to ask: Who has been excluded from this place that has welcomed us? Turning to Belinda's plea for a share in the wealth she helped to create, we might wonder whose hard work has enabled this institution to thrive.

In the end, the threads that bind these women to Harvard's history and to each other are admittedly thin—but surprisingly strong. What ties them together is perhaps best exemplified in the statute that established the Royall Professorship of Law. Written in 1815, those guidelines specified that the Royall Professor's ultimate purpose was to help students "become useful and distinguished supporters of our free system of government, as well as able and honorable advocates of the rights of the citizen."[33] Consider Belinda, one-time slave of Harvard's benefactor Isaac Royall, who once in 1783 and again in 1787 brought a plea to her government insisting that her rights be respected. And consider Phillis Wheatley, poet to Harvard and to the wider world, who in a verse addressed to King George's secretary of state explained that her love of American liberty stemmed from her experience of American slavery.[34] If a deep appreciation for human freedom is what a Harvard education entails, then surely these two women do belong amid all those distinguished alumni.

Notes

1. Samuel Eliot Morison, *Three Centuries of Harvard, 1636-1936* (1936; Cambridge, Mass.: Harvard University Press, 1946), 133.
2. Quoted in Morison, *Three Centuries of Harvard*, 135. In quoting here and elsewhere, I retain the spelling and capitalization of the sources.
3. Phillis Wheatley, "To the University of Cambridge, in New-England," in *Poems on Various Subjects, Religious and Moral* (London, 1773), 15-16. William H. Robinson, *Phillis Wheatley and Her Writings* (New York: Garland, 1984) includes a complete facsimile of the first edition of Wheatley's *Poems*.
4. William D. Piersen, *Black Yankees: The Development of an Afro-American Subculture in Eighteenth-Century New England* (Amherst: University of Massachusetts Press, 1988), 168; Lorenzo Johnston Greene, *The Negro in Colonial New England* (New York: Columbia University Press, 1942; rpt. with a preface by Benjamin Quarles, New York: Atheneum, 1968), 81.
5. Cotton Mather, *The Negro Christianized: An Essay to Excite and Assist that Good Work, the Instruction of Negro-Servants in Christianity* (Boston, 1706), 34-40. Mather's pamphlet was published some 60 years before Phillis Wheatley was "Christianized." The responses to Wheatley's accomplishments suggest that her contemporaries had no higher expectations for the intellectual potential of Africans than Mather had decades before; see, for example, the original London review of Wheatley's book, reprinted in William H. Robinson, ed., *Critical Essays on Phillis Wheatley* (Boston: G.K. Hall, 1982), 30-31. On white Anglo-Americans' beliefs about black intellectual inferiority, see Winthrop D.

Jordan, *White Over Black: American Attitudes Toward the Negro, 1550-1812* (New York: W.W. Norton, 1977), 187-90, 304-8.

6. *Memoir and Poems of Phillis Wheatley, a Native African and a Slave* (Boston, 1834). The *Memoir* was written by Margaretta Matilda Odell and is accessible in facsimile in Robinson, *Phillis Wheatley and Her Writings*, 431.

7. From a letter signed by John Wheatley and printed in the front matter of Phillis Wheatley, *Poems*, n.p.

8. Phillis Wheatley's year of birth is usually estimated as either 1753 or 1754. This account of Wheatley's education is based on Julian D. Mason, Jr., introduction to *The Poems of Phillis Wheatley*, rev. and enl. ed. (Chapel Hill: University of North Carolina Press, 1989), 3-5, and Vincent Carretta, introduction to Phillis Wheatley, *Complete Writings* (New York: Penguin, 2001), xiii-xiv. A useful biography is Robinson, "On Phillis Wheatley and Her Boston," in *Phillis Wheatley and Her Writings*, 3-69.

9. A person's educational opportunities in eighteenth-century New England were not circumscribed merely by gender and race but also by class. Working-class and slave women had no hope of maintaining the pretense of feminine delicacy to which elite women aspired. Though it is not about education per se, Laurel Thatcher Ulrich, "Sheep in the Parlor, Wheels on the Common: Pastoralism and Poverty in Eighteenth-Century Boston," in *Inequality in Early America*, ed. Carla Gardina Pestana and Sharon V. Salinger (Hanover, N.H.: University Press of New England, 1999), 182-200, illustrates the class lines I have in mind—those distinctions that sent some young women to spinning factories and others to embroidery schools. Although enslavement would seem to correspond with low class status, Wheatley's class position was surprisingly ambiguous. Susanna Wheatley apparently treated Phillis as something between a daughter and a cherished household pet: "[Phillis] was not devoted to menial occupations, as was at first intended; nor was she allowed to associate with the other domestics of the family, who were of her own color and condition, but was kept constantly about the person of her mistress." Odell, *Memoir*, facsimile in Robinson, *Phillis Wheatley and Her Writings*, 431.

10. Quoted in Linda K. Kerber, *Women of the Republic: Intellect and Ideology in Revolutionary America* (Chapel Hill: University of North Carolina Press, 1980), 191.

11. See, for example, Kerber, *Women of the Republic*, 189-231. A number of sources attempt to quantify literacy rates for New England women around this period; see Joel Perlmann and Dennis Shirley, "When Did New England Women Acquire Literacy?" *William & Mary Quarterly* 48 (1991): 50-67; Gloria L. Main, "An Inquiry into When and Why Women Learned to Write in Colonial New England," *Journal of Social History* 24 (1991): 579-89.

12. James Oliver Horton and Lois E. Horton, *In Hope of Liberty: Culture, Community, and Protest Among Northern Free Blacks, 1700-1860* (New York: Oxford University Press, 1997), 19-22.

13. A Lady of Boston [Mary Webb?], *Memoir of Mrs. Chloe Spear, a Native of Africa, Who Was Enslaved in Childhood, and Died in Boston* (Boston, 1832), 22-26.

14. On Wheatley's evangelical support network, see David Grimsted, "Anglo-American Racism and Phillis Wheatley's 'Sable Veil,' 'Length'ned Chain,' and 'Knitted Heart'," in *Women in the Age of the American Revolution*, ed. Ronald Hoffman and Peter J. Albert (Charlottesville: University Press of Virginia, 1989), 344-70, and James A. Rawley, "The World of Phillis Wheatley," *New England Quarterly* 50 (1977): 666-77.

15. Theodore Parsons and Eliphalet Pearson, "A Forensic Dispute on the Legality of Enslaving the Africans, Held at the Public Commencement in Cambridge, New-England," in *Blacks at Harvard: A Documentary History of African-American Experience at Harvard and Radcliffe*, ed. Werner Sollors, Caldwell Titcomb, and Thomas A. Underwood (New York: New York University Press, 1993), 17.

16. "Phillis Wheatley," in Sollors, Titcomb, and Underwood, eds., *Blacks at Harvard*, 9.

17. The most recent of the essays collected in Robinson, *Critical Essays*, reflect responses to Wheatley's poetry that range from ambivalent to hostile; for examples of the latter, see the selections by Angelene Jamison and Terrence Collins.

18. See the reading of Wheatley's "On Being Brought from Africa to America" in Marsha Watson, "A Classic Case: Phillis Wheatley and Her Poetry," *Early American Literature* 31 (1996): 122-23.

19. On African Americans and religion in New England generally, see Piersen, *Black Yankees*, 65-73; Erik R. Seeman, "'Justise Must Take Plase': Three African Americans Speak of Religion in Eighteenth-Century New England," *William & Mary Quarterly* 56 (1999): 395-406.

20. Noting that "Ethiopia" and "Gambia" are Wheatley's more familiar terms for her native land, Grimsted argues that the reference to Egypt in this poem is not synecdoche for Africa but instead an allusion to the Biblical land of slavery ("Anglo-American Racism and Phillis Wheatley," 357).

21. Massachusetts Archives, 239:12. There are several published variants of Belinda's petition. The most accessible (and tolerably accurate) transcription of the original text is in *Unchained Voices: An Anthology of Black Authors in the English-Speaking World of the Eighteenth Century*, ed. Vincent Carretta (Lexington: University Press of Kentucky, 1996), 142-43.

22. See Royall's entry in the 1771 Massachusetts tax inventory, originally published as Bettye Pruitt, ed., *The Massachusetts Tax Valuation List of 1771* (Boston: G.K. Hall, 1978). I used the online version in fall 1999: http://www.courses.fas.harvard.edu/hist1618/masstax/ masstax.html. Also see "A Medford Slave Roll," *Medford Historical Register* 27 (1914): 48. Biographies of Isaac Royall, Jr., and his family include James H. Stark, *The Loyalists of Massachusetts and the Other Side of the American Revolution* (1910; rpt., Clifton, N.J.: Augustus M. Kelley, 1972), 290-94; Edward Doubleday Harris, "The New England Royalls," *New England Historical Genealogical Register* 39 (1885): 348-58; Gladys N. Hoover, *The Elegant Royalls of Colonial New England* (New York: Vantage Press, 1974).

23. Hoover, *Elegant Royalls*, 65.

24. Royall will; Josiah Quincy, *The History of Harvard University*, 2 vols. (1840; New York: Arno Press, 1977), 1:319.

25. William Bentinck-Smith and Elizabeth Stouffer, *Harvard University History of Named Chairs*, vol. 3 (Cambridge, Mass.: Harvard University, 1995), 397. The delay stemmed from the fact that like other loyalist estates, Isaac Royall's property was in bureaucratic limbo for some years after the war.

26. "Gallery: A Royall Find," *Harvard Law Bulletin* (Summer 2001); also viewable at http:// www.law.harvard.edu/alumni/bulletin/2001/summer/gallery_main.html.

27. Royall will. I have added punctuation to the manuscript text to ease reading.

28. Nowhere does the language of the petition suggest that Belinda was a slave to a Royall heir in February 1783. Furthermore—and probably not coincidentally—by the time Belinda brought her petition to the legislature, public opinion had turned sharply against slavery. Many historians believe that several court cases decided in 1783 brought a de facto end to slavery, though there was no statutory abolition. See Timothy H. Breen, "Making History: The Force of Public Opinion and the Last Years of Slavery in Massachusetts," in *Through a Glass Darkly: Reflections on Personal Identity in Early America*, ed. Ronald Hoffman, Mechal Sobel, and Fredrika J. Teute (Chapel Hill: University of North Carolina Press, 1997), 67-95; Robert M. Spector, "The Quock Walker Cases (1781-1783)—Slavery, Its Abolition, and Negro Citizenship in Early Massachusetts," *Journal of Negro History* 53 (1968): 12-32.

29. Greene, *Negro in Colonial New England*, 218-34; Piersen, *Black Yankees*, 25-36; for a broader discussion of social relations in early New England, see Edmund S. Morgan, *The Puritan Family: Religion and Domestic Relations in Seventeenth-Century New England* (New York: Harper and Row, 1966).

30. Horton and Horton, *In Hope of Liberty*, 101-24; Joanne Pope Melish, *Disowning Slavery: Gradual Emancipation and "Race" in New England, 1780-1860* (Ithaca, N.Y.: Cornell University Press), 84-110.

31. Sidney Kaplan and Emma Nogrady Kaplan, *The Black Presence in the Era of the American Revolution,* rev. ed. (Amherst: University of Massachusetts Press, 1989), 244, 291; *Acts and Laws of the Commonwealth of Massachusetts* (Boston, 1893), 816.
32. Robinson, "On Phillis Wheatley and Her Boston," 53-65.
33. Quoted in Bentinck-Smith and Stouffer, *History of Named Chairs,* 397.
34. Wheatley, "To the Right Honourable William, Earl of Dartmouth, His Majesty's Principal Secretary of State for North America, &c." in *Poems,* 73-75.

SNAPSHOTS

From the Archives

ANNA QUINCY DESCRIBES THE "CAMBRIDGE WORTHIES"

Beverly Wilson Palmer

In the spring and summer of 1833, 21-year-old Anna Cabot Lowell Quincy kept a diary recording the social activities in Boston and Cambridge.[1] Because her father, Josiah, was then president of Harvard College, she was well positioned to observe the comings and goings in these communities. In Cambridge, a town of slightly over 6,000 residents, Harvard was then a small aspiring college. Only 212 students were enrolled as undergraduates, with 168 graduate students in the law, divinity, and medical schools. Professors and instructors for all of these schools totaled just 23 men.

Regularly, while the College was in session, Josiah Quincy and his family received visitors in their home, Wadsworth House, which still stands today inside Harvard Yard. At these receptions, which featured cake, wine, and fruit as refreshments for students, faculty, and friends, the public rooms were often crowded. In the following description of one of these affairs, Anna Quincy refers to her sister Sophia and to a series of Harvard men: undergraduate Thomas P. Rutledge of South Carolina, class of 1835; law students Joseph S. Jones of Shocco, North Carolina, and William Richard Chaplain ("Leicester") of Cambridge, Maryland. Francis Vinton, a West Point graduate, was also studying law at Harvard while stationed at Fort Independence in Boston. Betsy and the Major are servants in the Quincy household.

In this diary entry one can see a young woman who accepts, indeed enjoys, her role as both ironic observer and active participant in an academic setting. No Harvard male escapes Anna's satiric scrutiny. In her introduction to this volume, Laurel Thatcher Ulrich alludes to Virginia Woolf's statement from *A Room of One's Own* that "Women have served all these centuries as looking-glasses possessing the magic and delicious power of reflecting the figure of man at twice its natural size." But Anna's diary entry reduces these men and bears out Woolf's subsequent contention that if a woman "begins to tell the truth, the figure in the looking-glass shrinks; his fitness for life is diminished."[2] In fact, with the exception of Francis Vinton, who became a noted Episcopal clergyman in his day, none of the "Cambridge worthies" described here achieved any kind of fame or notoriety. Instead it is Anna Quincy's account that we will remember.

The "Cambridge Worthies"

Anna Quincy Diary,
March 21, 1833, Wadsworth House, Harvard College

Thursday 21st Came out of town—talked over the eveg &c— The day was lowring, chilly, dark, the roads were deep & boggy, the night was dark & foggy, & we of course did not anticipate any of "our hens" would <u>peck</u> their way out here— Indeed we should have been sorry to have seen any one from Boston— We had all the Cambridge worthies & all our elite beaux, & only regretted we had not more belles— Mr Rutlegdge first approached me, putting to flight some inferior being, who was daring to address me, we were soon joined by Mr Jones, who certainly would be classed by Mr [Gasport?] under the "<u>Voluables</u>"; these two youths amused <u>themselves</u> some time, & entertained me until the superior form of Mr Chaplain approached & then they spread their wings, biddy gutterfies, as they are, & left the scene to Chaplain—& to me As the elevated & the refined, however they surpass the ~~frivolous &~~ ridiculous & the unmeaning, in actual merit, & agreeableness, is not as well fitted to entertain in the pages of a journal, I more frequently record the sayings of a Jones & a Vinton, rather than a Chaplains, tho' far more worthy.

I therefore pass over the next half hour, during which we took a tour into the next apartment, wandered for some time gasing at the varied beauties of Nature & art & at length paused to moralise before the declaration of independance,— which if "you recollect yourself my good girl", hangs over the fire place, in which was enkindled a hospitable flame— But we were <u>above</u> such considerations & <u>stept</u> over the <u>fender</u>, in order to view more nearly same ancient worthy— While we were standing the <u>fire</u> of <u>patriotism</u>, Sophia & Mr Vinton approached, — & Mr Vinton with infinite humour, jocosely addressed us on the subject of our insensibility to all things around us, even to the elements.— The haughty

Leicester is the last person I should select to <u>rally</u> jocosely on any subject, & suddenly withdrawing from the offending fender, without taking any notice of Mr Vintons remarks, offered his arm, & "we sailed away to more secure repose"—& took our station before the shrine of <u>Lafayette</u>—[3]

Here we enjoyed the flow of soul for some time, & were deeply engaged in some interesting ~~disquis~~ topic, when without the least preparation, Mr Vintons <u>head</u> was thrust directly before us, in so startling a manner that even Leicester— started, & I almost leapt into the air— Barbarous man! He broke the illusion, merely to ask me who that young lady was—meaning Miss Randall. He then proceeded to remark that my sister was so kind, & "very obliging that she had gone upstairs to bring done a small glass bird for him"— Thinks I the man is demented entirely, what on Earth can he mean—

"Glass bird" repeated I, with a bewildered air, reflected <u>faintly</u> indeed ~~perhaps~~, from the glance of my elevated companion. "Yes," resumed Mr Vinton, "I believe it is a Peacock, at any rate it has a <u>long tail</u> of spun glass". This explanation, though it threw light upon me, seemed to cap the climax of Leicesters amasement. With folded arms, & knit brows, he looked down upon us, with a glance that might have melted the spun glass of the Peacocks tail. I hastened to explain the glassworkers powers & then turned the conversation— while Mr Vinton skipt off.— Soon after Miss Randall was prevailed upon to play— which she did extremely well. Soon after Sophia & Mr Vinton armed with the glass birds approached— Sophia declared that when she showed the wonderful bird with the glass tail to Leicester that he like Mr Meadows took no sort of notice of it—while Mr Vintons more present soul, exclaimed, "wonderful beautiful, exquiste"—and such is the praise of which <u>she</u> is silly enough to be vain— — Miss Randall again played—and is certainly a first rate performer I should think, tho' I must confess, mere instrumental music gives me but very little pleasure except when I am all alone.—

Talked to Rutledge some time—silly child—and then again to Mr Vinton, who is certainly an [amusing?] personage.— He informed me that he was certain we had "one comfort in our house"— "A great many, Mr Vinton, but to which do you allude" "Why" said he "I just looked in to the little parlour, & there I saw a woman, most industriously <u>plying</u> her <u>needle</u>, quite regardless of the company— I am sure she must be a treasure"!— <u>Betsy</u> certainly little imagined, that she was the object of Mr Vintons attention—but I agreed & then followed an account of some <u>old</u> <u>family</u> <u>servants'</u> of the <u>noble</u> <u>race</u> <u>of</u> <u>Vinton</u>! I then thought I would go a touch beyond—, so I told him that we had a still more distinguished, member and entered into a description of our coachman, who was a Major of artillery!— His astonishment was great, (second only to the Peacock with a glass tail)— "Is it possible" exclaimed he. "A major of Artillery! why, Miss Quincy if we were called in to service, that man would rank above me"! Just at this moment the Major appeared, bearing in his hand not a sword, but a waiter,[4] which he offered to us— As soon as he had passed & turned away—Mr Vinton raises his hand to make the military salute, & bowing low says "I pay my respects to my Superior officer"— It was quite smart of the youth I thought & certainly done very well.—

We then returned to the other room, where we had again a long & sentimental conversation, during which he enquired if I could inform him, how a gentleman was to know ~~how far~~ if he had penetrated into a ladys heart far enough to offer his own! I replied, "really Mr V I must leave that to yr own penetration". "Oh" said he "I was not referring to myself— I am now in a mere <u>butterfly</u> State, <u>roving</u> from flower to flower but it was more for the future I wished to be informed—" Leaving Mr Vinton in his butterfly state, I lightly flew off & had varied talks with various mortals, & wound up the evening with a talk with Mr Jones of which no trace is left on my memory— We had a pleasant evening & so ended the Levées of 1833.—

Notes

1. This extract is from the manuscript diary held at the Massachusetts Historical Society, Boston, Mass. The diary has been published as Anna Cabot Lowell Quincy, *A Woman's Wit and Whimsy: The 1833 Diary of Anna Cabot Lowell Quincy,* ed. Beverly Wilson Palmer (Boston: Northeastern University Press, 2003).
2. Virginia Woolf, *A Room of One's Own* (New York: Harcourt Brace Jovanovich, 1929; 1981), 37.
3. Items making up the "shrine of Lafayette" were likely two armchairs with flag seats that Harvard apparently acquired when the Marquis de Lafayette visited the College in August 1824. Inventory of furniture in Wadsworth House, Feb. 17, 1849, President's Papers, E. Everett letters, vol. 2, Harvard University Archives.
4. A tray for carrying dishes.

"FEMININE" CLOTHING AT HARVARD IN THE 1830s

Robin McElheny

The Harvard College laws of 1816 included the following curious entry: "If any [student] . . . shall put on indecent apparel or women's apparel . . . the Government may inflict any of the College censures, at their discretion."[1] This prohibition stands out because it is the only one that alludes to the gender of the (male) audience. What prompted it? Was the wearing of women's clothing frowned upon because it fell in the category of dissolute behavior? Or theatrical entertainment (also prohibited)? Or vanity? Was there a rash of cross-dressing at the time?

In 1838 Samuel Longfellow, Harvard class of 1839, drew a sketch of the "Summer Costume of the Cambridge Students." It depicts a person wearing a long-sleeved coat with a full skirt, attached cape, wide collar, and long sleeves. The coat is trimmed with fringe or lace. To complete the outfit, the person wears long pants and a wide-brimmed hat. The Harvard University Archives has just such a coat among its holdings. Made of green and white cotton gingham with white trim, it was supposedly worn by David Haskins, class of 1837, and given to the archives by his daughter in 1939, where it is described in the original shelf list as a "toga."[2]

At the time of the gift, Harvard historian Samuel Eliot Morison regarded the costume with suspicion, considering it "too sissy to have been worn by the deep-drinking young hellions of President Quincy's administration."[3] It

The Harvard "toga" (Harvard University Archives).

wasn't until an archivist found the following passage from Sidney Willard's *Memories of Youth and Manhood* that Morison was convinced that Harvard undergraduates would have worn such an unmasculine outfit. "In summer long gowns of calico or gingham were the covering that distinguished the collegian, not only about the College grounds, but in all parts of the village."[4]

In his own recollection, "The College Toga," David Haskins attributed its origins to "the creative genius and skilful fingers of 'Ma'am' Dana, the College tailoress of that day, who was the principal, if not the sole, manufacturer of the garment."[5]

Recent research by Sarah Carter, Harvard class of 2002, and an examination by costume historian Nancy Rexford provide a context for Willard's and Haskins's comments. Haskins's "toga" is an example of a "wrapper," a loose-fitting, informal housecoat dating back to the eighteenth century and worn by men and women. In fact, the toga is nearly identical to a "cloak dressing gown," the pattern for which appeared in an 1838 British sewing manual, *The Workwoman's Guide, containing instructions to the inexperienced in cutting out and completing those articles of wearing apparel, &c., which are usually made at home. . . .*[6] According to the *Guide,* the cloak dressing gown was suitable for men, women, and children. Possibly access to an earlier version of the *Guide* inspired Madam Dana to make the outfits that Harvard students of the 1830s found so appealing. Or perhaps cloak dressing gowns were popular enough in England and the United States that any sewing manual worth its purchase price included such a pattern.

No matter what the source of the College toga, its popularity among teenagers has a familiar ring, similar to the more recent popularity of sweat shirts and sweat pants. Clothing that in one setting is comfortable and practical in another setting attains a distinctive cachet. As Sarah Carter has written, "Then as now, college was a peer directed place in which rules were broken, followed and bent in a context of self expression. . . . It [the toga] highlights a unique student culture, the material facets of which are still virtually unexplored."[7]

Notes

1. Harvard University, Board of Overseers, *Laws of Harvard College, for the use of the students. With preliminary notices and an appendix* (Cambridge, Mass.: Printed at the University Press, by Hilliard and Metcalf, 1816), Harvard University Archives [hereafter, HUA] call no. HUD 816.48.
2. HUA call no. HUD 837.87.
3. Samuel Eliot Morison, "Summer Costume of Harvard Students a Century Ago," *Harvard Alumni Bulletin* (Feb. 10, 1939), n. p., HUA call no. HUK 137.
4. Sidney Willard, *Memories of Youth and Manhood* (Cambridge, Mass.: J. Bartlett, 1855), HUA call no. HUG 1876.9654 hd.
5. David Haskins, "The College Toga," *College Recollections and Stories,* place and date of publication unknown.
6. *The Workwoman's Guide . . . [by a lady]* (Guilford, Conn.: Opus Publications [1987], rpt.; originally published: London: Simpkin, Marshall, 1838).
7. Sarah Anne Carter, "Dressed for Undress: David Greene Haskin's 'Toga' and Its Context." Student paper submitted for History 1610, Harvard College (May 2002), HUA accession no. 14584.

JOHN LANGDON SIBLEY

on Taming Undergraduate Passions

Brian Sullivan

In entry after entry in his personal diary, Harvard librarian John Langdon Sibley recorded the behavior of Harvard men who inspired and dismayed him.[1] He offered a moving account of the humble beginnings of historian and Harvard president Jared Sparks and a stark appraisal of an esteemed Harvard alumnus and honorable judge who was stealing library materials. His greatest dismay, however, was reserved for the antics of Harvard students.

Born in Union, Maine, in 1804, Sibley graduated from Harvard College in 1825 and from the Divinity School in 1829. After a stint as the minister of Stow, Massachusetts, and as an editor of the *American Magazine of Useful and Entertaining Knowledge,* he returned to Harvard in 1841 as assistant librarian. He became head of the Harvard College Library 15 years later, serving until his retirement in 1877 at the age of 73.

Sibley's determination to locate, preserve, and publish sources relating to New England and Harvard history led to his multivolume work, *Biographical Sketches of the Graduates of Harvard College,* familiarly known as *Sibley's Harvard Graduates.* A bachelor until 1866 (when he married Charlotte Cook), Sibley inhabited quarters in Divinity Hall for nearly 33 years. From that perch he evaluated the behavior of Harvard undergraduates.

On January 12, 1860, he wrote:

On returning to Cambridge I learned that a special policeman who had been stationed for many weeks in the chapel, allowed a student to enter & place on the desk a Bible, which, it turns out, was stolen from Yale college, probably by way of exchange for one of the two, stolen from Appleton Chapel when it was entered sometime since. When the rogue was going away he seized him & requested him to let him put some iron manacles on his wrist, whereupon the student William Hathaway Forbes, from Milton, a member of the Junior Class struck him a dreadful blow in the face & forehead with "billy." The policeman presented his revolver fired it into the air & told him he would shoot him instantly if he did not suffer him to put the manacles on him. The student then wanted to be taken to the watchhouse. The officer said no. So they remained there from 2 to 6 o'clock, when Jones, the Janitor & Sexton, came to open the chapel & build the fire. Then Forbes appealed to Jones, who knew him, to prevail on the officer, whose face was covered with blood, to let him go. Jones replied that he was not a "man in authority." Accordingly the officer passed Forbes over to the Police Judge, & went home to bed. Judge Ladd would not admit him to bail, but sent him to jail, as Dr. Wyman testified that the officer was not out of danger, & if the blow had fallen a little differently it would have killed him. Forbes is not reckless but remarkable for his philanthropy & benevolence among the sick & poor students. So goes the report to-day.[2]

These comments were followed on January 14, 1860, by this entry:

It seems that the students had a meeting yesterday & passed spirited, able & specious resolutions, which appear in to-day's newspapers, in opposition to the governments employing armed police. The merits of the case seem to resolve themselves into this. Shall the students or the Faculty rule? Forbes would have escaped but for the pistol. The students say nothing about the impropriety of Forbes's being armed.[3]

No doubt, the Forbes incident reinforced concerns about the moral fiber of the undergraduates among Sibley and his colleagues. What was to be done to enhance their seemingly coarse character? A junior, Leonard Case Alden, A.B. 1861, offered a solution in an article in the July 1860 issue of *Harvard Magazine* (a periodical that predates today's version of the same name). Alden proposed what may have been a novel approach to elevating the social graces of the institution's male students—admitting women to Harvard College.

I intend only to notice slightly how the manners of both sexes would be benefited by being accustomed to meet in the recitation and reception rooms. . . . We very well know that a man's conduct towards men is often marked by coarseness and bluntness; and it is to be feared that women do not always treat those of their own sex with all possible consideration and courtesy. But intercourse between the sexes effects great changes. Awkwardness becomes gracefulness; coarseness is softened into politeness; and rough words are modulated into a kind and gentle language.

Do not tell me that it would be improper or indelicate to open our colleges to woman; do not pretend that her character would lose its charms by contact with coarser natures; do not endeavor to argue that alike our own interests and hers would be best separation. . . . if you shut woman out of College, you should also, for the sake of consistency, shut her out of the parlor and the reception-room. . . . will you tell us that, instead of cleansing the young men from the stain of licentiousness which rests upon them, we should only pollute the spotless purity of our sisters; and that, by our endeavor to repress the lust which now gratifies itself only upon the fallen, which should entrap the innocent in a fatal snare and turn the College into a brothel? . . . Public sentiment among the female portion of the college community would frown so severely upon every lapse from virtue that such a scandal would seldom, if ever, occur; and in this safeguard would be found not less effective than the watchful eye of a parent and the protecting influences of home.

The purifying of woman's presence and society [in the College] would be constantly and increasingly felt, and the young men, it is to be hoped, would soon learn to despise and tame the unholy passions which many of them now so shamelessly indulge.[4]

The Alden article appears to have met with some reaction. Another undergraduate, Frederic Baylies Allen, a member of the class of 1863, responded with the following verse in the October issue of *Harvard Magazine:*

Woman in College
As I sat on my window-seat, perched on high,
(For I room in attic, just next to the sky,)
Perusing the article for last July,
A very odd article met my eye,—
'T was a "Woman in College!"

I read it with care, laid the magazine down,
Leaned my head on my elbow, and mused thereon,
I suppose I slept for I saw in my snooze
A vision or a dream, which we'll call if you choose,—
"Woman in College."

'T was something as follows;—Old Jones rang the bell
With his usual vigor, when lo, strange to tell!
From entry of Stoughton and Holworthy too,
Massachusetts and Hollis, there burst in my view,—
The "Women in College."

Ah! you'd better believe, 't was a beautiful sight,
As they passed down the paths on their way to recite,
Brave youths and fair maidens in company go,
And their peg-tops and crinolines sway to and fro.—
Ah! 'tis jolly,—this "Women in College."

See that chap on the steps, with such impudent grace,
Explaining to Mary a difficult place,
One hand holds the book, while the other is placed,
With careless assurance, around the fair waist—
Of this "Woman in College."

But see these two girls! They're coming this way.
Just look at their head-gear! Now isn't that gay?
A wee bit of a cap, with a "63" on it,
Why bless me! That's surely the Soph'more class bonnet,
Of the "Women in College."

But they've met a gay Sophomore,—hear what they say.
"Why, Billy, my boy, how's your health to-day?
What's this sorrowful story, about you, we hear?
That you're summoned and sent to the country a year.
Away from the "Women in College"?

"Rather rough on you, Bill! You're an unlucky bird."
"Not a bit of it, Lucy! Why, have n't you heard
That lovely Miss Smith and Adelaide Brown

Are to rusticate with me,—a few miles from town?
Ain't it jolly, this "Women in College?". . .

And here I awoke. 'T was only a dream!
How dreary and cold the College did seem.
Ah, ladies! your presence would send a bright gleam
Of sunlight upon our dull, stupid routine
Of studies and deeds, and would make "all serene.". . .[5]

Regardless of undergraduate fantasies, women remained outside Harvard's lecture halls, and the men, unpurified. On May 15, 1868, Sibley recorded another incident involving the students:

Last evening, five tar barrels, one filled with shavings, kerosene, pistol-wickers, etc. carried into the southwest corner of Gore Hall, by the tower & piled up; but the students being discovered fled. At first it was thought a design was to set fire to the Library; but subsequently it seemed more probable that they were placed there to be carted to different parts of the college yard to be ignited simultaneously & excite a general alarm.[6]

There is no evidence that Sibley supported the admission of women, but in his own way he supported female education. College Library records show that he frequently checked out books on behalf of female readers who included the poet Caroline Orne and his housemaid Mary McCrossen.[7]

Notes

1. John Langdon Sibley's diary, Harvard University Archives [hereafter, HUA] call no. HUG 1791.72, is also known as his "Private Journal."
2. Sibley's Journal, 519.
3. Ibid.
4. *Harvard Magazine* 6, no. 56 (July 1860): 353, HUA call no. HUK 544.
5. *Harvard Magazine* 7, no. 58 (Oct. 1860): 59, HUA call no. HUK 544.
6. Sibley's Journal, 790.
7. Records of the Harvard College Library, Charging Records, HUA call no. UAIII 50.15.60.

II.

CREATING RADCLIFFE, DEFINING GENDER
1870–1910

TAKING UP THE CHALLENGE

The Origins of Radcliffe

Sally Schwager

Writing in 1962, on the eve of a dramatic new agreement between Harvard and Radcliffe, professor of history and former Harvard provost Paul Buck argued that the original scheme—the establishment of Radcliffe College in 1894 as a separate, degree-granting institution—had been "an illogical and wasteful adaptation." The separate women's college, he suggested, was a contrivance "forced upon the local friends of higher education for women by the obstinate resistance of the Harvard Governing Boards."[1]

Those friends of women's education had labored for decades to win access to Harvard, and finally, at the end of the nineteenth century, they believed that Harvard would agree to take over the instruction of women and grant them academic degrees. The private Harvard Annex, created in 1879 as an earlier compromise, had demonstrated women's ability to handle the intellectual work; the Woman's Education Association of Boston had raised substantial funds to support the education of women at Harvard; and the Annex was prepared to transfer its property to the College. President Charles William Eliot initially had seemed to support these efforts, but when confronted with the actual transfer of women, property, and the provision of academic degrees to Harvard College, he disavowed any such notion. "Eliot remained obdurate," wrote Buck, "and the antifeminism that he represented, or, at least, accepted, survived him."[2]

It also, of course, had preceded him. The establishment of Radcliffe College at the end of the nineteenth century was the culmination of a series of measures negotiated by the university in an effort to stave off women's challenges to the College. As early as the 1820s, several young women had made informal arrangements to study with Harvard professors. By the middle decades of the century, women schoolteachers and amateur scientists were studying privately in Harvard's new biology and botany laboratories. Cambridge women were invited to attend summer courses and evening lectures sponsored by the university. But women were denied access to the College as well as to the Medical School, the Law School, and the Divinity School. It soon became clear that Harvard would accommodate women only to the extent that their presence served the university's own purposes.[3]

In the decade following the Civil War, increased advocacy on the part of Boston and Cambridge women led to proposals for coeducation in the College and the founding of organizations such as the Woman's Education Association of Boston and the Society for the Collegiate Instruction of Women (the so-called Harvard Annex or just "the Annex") to promote the education of women at Harvard. Male faculty sympathetic to the women's cause appealed to Harvard's Board of Overseers in 1872, but the board declined even to investigate the question of coeducation.[4] The Woman's Education Association countered with a proposal whereby the university would grant degrees to women who might pass all of the examinations required of Harvard men. But Eliot refused to support any plan by which women would earn a Harvard degree, he explained, "because it would be as much to say that I thought the Harvard course as suitable for young women as for young men—which I do not."[5] Conversely, he had no scruples about exploiting nondegree programs and women's private tuitions to advance the work of the College. Eliot not only tolerated courses taught by Harvard faculty to women at the Annex, and later at Radcliffe, but shamelessly promoted them as "perks" when it helped him recruit new faculty for the university.[6]

The history of Radcliffe's origins, then, is a story of sustained advocacy on the part of women and a policy of containment on the part of the university. Their interplay is reflected in the work of the Boston and Cambridge women who were at the heart of the challenge and in the concessions that resulted. It began unceremoniously with a few young women arranging to attend the lectures of a Harvard professor.

ANTEBELLUM FORAYS

The extent to which women sought access to Harvard College in the years before the Civil War is difficult to assess. The College kept no records of isolated cases, but women's memoirs suggest that informal arrangements, though rare, were not unheard of. Ann Storrow, a Cambridge girl, attended the lectures of George Ticknor, Harvard's first professor of modern languages and literature, in the late 1820s or early 1830s. Lucretia Crocker, a science educator who taught at the State Normal School in West Newton and later at Antioch College, attended lectures and worked in the laboratory of Louis Agassiz, professor of zoology and geology, in the early 1850s. This informal arrangement may have been the impetus behind a petition submitted to the Corporation by Mary Peabody Mann in 1855, requesting that teachers from the normal school be allowed to attend Agassiz's lectures at Harvard. President James Walker disapproved, and the Corporation denied the petition.[7]

THE UNIVERSITY LECTURES

Women's interest in studying under Harvard scientists persisted, however, and for nearly a decade beginning in 1863, women were permitted to attend lectures in an adjunct program established by President Thomas Hill. The University Lectures, given by Harvard professors and other scholars, were predominantly scientific in subject. Women, to the surprise of many, consistently constituted the majority of the students. By 1870, 74 courses of lectures had been presented, and in that year alone women accounted for 72 percent of the 155 students enrolled.[8]

Many of the women who attended this series were teachers or amateur scientists working without institutional affiliation. For these students, the program was one of the few opportunities available to study with professional scientists. As historian Sally Gregory Kohlstedt has pointed out, for much of the nineteenth century women scientists typically pursued their work in relative isolation. Barred from professional societies as well as from university departments, women scientists had few opportunities to publish or to work except in support roles. As a consequence, many women scholars became schoolteachers, textbook writers, or educational reformers. For these women, contact with Harvard professors provided "a certain validation of their interest" as well as important substantive training.[9]

President Hill's University Lectures later were hailed as "the germ of the graduate school."[10] The series had been part of a larger reform effort that Hill considered the centerpiece of his plan to make Harvard "a university of a high order."[11] The program was not, however, embraced by Charles W. Eliot, who assumed the presidency in 1869. Shortly after his inauguration, Eliot pronounced the University Lectures a "hopeless failure." Eliot's reform objective was to provide systematic graduate training in the sciences to graduates of Harvard and other institutions—not to attract a preponderance of women science teachers. He declared the University Lectures "under-enrolled" and suspended them in 1872.[12]

ELIOT'S INAUGURAL ADDRESS

Eliot had set the tone for his administration's attitude toward the higher education of women in his inaugural address of 1869. The two-hour speech, which the *Boston Post* hailed as "a turning point in higher education," contained only two paragraphs regarding the education of women. Eliot maintained that it would be irresponsible for the university to sponsor the collegiate education of women. "The world knows next to nothing about the natural mental capacities of the female sex," he argued. "Only after generations of civil freedom and social equality will it be possible to obtain the data necessary for an adequate discussion of women's natural tendencies, tastes, and capabilities." Eliot thus exempted the university from the responsibility to educate women. He declared, simply, that it was not the business of the university to "decide this mooted point . . . a matter concerning which prejudices are deep, and opinion inflammable, and experience scanty."[13]

Women's supporters responded that Eliot seemed to be blind to women's intellectual successes in coeducational academies, colleges, and universities across the country. Had he looked at the evidence, wrote Thomas Wentworth Higginson in *The Woman's Journal*, "he must have seen that instead of this being 'a matter concerning which prejudices are deep, and opinion inflammable, and experience scanty,' it is, on the other hand, a matter where prejudices are turning out to be shallow, and opinion is becoming reasonable, and experience is very large, and accumulating day by day."[14] Teachers' associations, heads of girls' schools, and the wives and daughters of many of Eliot's faculty continued to rail against his position. "Let women be able through all the advanced methods of higher education, to determine her actual and relative mental status, that she may have a helpful consciousness of what she is and what she can do," they challenged.[15]

UNIVERSITY COURSES OF INSTRUCTION

But Eliot held the line, offering only a modest appeasement. As a gesture of the university's commitment to fostering liberal culture and improved preparation for women teachers, he would devise "a safe, promising, and instructive experiment." Women, he announced, would be allowed to enroll in the new University Courses of Instruction, a series of lectures on literature and philosophy.[16]

The program, however, was poorly conceived and poorly funded. Few people outside Harvard's immediate neighborhood knew of its existence, and its relation to advanced study was vague. Only thirteen people enrolled in the program: six men and seven women. These women, however, were representative of the intellectually ambitious teachers and reformers who continued to campaign for women's access to Harvard. Mary Allen, an abolitionist and teacher, had recently returned from working in the freedmen's schools in Charleston, South Carolina; Harriet Pitman, the daughter of local philanthropists, served for a time as a teacher with Anna Eliot Ticknor's Society to Encourage Studies at Home and later attended the Harvard Annex. Charlotte Brooks organized and hosted the first meeting of the Woman's Education Association, whose purpose was to secure the Harvard degree for women.[17]

Eliot, meanwhile, turned his attention to more formal mechanisms for graduate study within the College, and his "safe, promising, and instructive experiment" was disbanded after its second year. In 1872 the Governing Boards approved a Graduate Department and established higher degrees.[18]

The consolidation of all advanced courses into the Graduate Department meant, of course, that women teachers and other unmatriculated students lost access to instruction at Harvard. Although women teachers would continue to study for a time in special summer courses taught at the Botanic Gardens, at the Bussey estate in Jamaica Plain, and in a summer course in chemistry, opportunities for most women declined in the 1870s. When specialized study was an ancillary feature at Harvard, women enjoyed more access to advanced study than they did after the graduate program had become a flourishing and important department of the university. Moreover, even the summer program for local teachers changed its policy regarding women students when the Summer School became a permanent feature of the university in 1886. The mounting exclusion of women reinforced Harvard's growing exclusiveness. By 1891 only Harvard undergraduates and Harvard graduate students were admitted to summer courses, and the phasing out of women and of male students not affiliated with Harvard was completed.[19]

HARVARD WOMEN AND THE FOUNDING OF THE WEA

To many women, however, it had been clear from the beginning of the University Courses that President Eliot's provision was inadequate. Informal studies in liberal culture through adjunct, nonaccredited lectures seemed a fitting solution to Eliot and to many of the Harvard faculty, but the network of educated Boston and Cambridge women who championed Harvard degrees for women found it wanting. Meeting together, they lamented "the great and crying want, which as each woman felt it in her own life she knew existed for all women, of more and better wider and higher education." And they felt it only natural that the university in Cambridge should embrace their ambitions for themselves and for subsequent generations of women.[20]

The Boston and Cambridge women who organized the Woman's Education Association of Boston in 1872 were accustomed to working together on behalf of educational, literary, and scientific projects—many of which they pursued in association with their husbands and other kin at Harvard. These were the nineteenth-century "Harvard women." They were the wives, mothers, daughters, and sisters of men affiliated with the College. Many were writers or scholars in their own right, and their own intellectual quests informed their activism on behalf of women and girls. They represented a long tradition of private study and intellectual pursuits among the women from learned families in New England, and although many of them held conservative views about women and politics, they believed that women held an equal right with men to the best possible education.[21]

Two such Harvard women, Zina Fay Peirce and Charlotte Brooks, invited a group of their friends and associates on December 22, 1871, to the first meeting of the Committee on Better Education of Women, a group which was organized shortly thereafter as the Woman's Education Association of Boston (WEA). Among the guests who gathered at this meeting were Elizabeth Cary Agassiz, later Radcliffe's first president; future Radcliffe supporters Mary Hemenway and Mrs. Charles G. Loring; Emily Otis Eliot, wife of Harvard Overseer Samuel Eliot; and science educator Lucretia Crocker—all of whom had ties both to Harvard University and to the movement for women's higher education.[22]

These women and others who joined them in forming the WEA were related not only through their educational work and, in many cases, through family connections but also through their shared experience of having studied with Harvard professors. Zina Fay had been a student of Professor Louis Agassiz in 1860 and 1861 at the school run by Elizabeth Agassiz in her home on Quincy Street, opposite Harvard Yard. In 1862 Fay married the philosopher Charles Saunders Peirce, the Agassizs' young friend and colleague. Charlotte Brooks studied philosophy under Charles Peirce and the other Harvard philosophers who taught in the University Courses of Instruction. Lucretia Crocker had, of course, studied with Louis Agassiz in the 1850s. And Elizabeth Cary Agassiz as a young woman in the 1840s had been guided in her studies by Professor Cornelius Felton, her brother-in-law and later president of Harvard University.[23]

It was therefore natural that the committee led by Peirce and Brooks would seek support from their friends at Harvard when they resolved to sponsor a conference on women's education in 1872. It also made sense that they would look for leadership from two very popular men who had supported them in other projects—the Reverend Phillips Brooks and Samuel Eliot. When asked to present speeches on the subject of women's education, however, the men demurred. Brooks declined on the grounds that "not having thought upon the subject of Women's Education [he was] not prepared to speak." Samuel Eliot agreed to preside at the meeting in Wesleyan Hall in Boston, but he limited his remarks to praise of the lectures that were available to women under the auspices of the University Courses of Instruction.[24]

The women of the committee reportedly were disappointed by this narrow perspective on their need for higher education. Professors Frederic Hedge and Francis Child, along with Samuel Eliot, observed that women were, indeed, the majority of those attending the lectures at Harvard. But they also revealed their entrenched bias against admitting women to the University. "We were told," reported the women, "not to disturb the present system of education, which is the result of the wisdom and experience of the past, and bears so large a part in the molding of our republican life." The men at the meeting were in agreement, however, on the need for a more advanced girls' high school in Boston.[25]

Eight days later, Peirce, Brooks, and their committee of 15 women adopted a constitution, reorganized themselves into the Woman's Education Association, and directly confronted Harvard by inviting President Eliot to a meeting later that week to discuss women's access to the College. Eliot, though called on short notice, arrived at the January 1872 meeting with minutely detailed notes to argue against the education of women at Harvard. He argued first that statistics regarding women who had sought instruction at Harvard College demonstrated that not enough women wanted to take the college course to make it worthwhile. Second, he stated flatly that the lower-level classes at Harvard were overcrowded already, and that consequently there was no space available for women students. The women could not help but note the inconsistency of these two arguments and later ridiculed Eliot's logic in the press. Furthermore, they asked, how was Harvard to gauge women's desire to attend Harvard College?[26]

Zina Fay Peirce enlisted Eliot's own argument about the crowded condition of Harvard's classes to propose an alternative path to the Harvard degree. She asked Eliot if Harvard would give its degree to women who could educate themselves and pass all of the examinations required of Harvard men. Eliot is reported to have said that he saw "no difficulty about that," and Peirce's Committee on Intellectual Education immediately enlisted 12 Harvard professors and several other Boston educators to help them prepare a proposal. They developed a plan whereby women would pursue Harvard courses in day classes held in Boston and then would be examined by Harvard professors. But when the WEA presented their plan to Eliot, he reversed himself. Eliot warned that the Corporation would not approve of their plan; and moreover, even if they were willing, he would oppose it. The matter was officially considered at the Corporation meeting in March, and the president was instructed to reply that: "1) a certain amount of time in residence at Harvard College was required for the degree; and 2) the University does not propose to give its degrees to women."[27]

A FACULTY PROPOSAL FOR COEDUCATION

The women's challenge to Harvard College was not settled, however, by Eliot's report to the WEA. Several members of the Harvard faculty had by now become strong advocates of coeducation at Harvard, and both the popular press and professional journals actively promoted the idea. James Freeman Clarke, a prominent Unitarian minister in Boston and a member of the Board of Overseers, took up the cause, and the Woman's Education Association simultaneously launched a campaign to negotiate further with the Corporation. At the April 1872 meeting of the board, Clarke presented a motion that a committee of the Board of Overseers be appointed "to inquire into the practical operation of the system of the coeducation of the sexes." The motion was passed, and the committee was asked to report its findings and its opinions on the adoption of the system by Harvard.[28]

Clarke, whose 20-year-old daughter Cora was studying botany with professors at Harvard and whose wife, Anna Huidekoper Clarke, was a founding member of the WEA, had long supported women's rights and women's higher education. These credentials apparently did not impress the Overseers, as the inquiry soon unraveled. Eliot, in an address to the annual meeting of the Social Science Association in May, argued against the education of women at Harvard on the grounds, among others, that moral injury would be sustained and that religious tenets would be violated. It was reported that nine-tenths of the Board of Overseers and the whole of the College faculty would obstinately resist any effort to bring women to campus or to award them the Harvard degree. Former Harvard president James Walker, on behalf of the investigative committee, reported to the Board of Overseers in September that James Freeman Clarke had "ceased to be a member" and that the remaining members unanimously recommended that no further action on the matter of coeducation be taken. The committee was discharged, and a minority report by Clarke was suppressed.[29]

Clarke had argued in his report that friends of Harvard had daughters as well as sons to educate; that it was more appropriate for men to work in the company of women than to be isolated and removed from their refining influence; and that Harvard's elective system made the introduction of women into the College particularly suitable, as the course of study could be adapted to particular needs and interests. His arguments, however, failed to influence the Overseers or the president. *The Woman's Journal* reported that Eliot had refused to have a full report of the debate published and claimed that he also was unwilling to publish a paper in favor of coeducation by Thomas Wentworth Higginson. The Boston press vigorously censured Eliot for his extreme views, and Eliot's speech to the Social Science Association led women's rights advocate Julia Ward Howe to inform him that, in her opinion, he was "possessed by the very Satan of human society." In defiance of Eliot's proclamation, suffragist Mary Livermore's daughter applied to Harvard and was promptly rejected on account of her sex. The issue had become of concern to the Boston public, and public opinion was critical of Harvard's intransigence. But popular support wielded little sway over Harvard, and even before Clarke's minority report appeared, the Woman's Education Association had begun to formulate a more feasible interim plan.[30]

THE HARVARD EXAMINATIONS FOR WOMEN

Their idea was to provide a series of examinations—but not instruction—that would be sponsored by Harvard for young women of college age. Unlike the WEA's earlier examination proposal that had provided for a Harvard degree, this new plan would simply certify that women had passed exams equivalent to the Harvard entrance exams. The concept had been suggested by Samuel Eliot as a result of his research into the University Examinations for Women in England. A similar examination sponsored by Harvard, it was argued, would raise the standard of work at girls' schools, academies, and the public high schools. Moreover, the concept might appeal to the Harvard faculty, who, by preparing and correcting the examinations, would establish a national standard for girls' education.[31]

Several members of the Woman's Education Association vehemently opposed this compromise, however, and the issue of whether to continue to press for a Harvard degree or to switch to other means for improving the education of women divided the association. Zina Fay Peirce, lamenting the readiness of her associates to compromise, resigned from her post as chairwoman of the Intellectual Committee. Elizabeth Cary Agassiz, who succeeded her, reflected the opinion of the majority who were unwilling to adopt an adversarial stance in relation to the university. Both Peirce and Agassiz were devoted to the cause of women's higher education, but their approaches differed. Agassiz and her associates—women like Anna C. Lowell and Mary Parkman who previously had worked with the Sanitary Commission and the freedmen's schools; Lucretia Crocker, Harriet Caryl, and Margaret Badger, prominent Boston teachers and reformers; and Catherine Ireland, who had taken over and expanded the Agassiz's school—were what historian Karen Blair has called "feminists under the skin." They were intent on advancing women's opportunities, but they avoided ideological labels that might hinder their efforts. Determined not to jeopardize the potential for amicable negotiations with Harvard, the WEA denied membership to Julia Ward Howe, Caroline Dall, Ednah Dow Cheney, Abby May, Elizabeth Peabody, and Mary Peabody Mann because they were known suffragists and thus controversial figures.[32]

The Harvard Corporation, meanwhile, agreed to conduct the examinations—but only on the conditions that Harvard's role be limited to writing the exam questions and that the WEA would cover all expenses. A Harvard faculty committee was put in charge, and the first Harvard Examinations for Women were administered in 1874. President Eliot wrote in his annual report that these examinations would provide for girls' schools what entrance examinations had done for boys' preparatory schools: set a standard and prescribe a judicious program of study. "The experiment is an interesting one," he wrote, "which should cause no interference with the work of the University."[33]

The Harvard Examinations for Women evoked mixed reviews, however. To the women who took the examinations between 1874 and 1883, the experience could mean significant personal or professional advantage. The majority expected to teach upon completion of the exams, and many who already were teachers received better posts as a result of passing the exams. Eugenie Homer and her friend Helen Cabot, after taking the exams in 1874, went on to receive training in chemistry at the Woman's Laboratory at the Massachusetts Institute of Technology, and Homer later continued her studies at the Harvard Annex. Susan Monroe was offered a teaching position at Wellesley College after taking the advanced section of the Harvard Examinations in 1875. Harriet Williams taught Greek and Latin at Smith College after passing the preliminary and advanced exams.[34]

At the same time, women critics of the compromise protested that they aspired to instruction at Harvard, not to examinations in a rented room in Boston. When the second administration of the exams was announced, one writer to *The Woman's Journal* wryly observed, "thus women have, again, the opportunity to show whether they can do as well without the instruction of Harvard, as the regular students can with it." Attracting candidates, moreover, proved to be difficult. In spite of significant advertising, only seven women took the first examination held in Boston in June 1874; and the Harvard Examinations, which were moved the next year to Cambridge in the hope of attracting more participants, never drew more than eleven candidates in a given year. Hoping to increase their clientele, the WEA proposed a plan to offer women the *actual* Harvard entrance examinations, arguing that the new women's colleges might then adopt the examinations as their standard for admission. President Eliot resisted the idea, however, as he feared that women who passed Harvard's own entrance examinations might then seek admission to the College. In 1879, however, the development of a new program in Cambridge under the leadership of Elizabeth Cary Agassiz promised to avert this danger.[35]

HARVARD WOMEN AND THE FOUNDING OF THE HARVARD ANNEX

The Harvard Annex, the program that was established in 1879, was marked by confusion about its relationship to Harvard University from the outset. The very name by which this organization quickly and almost mysteriously came to be known was misleading: the Harvard Annex had no official relationship to the university. It was, as its proper name indicated, a program of Private Collegiate Instruction for Women in which a small group of Harvard professors agreed to repeat their lectures to groups of private women students. Thirteen members of the faculty were enlisted to teach the first year, and courses were offered in ancient and modern languages, English, philosophy, and political economics. Elizabeth Cary Agassiz led the program with a committee of friends and associates, the majority of whom were wives or daughters of Harvard professors: Ellen Hooper Gurney, wife of Professor Ephraim Gurney; Mary H. Cooke, wife of Professor Josiah Cooke; Mary Greenough, wife of Professor James B. Greenough; Alice Mary Longfellow, daughter of Henry Wadsworth Longfellow; Lilian Horsford, daughter of former Professor Eban Horsford; and Stella Gilman, wife of Cambridge author and principal of the Gilman School for Girls, Arthur Gilman. He had helped to organize the new program and served as its secretary.[36]

The public and the press, however, immediately picked up on its Harvard connections and touted the program as the "Harvard collegiate course for women." When the first announcement was issued in February 1879 under the banner, "Private Collegiate Instruction for Women by Professors and Other Instructors of Harvard College," the *New England Journal of Education* heralded it as "the entering wedge of joint-education" at Harvard. This notion was fueled by conversation in Cambridge about a brilliant young woman, Abby Leach, who had arranged that fall to study Latin, Greek, and English literature with Professors James B. Greenough, William W. Goodwin, and Francis J. Child, respectively. Leach's work was praised as being equal to the most advanced work in the College, and supporters celebrated her example in comments that were widely quoted in the press. Mary Hughes, a prospective student who had read about the new program in the *Cambridge Tribune,* wrote to Arthur Gilman inquiring about "the new plan of opening Harvard College to lady students." Even Elizabeth Agassiz referred to the program as "Harvard Education for Women."[37]

President Eliot had expressed concern about the public's predilection to highlight the university's role when he read a draft of the circular announcing the program. He insisted that they change the phrase, "the ladies of the Committee," which he feared might be construed to mean that there also were men on this steering group. Eliot was particularly anxious to avoid confusion about the source of the graduation certificates that were to be awarded to women students. "I think it should be clearly stated that they are to be given by the Committee or its officers," he instructed the committee. "People are incredibly apt to misunderstand such announcements. It is impossible to make them too plain and full."[38]

The fact that Harvard was *not* more formally associated with the new opportunity for women also was criticized. Many saw this new effort not as a wedge in the door but as a subterfuge that could impede women from gaining admission to the legitimate Harvard program. A graduate of the University of Illinois wrote that she found it incredible that Annex women would do as much work as young men "without being regarded as students, without a student's use of the library, and with no prospect of a degree." The *Springfield Republican* called the Annex a "postern-gate and back door contrivance to preserve the prestige of 'the superior sex'."[39]

Elizabeth Cary Agassiz and her committee, however, were very hopeful about the success—and the significance—of the program. They believed that the Annex program would offer women opportunities for advanced study that were greater in both quality and variety than those available at any other institution in the country. Agassiz refused to allow a "ladies' degree" to be created for the Annex, and she maintained from the beginning that women deserved "the largest liberty of instruction." She was confident that the opportunities of Harvard, with full equality of academic standards, would finally be made available to women.[40]

ELIZABETH CARY AGASSIZ AND THE AGASSIZ SCHOOL

Elizabeth Cary Agassiz was 56 years old when she undertook the leadership of the Annex. She had been working on behalf of improved education for girls since the 1850s, and it was she who ultimately would negotiate the agreement for the founding of Radcliffe College in 1894. At the time of the Annex's founding, she was writing a two-volume biography of her husband, the Swiss-born naturalist Louis Agassiz, who had died in 1873.[41]

Much of her time during the late 1850s and early 1860s, however, was devoted to running the Agassiz School for Girls, which she opened in her Cambridge home in 1855 and directed until 1863. Elizabeth Agassiz directed every aspect of the school, from financial accounting to faculty recruitment; and under her leadership the school was extremely successful, both academically and financially. The school promoted progressive practices and attitudes about the education of girls, and, in fact, its faculty included several of the Harvard professors who later would agree to teach at the Harvard Annex.[42]

Agassiz's educational ideas undoubtedly were informed by her own early experiences and her family's progressive attitudes regarding education. She had witnessed the teaching of her younger siblings at an experimental school taught by Mary Peabody, sister of the educational reformer Elizabeth Palmer Peabody and protégé of Horace Mann, whom Mary later married. Elizabeth Cary Agassiz's cousins studied with progressive educator and Transcendentalist Bronson Alcott at his celebrated Temple School. Her sisters, Mollie, Sallie, and Emma Cary, were sent to George Emerson's pioneering school for girls. Lizzie (the name by which Elizabeth Cary Agassiz was known to family and friends throughout her life) was educated at home, and under the tutelage of the family's governess, Miss Lyman, she learned to make studying a habit of life, independent of school. In 1834, she joined her sister and her cousin at Elizabeth Peabody's afternoon Historical School, where Peabody employed Bronson Alcott's Socratic method to teach her young women students to think critically. A later biographer noted that at Miss Peabody's school, "Lizzie Cary learned to keep her mind awake, to study under her own volition and never to imagine that she had finished her education."[43]

This independence and progressive attitude characterized Elizabeth Cary Agassiz's later work at the Harvard Annex and at Radcliffe. She considered her management of the Agassiz School as "training" for her new tasks at the Annex and her collaboration with Harvard professors in this work as the model for Radcliffe College. "But for the school," she wrote, "the college (so far as I am concerned) would never have existed." Moreover, her confidence in the purposefulness, independence, and scholarly abilities of young women was reflected in her design for the new program. "I am as independent as the air," wrote Abby Parsons to her parents in 1879, describing life at the new Annex. Elizabeth Agassiz always referred to Parsons and the other Annex students as her "Harvard girls," for she believed that they were worthy of the highest intellectual advantages and deserved the freedom to order their own lives and learning.[44]

THE ANNEX STUDENTS

Abby Parsons' parents undoubtedly were relieved to receive such happy news from their daughter after her first few months at the Annex in 1879. Her father James Parsons, a high school principal, had personally prepared his daughter to meet Harvard's entrance requirements and had written to President Eliot only a year or so earlier to ask if there was any prospect of girls being allowed to study in Harvard College. To his disappointment, Eliot had responded that there was "no such prospect, near or remote." Parsons had thus sent his daughter to the Annex with some hesitation, as he was distressed that not all of the courses available at Harvard were offered to women in the Annex. Mary Byrd, a graduate of the University of Michigan, also was apprehensive about Harvard attitudes toward women. "I wish, if possible, to learn beforehand how much discomfort I shall find in a school where coeducation is regarded as something strange and unnatural," she wrote.[45]

Mary Byrd, like several other of the college-trained women who applied to the Annex, feared that the atmosphere in Cambridge might be hostile; but the lure of study with Harvard professors was powerful and proved to be advantageous. Byrd came to the Annex as a graduate student in 1882 and studied for a year under the direction of Edward Pickering at the Harvard College Observatory. She left to teach at Carleton College and later became director of the observatory at Smith College. Emily Norcross, who had received her bachelor's degree from Wellesley in 1880, also taught at Smith after pursuing classical studies in the Annex. Two years later, Grace Chester, a biologist who had studied at the Annex, joined the Smith College faculty.[46]

In all, 27 students enrolled in 1879, 25 of whom completed the first year. The Annex, like Harvard College, drew its student body from a predominantly local, urban population. But unlike Harvard (and unlike nearby Smith and Wellesley), a significant number of the women who studied at the Annex were older "special students" or "graduate-specials" who came to pursue focused study for a year or two. Among this class of "specials" in the first year of the Annex were Ellen Gurney, Lilian Horsford, and Alice Mary Longfellow, all members of the Executive Committee. Gurney was by far the most advanced of all Annex students in Greek that year, studying along with Abby Leach under Professor William Goodwin.[47]

Abby Parsons, Annie Barber, and Annie Ware Winsor were among the younger women who came to the Annex to pursue a regular four-year course of study. They were academically serious students whose families distinctly supported their college ambitions. Annie Barber recalled that her mother invariably had told friends that she would send her daughter to Harvard. "When Annie is ready for Harvard, Harvard will be ready for Annie," she had insisted. Annie Winsor was encouraged in her studies by several generations of women in her family who had attended normal schools and academies and then had served as teachers. Winsor later wrote about this legacy and highlighted the Annex students' shared commitment to serious study—a commitment that distinguished them from the men at Harvard. "A little common-sense and mathematics will show . . . that the Annex girl, coming to the Annex as she does because she chooses to study, is likely to do faithful and good work; while no such presumption can be made about the College man, for he comes to College from every variety of reason and mostly not from love of study," she wrote.[48]

Clearly, these young women felt themselves to be participants in an important undertaking. No other women ever had come so near to being Harvard students; but, ironically, having reached this goal, they experienced new conflicts about their intellectual and professional ambitions and about the roles that they were expected to fulfill as adult women. Annie Winsor sat down with her diary one evening, apparently in a mood of triumph: "And now my plans are pretty well made for my work in life," she wrote. "I have set out to outfit myself to be a professor of English. Bryn Mawr is in my eye." But then she wrote an addendum: "Of course if I am married I shall not be a professor, but my studies will not hurt me for that future."[49]

CHALLENGES AT THE ANNEX

The situation of the Harvard Annex was fraught with uncertainty resulting from the Annex's lack of authority and its dependence on the good will of Harvard professors. The organization of the Annex was intentionally informal in anticipation of the time "when, as was fondly hoped," wrote Arthur Gilman, "the President and Fellows of Harvard College would undertake the work of teaching women." This, of course, had long been the hope of the Woman's Education Association. Within two years, by 1881, the managers had determined that their "experiment" was a success, and Elizabeth Agassiz was formally instructed to speak with President Eliot about taking over the Annex. Eliot must have raised the issue of an endowment, for coming out of their meeting, Agassiz recommended that the Annex ask the Corporation whether it would be willing to take over their work and inquire "how large a sum of money would be required."[50]

The Annex managers also advised the Corporation that the program could not continue in its current state: the difficulties of enlisting professors and guaranteeing continuity of the program were insurmountable. Although all 53 members of the Harvard faculty had been invited to teach in the Annex and 44 had agreed to contribute in some form, only 13 had actually taught in the first term. Most professors taught only one course, and the program grew to include only 20 or 30 courses per year. By comparison, the number of courses in Harvard College was over 120.[51]

Furthermore, professors' attitudes toward the instruction of women varied—even among those who supported the Annex. Barrett Wendell's examination questions were embarrassingly superficial and skewed toward the students' so-called feminine natures. George Martin agreed to teach with the provision that he would have "no examination books to read and no papers to make out." John Williams White decided to abandon his Greek class in the middle of the year. Other professors could offer only one or two hours a week to the program, and as a consequence Annex students spent eight to ten hours a week with their instructors, compared to fifteen or sixteen hours a week in the College. Abby Parsons wrote that it was impossible for the students to "keep up with the yard students in two recitations a week." She also had concluded after only two months at the Annex that her history composition would be badly treated. "You know," she explained to her parents, "that ridicule is the Harvard College theory."[52]

The Corporation, meanwhile, declined to take action on the Annex's request, and by March 1882 Elizabeth Agassiz and the other managers were reconciled to the necessity of raising funds to continue their work, as it stood, for several more years. Arthur Gilman proposed an endowment drive to support a more independent women's institution. Elizabeth Cary Agassiz intervened, however, and reiterated her long-held position that the goal of their efforts was to provide a Harvard education to women. She explained to Gilman that although she, too, had at one point considered the idea of running a separate program with a supplementary faculty, she had come to fear such a step. "The more I think of this, the more I fear that we shall drift into the building up of another female college, distinct from the University," she explained. "I believe this would be a great mistake. . . . We must be careful to avoid this rock," she warned.[53]

The Annex, therefore, was reorganized and incorporated in 1882 as the Society for the Collegiate Instruction of Women, with Elizabeth Agassiz elected president, Arthur Gilman secretary, and Lilian Horsford treasurer. The charter placed the Annex in a position to raise an endowment, and they hoped that this would convince Harvard to establish the work on a permanent basis.[54]

The endowment drive was immediately adopted by the Woman's Education Association as a major campaign. Subscriptions of $5,000 each had already been received from Mary Hemenway, Ellen Mason, Pauline Agassiz Shaw, Thomas Appleton, and the George O. Hovey estate. Supporters of the Annex pointed out that American women had given considerably over one million dollars to colleges for men, including over $325,000 to Harvard. The WEA beseeched them to turn their attention instead to the Annex, and Elizabeth Agassiz claimed that this support made her feel "doubly sure of our permanent success."[55]

Such success was not swift in coming, however. Only two-thirds of the required sum had been raised by February 1884 when the executive committee of the Annex met to discuss its future. Thoughts of petitioning Harvard were put aside, and the issue was again tabled at the annual meeting in 1885. Fearing that the Corporation would not accept their proposals unless a larger endowment were attached, they discussed instead the use of the endowment income to offset current expenses, and a committee was established to determine what might be salvaged. The next major negotiations with Harvard would not take place until 1893, when the topic of discussion would not be the education of women in Harvard College, but rather the establishment of a new women's institution— Radcliffe College.[56]

THE RADCLIFFE COMPROMISE

By 1890 it had become clear to the Annex managers that the program could not survive. The Annex had grown into a school of over 200 students; it owned land, a large building (Fay House), and had an endowment of approximately $75,000. Elizabeth Agassiz explained that in spite of such success, the Annex program was untenable. The managers could not guarantee stable instruction, they could not afford to offer postgraduate courses, and the Annex certificate was considered by most to be a poor substitute for a college degree.

Elizabeth Agassiz initiated a series of conversations with President Eliot, and the Woman's Education Association, which was hopeful that their goal might finally be within reach, launched a new fund-raising effort to raise an additional endowment of $250,000. Eliot's response to their effort, however, was equivocal. On the one hand, he suggested that the university might take over the Annex if it could be made self-supporting; on the other hand, he explicitly stated that he had no authority concerning the possibility of uniting the Annex with the University and claimed that he did not know the Corporation's and Overseers' positions on the matter. The Woman's Education Association nevertheless continued its efforts, and in March 1893, the Annex offered the Corporation all of its present property—an invested capital of $150,000 with real estate. They promised, further, that they would continue to raise funds for ongoing support and future development.[57]

The immediate approval of the Corporation was not to be won, however, by this promise or by the property of the Annex, which was so insignificant that it could not possibly have been considered as the basis of bargaining power. As Le Baron Russell Briggs later wrote, the Annex "had nothing to offer Harvard but girls, whom Harvard did not want."[58]

Instead, after a series of negotiations the Corporation agreed to consider the establishment of a new institution, "X. College," which would be self-governing in all respects and which would offer its own diplomas, to be countersigned by the president of Harvard. The President and Fellows of Harvard College would serve as "Visitors" of the college and would approve all faculty appointments. This organizational interdependence, it was argued, would give the women's institution all of the security and status it might require for practical purposes, and yet it still would maintain the independence of the Harvard Corporation from the enterprise of educating women—a condition that was not subject to negotiation.[59]

This plan was not, of course, the plan that had been promoted by the WEA, nor was it the plan that the Annex had set out to secure. The idea that the Annex grant academic degrees to its graduates had been proposed earlier, in 1886, but was defeated because of the desire on the part of Elizabeth Agassiz and other board members to secure the Harvard degree for women. Agassiz repeatedly had insisted that she saw no purpose in establishing another women's college, but now it appeared that the Annex had no choice in the matter. The Annex committee voted on October 31, 1893, to accept the Corporation proposal, and the new college for women was christened "Radcliffe College." The proposal was approved by the Overseers on December 6, 1893, and, in spite of protests by the WEA, a committee of Annex alumnae, and the Association of Collegiate Alumnae, the charter for Radcliffe College was signed by the governor of Massachusetts on March 23, 1894.[60]

On May 25, 1894, two months after the approval of Radcliffe College by the commonwealth of Massachusetts, the Harvard Board of Overseers adopted a resolution that the degree of Bachelor of Arts should not be given to women by the university under any circumstances. They also rejected a proposal that a separate degree be developed by the Faculty of Arts and Sciences that might entitle women to earn a Harvard degree for postgraduate work. The Overseers did, however, allow a provision that Radcliffe graduate students might, under certain conditions, study in graduate courses at Harvard. One of the conditions was that the new privilege could be revoked at any time.[61]

IN RETROSPECT

As it was conceived, Radcliffe College by its very status as an "affiliate" rather than an integral part of Harvard, by its financial uncertainty, and by its lack of privileges and political rights within the university reflected the precarious-ness of women's role in the intellectual life of the nineteenth century. It was not clear to the women who had sought admission to Harvard University in the 1870s, 1880s, and 1890s what their ultimate relationship to the university would be in the next century. The terms under which women might receive postgraduate training at Harvard still were unclear, alumnae continued to press for the Harvard Ph.D., and women students did not know what new roles might be available to them as college graduates.

Moreover, the odd arrangement between Harvard and Radcliffe served to reinforce the larger social debate pertaining to women's intellectual abilities and social roles. Harvard president Charles Eliot claimed that the establish-ment of Radcliffe College did not deny women greater opportunities. Rather, he suggested, the separate women's college would serve to enhance and stimulate women's own distinctive intellectual natures. He argued that the movement of nineteenth-century women to gain access to programs designed for the education of men, and the concomitant efforts of women's colleges to imitate the curricula and purposes of the men's colleges, would prove eventually to have been a misguided endeavor. "The prime motive of the higher education of women," Eliot declared, "should be recognized as the development in women of the capacities and powers which will fit them to make family life and social life more intelligent, more enjoyable, happier, and more productive."[62]

Such arguments concerning woman's special needs and accolades regarding her domestic virtues had changed little from the emergence of women's collegiate education in the years before the Civil War to the consummation of the agreement between Harvard and Radcliffe at the close of the nineteenth century. The purpose of educating women according to President Eliot, and according to dean Le Baron R. Briggs, who succeeded Elizabeth Agassiz as president of Radcliffe College in 1903, was to enhance women's ability to serve in their traditional roles as wives, mothers, and teachers of the young. The status and relation of men to women, and the distinctive purposes proposed for women's education throughout the nine-teenth century, were more constant and more enduring than any other aspect of the college curriculum or university structure. The purpose of educating women continued to be cast in terms of women's relationship to men and women's responsibilities to others. "Can any greater gift be made to man than to keep him in the presence of a highly trained and spiritual woman?" asked President Eliot of the Radcliffe graduating class in 1898. Can any responsibil-ity or occupation bring educated women more happiness and influence, asked Briggs in 1904, than their work "as sisters, as wives, as mothers, as friends, as helpers to all that is noble?"[63]

Still, these first college women looked back on the century they were leaving as one that had been generous to them. It had granted them new opportunities, a larger share in the culture's learning and intellectual life, and a somewhat wider choice of occupations that could lead to personal independence. Elizabeth Agassiz beheld these new possibilities as "great gifts which the nineteenth century has given women," and she celebrated the gains that the establishment of Radcliffe represented. "I am very happy about Radcliffe College," she wrote to a former Annex student. "In my own youth," she later elaborated, "the path which you . . . tread without let or hindrance, almost without comment or criticism, would have been absolutely beyond the reach of girls of average acquirements and positions."[64]

In the context of the tremendous changes that she had known in her own lifetime, Elizabeth Agassiz did not doubt that Radcliffe would soon be absorbed by Harvard. She had assured the Annex alumnae when Radcliffe was established that she felt the arrangement to be only a temporary solution—the best that was within their immediate reach. To Agassiz and to the other Harvard women, the founding of the Harvard Annex and the establishment of Radcliffe were part of the brilliant and ongoing success story of the nineteenth century. Their work on behalf of women's education was rooted in a personal faith and confidence in the capacities of women, in the strength of education as a moral force, and in the progress of the age in which they lived.

When President Agassiz framed her parting words to the last Radcliffe class to graduate in the nineteenth century, she reiterated this hope and trust: "Among the numerous and startling changes that have marked this century," she remarked, "the progress in the education of women has been singularly striking and novel. For one whose life has kept pace with that of the century, beginning with its earlier years and sharing now in its decline, the retrospect as regards women is simply amazing."[65]

Harvard, however, was hardly progressive in its attitude toward the higher education of women. The advances it did promote invariably served the university's own institutional interests, and the obstacles it installed led to uncertainties that would continue to condition women's education at Harvard and at Radcliffe for another hundred years. The Eliot era, which generally has been acclaimed as a period of unprecedented reform, and one that was critical in the shaping of American higher education, takes on a new aspect when examined from this vantage. The challenges of the nineteenth-century Harvard women call into question the extent of reform-mindedness at Harvard.

Notes

1. Paul Buck, "Harvard Attitudes Toward Radcliffe in the Early Years," paper read before the Massachusetts Historical Society at the May 1962 meeting, *Proceedings of the Massachusetts Historical Society* (1962), 34. The provisions of the 1963 agreement included the granting of Harvard degrees to Radcliffe seniors, a merger of the Radcliffe Graduate School and the Harvard Graduate School of Arts and Sciences, and the opening of all programs of the Harvard Business School to women. See Agreements Between the President and Fellows of Harvard College and the Trustees of Radcliffe College, Radcliffe College Archives [hereafter, RCA]. The 1963 agreement is discussed in Dorothy Elia Howells, *A Century to Celebrate: Radcliffe College, 1879-1979* (Cambridge, Mass.: Radcliffe College, 1978), 33. For an extended discussion of the controversy surrounding the 1894 agreement and the establishment of Radcliffe College, see Sally Schwager, "'Harvard Women': A History of the Founding of Radcliffe College" (Ed.D. diss., Harvard University, 1982), 326-68.
2. Buck, "Harvard Attitudes Toward Radcliffe," 49.
3. Schwager, "'Harvard Women'," 80-98. For action on petitions to the Medical School, see Channing to Harvard Corporation, July 19, 1847 and vote of the Corporation, misc. series, Harvard University Overseers' Records [hereafter, OR], 63; Holmes to Corporation, Dec. 11, 1847, misc. series OR, 239; Hunt to Corporation, Dec. 17, 1847, misc. series, 240. For the Divinity School, see Corporation Report dated Aug. 14, 1869, Harvard University Corporation Records [hereafter, CR], 136; *Annual Report of the President of Harvard University* (1870), 29-30; and Corporation Report dated June 24, 1872, CR, 389, all in Harvard University Archives [hereafter, HUA].
4. For discussion of coeducation proposals, see Schwager, "'Harvard Women'," 98-105. For official responses to the 1872 proposal for coeducation, see CR, 11:364-67, and OR, 11:69-70.
5. The WEA proposal was considered by the Corporation in 1872. See CR, March 25, 1872, 11:364. For Eliot's response, see *Boston Daily Advertiser* article by Zina Fay Peirce, reprinted in *The Woman's Journal*, April 17, 1875. Eliot held to this belief that men and women should be educated differently throughout his career. For statements of his opinion, see Charles W. Eliot, address delivered at Smith College, June 16, 1879, quoted in L. Clark Seeyle, *The Early History of Smith College, 1871-1910* (Boston: Houghton Mifflin, 1923), 47-49; and "Higher Education for Women," in William Allan Neilson, ed., *Charles W. Eliot: The Man and His Beliefs*, vol. 1 (New York: Harper & Bros., 1926), 160-67 (originally published in *Harper's Bazaar*, 1908). On the scientific ideas that underlay Eliot's position, see Cynthia Eagle Russett, *Sexual Science: The Victorian Construction of Womanhood* (Cambridge, Mass.: Harvard University Press, 1989). A number of men and women educators challenged Eliot on this point, most eloquently president M. Carey Thomas of Bryn Mawr. For her response to Eliot, see Thomas's 1900 address, reprinted as "Should the Higher Education of Women Differ from That of Men?" *Educational Review* 21 (1901): 1-10. The best discussion of Thomas's criticism of Eliot is Helen Lefkowitz Horowitz, *The Power and Passion of M. Carey Thomas* (New York: Alfred A. Knopf, 1994), 317 and 321-22.
6. Charles W. Eliot to Edward Cummings, Jan. 19, 1891; Eliot to William Ashley, May 12, 1892; Eliot to Fred Norris Robinson, March 25, 1896; Eliot to George James Peirce, Feb. 4, 1897; Eliot to Thomas N. Carver, May 15, 1900, letter press volume, Eliot Papers, HUA.

Sociologist Lawrence Nichols notes that the practice of recruiting faculty with the promise of added compensation from Radcliffe continued under President Lowell. See Lawrence T. Nichols, "Sociology in the Women's Annex: Inequality and Integration at Harvard and Radcliffe, 1879-1947," *American Sociologist* (Fall 1997), 8. I am grateful to Margaret Rossiter for this reference.

7. *Letters of Ann Gillam Storrow to Jared Sparks,* ed. Frances Bradshaw Blanchard, Smith College Studies in History 6, no. 3 (Northampton, Mass.: Smith College, 1921), 210, as cited in David B. Tyack, *George Ticknor and the Boston Brahmins* (Cambridge, Mass.: Harvard University Press, 1967), 91. Ticknor's openness reflected his larger reform agenda. See Tyack, *George Ticknor,* chap. 3, and Julie A. Reuben, *The Making of the Modern University* (Chicago: University of Chicago Press, 1996), 24-25. On Crocker, see Ednah D. Cheney, "The Women of Boston," in *The Memorial History of Boston Including Suffolk County, Massachusetts 1630-1880,* vol. 4, ed. Justin Winsor (Boston: James R. Osgood & Co., 1881), 345; and Norma Kidd Green, "Lucretia Crocker," in *Notable American Women, 1607-1950,* ed. Edward T. James and Janet Wilson James (Cambridge, Mass.: Harvard University Press, 1971), 407-9. On Mary Mann's appeal, see Edward Lurie, *Louis Agassiz: A Life in Science* (Baltimore, Md.: Johns Hopkins University Press, 1988), 200-201. Crocker later became a founding member of the WEA and one of the first women elected to the Boston School Committee. See Ednah Dow Cheney, *Memoirs of Lucretia Crocker and Abby W. May* (Boston: Massachusetts School Suffrage Association, 1893), and Polly Welts Kaufman, *Boston Women and City School Politics, 1872-1905* (New York: Garland Publishing, 1994).

8. Samuel Eliot Morison, ed., *The Development of Harvard University Since the Inauguration of President Eliot, 1869-1929* (Cambridge, Mass.: Harvard University Press, 1930), 453; and *Annual Report of the President of Harvard University* (1870), 18, HUA. See also Mary Hume Maguire, "The Curtain-Raiser to the Founding of Radcliffe College: The Search for a 'Safe, Promising, and Instructive Experiment'," *Proceedings of the Cambridge Historical Society* 36 (1957): 29. I have benefited from Maguire's careful documentation of women's participation in this and several other university programs that I discuss herein; I disagree, however, with her overall conclusion that Harvard was a liberal benefactor of women's higher education.

9. Sally Gregory Kohlstedt, "In from the Periphery: American Women in Science, 1830-1880," *Signs: Journal of Women in Culture and Society* 4, no. 1 (Autumn 1978): 81-96. See also Margaret W. Rossiter, "'Women's Work' in Science, 1880-1910," *Isis* 71 (1980), reprinted in *History of Women in the Sciences: Readings from "Isis,"* ed. Sally Gregory Kohlstedt (Chicago: University of Chicago Press, 1999), 287-304; and Mary R. S. Creese, *Ladies in the Laboratory? American and British Women in Science, 1800-1900* (London: Scarecrow Press, 1998).

10. The term was used by Eliot and others. See Francis G. Peabody, "The Germ of the Graduate School," *Harvard Graduates' Magazine* (Dec. 1918), 176-81. For an excellent discussion of this program in the context of university reform and the development of the graduate department at Harvard, see Hugh Hawkins, *Between Harvard and America: The Educational Leadership of Charles W. Eliot* (New York: Oxford University Press, 1972), 38.

11. *Annual Report of the President of Harvard University* (1868), 8; and Hawkins, *Between Harvard and America,* 38.

12. *Annual Report of the President of Harvard University* (1870), 19-30; and *Annual Report* (1872), 13. See also Morison, *Development of Harvard University,* 453.

13. Charles William Eliot, "Inaugural Address," reprinted as *A Turning Point in Higher Education: The Inaugural Address of Charles William Eliot as President of Harvard College, October 19, 1869,* ed. Nathan Pusey (Cambridge, Mass.: Harvard University Press, 1969), 17-18. The *Boston Post* epithet is cited in Samuel Eliot Morison, *Three Centuries of Harvard, 1636-1936* (1936; Cambridge, Mass.: Harvard University Press, 1946), 328.

14. For a reprint of Higginson's remarks and discussion, see *The Schoolmaster: A Journal of Educational Literature and News* 3, no. 20 (Jan. 15, 1870): 5-6.

15. *The Woman's Journal* (Nov. 27, 1875); for other critics' responses to Eliot, see *The Schoolmaster* 3, no. 20 (Jan. 15, 1870): 5-7; and *The American Educational Monthly* 10 (Nov. 1873): 509-13.

16. Eliot, "Inaugural Address," 18.

17. The *Harvard University Catalogue* (1870), 102-3, lists the University Courses of Instruction and the students enrolled in both courses. Maguire, "The Curtain-Raiser," 28, reports her conversation with Allen's daughter, Mary Faben Boles (Radcliffe, 1903) regarding Allen's teaching in Charleston. On Allen's enrollment in the program see also Mary Chandler Faben Boles' report in "Class Notes—1903," *Radcliffe Quarterly* 51, no. 4 (Nov.-Dec. 1967): 29, and Faben alumna folder, RCA. On Pitman, see receipt for tuition of $50 made out to Miss Harriet Minot Pitman for the second term of courses in modern literature, Pitman alumna folder, RCA. For evidence of her work with the Society to Encourage Studies at Home, see *Society to Encourage Studies at Home Founded in 1873 by Anna Eliot Ticknor* (Cambridge, Mass.: Riverside Press, 1897), 186. On the society's work, see Schwager, "'Harvard Women'," chap. 2. Charlotte Brooks (Mrs. B. F. Brooks) hosted the "Committee on Better Education of Women" in December 1871. The committee was reorganized as the WEA in January 1872. See WEA, Minutes of Committees, quoted in Elizabeth Briggs's notes under heading, "Massachusetts Historical Society, Minutes of Committees," Elizabeth Briggs Papers, RCA.

18. Morison, *Development of Harvard University*, 454. For discussion of faculty opposition to Eliot's plan and the subsequent growth of the Graduate School, see also Morison, *Three Centuries of Harvard*, 334-36; and Hawkins, *Between Harvard and America*, 54-58.

19. On summer courses, see Morison, *Three Centuries of Harvard*, 390, and *The Woman's Journal* (Dec. 11, 1875). In 1875, 11 women studied chemistry and 30 studied botany. See *Harvard University Catalogue (1874-75)*, 147-48, HUA. President Eliot advocated botany as an avocation for young ladies and encouraged women's organizations to contribute funds to the Bussey Institution (endowed to provide Harvard with space and funds for an undergraduate school of agriculture and horticulture), whose financial condition was precarious. Women were admitted, however, only to three courses held in the summer, and, unlike their male classmates, they received no Harvard credit. See Morison, *Development of Harvard University*, 508-17; *Annual Report of the President of Harvard University* for 1870, 1871, and 1872; and vote to admit women to the three courses in CR, April 28, 1871, 288, HUA. In 1875 women were invited to attend a new evening readings series on "masterpieces of literature." Eliot introduced the program to provide extra teaching and earnings for some faculty. It also served, like earlier initiatives, as a gesture of Harvard's accommodation of women. See *Annual Report of the President* (1875), and *Harvard University Catalogue* (1875-76, 1876-77, 1878-79), HUA. The pattern of declining access for women at Harvard confirms what Patricia Graham has observed more generally regarding the differential impact on men and women of changes in the structure of higher education. See Patricia Albjerg Graham, "Expansion and Exclusion: A History of Women in American Higher Education," *Signs* 3, no. 4 (Summer 1978): 759-73. Eliot's wholesale exclusion of women from Harvard's mandate contrasts sharply with his meritocratic ideals as applied to men. For an interesting discussion, see Kim Townsend, *Manhood at Harvard: William James and Others* (Cambridge, Mass.: Harvard University Press, 1996), 83-97. On patterns of exclusion earlier in the century, see Ronald Story, *Harvard and the Boston Upper Class: The Forging of an Aristocracy, 1800-1870* (Middletown, Conn.: Wesleyan University Press, 1980), chaps. 6-7.

20. Woman's Education Association, *First Annual Report, for the Year Ending January 16, 1873* (Boston: W. L. Deland, 1873), 5.

21. For evidence of the tradition of learned women in Boston, see Ednah D. Cheney, "The Women of Boston," and Schwager, "'Harvard Women'," chap. 1. On New England women more generally, see Catherine E. Kelly, *In the New England Fashion: Reshaping Women's Lives in the Nineteenth Century* (Ithaca, N.Y.: Cornell University Press, 1999). For a discussion of the liberal educational reforms of Harvard men, see for example, Daniel

Walker Howe, *The Unitarian Conscience: Harvard Moral Philosophy, 1805-1861* (Cambridge, Mass.: Harvard University Press), chap. 9. On family connections and the pattern of Harvard professors who married prominent (and wealthy) Boston women, see Story, *Harvard and the Boston Upper Class*, 86-87. Peter Dobkin Hall discusses this pattern as an aspect of the changing social order: see *The Organization of American Culture, 1700-1900: Private Institutions, Elites, and the Origins of American Nationality* (New York: New York University Press, 1984), 198-206. On kinship networks among Boston's aristocracy, see Betty G. Farrell, *Elite Families: Class and Power in Nineteenth-Century Boston* (Albany, N.Y.: SUNY Press, 1993), chap. 4. I have chosen to call these women "Harvard women" to emphasize both their close association to the university and, in many cases, their study under Harvard professors. They did not use the term to describe themselves, though Elizabeth Cary Agassiz referred to the Annex students as "the Harvard girls." See Elizabeth Cary Agassiz [hereafter, ECA], diary entry for Sept. 24, 1879, Elizabeth Cary Agassiz Papers, Schlesinger Library, Radcliffe College [hereafter, SL].

22. WEA, Minutes of Committees, Elizabeth Briggs papers, RCA. For officers and charter members, see WEA, *First Annual Report*, 16-17.

23. On the Agassiz School and its students, see Georgina Schuyler, typescript of speech given at memorial meeting, Dec. 8, 1907, Rosamond Lamb Papers, SL; Ellen Emerson to ECA, Sept. 26, 1905, Elizabeth Cary Agassiz Papers, SL; Elizabeth Cary Agassiz, ed., *Louis Agassiz: His Life and Correspondence*, 2 vols. (Boston: Houghton Mifflin, 1885), 526-30; and Louise Hall Tharp, *Adventurous Alliance: The Story of the Agassiz Family of Boston* (Boston: Little, Brown, 1959), 139-44. Elizabeth Agassiz later wrote of how important Felton's tutelage had been to her life and education: ECA to Mary Perkins Cary, Feb. 11, 1868, box 2, folder 17, Elizabeth Cary Agassiz Papers, SL. Felton served as Harvard's president from 1860 until his death in 1862.

24. WEA, Minutes of Committees, Elizabeth Briggs Papers, RCA.

25. Ibid. See also newspaper report, "The Woman's Education Association," dated Jan. 16, 1873, and signed by J. Marcou, H. L. Cabot, and A. C. Lowell, Harvard Examinations for Women folder, RCA; WEA, *First Annual Report*, 8.

26. This meeting was not officially reported by the WEA. The only source regarding its details is an article by Peirce published in the *Boston Daily Advertiser* and reprinted in *The Woman's Journal*, April 17, 1875. Eliot appears not to have denied the substance of Peirce's article. Within the year, the WEA grew to a membership of 107 women. See List of Members, WEA, *First Annual Report*, 16-17.

27. On the development of the plan, see Peirce's article in *The Woman's Journal*, April 17, 1875; and WEA, *First Annual Report*, 9. On Harvard's action, see CR, 11:364.

28. OR, 11:39-40; see also *Reports to the Overseers*, 3:75-76.

29. The women in Clarke's family may have encouraged his commitment to women's education. Cora H. Clarke was to become a well-regarded botanist and entomologist and in 1884 was named a fellow of the AAAS. See Margaret W. Rossiter, *Women Scientists in America: Struggles and Strategies to 1940* (Baltimore, Md.: Johns Hopkins University Press, 1982), 77; and WEA, *First Annual Report*, 16. For report of Eliot's address, see *The Woman's Journal*, July 26, 1873. On action by the Board, see OR, 11:69-70.

30. On suppression and discussion of Clarke's report, see *American Educational Monthly* 10 (Nov. 1873): 509-12; and references in obituaries, *Boston Herald*, June 9, 1888, and *Boston Transcript*, June 9, 1888. No reference to the report exists in the Corporation Records or in the Minutes of the Board of Overseers. On Eliot's speech, see also *Boston Daily Advertiser*, May 16, 1873.

31. The most comprehensive description of the Harvard Examinations is an unsigned manuscript (probably written by Katharine P. Loring), dated Jan. 1, 1884, Harvard Examinations for Women folder, RCA. See also *Annual Reports* of the Woman's Education Association for the years 1873-1884; Elizabeth Briggs notes, RCA; and Maguire, "The Curtain-Raiser," 32-38. *Reports of the President of Harvard University* for the years 1872-1878 also include some information. Samuel Eliot, first cousin of Charles W. Eliot, was a

lecturer in history at Harvard from 1869 to 1873. Earlier he had served as professor of history and then president of Trinity College, president of the Perkins' Institution and Massachusetts School for the Blind, and Harvard Overseer. In 1873 he became master of Girls' High School in Boston. See Walter Graeme Eliot, *Eliot Family* (New York: Livingston, Middleditch, 1887), 90-91.

32. On controversy within the WEA, see *The Woman's Journal*, July 26, 1873, Sept. 20, 1873, and April 17, 1875. On the women on Agassiz's committee, see: Ednah D. Cheney, "The Women of Boston," 344-45 and 353; Harriet Dix et al., eds., *A Memorial of Harriet Elizabeth Caryl, 1834-1918* (Boston: privately printed, 1919); Olive White, *Centennial History of the Girls' High School of Boston* (Boston: Paul Blanchard, 1952); and Emily Greene Balch, ed., *Catherine Ireland, 1838-1925* (Boston: privately printed, 1929). Elizabeth Cary Agassiz repeatedly hailed women whose reform activities were conducted with "quiet unobtrusiveness." See, for example, her memorial to Anna Eliot Ticknor in *The Society to Encourage Studies at Home*, 6. For quotation, see Karen Blair, *The Clubwoman as Feminist: True Womanhood Redefined, 1868-1914* (New York: Holmes & Meier, 1980), 1. Peirce resigned from the WEA in protest when Howe and the others were rejected. See *The Woman's Journal*, April 17, 1875.

33. Corporation Minutes for Aug. 7, 1872, CR, 11:402-3; OR, 22:64-65; *Annual Report of the President* (1872), 26-28, HUA. See also Maguire, "The Curtain-Raiser," 32.

34. Minutes of the Committee on Harvard Examinations, Jan. 14, 1884, and "Report on the Committee on Harvard Examinations for Women," Harvard Examinations for Women folder, RCA.

35. For critics' arguments, see *The Woman's Journal*, July 26, 1873; July 5, 1873; and June 5, 1875; and Thomas Wentworth Higginson, in *New England Journal of Education* 1, no. 2 (Jan. 9, 1875): 21. On the history of the exams and the decision to end them in 1883, see "Report of the Committee on Harvard Examinations for Women," June 1, 1884; Minutes of the Harvard Examinations Committee for Dec. 1, 1882; Eugenie Homer to Elizabeth Briggs, April 25, 1932, Briggs' notes on the Harvard Examinations, Elizabeth Briggs Papers, RCA. On Williams' tenure at Smith, see "Officers of Instruction and Administration," *Smith College Alumnae Association Biographical Register* 30, no. 1 (Nov. 1935), Smith College Archives, Northampton, Mass. For a detailed discussion of the Harvard Examinations and their relation to the Annex, see Schwager, "'Harvard Women'," 108-26.

36. The origin of the sobriquet is unknown; one version attributes it to an unknown Harvard student: Lucy Paton, *Elizabeth Cary Agassiz: A Biography* (Boston: Houghton Mifflin, 1919), 203-4; and Mary E. Howard, "It Happened Seventy-Five Years Ago," *Radcliffe Quarterly* (Nov. 1954), 9. Details of the program and names of the managing committee appear in the first circular, dated Feb. 22, 1879, RCA. For WEA membership, see *Annual Report of the Woman's Education Association for the Year Ending January 13, 1881* (Boston: Cochrane & Sampson, Printers, 1881), 27-29. Arthur Gilman, in his own histories of the Annex, claimed a more central and exclusive role in its founding than probably is deserved. For an extensive discussion of the Gilmans' role and the historiography, see Schwager, "'Harvard Women'," chap. 4.

37. *New England Journal of Education* 9, no. 24 (June 12, 1879). Thomas Wentworth Higginson, in *The Woman's Journal* 10, no. 9 (March 1, 1879): 1. On Leach, see also Mary Hume Maguire, "The Uniqueness of Radcliffe," *Radcliffe Quarterly* (May 1948), 2-3. Leach had a long and distinguished career as head of the Greek Department at Vassar College. See Ann Townsend Zwart, "Abby Leach," in *Notable American Women, 1607-1950*, vol. 2, ed. Edward T. James and Janet Wilson James (Cambridge: Harvard University Press, 1971), 379-80. Mary E. Hughes to Arthur Gilman, March 13, 1879, box 1, Arthur Gilman Papers, Massachusetts Historical Society [hereafter, MHS]. ECA, diary entry, Feb. 11, 1879, Elizabeth Cary Agassiz Papers.

38. Charles W. Eliot to Arthur Gilman, Feb. 7, and Feb. 18, 1879, box 1, Gilman Papers.

39. Mrs. R.A. Reynolds, *The Woman's Journal* (May 10, 1879): 147; *Springfield Republican* article reprinted in *The Woman's Journal* (March 15, 1879): 84.

40. Mary Gilpin Armstrong, "Alice Longfellow's 'Adopted Child': Her Last Interview—On Radcliffe," *Boston Sunday Globe,* Dec. 16, 1928, RCA. Hugh Hawkins, "Elizabeth Cary Agassiz," in *Notable American Women,* 1:24. The "ladies' degree" was introduced with coeducation in the antebellum colleges. The degree typically substituted French for Greek and Latin. See Roger Geiger, "The 'Superior Instruction of Women' 1836-1890," in *The American College in the Nineteenth Century,* ed. Roger Geiger (Nashville, Tenn.: Vanderbilt University Press, 2000), 185-92. For an important discussion of regional differences, see Christie Anne Farnham, *The Education of the Southern Belle: Higher Education and Student Socialization in the Antebellum South* (New York: New York University Press, 1994), chap. 1.

41. The only full-length study of Elizabeth Cary Agassiz is Paton's *Elizabeth Cary Agassiz.* This work was the result of a commission formed by Radcliffe College in 1917, and it has served since then as the major source of information on Agassiz's life and her work at Radcliffe. It is not, however, a critical biography. Several popular biographical accounts and family reflections contain useful information as well. See, for example, Emma Forbes Cary, "A Sketch of Mrs. Louis Agassiz," in Caroline Gardiner Curtis, *Memories of Fifty Years in the Last Century* (Boston: privately printed, 1947), 116-17; Louise Hall Tharp, *Adventurous Alliance: The Story of the Agassiz Family of Boston* (Boston: Little, Brown, 1959); and Mary Caroline Crawford, *Famous Families of Massachusetts,* 2 vols. (Boston: Little, Brown, & Co., 1930), 1:214-32. The best biographical essay is Hawkins, "Elizabeth Cary Agassiz," in *Notable American Women,* 1:22-25.

42. Elizabeth Cary Agassiz, *Louis Agassiz: His Life and Correspondence,* 2 vols. (Boston: Houghton, Mifflin and Company, 1885), 1:526-27; Edward Lurie, *Louis Agassiz: A Life in Science* (Baltimore, Md.: Johns Hopkins University Press, 1988), 201. On students at the Agassiz School, see Nellie to Mother, Sept. 29, 1856, Sarah Ellen Browne Papers, SL; Charlotte Whiton, quoted in Tharp, *Adventurous Alliance,* 143. Faculty who taught in the school included Professors Felton, Schmidt, Monti, Gurney, Lowell, and Child. Other faculty members were Helen Clapp, Katherine Howard, Emily Howard, Augusta Curtis, Catherine Ireland, Ida Agassiz Higginson, Mlle. Le Clère, and William J. Stillman: see Paton, *Elizabeth Cary Agassiz,* 396-97.

43. Tharp, *Adventurous Alliance,* 28-30.

44. Elizabeth Cary Agassiz to Emma F. Cary and Louisa Fulton [June 26, 1903], quoted in Paton, *Elizabeth Cary Agassiz,* 350-51. The identification of the Annex with the Agassiz School also is noted by Elizabeth's sister, Emma Forbes Cary, in her "Sketch of Mrs. Louis Agassiz," 124. For student quotes, see Abby Parsons MacDuffie, *The Little Pilgrim* (New York: privately printed, 1938), 27; and Cora Burr Hardon, student memoir dated May 1939, RCA. For a student description of the Annex, see Eleanor Pearson, "Harvard Annex Letter," *The Wellesley Prelude* 1, no 7 (Oct. 17, 1889): 99-101.

45. MacDuffie, *The Little Pilgrim,* 9; and James C. Parsons to Arthur Gilman, March 4, April 3, and April 26, 1879; Mary Byrd to Arthur Gilman, March 14, and June 19, 1882, all in box 1, Arthur Gilman Papers.

46. On Byrd, see Bessie Zaban Jones and Lyle Gifford Boyd, *The Harvard College Observatory, 1839-1919* (Cambridge, Mass.: Harvard University Press, 1971), 414. On careers of graduate students, see alumnae surveys dated 1928, 1931, 1934, 1937, and 1940; and Memorial Biographies, alumnae folders, RCA.

47. Number of students calculated from Class Lists, first and second terms, 1879-1880, Registrar's Records, RCA. For statistics on special students at the Annex, see annual reports by year, RCA. In 1912, a committee headed by William Byerly investigated "the Special Student question" at Radcliffe. The report indicated that "Specials" still were numerous at Radcliffe: for the 15 previous years they had formed about 25 percent of the student body. See Byerly Report (1913), RCA.

48. Annie Barber Clarke, "A Member of Radcliffe's First Class Speaks for Herself," *Radcliffe Quarterly* (Nov. 1954), 16; see also undated letter in Annie Barber student diary, following entry for Jan. 3, 1880, RCA. Annie Winsor, "Annex vs. College," student theme dated Nov.

17, 1886, box 1, folder 2, Annie Ware Winsor Allen Papers, RCA. The role of educated mothers in promoting the careers of their daughters warrants further study. The Annex and Radcliffe data suggest that mothers who were educated in the nineteenth-century female academies, seminaries, and normal schools—and those who had served as teachers—provided important impetus to their daughters' decisions to attend college. For discussion, see Schwager, "'Harvard Women'," chap. 5.

49. Annie Winsor, entry for Jan. 9, 1885, Annie Ware Winsor Allen diary, SL. See also, Annie Winsor, sophomore theme dated Dec. 1, 1884, box 1, folder 1, Annie Ware Winsor Allen Papers, RCA.

50. Arthur Gilman, "In the Beginning," *Radcliffe Magazine* 7 (June 1905): 80-81; and Arthur Gilman Private Records, entry for May 30, 1881, Radcliffe College Documents, RCA.

51. Arthur Gilman Private Records, entry for June 4, 1881; Arthur Gilman to President Eliot, June 14, 1881, and enclosure addressed to the President and Fellows of Harvard College, copies in Arthur Gilman Private Records, pp. 50-52, Radcliffe College Documents, RCA. Arthur Gilman to Joseph B. Warner, Dec. 11, 1893, Radcliffe College Documents; "Report of the Work of the First Year," dated Nov. 10, 1880, RCA. The number of Harvard courses is approximated from my count of those listed in the *Harvard University Catalogue* (1879-80), 77-90.

52. Barrett Wendell's comments date to 1884. See comments written on first sophomore theme, dated Dec. 1, 1884, box 1, folder 1, Annie Ware Winsor Allen Papers, RCA. George Martin Lane to Arthur Gilman, n.d. [received March 19, 1879], Radcliffe College Documents, RCA. On Williams, see William E. Byerly to Arthur Gilman, Dec. 21, 1883, box 2, Arthur Gilman Papers. John Tetlow, "The Eastern Colleges for Women: Their Aims, Means, and Methods," Part I, *Education* 1 (May-June 1881): 483-84, describes scheduling in the Annex and compares the work of the Annex to that of Vassar, Smith, Wellesley, and the College of Liberal Arts of Boston University. Abby Parsons to her parents, Oct. 26, 1879, quoted in MacDuffie, *The Little Pilgrim*, 18-20.

53. Arthur Gilman, "Report of the Secretary," in *Private Collegiate Instruction for Women Second Year Reports*, 11, RCA. Elizabeth Cary Agassiz to Arthur Gilman, March 24, 1882, as quoted in Paton, *Elizabeth Cary Agassiz*, 205-6.

54. See notes on meeting of Managers and Advisory Board, Arthur Gilman Private Records; and Academic Board Meeting Minutes, Radcliffe College Documents, RCA.

55. On endowment drive, see minutes of the Executive President's Office, Council Records, vol. 1; and circular dated Feb. 22, 1883, RCA. On WEA's campaign and ECA's response, see Woman's Education Association, *Annual Report for the Year Ending January 8, 1885*, p. 5.

56. Society for the Collegiate Instruction of Women, "Subscription List," dated Feb. 22, 1884, RCA; minutes of the Executive Committee, Feb. 4, 1884, Council Records, vol. 1; minutes of the annual meeting, 1885, Minutes of the Trustees, RCA.

57. Charles W. Eliot to Annie Barber, Jan. 24, 1893, letter press volume, Eliot Papers, HUA (copy of this letter also in folder 3, Elizabeth Briggs Papers, RCA). Elizabeth Agassiz to C. W. Eliot, March 25, [1893], letter press volume, Eliot Papers, HUA. For detailed discussion of the negotiations, see Schwager, "'Harvard Women'," chap. 6.

58. Le Baron Russell Briggs, "Not Always to the Swift," *Radcliffe Quarterly* 11, no. 2 (April 1927): 20.

59. C. W. Eliot to Mrs. Louis Agassiz, May 29, 2893, letter press volume, Eliot Papers, HUA.

60. For vote by the Annex, see Minutes of the (Associates) Trustees, Oct. 31, 1893; also Arthur Gilman to Charles W. Eliot, Nov. 1893 (copy), Arthur Gilman scrapbook, RCA; and WEA, *Annual Report for the Year Ending Jan. 18, 1894*, pp. 15-16. In 1640, Lady Mowlson (neé Radcliffe) had contributed 100 pounds sterling to Harvard for a scholarship fund and hence was considered the first woman benefactor of Harvard College. For Overseers' vote, see OR, Dec. 6, 1893, 13: 138, HUA. For a detailed discussion of alumnae and other protests, see Schwager, "'Harvard Women'," 347-66. For accounts of the hearings regarding the charter and actions by the commonwealth, see Mary Coes, "Radcliffe

College," *Harvard Graduates Magazine* 2, no. 8 (June 1894): 551-52; Arthur Gilman, "Incorporation of Radcliffe College," dated July 31, 1909, Radcliffe College Documents, RCA; and Paton, *Elizabeth Cary Agassiz,* 249-56.

61. OR, May 24, 1894, 13:154-55.

62. Charles W. Eliot, Radcliffe Commencement Address, 1894, reprinted in *Harvard Graduates' Magazine* 3, no. 9 (Sept. 1894): 105; and "Higher Education for Women," in Neilson, ed., *Charles W. Eliot* 1:166-67.

63. Charles W. Eliot, Radcliffe Commencement Address, 1898, reprinted in *Harvard Graduates' Magazine* 7, no. 25 (Sept. 1898): 83; Le Baron Russell Briggs, "Commencement Address at Wellesley College," in *Routine and Ideals* (Boston: Houghton, Mifflin and Company), 129.

64. Elizabeth Cary Agassiz, Radcliffe Commencement Address, 1898, reprinted in *Harvard Graduates' Magazine* 7, no. 25 (Sept. 1898): 82. Elizabeth Agassiz to Abby Parsons McDuffie, March 18, 1894, Radcliffe College documents, RCA. Elizabeth Cary Agassiz, Radcliffe Commencement Address, June 1899, reprinted in *Harvard Graduates' Magazine* 8, no. 29 (Sept. 1899): 66-67.

65. Agassiz, Radcliffe Commencement Address, June 1899, 66-67.

HARVARD MEN

From Dudes to Rough Riders

Kristin Hoganson

As the nineteenth century drew to a close, Harvard president Charles William Eliot struggled to transform his institution from a gentlemen's club to a world-class research university. But despite those ambitions, Harvard remained a bastion of privilege. To many observers from beyond the confines of Cambridge, Harvard men appeared aristocratic in an age of mass politics, contemplative in an age of action, leisured in an age of enterprise, and overly refined in an age that valued robust masculinity in men. They appeared, in short, to be "dudes." The 1895 *Century Dictionary* defined the "dude" as a "fop or exquisite, characterized by affected refinements of dress, speech, manners and gait."[1] He was educated, professional, and well-to-do; urban, dandified, soft, and elitist. And he was becoming an increasingly marginal figure in the nation's political life—or at least some feared this possibility. In 1896, the *Forum,* a magazine aimed at a rather dudish audience, worried that college men were learning to be critics, not leaders.[2] Writing in the equally highbrow *Outlook,* settlement house leader Jane Addams blamed the rise of the ward boss on the political inefficacy of educated men.[3]

And these were the criticisms of sympathizers. Populist stump speakers such as Mary Elizabeth Lease expressed nothing but contempt for the "silk-hatted dude and the soft-handed son of idleness" who profited from the toil of real men.[4] Party regulars raged against the civil service reformers who wished to reserve administrative positions for the well educated by calling them "Miss Nancys," "eunuchs," members of a "third sex," and "dudes."[5] All these epithets reflected the belief that educated reformers' intellectual and moral approach to politics rendered them less manly than the party loyalists who fought for power in the trenches.[6]

This is not to say that Harvard graduates lacked political power. In aggregate, they enjoyed the benefits of great wealth, prestigious family connections, and public prominence. Their privileged social positions made them poor objects of sympathy. Nonetheless, Harvard men did suffer from status anxieties that were very real to them. They faced the challenge of holding on to—not to mention augmenting—their power in an age in which a Harvard education could be seen as a liability as much as an asset. Above all, those who desired political careers had to struggle to establish their credibility in the eyes of a male electorate that valued democratic, practical, and masculine attributes in its leaders. To preserve their political authority, Harvard men had to overcome the "dudish" stereotype and align themselves with more robust ideals of manhood. Henry Cabot Lodge and Theodore Roosevelt serve as cases in point.

Lodge, a bookish man from a Boston Brahmin family, was in some respects a quintessential dude during his undergraduate years. He once cavorted in petticoats in a Hasty Pudding show, and his academic record was such that, after earning his B.A. from Harvard in 1871, he stayed on to receive a Ph.D. in political science in 1876 and then lingered a few more years teaching American history. But Lodge did not limit himself to theatrical and intellectual pursuits. He also spent time sparring in the gymnasium and boating on the Charles.[7] In later years, when he ran successfully for the Massachusetts legislature, the House of Representatives, and the Senate, he felt compelled to emphasize these more robust interests in order to cast himself as a man's man, a challenge given his petite stature, delicate muscle tone, plush life style, and bouts of ill health. (Even when Lodge was in his mid-40s, his anxious mother fretted about his upset digestion.[8])

Invited to speak at an 1896 alumni dinner, Lodge extolled the virtue of rough and tumble sports: "The time given to athletic contests and the injuries incurred on the playing-field are part of the price which the English-speaking race has paid for being world-conquerors." Lodge made it clear that rigorous sports would do more than benefit the race and the nation; they would benefit Harvard as well. "In the future of the United States I want Harvard to be in the forefront," Lodge continued. "I want her to wield the influence and take the part to which her traditions and her past, to which all she is and all she hopes to be, entitle her."[9] According to Lodge, the means to accomplish that objective lay on the football field, not in the library.

Lodge found a kindred spirit in Theodore Roosevelt, Harvard class of 1880. Roosevelt came from a socially prominent New York City family, and at Harvard he continued to circulate in the most exclusive circles.[10] He did well academically, winning election to Phi Beta Kappa, but like Lodge he also made a point of visiting Hemenway Gymnasium and practicing his sculling. These latter activities helped him present himself as something other than an asthmatic, nearsighted, bookwormish dandy with a high, squeaky voice. This is not to say he escaped ridicule altogether—when he won a seat in the New York State Assembly shortly after graduating from college, the press derided him as a dude.[11] Nevertheless, along with his ranching experiences in the Dakota territory, his earlier efforts to build his body helped the youthful Roosevelt counter this negative image.

For Roosevelt, no less than Lodge, rehabilitating the Harvard man entailed supporting collegiate athletics. Even from the White House, Roosevelt followed Harvard teams and lobbied his alma mater in behalf of the football program.[12] Roosevelt valued college sports because he worried about "overcivilization," meaning the tendency of industrial society to weaken the bourgeois men who benefited most from its comforts. Looking beyond the confines of his class, Roosevelt expressed concerns about the challenges posed by working-class men—especially immigrant and African American men—whose manual labor seemed to be building hardier physiques than those attained by white-collar workers in their sedentary office jobs. Seen from within a Darwinian framework, elite men's apparent softness foretold their inevitable decline. To preserve their class, racial, and even national standing, they must build their bodies. And college sports appeared to be an ideal means of doing so. In advocating body building—or, as he put it, "the strenuous life"—Roosevelt was in keeping with the currents of his time. Whereas Northern middle-class and wealthy men of the mid-nineteenth century had placed a premium on moral earnestness in men, at the turn of the century they placed greater emphasis on a fighting spirit. Right or wrong, what mattered most in assessing a man's worth was his tenacity.[13]

Roosevelt did not stop with supporting collegiate athletics. In his efforts to foster a more vigorous manhood among wealthy white men, he exhorted them to embark on strenuous endeavors beyond the playing field. In an 1894 article, "The Manly Virtues and Practical Politics," Roosevelt exhorted educated men to enter the "battles of the political world," to go out into the "rough hurly-burly of the caucus, the primary, and the political meeting."

Roosevelt admitted that it was pleasant to associate merely with cultivated, refined men, but he admonished his peers to mingle on equal terms with coarse men and to develop the "rougher, manlier virtues, and above all the virtue of personal courage, physical as well as moral," for these "manly virtues" were essential in politics. "We must be vigorous in mind and body, able to hold our own in rough conflict with our fellows, able to suffer punishment without flinching, and, at need, to repay it with full interest."[14] To succeed in politics, concluded Roosevelt, college men must demonstrate the hardy virtues of the soldier. And what better way to do this than to become soldiers?

In 1895, distraught over the refusal of Harvard's student newspaper, the *Crimson,* to jump on the martial bandwagon during a war scare with Great Britain, Roosevelt wrote Lodge about the need to save Harvard from "degradation." "The clamor of the peace faction has convinced me that this country needs a war," he wrote.[15] Harvard needed war most of all. Roosevelt made this point the following year when he wrote Lodge that pacifistic Harvard professors were "rapidly confirming me in the feeling that there ought to be a war."[16] Upon expressing such sentiments publicly, in a letter to the *Crimson,* he met a mixed response: on the one hand, he reported that 20 to 30 Harvard men had thanked him for having written it; on the other hand, he wrote Lodge that the *Harvard Graduate's Magazine* "is now assailing me with the ineffective bitterness proper to beings whose cult is nonvirility." President Eliot, he continued, had attacked the two of them as "degenerate sons of Harvard."[17] Roosevelt reciprocated Eliot's animosity, blaming him and other "futile sentimentalists" for "producing a flabby, timid type of character, which eats away the great fighting features of our race."[18] Roosevelt's deep attachment to Harvard made its dudish reputation—and even worse, its dudish attributes—hard to bear. Pleased and yet frustrated by a militaristic article from the *Yale Alumni Weekly,* Roosevelt confessed to a friend: "I wish I could get some of the Yale spirit into Harvard."[19]

Even in the face of vigorous alumni lobbying, President Eliot lacked Lodge's and Roosevelt's commitment to promoting dangerous sports and a military ethos on campus. Valuing the life of the mind more than the feats of the body, he deplored the tendency to regard intercollegiate athletic competitions as indicators of institutional standing. He criticized the football program for teaching the ethics of war and suggested that instruction in dance would actually be more relevant to military service.[20] (Not only did this position reflect his academic inclinations; it also helped downplay the significance of Harvard's long losing streak to the Yale football team.) Yet even Eliot could not stop efforts to beef up Harvard men. During his lengthy tenure as president (1869-1909), a crew coach won an honorary degree and the football coach started receiving a salary larger than that of any faculty member.[21] In trying to nurture manliness through academic achievement and professionalism, Eliot was swimming against the currents of his time. These currents grew still stronger when the United States went to war in 1898.

The United States entered the Cuban war for independence against Spain near the end of Harvard's spring term. From the passage of the war resolution on April 25 to the Spanish surrender in Santiago on July 17, the conflict that came to be known in the United States as the Spanish-American War (thereby negating the Cubans' central role) lasted less than three months. In hindsight, the Spanish-American War appears to have been the opening wedge for U.S. empire building in the Caribbean and the Pacific: it led to the passage of a Hawaiian annexation treaty and the acquisition of Guam, the Philippines, Puerto Rico, and a base at Guantánamo Bay, Cuba. But more than acquisitive ambitions lay behind the widespread enthusiasm for the war. For many Americans, it served as an opportunity to build strenuous character in dandified American men. In particular, bourgeois commentators from the Northeast looked to military service as a chance for dudes to prove themselves as citizens and leaders. They viewed war as an opportunity for elite men to dispel the fears expressed by political scientist Franklin H. Giddings: that "mere intellectual struggles would leave our youth anaemic bookworms, unfit for the serious work of practical politics."[22] War, they hoped, could help college men regain a favorable image.

To prove the dude's martial character, his supporters first had to disprove charges that he feared war and shunned military service. Such charges gained credence because of some well-publicized remarks by Charles Eliot Norton, a Harvard humanities professor. Norton, who had been appointed to his position years earlier by his cousin, President Eliot, won national notoriety for his institution after turning aside from his prepared lecture notes to denounce the war with Spain as an "inglorious" conflict. Even worse, judging from the ensuing brouhaha, he said he did not think his students should rush to enlist. The response was vitriolic. One critic found Norton so wanting in virility that it characterized him as "a true type of that fine flower of culture which is worshiped with extravagant and idolatrous rites in Boston and Cambridge. It is eminently graceful and generally sterile."[23] Another found it "unseemly" that the sons of "men with blood in their veins" be "instructed in the principles of life by such anaemic educators."[24]

The criticisms went beyond Norton to the college that employed him. In an article titled "Disloyalty at Harvard," the *New York Sun* questioned the value of a Harvard education. "Is that the spirit which American parents desire to have instilled into their sons?" The article went on to condemn Harvard for teaching a "spirit of critical disparagement," rather than the "impulse of patriotism, so essential in the preservation of the nation and their own manliness."[25] Another newspaper that took great offense at Norton's remarks connected Harvard's recent loss to Cornell and Yale in crew to Norton's unmanly utterances:

> A man can't row with a gelatine back. Neither can eight men, no matter how hard the little coxswain curses nor how dexterously he steers. It takes eight men with piano-wire sinews and cast-iron jaws and fight in every fiber of them to win the race. The clammy, chilly influence of Charles Eliot Norton will not produce iron jaws nor iron backs nor anything else that helps men win races, or go through rush lines, or fight for the flag.

After casting Harvard men as less manly than their Ivy League rivals, thanks to the gelatinous influence of one of their professors, the author offered his own advice to Harvard freshmen: "Stop contemplating the aesthetic beauties and peaceful calm of your Charles Eliot Nortons, get under the influence of your Teddy Roosevelt, shed your aristocratic swaddling clothes and live and train and rough it, like the husky boys from Cornell."[26] He could have added "or transfer to Brown," for another clipping in Norton's papers held up Brown's president E. Benjamin Andrews—who declared his desire to enlist with his students and "march with them to the front"—as a role model for men such as Norton.[27]

Norton did have his admirers. A former student, Samuel C. Bennett, rallied to the side of his beloved professor in the height of the storm. Reflecting on his undergraduate experiences 20 years earlier, Bennett remarked: "I learned one thing in that course, and learned it by a study from life—and that is how beautiful a thing it is to be a gentleman."[28] Hannah J. Bailey, head of the Woman's Christian Temperance Union's Department of Peace and Arbitration, wrote to express her gratitude "for the brave stand you have taken against the present war with Spain." Bailey applauded Norton for understanding the true object of belles-lettres—refinement.[29]

Norton's admiring correspondents, many of them women, held fast to the older, genteel ideals of manhood that were being displaced by the martial ideals of the late nineteenth century. Whereas Norton spoke passionately about aesthetics, the American public seemed more concerned with practicality. Norton was an elderly man (he retired from Harvard at the end of the term) in a time that valorized the robustness of the young. He was unabashedly elitist in a country riven by class, ethnic, and racial divisions. He valued the life of the mind in a university that, despite his cousin's efforts, was increasingly emphasizing the cultivation of the body. And Norton was an advocate of peace in a time of war. His supporters might wallow in nostalgia about the beauties of gentlemen and the uplifting capacities of belles-lettres, but detractors ridiculed him as a symbol of the irrelevance of Harvard men in the contemporary world.

In response to the Norton scandal, even Harvard men with no sympathy for the professor rallied to the defense of their institution and class.[30] One alumnus credited Norton with being a fine art historian but then dismissed his worth as "a man of affairs," saying that the patriotic Harvard men who had served in the Civil War and those who now were serving in the Spanish War should be seen as more representative of the institution.[31] Besides pointing to the achievements of past generations of Harvard men, the college's militaristic advocates maintained that the current crop of undergraduates was up to par, that, "captious professors" notwithstanding, Harvard boys were "all right."[32] To support this point, still another Harvard man wrote a letter to his local paper pointing out that, with the encouragement of the faculty, enough students to fill two regiments had volunteered.[33] "As a Harvard man," wrote an equally militant alumnus to the *New York Times,* "I feel naturally angry that such views should get associated with Harvard, especially at a time when two of her graduates, Secretary Long and Assistant Secretary Roosevelt, are working so hard and with so much ability for the navy, and, incidentally, doing great Honor to Harvard."[34]

In their efforts to show that Harvard men were made of sterner stuff than reputed, those who trumpeted their military service often emphasized that they had spurned soft commissions and had enlisted in the ranks. Henry L. Higginson (a Union veteran and fellow of the Harvard Corporation) wrote an exuberant letter to Senator Henry Cabot Lodge, reporting that some Harvard students he knew had enlisted as privates:

> We of '61 got commissions and these boys go us one better and enlist! . . . Here I sit in the dude club—sports—loafers—athletes—dandies—raised in cotton wool . . . a little club and 40 men have already gone—11% of the club, which has many old men as well as young—20 seniors of Harvard college and many of the other schools are in the service—chiefly privates.[35]

On the floor of the Senate, William J. Sewell of New Jersey applauded the "dude's" willingness to serve in the ranks:

> The darling of the parlor, the athlete at Yale, Harvard, or Princeton, are lined to-day on the picket line before Santiago with the farmer and the mechanic, each equal, each claiming no more right as an American citizen, and each anxious and eager for the fray. It is the most sublime spectacle, I say to the Senate of the United States, that ever has been witnessed that our very best blood, our brightest young men, claim the right of citizenship to the extent that they go to the front line of battle and vie with anybody and everybody, no matter from what rank of society.[36]

Higginson and Sewell were pleased to believe that, contrary to the stereotype, Ivy League graduates did not shirk the harsh duties of citizenship. Equally gratifying were the reports that college men's constitutions were as robust as those of the working class. What had fostered this hardy manhood? Athletics. A typically admiring newspaper claimed that the Rough Riders' "rich society men and students from Harvard College" had "given a superb account of themselves. . . . in riding, shooting and agility of movement in general they show the results of their long experience on the polo field and in college athleticism."[37]

If any doubts remained, the public need look only at the Rough Riders, the most touted proof of college men's fiber. Led by Colonel Leonard Wood (an 1884 Harvard Medical School graduate) with Theodore Roosevelt as second in command, the Rough Riders captured the public's imagination, thanks to Roosevelt's publicity skills. He presented his regiment as a model fraternity, in which the privileged college man bonded with the lower-class Western cowboy. In his book *The Rough Riders*, Roosevelt emphasized the college backgrounds of many of his recruits. "Harvard being my own college, I had such a swarm of applications from it that I could not take one in ten," he wrote. "What particularly pleased me, not only in the Harvard but the Yale and Princeton men, and, indeed, in these recruits from the older States generally, was that they did not ask for commissions. With hardly an exception they entered upon their duties as troopers in the spirit which they held to the end, merely endeavoring to show that no work could be too hard, too disagreeable, or too dangerous for them to perform."[38] In his farewell remarks to the troops, reprinted by admiring newspapers, he proclaimed: "You are men of widely different pursuits, yet you stand here side by side. You fought shoulder to shoulder. No man asked quarter for himself, and each one went in to show that he was as good as his neighbor."[39] The message was clear: it was not the hardened bronco buster who had proven himself to the watching nation—there was no need for that—but the supposedly effete Ivy League graduate who had shown he was as good—that is, as masculine—as his fellows.

To Roosevelt's immense satisfaction, the U.S. press tended to take him at his word, further popularizing the idea that the rough-riding college man had demonstrated his stuff in combat. The *Cleveland Leader* sang the college man's praises in rhyme:

> They laughed when we said we were going,
> They scoffed when we answered the call;
> We might do at tennis and rowing,
> But as warriors! O, no—not at all!
> Ah, let them look there in the ditches,
> Blood-stained by the dudes in the van,
> And learn that a chap may have riches
> And still be a man![40]

If prior to the war, dudes seemed refined to the point of effeminacy, after the war they found it easier to claim manhood.

Richard Harding Davis, a popular novelist and well-known reporter, encapsulated this change of view in his description of a college and club man turned sergeant. "There was not a mule-skinner or cow-puncher in the regiment that did not recognize in him something of himself and something finer and better than himself."[41] Roosevelt was even more partisan in his praise, naming his alma mater as the foremost crucible of manhood. "I think the Harvard boys have averaged the best of all," he wrote his sister from Santiago.[42] Men such as Davis (who had studied at Johns Hopkins) and Roosevelt believed that military service revealed a class of natural commanders—more likely elite men than not.

The war did more than reshape the dude's public image; it gave dudes some experience in leading men from widely divergent backgrounds. Theodore Roosevelt saw the war as a test of his ability to lead men from different walks of life. Of course, he believed he passed the test with flying colors. "These men would follow me anywhere now," boasted Roosevelt to Lodge.[43] After the war, he made the most of his military record when running for office. In his successful campaign for governor of New York, he traveled with six Rough Riders in full uniform and told war stories at whistle stops. He appeared at the 1900 Republican convention in a wide-rimmed hat that evoked his Rough Rider headgear. His supporters joined with him in milking his military record for all it was worth.[44] To introduce Roosevelt to the convention, Senator Chauncey M. Depew of New York started with the obstacles that Roosevelt had to surmount: he was a child of Fifth Avenue, a child of the clubs, a "child of the exclusiveness of Harvard College." But this child of privilege had overcome his disadvantages and had reinvented himself. Summing up the transformation, Depew said: "the dude had become a cowboy, the cowboy had become a soldier, the soldier had become a hero."[45]

Roosevelt reaped unparalleled political profits from his military service, but even "dudes" who did not serve regarded the war as an opportunity to bolster their images. This can be seen in the case of Henry Cabot Lodge. He expressed a burning desire to jump into the fray but stayed in the Senate instead, where he expounded on the glories of war and became a leading advocate of taking the Philippines, a former Spanish colony. He posed as a manly fighter, especially in comparison to anti-imperialists and the Filipinos, whom he depicted as comparatively effeminate. And he praised the Rough Riders, foremost among them his long-time friend Theodore Roosevelt, in terms that made it clear they represented men such as himself. In his history of the war, rushed to press shortly after the end of hostilities, Lodge emphasized that the regiment included graduates of Yale and Harvard. "All have the spirit of adventure strong within them, and they are there in the Cuban chaparral because they seek perils, because they are patriotic, because, as some think, every gentleman owes a debt to his country, and this is the time to pay it."[46]

If college men in general found themselves more likely to be associated with military prowess than effeteness after the war, Harvard men benefited particularly from this image transformation. Before the war, Harvard brought to mind the image of effete and unpatriotic Professor Norton. After the war, President William McKinley praised Harvard for its "potent influence in the community and throughout the United States" and applauded its graduates who had served in the military.[47] Even President Eliot struck a martial tone in his 1898 commencement speech, eliciting prolonged applause from the audience.[48] Military service regendered Harvard men, transforming them from symbols of effeminacy to symbols of powerful masculinity. This new association with militant manhood helped give them the credibility necessary to lead in the dawning years of the twentieth century.

Notes

1. *Century Dictionary* (1791; New York: Century Co., 1895), vol. 3.
2. Charles F. Thwing, "Drawbacks of a College Education," *Forum* (Dec. 22, 1896), 483-92.
3. Jane Addams, "Why the Ward Boss Rules," *Outlook* 58 (April 2, 1898): 882.
4. Lease cited in Scott G. McNall, *The Road to Rebellion: Class Formation and Kansas Populism, 1865-1900* (Chicago: University of Chicago Press, 1988), 214.
5. Matthew Josephson, *The Politicos, 1865-1896* (New York: Harcourt, Brace, 1938), 319, 356, 384; John G. Sproat, *"The Best Men": Liberal Reformers in the Gilded Age* (New York: Oxford University Press, 1968), 57-58.
6. Richard Hofstadter, *Anti-intellectualism in American Life* (New York: Alfred A. Knopf, 1979), 186-89.
7. Charles S. Groves, *Henry Cabot Lodge the Statesman* (Boston: Small, Maynard, 1925), 7.
8. Theodore Roosevelt to Henry Cabot Lodge, May 12, 1895, folder, T. Roosevelt Correspondence, Feb.-June 1895, Theodore Roosevelt Correspondence, Henry Cabot Lodge Papers, Massachusetts Historical Society [hereafter, MHS].
9. Henry Cabot Lodge, "Speech at the Alumni Dinner," June 1896, *Speeches and Addresses, 1884-1909* (Boston: Houghton Mifflin, 1909), 291-94.
10. Kathleen M. Dalton, "Theodore Roosevelt, Knickerbocker Aristocrat," *New York History* 67 (Jan. 1986): 39-65.
11. Serge Ricard, "War and Myth: Rough Riding at San Juan," *Interface: Essays on History, Myth and Art in American Literature,* ed. Daniel Royot (Montpellier, France: Publications de la Recherche, 1985), 61-69.
12. Kim Townsend, *Manhood at Harvard: William James and Others* (New York: W.W. Norton, 1996), 275.
13. On the growing valorization of male toughness, see E. Anthony Rotundo, *American Manhood: Transformations in Masculinity from the Revolution to the Modern Era* (New York: Basic Books, 1993), 225-34; Gail Bederman, *Manliness and Civilization: A Cultural History of Gender and Race in the United States, 1880-1917* (Chicago: University of Chicago Press, 1995), 71-88, 170-216; Elliott J. Gorn, *The Manly Art: Bare-Knuckle Prize Fighting in America* (Ithaca, N.Y.: Cornell University Press, 1986), 179-98.
14. Theodore Roosevelt, "The Manly Virtues and Practical Politics," *Forum* 17 (July 1894): 551-57.
15. Theodore Roosevelt to Henry Cabot Lodge, Dec. 27, 1895, folder: T. Roosevelt Correspondence, Dec. 1895, Theodore Roosevelt Correspondence, Henry Cabot Lodge Papers, MHS.
16. Theodore Roosevelt to Henry Cabot Lodge, Jan. 2, 1896, folder: T. Roosevelt Correspondence, Jan.-Feb. 1896, Theodore Roosevelt Correspondence, Henry Cabot Lodge Papers, MHS.
17. Theodore Roosevelt to Henry Cabot Lodge, Jan. 10, 19, April 29, 1896, in folders T. Roosevelt Correspondence, Jan.-Feb., 1896 and T. Roosevelt Correspondence, March-June, 1896, Theodore Roosevelt Correspondence, Henry Cabot Lodge Papers, MHS.
18. Theodore Roosevelt to Henry Cabot Lodge, April 29, 1896, *Selections from the Correspondence of Theodore Roosevelt and Henry Cabot Lodge, 1884-1918,* ed. Henry Cabot Lodge, 2 vols. (New York: Charles Scribner's Sons, 1925), 1:218.
19. Theodore Roosevelt to Mr. De Forest, April 13, 1898, *The Letters of Theodore Roosevelt,* ed. Elting E. Morison, 8 vols. (Cambridge, Mass.: Harvard University Press, 1951), 2:815.
20. Townsend, *Manhood at Harvard,* 97, 110-11.
21. Ibid., 108.
22. Franklin H. Giddings, "Imperialism?" *Political Science Quarterly* 13 (Dec. 1898): 585-605, quotation at 587.
23. "C. E. Norton and Maximo Gomez," *New York Times* clipping, May 1, 1898, Records of the Hour, War Time, 1898, vol. 1, p. 8, compiled by Sara Norton, Letters to Charles Eliot Norton, Houghton Library [hereafter, HL], Harvard University.

24. "Prigs Prate of Patriotism," clipping from *Commercial Tribune,* ibid., 17.

25. "Disloyalty at Harvard," *New York Sun* clipping, April 30, 1898, ibid., 2.

26. "Norton and the Boat Race," clipping enclosed in James A. Burnham to Charles E. Norton, June 24, 1898, document 903, Letters to Charles Eliot Norton, HL.

27. "A Real American at Brown," clipping in Records of the Hour, War Time, 1898, vol. 1, p. 10, compiled by Sara Norton, Letters to Charles Eliot Norton, HL.

28. Samuel C. Bennett to Charles E. Norton, July 22, 1898, document 447, Letters to Charles Eliot Norton, HL.

29. Hannah J. Bailey to Charles E. Norton, Aug. 3, 1898, document 346, Letters to Charles Eliot Norton, HL.

30. G. C. Mead, "Criticizes Prof. Norton," *New York Times,* May 4, 1898, p. 6.

31. Alexander Blackburn, "Do Not Represent New England," clipping from the *Portland Oregonian* enclosed in J. H. Murphy to C. E. Norton, May 10, 1899, document 4923, Letters to Charles Eliot Norton, HL.

32. Records of the Hour, War Time, 1898, compiled by Sara Norton, vol. 1, p. 2, Letters to Charles Eliot Norton, HL.

33. Letter to the editor of the *Sentinel,* May 10, 1898, clipping, ibid.

34. Mead, "Criticizes Prof. Norton," 6.

35. H. L. Higginson to Henry C. Lodge, July 1, 1898, folder: Higginson, H.L., May-Sept., 1898, box 16, Henry Cabot Lodge Papers, MHS.

36. Senator Sewell, *Congressional Record,* June 29, 1898, 31, part 7, 6450.

37. Clipping from the *Transcript,* Athol, Mass., June 7, 1898, from the scrapbook of Mary M. Goodrich, Theodore Roosevelt Collection, HL.

38. Theodore Roosevelt, *The Rough Riders* (New York: G. P. Putnam's Sons, 1901), 19.

39. Clipping, "Good-bye to Rough Riders," Sept. 13, 1898, Scrapbook of Emily Carow, Theodore Roosevelt Collection, HL.

40. "Dudes Before Santiago," *Cleveland Leader,* in *Spanish-American War Songs,* ed. Sidney A. Witherbee (Detroit: Sidney A. Witherbee, 1898), 31.

41. Richard Harding Davis, *The Cuban and Porto Rican Campaigns* (New York: Charles Scribner's Sons, 1898), 286-88.

42. Davis, *The Cuban and Porto Rican Campaigns,* 286-88.

43. Theodore Roosevelt to Bye, July 28, 1898, *Letters from Theodore Roosevelt to Anna Roosevelt Cowles, 1870-1918* (New York: Charles Scribner's Sons, 1924), 222.

44. Theodore Roosevelt to Henry Cabot Lodge, July 5, 1898, *The Letters of Theodore Roosevelt,* ed. Morison, 2:849.

45. Edmund Morris, *The Rise of Theodore Roosevelt* (New York: Ballantine Books, 1979), 683, 722.

46. L. White Busbey et al., *The Battle of 1900* (Chicago: Monarch Book Co., 1900).

47. Henry Cabot Lodge, *The War with Spain* (New York: Harper and Brothers, 1900), 114.

48. George B. Cortelyou, Diary, Feb. 17, 1899, folder: diary, 1899, box 52, George B. Cortelyou Papers, Library of Congress.

49. Theodore Roosevelt to Charles William Eliot, June 27, 1898, *The Letters of Theodore Roosevelt,* ed. Morison, 2:861.

THE GREAT DEBATE

Charles W. Eliot and M. Carey Thomas

Helen Lefkowitz Horowitz

Sometimes, as when two students are pitted against each other as debaters in a tournament, we can delight in the play of words alone. But words usually matter because they are words that flow into actions. In the case of the words of educational leaders, they shape and reflect college policy. They set the terms by which opportunity is offered or denied to a group. They mold curriculum and thus the building blocks of educated intelligence. Thus it was in 1899 when the president of Harvard University and the president of Bryn Mawr College squared off on the subject of the education of women. Their words in 1899 mattered a great deal. An exploration of M. Carey Thomas's response to Charles William Eliot in 1899 allows us to see the alternative to Harvard's nonrecognition of women within the university not from our hindsight 100 years later, but rather from her and Bryn Mawr College's perspective at the time.

For three decades Eliot had been a great and good president of Harvard. His innovations had moved a fine provincial college into the first rank of world universities. He had nurtured creative scholarship and attracted much of the best talent to teach, engage in research, and write in his institution. He had encouraged great professional schools and their innovative practices such as the case method in law. He had introduced the full elective system for undergraduates, opening up the curriculum to new lines of inquiry and theory. He had broadened the student body to a much wider mix of male undergraduates, including many sons of immigrants and non-Christians. He had even allowed a scheme in 1878 that opened instruction by Harvard faculty to women students through "The Society for the Collegiate Instruction of Women," familiarly called the Annex.[1]

About Harvard, the mission of the modern university, the elective system, and more open admissions, Eliot spoke eloquently. When he turned to the education of women, however, his words, both in private and in public, expressed his class and gender prejudices.

His reservations about coeducation came out in a private conversation in Baltimore to the wife of a founding Johns Hopkins trustee. She wrote to her daughter, "Eliot says . . . that coeducation does very well in communities where persons are more on an equality, but in a large city where persons of all classes are thrown together it works badly, unpleasant associations are formed, and disastrous marriages are often the result."[2]

In 1879, at the time of the Annex's founding, Eliot considered college education for women and coeducation at the first Smith commencement. He stated that, although he believed that young women should receive the best education that they can physically and mentally stand, he regarded college education for them as an experiment. He feared for their health, and applauded the steps taken at Smith to secure it. Echoing his Baltimore conversation, Eliot stated that separate education insured that parents could influence the marriages of their children "by taking care of the antecedent associations of their sons or daughters," a course best secured in single-sex institutions. But there remained the concern that women's colleges could address: whether or not time away from home spent "in the enjoyment of keen intellectual sympathy will produce in women discontent with the domestic life which is their ordinary lot."

When he turned to reflect on coeducation, he applauded the unfounded assertion that coeducation "finds no acceptance in New England, with the most insignificant exceptions." (This at a time when Boston University had been established as coeducational under Methodist auspices.) Coming closer to his concerns, he reminded his audience that "Harvard and Yale never undertook to make social experiments, or to solve new problems relating to sex; they never had to face the grave difficulties which attend all attempts to teach together sets of persons who, like young men and young women, differ widely in regard to sensibility, quickness, docility and conscientiousness." That young women were entering the Annex and thus Harvard's doorstep was dismissed in this fashion: few New England women chose to come to colleges for men open to them "unless by exception as day-scholars living at their own homes."[3]

What is interesting in Eliot's address of 1879 is his desire to protect Harvard for men and his concern with the social life of students and cross-class marriages. His outlook mirrored some of the concerns then prevalent at Harvard. Harvard saw itself in the late nineteenth century as a nursery of leadership and scholarship. In the minds of the men who composed the board of trustees, women had no place in either realm. Women should receive higher learning in order to foster their domestic roles or their work as teachers, but they should not do so at the sacred grove reserved for the future ruling elite and intelligentsia. Precious resources designated for men should not be dissipated. Nor should the sexes be mixed in classrooms during the college years, especially in nondenominational institutions such as Harvard, where the opening up of admissions meant that one could not assure the social pedigree of members of the student body.[4]

In 1885 Bryn Mawr College opened its doors. Its founding trustees, many of whom had served at Johns Hopkins University, were orthodox Quaker men who supported Eliot's belief in the value of separate collegiate institutions for men and women for many of his reasons. In the case of Bryn Mawr College, they had been asked to administer the bequest for a Quaker college for women placed in a suburb outside Philadelphia. They did so in a physical setting as much like Smith College as possible. They agreed in 1884, however, to allow a Quaker daughter to serve as dean and thereby to shape the intellectual terms of the institution: the graduate school, the graduate and undergraduate curriculum, and the composition of the faculty. She was an extraordinary young woman: M. Carey Thomas, the daughter, niece, and cousin of members of the board, had graduated from Cornell and had earned her Ph.D. in philology in 1883 from the University of Zurich, the first woman ever to do so summa cum laude.[5]

As she planned Bryn Mawr, she took a tour of selected institutions of higher education: Smith, Wellesley, Vassar, and the Annex. In Cambridge she admired Harvard for offering students the "higher learning" from professors immersed in original work. One of them, Professor William Byerly, a great friend of the Annex, had been her mathematics professor at Cornell. She therefore believed that the Annex provided Bryn Mawr with the best precedent. Yet in 1884 it could not be a full model for it did not offer "the attractions of college life," that mix of residential life and extracurricular activity and positive ethos that she had found so engaging at Wellesley and Vassar.[6] In the next decade, as Thomas built the institutional fabric of Bryn

Mawr, she tracked the Annex closely as she received reports from interested women.

Under dean Agnes Irwin, Radcliffe began to take a series of important steps to build the extracurricular and residential life on the quadrangle on Brattle and James Streets and the residential campus on Garden Street. In so doing, Radcliffe simultaneously opened access to students beyond the local area and created the material ground for college life. While much of Radcliffe's promise was to be realized only in the first decade of the twentieth century, by 1899 plans were underway.[7] The Radcliffe College that was emerging seriously challenged Bryn Mawr's vaunted position as the most intellectually vital of the women's colleges.

In 1899 both Eliot and Thomas attended the inauguration of Caroline Hazard as president of Wellesley College. Thomas spoke at the luncheon in Hazard's honor and Eliot gave the inaugural address. By 1899 Eliot had a secure reputation as the most highly respected educational leader in the nation. Not only had he transformed Harvard; he also had worked tirelessly to reform American high schools so that they could properly prepare young people for college. At the time of his Wellesley speech, Eliot was presiding over a Harvard University that had made room for Radcliffe College and accepted its plans for expansion and development. He was just about to appoint to be Radcliffe's president Le Baron Russell Briggs, Harvard's dean of the faculty and a man who would greatly assist Radcliffe as it became visible and respectable in the university. Oddly, then, Eliot used the Wellesley inauguration to voice his doubts about offering the liberal arts to women.

Eliot began by stating that, as the president of a long-established men's college, he ought to be "diffident" about giving advice to a "young college for women." Somehow he turned this humble statement into a pronounced judgment: in contrast to a man's college,

> A woman's college can have no such guidance from venerable experience, and no such clear sight of the goal to which its efforts should be directed. The so-called learned professions are very imperfectly open to women, and the scientific professions are even less accessible; and society, as a whole, has not made up its mind in what intellectual fields women may be safely and profitably employed on a large scale.

Although a man's college is clearly indispensable to society, he continued, those for women are still regarded as "luxuries or superfluities which some rather peculiar well-to-do girls desire to avail themselves of" or as a means of helping a "few exceptional girls" earn a living. The higher education of women, as a result, is not seen either by parents or by the larger public as the "solid investment" that they accord that of men.

Faced with irrelevance, what should women's colleges do? Eliot went on to instruct. Women's colleges should become schools of manners, especially necessary because women must rely on their "delicate qualities" rather than on their strength. Eliot raised the possibility that, if they succeeded, women's institutions could lead the way in teaching men's colleges how to foster the proper behavior of young people. Women's colleges should encourage religion, especially that favored by Congregational worship, avoiding the "gregarious religious excitement so unwholesome for young women."

Most important, according to Eliot, women's colleges should cease to imitate colleges for men. They should stop all competitive enticements to learning such as "grades, frequent examinations, prizes, and competitive scholarships," since women work hard without such goads. Eliot then stuck the knife home. Women's colleges should concentrate on an education that will not injure women's "bodily powers and functions." Eliot continued,

> It remains to demonstrate what are the most appropriate, pleasing, and profitable studies for women, both from the point of view of the individual and the point of view of society; and this demonstration must be entirely freed from the influence of comparisons with the intellectual capacities and tastes of men. It would be a wonder, indeed, if the intellectual capacities of women were not at least as unlike those of men as their bodily capacities are.[8]

Sitting in her academic robes as part of the ceremonial delegation, Carey Thomas listened to Eliot's speech with mounting fury. She wrote to her intimate friend Mary Garrett after the ceremony, "Eliot disgraced himself. He said the traditions of past learning and scholarship were of no use to women's education, that women's words were as unlike men's as their bodies, that women's colleges ought to be schools of <u>manners</u> and really was hateful." In a subsequent letter she recalled Eliot's Wellesley speech as "so brutal, it made me hot from head to foot."[9]

In 1899, at age 42, Thomas had been president of Bryn Mawr College for five years. She had spent her life trying to demonstrate that women's capacity of mind was equal to that of men and that women had a right to a man's education.

To M. Carey Thomas, Eliot was no abstract being on a podium, but a person who once stood as an obstacle in her course. The wife of the Johns

Hopkins' trustee who had written to her daughter with Eliot's objections to coeducation was Mary Whitall Thomas; the daughter was her 17-year-old Martha Carey Thomas. Eliot was one of the critical voices that had insured that Johns Hopkins opened only to male undergraduates, making it necessary for the daughter to go elsewhere for college.

As she returned to Bryn Mawr after the Wellesley ceremonies, M. Carey Thomas offered her reply in the chapel talk that opened the college year. Thomas began by accepting Eliot's statement that it was the mission of a college to teach manners. In the "mutual association" of new and returning students in the residence halls, she hoped there would "be fashioned and perfected the type of Bryn Mawr women which will, we hope, become as well known and universally admired a type as the Oxford and Cambridge man." In the halls younger students would be influenced by "the scholarly point of view of the older students," and they would learn good manners. Bryn Mawr was to become a school of "good breeding. . . . Manners do, as President Eliot says, matter immensely and if the Bryn Mawr woman should add to scholarship and character gentle breeding and could join high standards of behavior and usages of culture and gentle observances to high standards of scholarship we should have the type we are seeking to create."

Having established this, she went on to her central point. She attacked Eliot's premise that the world of knowledge "existing from the time of the Egyptians to the present existed only for men," and that therefore the curriculum and methods of men's colleges were no guide for women. This was, Thomas retorted, nonsense. "He might as well have told the president of Wellesley to invent a new Christian religion for Wellesley or new symphonies and operas, a new Beethoven and Wagner, new statues and pictures, a new Phidias and a new Titian, new tennis, new golf. . . . in short, a new intellectual heavens and earth."[10]

Thomas firmly believed that women should take no separate courses, such as psychology or domestic science, to prepare them for life's tasks, nor should existing subjects be presented from a women's point of view. Women's education must be identical to that of men. The life of the mind has no gender. As she later put it, "Science and literature and philology are what they are and inalterable." Although science and culture belong to women, they have been robbed of opportunity. "The life of the intellect and spirit has been lived only by men. The world of scholarship and research has been a man's world." Her task was to change that. Women's colleges have a special mission. They uphold the highest standards. They offer a place where the woman student can be the focus. They give employment to women scholars and researchers.

As women enter professions, the education they receive must be the same as men's:

> Given two bridge-buildings, a man and a woman, given a certain bridge to be built, and given as always the unchangeable laws of mechanics . . . it is simply inconceivable that the preliminary instruction given to the two bridge-builders should differ in quantity, quality, or method of presentation because while the bridge is building one will wear knickerbockers and the other a rainy-day skirt.

Driving home her point, she argued for identical medical education for men and women: "There is no reason to believe that typhoid or scarlet fever or phthisis can be successfully treated by a woman physician in one way and by a man physician in another way. There is indeed every reason to believe that unless treated in the best way, the patient may die, the sex of the doctor affecting the result even less than the sex of the patient." The career paths of women and men must be identical. Thus all fields and positions should be open to women. Because the world of knowledge is the same for both sexes, "the objects of competition are one and the same for both men and women— instructorships and professors' chairs, scholarly fame, and power to advance, however little, the outposts of knowledge."[11]

Throughout her life M. Carey Thomas remained committed to complete equality in educational and professional opportunity for men and women. In 1899, as she confronted Eliot, she feared that acknowledgment of any difference between men and women and any accommodation of that difference in curriculum could threaten women's chances. She shared with her age—and with Eliot—a positivist belief in science. Truth existed and could be fathomed by human intelligence. She had been trained abroad in philology, the nineteenth-century science of language. She believed that an education based on experimental methods could find the true patterns underlying language, build sound bridges, and cure typhoid fever. That education was to be open on equal terms to women and men. They were to learn the same methods, rules, and content in the same manner.

Through the conflicting perspectives of Eliot and Thomas, one can see the way that the battle lines over gender were drawn at the turn of the century by America's most progressive educators. In 1899 to focus on women's distinctiveness was to question their right to the world's culture and knowledge. To assert that right required that one deny that gender existed in the realm of intellect and art.

It is interesting to think about Eliot's position in the light of more recent debates over women's studies. Although most of what Eliot said in 1899 is abhorrent because it limits women's intellectual and professional opportunities, we might wish to reconsider one statement: "It remains to demonstrate what are the most appropriate, pleasing, and profitable studies for women, both from the point of view of the individual and the point of view of society; and this demonstration must be entirely freed from the influence of comparisons with the intellectual capacities and tastes of men." It is possible to read these words as an invitation to reconsider women's difference in a positive way.

Thomas herself, I think, would have led this reconsideration. In 1913 in one of her chapel talks, she spoke to Bryn Mawr students about the new movement of feminism. It meant not the narrow pursuit of legal rights but women's broader effort to open opportunity and to inject a distinctive perspective. It was a worldwide movement of women and men that sees "the emergence into the life of the state, . . . into literature, into scholarship, medicine, philosophy, art, wherever the human spirit manifests itself, of the woman's point of view." It was more than women getting the vote and attaining equal opportunity and pay; it was "the coming into our social, artistic, literary, civic life of the woman's point of view for the first time honestly expressed."[12]

In 1921 she gave an address of welcome for Madame Marie Curie at a gathering of university women in Carnegie Hall. She celebrated "the coming to its own of a new group-consciousness on the part of women. . . . a wholly new sex solidarity." At the end of the international struggle for education and the vote, women were seeking freedom "to act as we think best . . . the right to dispose of our own lives and bodies . . . to live worthily and unashamed."

Through suffrage work, Thomas had come to understand that women as a group had interests different from men. "These differences cannot be ignored. For the sake of us all, men and women alike, they <u>must not</u> be ignored. Our different woman's outlook must be written large into the laws and life of all civilized nations."[13] Thomas here argues not only for a positive understanding of women's intellectual, aesthetic, and political differences, but also for an infusion of that difference into the world of public affairs.

As we think about the way that women stood at Harvard's gates and breached them over a century ago, we can return to the great debate between Eliot and Thomas, and then circle back, realizing that some words indeed matter a great deal.

Notes

1. I have considered Eliot's reforms at Harvard in *Campus Life: Undergraduate Cultures from the End of the Eighteenth Century to the Present* (New York: Alfred A. Knopf, 1987), 70-73; I have treated the founding of the Annex in *Alma Mater: Design and Experience in the Women's Colleges from Their Nineteenth-Century Beginnings to the 1930s* (New York: Alfred A. Knopf, 1984), 95-104.
2. Mary Whitall Thomas to M. Carey Thomas, June 10, 1874, in *The Papers of M. Carey Thomas in the Bryn Mawr College Archives,* ed. Lucy Fisher West, 217 reels (Woodbridge, Conn.: Research Publications, Inc., 1982), reel 61, frame 247.
3. Eliot's address at Smith was printed in the Springfield *Republican,* June 19, 1879, under the title "Elective Studies for Women."
4. Horowitz, *Alma Mater,* 97.
5. I have documented M. Carey Thomas' life in *The Power and Passion of M. Carey Thomas* (New York, Alfred A. Knopf, 1994).
6. M. Carey Thomas, Report to the President and Trustees, Bryn Mawr College, June 7, 1884, p. 24, M. Carey Thomas Professional Papers, Bryn Mawr Organization, Bryn Mawr College Archives, Bryn Mawr, Pa.; Horowitz, *Alma Mater,* 115; Horowitz, *M. Carey Thomas,* 191-92.
7. For a full discussion of these developments, see Horowitz, *Alma Mater,* 237-47.
8. *A Record of the Exercises Attending the Inauguration of Caroline Hazard, Litt. D., as President of Wellesley College, III October MDCCCXCIX* (Cambridge, Mass.: Riverside Press, 1899), 14-19.
9. M. Carey Thomas to Mary E. Garrett, Oct. 3, 1899, Papers of M. Carey Thomas, reel 22, frame 540; M. Carey Thomas to Mary E. Garrett, Nov. 3, 1899, ibid., reel 22, frame 640.
10. Address to Students at the Opening of the Academic Year 1899-1900, Oct. 10, 1899, typescript, ibid., reel 182. This talk, published as "The Bryn Mawr Woman," in *The Educated Woman in America,* ed. Barbara Cross, Classics in Education no. 25 (New York: Teachers' College Press of Columbia University, 1965), 139-44, first introduced me to M. Carey Thomas.
11. M. Carey Thomas, "Should the Higher Education of Women Differ from That of Men?" *Educational Review* 21 (1901): 1-10.
12. M. Carey Thomas, Chapel Address, 1913, Bryn Mawr College Archives.
13. M. Carey Thomas, "The Woman's Programme," May 18, 1921, *Bryn Mawr Bulletin* (June 1921), 7-17.

RADCLIFFE WOMEN AT PLAY

Gloria Bruce

Radcliffe's development from an academic Annex to a full-fledged college took place between 1879 and 1910. It was in those early decades that Radcliffe women shaped their femininity and defined what it meant to be a Harvard-educated woman in almost complete isolation from Harvard men. Since Radcliffe academics were inherently male-oriented (planned for men, taught by men), the single-sex environment of extracurricular activities, known then simply as college life, allowed this formation of female identity.

The first few classes of the 1880s were very small and academically oriented, and there was no college life to speak of. This was an era when some felt that letting women into Harvard was akin to "opening a Protestant Chapel in Vatican City," so female students had to prove themselves to a tradition-bound university by working hard and staying invisible.[1] However, it was by pursuing this very intellectualism and invisibility that students risked being labeled bluestockings—the derisive term for educated women who supposedly lost their looks, their charm, and all else womanly in the pursuit of higher knowledge. Once the hard work of establishing their intellectual credibility was done, students desired the world to know they could banish the *Harvard Lampoon*'s dowdy "Miss Bluesock" and, as the 1898 class poet put it, "wear their learning as their gowns—becomingly."[2]

In 1884 students at the Harvard Annex started a social group that would be the foundation of Radcliffe's extracurricular culture and would change the way students thought about themselves.[3] The students gave their new organization the telling name "Idler," declaring that they would perform "theatricals" at every meeting. The rousing success of the Idler, which endured into the 1950s and drew most of the student body to its twice-monthly dances and plays, spurred the blossoming of college life at Radcliffe. Before long the ideal Radcliffe student was what Helen Lefkowitz Horowitz calls the "all-round girl," balancing academics with drama, athletics, and cultural clubs on a campus that mirrored her development, adding a theater, gymnasium, and dormitory by 1905. Though historians of the Seven Sisters (the elite women's colleges—Radcliffe, Vassar, Smith, Mount Holyoke, Wellesley, Bryn Mawr, and Barnard) often fail to mention the fact, Radcliffe soon boasted an extracurricular life rivaling that of Wellesley or Smith in scope if not in size. Its organizations suited the qualities of the "New Woman" rather than the bluestocking. Womanly philanthropy in the Progressive mode could be exercised in the Emmanuel Club or the YWCA, genteel leisure in the Tennis Club, musical accomplishment in the Mandolin Club, and light literary debate in the English Club.

Nearly all of Radcliffe's organizations, including such unlikely candidates as the Athletic Association, put on plays from time to time, as fund-raisers or as simple diversions. As is the case at Harvard today, it was a rare weekend that had no play or operetta scheduled. Combining fantasy, performance, and creative leadership, theater was understandably popular among young women trying to squeeze as much freedom as possible into their four years away from domestic life. But it also won administrative approval as an appropriate "womanly" activity, bolstering Radcliffe's public image by emphasizing the artistic, literary, and graceful aspects of the female scholar. In the minds of college presidents and deans, acting was a safe arena in which to explore identity, because at the time many critics and theatergoers viewed it as a particularly feminine art. As one author put it, women were naturally more attuned to superficiality, emotion, and "the histrionic tendency," whereas men dealt with the "realities of life."[4] Though hardly an example of progressive thinking, this logic did make theater an activity that could distinguish womanly Radcliffe from manly Harvard.

For students, however, theater was a ground to test new identities, not merely a place to help project a proper feminine tone. Actresses and directors in the Idler and Glee Clubs used an activity labeled feminine on the surface to subvert gender roles and to claim certain nontraditional behaviors as womanly. Behind every production were women in creative, leadership, and managerial roles generally held only by men outside the college setting. The students approached their work with a professionalism that eschewed feminine frivolity; Harvard graduate and *Boston Evening Transcript* drama critic H. K. Moderwell admitted in 1914 that "the Idlers took themselves seriously enough to belie their name," producing "amateur work so well done [that it] tempts one to praise it in a serious tone of voice."[5] Students built sets, directed rehearsals, managed publicity, and wrote scripts and scores. Student-written shows, such as the operettas written by Josephine Sherwood of the class of 1899, were performed for the public, favorably reviewed in area newspapers, and even published and put on in outside venues. Alumnae Beulah Dix, Mabel Daniels, and Josephine Preston Peabody went on to distinguish themselves in the fields of playwriting and composing. Josephine Sherwood, considered without peer as an actress in her Radcliffe days, pursued a successful career on stage and screen, winning an Oscar for her supporting performance in the 1944 film *Harvey*. The majority of Radcliffe students never took their skills beyond the stage of the Agassiz Theater, but they still recognized their rare opportunity to be seen and heard in the public space, to step forth as individuals, to try on different roles—in other words, to be the opposite of the ideal nineteenth-century woman.

While the very nature of theatre was liberating for students, one characteristic of Radcliffe drama stands out as the most transgressive, or at least the most likely to make administrators shudder. By curious consensus of a tradition-bound faculty and an independent-minded student body, men were absolutely forbidden to perform in Radcliffe shows in the period before the First World War (in fact, they were often barred from attending performances). This restriction did not stop Radcliffe women from taking on heroic, dramatic, and romantic male roles on stage. Building on the long tradition of professional actresses playing "breeches parts" (often young, pretty-boy roles such as Romeo), Radcliffe students created their own gender structure in which certain women usually played men and won great praise for doing so, and others, like Sherwood, always played more "traditional" women. Yearbooks and photographs from 1890 to 1910 make it clear that cross-dressing on stage was widespread and often carried off with uncanny accuracy; this was no female version of Hasty Pudding drag.

It was here that the idea of theater as feminine broke down, and here that Radcliffe administrators decided the attempt to be well rounded had endangered the still-present need for a low profile of respectable scholarly womanhood. In 1894 a committee of Radcliffe officials including Elizabeth Cary Agassiz laid down costuming rules that would dominate gender roles on stage for years. As elaborated in 1897 by dean Agnes Irwin, Radcliffe students were "forbidden to wear men's costumes at their theatricals or other entertainments, with the exception of such costumes as consist of long flowing garments. The students may wear gymnasium suits, or may wear full knickerbockers. . . . These should be taken off immediately after the play. The students are recommended to ask no visitors."[6] Students generally greeted the "bloomer rule" as the amusing preference of an older, stiffer generation and delighted in finding loopholes, but the restriction served as a reminder that they were, in fact, only playing at being men.

Gymnasium bloomers—heavy, dark, and almost universally unflattering garments consisting of voluminous below-the-knee knickers—are a convenient symbol of Radcliffe's struggle to define its young women as attractive yet intelligent, active yet controllable, well rounded but well aware of the boundaries between the sexes. Somewhere between a skirt and trousers, bloomers served as a link between the feminine pursuit of drama and the more masculine realm of Radcliffe's other most popular activity—sports. This popularity was to some degree forced; starting in the 1890s, every student had to engage in some form of organized physical activity. This was to counteract assertions by medical professionals that the scholarly woman, in addition to being unattractive and awkward as social critics believed, was also at risk of illness and reproductive disorders. The infamous 1873 book *Sex and Education* contained the dubious research of a Harvard Overseer who believed that "physiology protest[ed] against" female higher education and that a student at a women's college was likely to end up "an invalid" if not dead, like the "Miss A" and "Miss B" he studied.[7] Officials at the women's colleges saw no truth to the charge that studying sapped a woman's vital force, but they nevertheless immediately instituted physical education programs to ensure the health of their students. Radcliffe was no exception, requiring freshmen to don bloomers for calisthenics and encouraging the growth of basketball, field hockey, and tennis teams on the intramural and varsity levels.

A photograph of a class basketball game at Radcliffe in 1897 shows several women in a blur of dark serge, getting their bloomers dirty as they wrestle for the ball on the basketball "field" that preceded the Radcliffe gymnasium. While athletics flourished at Radcliffe (the construction of Hemenway Gymnasium in 1898 gave sports legitimacy and eliminated the need to play basketball in the chemistry lab), administrators never seemed quite as comfortable as students did with the ambitious, unpredictable, even violent elements of the sporting life. Team games had undeniable benefits. They gave the wan bluestocking vigor, grace, and bloom while promoting the class spirit and "democracy" that were a point of pride for women's colleges. But unlike the gymnastics, dance, and Indian club exercises that performed

Radcliffe women playing basketball, 1897 (Radcliffe College Archives).

the essential job of maintaining good health, competitive sports included yelling, running, and "the exultation of brute force and skill."[8]

According to Professor Charles Eliot Norton, supported in his views by Harvard president Charles William Eliot, such qualities were "barbarian" and increasingly embarrassing for Harvard men, let alone their supposedly gentler counterparts up Garden Street. Radcliffe president Le Baron Russell Briggs warned that "few things are more pitiable than a woman's deliberate imitation of the sporting man."[9] Competitiveness, individual drive, and sheer physical strength were, in the minds of administrators, traits that the New Woman would do best not to develop.

Accordingly, Presidents Agassiz and Briggs and their deans devised controls for sports, stricter than the rules applied to theater in proportion to the increased danger of "unwomanliness." Administrators were still conscious of the power of appearances. The construction of the gymnasium kept bloomer-clad women, shrieking cheerleaders, and sweating point guards out of the view of passers-by. One student pointed out the irony that gym bloomers "were taken to indicate moral stability or moral laxity, according to the occasion in which they figured."[10] Bloomers were the dress of choice for Idler performances, yet students risked a lecture from the formidable dean Agnes Irwin if they were caught wearing them outside the gymnasium. An 1899 photograph of a class basketball team shows players sitting demurely in standard uniform of blouse and bloomers, covered from neck to ankles. Though Dean Irwin knew students played in this garb, she was shocked that the team captain allowed it to be captured on film. The captain was "called on the carpet . . . and took the whole blame." The rest of the team, however, "refused to be humiliated or apologetic," and quite a few pictures of teams in the offending bisected garments made it into student-produced yearbooks.[11] Students rarely flouted administrators directly, sharing as they did a vision of Radcliffe women as well bred and only mildly assertive, but they loved to think their way around the rules. Student actresses who wanted to dress like men wore ankle-length overcoats instead of bloomers. At a 1907 basketball game, student athletes who wanted to shout and cheer like men "while obeying the college rule that there shall be no applause . . . sang songs . . . thereby, in their enthusiasm keeping only the letter of the law."[12]

Such good-natured protest notwithstanding, students counteracted the "manly" nature of athletics by keeping their activities within certain unspoken boundaries. The Radcliffe Rugby Football Club was far in the future; early students pursued only those few sports such as tennis and field hockey that had been generally deemed acceptable for women. Athletic competitions included events unlikely to have taken place at Harvard, such as "fancy marching" and "a cereal-feeding contest." And there were limits on rewards for individual achievement, as if students sensed that an athletic star was perhaps a bit too mannish for comfort. Whereas individual actresses such as Josephine Sherwood and Mabel Daniels are praised and immortalized in *Radcliffe Magazine* articles and yearbook portraits, it is difficult to find a photograph or detailed description of an individual athlete in the archives. In 1897 the freshman class managed the coup of winning the Athletic Association banner for the year, but no individual women are named in the description of the feat as the young women cry "We got it, we did!"[13] It was this "we" mentality, along with the salutary effects of sports on health and image, that kept team sports within the realm of respectability.

With individual achievement and even intercollegiate competition de-emphasized (Radcliffe teams did play Smith, Wellesley, and local high schools, but the great majority of games were intramural), students and administrators were able to find common cause in support of class teams. These class organizations allowed women to take leadership roles and enjoy competition, but they also served the administrative goal of encouraging "democratic" class and college spirit. For students, the opportunity to jump, yell, run, sweat, and compete was a cherished part of the college experience, vastly removed from the indoor, sedentary lives they might have led before. For administrators, athletics and their accompanying ambition were dangerous but ultimately allowable because they served a purpose and were temporary. Unlike theater, which a young woman could hope to pursue in some fashion after graduation, sports were closed to women outside of college, except for some light tennis or golf. For better or for worse, the sporting life was viewed as a passing fever, as President Briggs summed it up: "A slight athletic swagger in a young woman with a basketball halo does not mean that she will be mannish for life. It subsides, like the puffed cheeks of mumps . . . rather grotesque while it lasts, but not at all prophetic."[14]

Image aside, however, athletics and theater had the simple and crucial function of allowing women to enjoy and express themselves. They could take on behaviors coded "male"—wearing trousers, directing a play, building up muscle, *really* wanting to win the basketball championship—and make them their own. At the same time, students fostered the solidarity and college spirit that made early Radcliffe a cherished place for so many and eased some of the administrators' discomfort.

Students and college officials could disagree on what it meant to be a feminine athlete, or whether it was proper to play a man on stage, but they were united in the belief that these activities enhanced college pride. Sports and theater served the common goals of encouraging democracy and banishing the bluestocking stigma, portraying Radcliffe women as well rounded, socially attractive, and healthy females ready to become the wives, mothers, educators, and career women of the twentieth century. They helped transform Radcliffe from a hidden academic annex of Harvard into a vibrant place where students fostered character, career, and cultural knowledge. A student said it best, speaking of drama but reflecting the impact of all extracurricular activities: "Out of each production everyone comes out just a little more thoroughly a part of Radcliffe."[15]

Notes

1. Elaine Kendall, *"Peculiar Institutions": An Informal History of the Seven Sister Colleges* (New York: G. P. Putnam's Sons, 1976), 62.
2. Margaret Leonard, "Class Poem," *Radcliffe College Yearbook* (1898), 43.

3. Idler Club, records of secretary, 1884/1885-1890/1891, p. 19, in box 7, folder 1, Student Activities Collection, RG XXX, series 1, Radcliffe College Archives, Cambridge, Mass.

4. W. L. George, *Woman and Tomorrow* (London: Herbert Jenkins, 1913), 111.

5. H. K. Moderwell, revision of "The Chinese Lantern," *Boston Evening Transcript*, March 11, 1914, II:6.

6. Idler records, note on costumes between pp. 22-23 (c. 1907), Radcliffe College Archives.

7. Edward H. Clarke, *Sex in Education: Or, A Fair Chance for the Girls* (Boston: James R. Osgood, 1873; rpt., New York: Arno Books, 1972), 127, 68.

8. Charles Eliot Norton, "Commencement Address," *Radcliffe College Yearbook* (1901), 53-54.

9. Le Baron Russell Briggs, *Girls and Education* (Boston: Houghton Mifflin, 1911), 110.

10. Grace Hollingsworth Tucker, "The Gods Serve Hebe," *Radcliffe Quarterly* 17, no. 3 (Oct. 1933): 192.

11. Cornelia James Cannon, "Class Notes—Reminiscences," *Radcliffe Quarterly* (Feb. 1955), 30.

12. "My first championship game," undated clipping, Scrapbook, p. 46, Eva Alberta Mooar Papers, SC-44, Radcliffe College Archives.

13. Agnes B. Morgan, "Class History," *Radcliffe College Yearbook* (1901), 15.

14. Briggs, *Girls and Education*, 113.

15. Quoted in Dorothy Elia Howells, *A Century to Celebrate: Radcliffe College, 1879-1979* (Cambridge, Mass.: Radcliffe College, 1978), 71.

"CLOTHES MAKE THE MAN"

Cross-Dressing on the Radcliffe Stage

Karen Lepri

Radcliffe students' fascination with the stage prepared them to be pioneers on the imaginative frontier beyond the boundaries of men's and women's gender roles in the Victorian era. Evidence of their "gender consciousness," a term we can use only in retrospect, surfaces repeatedly, particularly in the texts that discuss theatrical cross-dressing. As Radcliffe students appropriated the right to go to college, they also laid claim to their brothers' breeches and all the inherent behaviors that go with wearing pants—behaviors not found in the realm of conventional femininity. Radcliffe women's cross-dressing experiences contradicted the expectations of femininity held by the college and the public at that time. In the tension between what students described in their writings about dramatics and how others expected them to act lies the importance of their sartorial transgression.

Elizabeth Briggs, Harvard Annex class of 1887 and founding member of the Idler Club, recalled her first fond memories of dramatics at the Annex in a 1910 article titled "The Beginning of the Idler." "The standard was high, nothing less than Shakespeare," she claimed with pride, adding, "Annie Winsor was a gallant Henry V." In *The Spirit of '76*, a woman-suffrage play, gender roles were even more confused. "Sarah Hanks, a lovely heroine, was wooed and won by Gertrude Tyler, a handsome and convincing lover, with the aid of a cradle-rocking and sock-darning father, myself."[1]

Briggs laughed at the double irony of not only having acted a man, but a sewing, child-nurturing man—possibly a gender confusion she saw fit for herself. Briggs and other founders of the Idler Club initiated the belief that cross-dressing required the highest acting skills. No one could question the talent of a young woman who transformed herself into a convincing old man.

The interest in cross-dressing began early and remained deep. The author of a 1918 review of the freshman play *Adventures of Ursula* was astonished by the transforming power of dress on a young student: "Grace Cobb, who played Lady Ursula, was so much more charming when masquerading as her younger brother. She seemed flat and colorless as a girl, but the minute she donned breeches she revived and in acts two and three she gave us the most delightful impersonation of this impetuous and amusing eighteenth century Rosalind." The author favored other performances that "gave the most masculine illusion as to appearance and voice."[2]

Full-cast pictures demonstrate how elaborately these women transformed themselves. Although pants were often against the rules, the full beards, scraggly mustaches, makeup, and facial expressions all distract the viewer from noticing that the character is wearing a robe instead of pants or that he is really a she. The pictures tell a story that both corroborates and magnifies the tale told by surviving texts. The marvelous bearded faces speak profoundly of the metamorphosing experience, the material reality, and the satisfaction of playing male parts.

Katharine Searle argued that "however absurd cold outsiders think college girls in their disguises, they must admit that they can adapt themselves to other ranks, ages, and periods in their acting more agreeably than college men of the same years."[3] But she also suggested that part of the difference could be attributed to status. "It may be a pleasant change sometimes for a boy to act a girl. This can never be the rapture for him that it is for a girl to pretend she is a man."[4] The "girl" pretends she is a "man"—someone older, more powerful, and deserving higher status in society. However, the "boy" becomes a "girl"—a young woman, someone without autonomy or rank.

Pleased with the privileges she gained by cross-dressing, even if only on stage, Searle sought men's roles. Luckily, friends like Beulah Dix wrote heroic though comical parts for her to play. She justified her affection for these parts, "afraid that a gentlemanly renegade of some sort must be hidden in my ancestral tree, [for] I took to these parts with such unnatural naturalness."[5] When she described a scene in which she, a heroine who cross-dressed, had to punch a male character, Searle revealed the source of her manliness to be internal and quite possibly uncontrollable. "Litterly always instructed me to 'bang away'," she excused herself; "I did so, and broke several pairs of her glasses and gave her each time a real fright and a red ear. . . . It was the torrent, tempest and whirlwind of my genius that bore me away."[6] In her account, as in others', the border between the male character and the female actress blurs as the woman transcribes masculine traits onto herself.

By emphasizing the intuitive over the rational in women, these actors evoked traditional "separate spheres" rhetoric while simultaneously advocating cross-dressing. Upon entering the imaginary realm of recreation and confidence on stage, they claimed women naturally gave more splendid performances. "Imagination, which is supposed to take the place of reason in so many of us, has in acting free play," argued Katharine Searle, depicting the stage as a place open to creativity, a value that was possibly disregarded in the classroom.[7] On stage, imagination and the rational desire to transcend a subjected position collaborated to produce a transgender experience.

In response to the depth of this transformative mental experience, many students personalized their memory of playing male roles. Beulah Dix wrote in an 1895 letter, "I wish you could have seen me. I wore a red wig, foot-ball length, and instead of a mustache I blackened the lower part of my face, giving myself an unshorn appearance that was very fetching." After the first act, she explained, "Elsie had a curtain call and Elizabeth Marsh passed her up a great bunch of carnations that we <u>men</u> clubbed together and bought for her."[8] Through acting, she had assumed another gender identity to the point of giving flowers to the heroine. Years later in a memoir, Dix declared, "I was the swashbuckling hero"—not "I played" or "I acted," but "I was."[9]

The homoerotic tone of some letters and memoirs represents one of the ways in which Radcliffe dramatists expanded their masculine roles from plays into relationships in daily life.[10] Students of Radcliffe in the Victorian era, a time known for women's intimate social circles, expressed a deep attraction to love scenes onstage and intimate friendships offstage.[11] Many social events required the same male-female role play as their theatricals. Beulah Dix informed her cousin of the "grand jubilation the day Mid Years ended":

We . . . danced and sang and romped. No men invited, just us by ourselves having a good time. . . . in my rash confidence [I] allowed one of the girls to seduce me into waltzing with her. It was very pleasant while it lasted but when she stopped I went right on going and almost landed on my nose. She got me onto the sofa and the dizziness wore off in time. I am very glad of the experience. I can now conceive of a drunken man's sensations.[12]

"No men invited" opened the dance floor to seductions and experiences usually limited to the stage. Such confrontations, be they exciting or confusing, were always good lessons on playing more than one part.

Radcliffe students constructed and idolized the images of certain actresses, creating a world of masculine and feminine role models for actresses to follow. Beulah Marie Dix assembled her famed cast as follows: "Katharine Searle was our gallant hero, to whom we all lost our hearts, and Josephine Sherwood our sweet heroine, and Ruth Delano—ah! you should have seen Ruth Delano play the sea-dog in *Diccon Goodnaught*, swathed in convincing layers of waistcoats and peajackets."[13]

Dix's memories and fondness for her friends were deeply entrenched in the gendered personas they assumed onstage, especially in the plays she wrote for them, such as *Diccon Goodnaught* and *Cicely's Cavalier*. The place they held in her memory was not merely imaginary but also social. Constructing masculine-feminine categories, students restricted some women to men's roles and some to women's. One student noted that the beloved Josephine Sherwood Hull "does one thing—the heroine that calls for grace and winsomeness, for wit and appealing femininity—and she does that so well that we have rarely let her try anything else."[14]

On the masculine side of the student body stood Ruth Delano. In 1901 a fellow student memorialized her as an actress who could bring the audience beyond the material reality of the stage and biological sex into a world of infinite possibilities made real. She remembered Delano not merely as a Radcliffe student but more importantly as

a high-bred youth, careless, graceful, keenly alive, with a sense of humor, yet capable of earnestness that astonishes the audience into breathless intensity; or else an old man, cantankerous; or dignified; or senile; an astute Baron, a man of the world, able to play a desperate game, and win or lose gracefully; or a Puritan sea captain, rough, sheepish and loveable; or a choleric father, Sir Anthony, who reflects all the depravity of the 18th century; which ever it may be, the character is complete, convincing, an actual creation.[15]

This review evokes an amazing declaration—that each time Delano assumed one of these male characters she not only recreated herself, but also

Radcliffe student actor Alice Heustis Wilbur, in costume, 1894 (Radcliffe College Archives).

possessed the power to transport the audience beyond the concrete time and place of the stage and the sex of the cast.

Katharine Searle (circa 1900) and Marjorie Smith, class of 1911, were admired for their "true" dramatic ability—in other words, their talent in rendering men as well as women—perfect dramatic hermaphroditism.[16] This versatility was crucial to the process of defining a place at Harvard and Radcliffe as a woman who had simultaneously to represent her sex and seek an education in a male-dominated academic world. In the words of athletics advocate and Radcliffe gym instructor Dudley Sargent, "There is a time in the life of a girl . . . when it is better for her and her community to be something of a boy rather than too much of a girl."[17] Radcliffe students understood the need for flexibility and admired its extremity on stage. An actress's "genuine dramatic instinct" naturally manifested itself in gender versatility. At Radcliffe, those born to act were born to stretch gender boundaries.[18]

The students' admiration for cross-dressing, enthusiasm for all-female romance, and the creation of role models in actresses according to gender all demonstrate how progressively Radcliffe students thought about their role as women at the turn of the twentieth century. As college students, they were more exposed than most young women to ideas about suffrage, women in the professions, and other feminist causes. Students wrote sarcastically about roles and expectations, releasing the frustrations they felt as young women.

As Gloria Bruce has shown, college women were some of the first to benefit from the Dress Reform Movement, which brought bloomers and gym suits to the gymnasium and the fields.[19] As designers and moralists debated the question of how high bloomers should join between ladies' legs, Radcliffe administrators battled over the propriety of pants in student plays. In both groups, the problem was well understood—open legs would lead to new freedoms and behaviors unacceptable for educated young women. Not only could a woman walk, jump, sit, and move entirely differently while wearing pants, but she also would appear dangerously seductive, marked by a new silhouette so close to the shape of the body itself.

A photograph taken in the spring of 1894 stuck conspicuously in an album offers a clue to the original decision to regulate pants. The photo captured Alice Heustis, who graduated that June and married in the same month, dressed and posed as the most convincing gentleman found in all visual evidence preserved in the Radcliffe archives. Her hair, mustache, full suit and pose—hand on hip, leg extended, and lips pursed—proposed a trespass of gender boundaries that officials could not ignore.[20]

Beulah Dix expressed frustration with the rule against pants.[21] Without pants, she felt quite ugly and out of place, barricaded from the path to new freedoms and confidence. In a letter to her cousin, she complained about the college's puritanical restrictions:

> Next Friday Elsie Tetlow's play is to be given, and we are on the fly with rehearsals. . . . I play a young man who sighs like a September gale etc. It's a clever little farce, but it will be spoiled by the prudery of the corporation. We can't wear trousers but must appear in full bloomers or scant skirts, hang them! One of the girls has a brother as obliging as herself from whom she

intends to borrow a dress coat, vest, and shirt. With that and my own black skirt I shall present a curious half and half appearance like a Centaur or a Siren or a Harpy, for that matter.[22]

Dix blamed the college for her failure to render successfully the young man she played. A year later, excited by the radical costuming she saw at an Idler show, she wrote, "Riding boots and trousers have appeared upon the stage."[23] In her letters, the clothing takes on a life of its own, appearing, disappearing, and being forbidden to return. Undoubtedly, the students' blatant disregard of the 1894 ruling motivated the Students' Committee to reinstate their regulation in 1897.

When students brought cross-dressing noticeably into the public eye, eyebrows rose. In one review, the author excitedly described Rebecca Hooper Eastman's rendering of a male character, reveling in "Her smile, her swagger, and . . . wildfire."[24] Although the college supported dramatics, proper society did not agree that a theatrical life was a righteous path for young, educated, middle- to upper-class women. Beulah Dix recalled a cautioning lecture by "Major Brewer who spoke at Radcliffe last year . . . [and] insinuated pretty strongly that the theatre was the road to hell."[25]

Despite such moral condemnations, some men preferred to watch women onstage. Josephine Sherwood received two curious letters from admirers after a Radcliffe performance in 1898. One man remarked, "You girls beat the boys art and art at this sort of performance. I have seen many Harvard theatricals, but never any that equaled this. Hasty Pudding [Harvard's theatrical club] may be good in its way, but divine ambrosia is better; and nectar from the hands of Hebe has a finer flavor and produces a more exquisite exhilaration than bottled beer."[26] Another young man wrote of a theatrical performance, "It might be called the Pureè of Radcliffe—because it is so vastly ahead of the Pudding plays . . . and truly Miss C.P. Folsom? How could you get yourself up as such a splendid villain?"[27]

Questions and conflicts about the changing public perception of women onstage led to the advent of coed casting beginning around 1912.[28] The choice to bring Harvard and Radcliffe students together in theatricals may seem an obvious one today. However, both moral concern about young men and women socializing and acting together and the enthusiasm of single-sex student bodies separated the two dramatics groups until that time. When Professor George Pierce Baker founded the coeducational Workshop 47, he saw no good reason to maintain the tradition of cross-dressing. The president of Radcliffe agreed on the propriety of coed productions, noting, "The

Harvard Dramatic Club, because of the seriousness of its attempts and of Mr. Baker's interests in it, and because of the unsatisfactoriness of boys in girls parts, has had the girls parts taken by girls."[29]

Despite the new trend of coed casting, Radcliffe's Idler Club continued to produce all-women theatricals until 1953, although those performances inevitably lost the radical daring and enthusiasm heralded by the earlier students. With the suffrage victory, the ensuing muffling of the feminist movement, and the great changes in moral expectations in the 1920s and 1930s, cross-dressing lost its power of transgression. One alumna expressed disappointment over how such changes had stripped the humor and power of their gender-crossing in an article called "Clothes Make the Man." After the 1931 alumnae revival of *The Amazons,* the play with which they most identified and most liked to perform, she wrote:

> There was only one shock about the performance, which went without a hitch at both shows and received great applause, and that was, we are afraid, that there was no shock at all. We howled with delight years ago, at visions of maidens going about attired more or less casually as boys. But we are used now to girls in exactly that blend of knickers and semi-bob that we barely realize they were supposed to be dressed as boys. Eheu fugaces! However the female costumes more than made up, for they were carefully 1890, and entertaining accordingly.[30]

Change in dress styles signaled a change in what *made* a man. Pants were not the social and biological indicator that they had been earlier, even though they were still far from incorporated into the average schoolgirl's dress.[31] In retrospect, the feminine dress most shocked the women audience members, making them laugh at the silliness of the conventionally long skirts and tight-fitting corsets. From the liberated perspective, it was more difficult to believe one would choose those garments over the comfort of trousers.

One could say it was the years of romping and howling on stage, with silliness or with dignity, that flexed and pressed the confining constraints of gender categories until the temporary burst in the 1920s. As early as 1884, when Annie Winsor and Elizabeth Briggs decided it was time to start acting, they made a greater, more serious gesture than a mere Shakespearean production. For in due course, there followed a whirlwind of Radcliffe women filled with talent, enthusiasm, and the determination to be what others saw them as not. First, they would be college students—the students of Harvard professors—but to do that successfully, it was necessary to form a language of the body that communicated beyond the contemporary confines of femininity. To be students, they needed to find a voice as both man and woman and to write, speak, and walk as both. They found entertainment, excitement, confidence, romance, personal heroes, superior approval, and, for some, even a career in their world around the stage because of the ability to create two sexes out of one.

Notes

1. Elizabeth Briggs, "The Beginnings of the Idler," *Radcliffe Magazine* 12 (June 1910): 178.
2. R.L.F. [Rachel Lyman Field], "The Freshman Play," *Radcliffe Magazine* 20 (April 1918): 98.
3. Katherine Searle, "College Plays," *Radcliffe Magazine* 7 (Dec. 1904): 17.
4. Ibid., 18.
5. Ibid., 20.
6. Ibid., 21.
7. Ibid.
8. Beulah Marie Dix to Mary Ruggles Chandler, Nov. 1895, typescript transcribed by Radcliffe Archives, Alumnae Association Class Collections of 1897, Radcliffe College Archives [hereafter, RCA].
9. Beulah Dix Flebbe, "Recollections of a Prominent Graduate," *Radcliffe Magazine* 13 (June 1911): 187.
10. Helen Lefkowitz Horowitz, *Alma Mater: Design and Experience in the Women's Colleges from their Nineteenth-Century Beginnings to the 1930s* (New York: Alfred A. Knopf, 1984), 58-68.
11. Carroll Smith-Rosenberg, "The Female World of Love and Ritual: Relations between Women in Nineteenth Century America," *Disorderly Conduct: Visions of Gender in Victorian America* (New York: Alfred A. Knopf, 1985), 53-76.
12. Dix to Chandler, March 3, 1895.
13. Flebbe, "Recollections of a Prominent Graduate," 187.
14. Elizabeth Stevens, "Radcliffe Dramatics: A Five-Year Perspective," *Radcliffe Magazine* 3 (March 1901): 78.
15. Ibid., 79.
16. Ibid.
17. Kim Townsend, *Manhood at Harvard: William James and Others* (New York: W.W. Norton, 1996), 225.
18. Caroline Solis, "Monsieur Beaucaire," *Radcliffe Magazine* 13 (April 1911): 129.
19. Gloria Bruce, "Radcliffe Women at Play," this volume; Patricia Campbell Warner, "The Gym Suit: Freedom at Last," *Dress in American Culture*, ed. Patricia A. Cunningham and Susan Voso Lab (Bowling Green, Ohio: Bowling Green State University Popular Press, 1993), 154-57.
20. Photograph taken from Alumnae Class Collections album, RCA.
21. Beulah Marie Dix, Cambridge, to Mary Ruggles Chandler, Chelsea, Nov. 1895, typescript transcribed by Karen Lepri, Radcliffe Archives, Alumnae Association Class Collections of 1897, RCA.
22. Beulah Marie Dix, Cambridge, to Mary Ruggles Chandler, Chelsea, Oct. 1895, typescript transcribed by Karen Lepri, Radcliffe Archives, Alumnae Association Class Collections of 1897, RCA.

23. Beulah Marie Dix, Cambridge, to Mary Ruggles Chandler, Chelsea, Nov. 8, 1896, Beulah Dix Flebbe Papers, RCA.
24. N.a., n.p., n.d, review from 1900, folder of reviews, Josephine Sherwood Hull Collection, Schlesinger Library [hereafter, JSH Collection].
25. Beulah Marie Dix, Cambridge, to Mary Ruggles Chandler, Cambridge, March 3, 1895, Beulah Dix Flebbe Papers, RCA.
26. W. J. Rolfe, Cambridge, to Josephine Sherwood Hull, Cambridge, May 28, 1898, JSH Collection.
27. Henry L. Raud, Cambridge, to Josephine Sherwood Hull, Cambridge, May 28, 1898, JSH Collection.
28. Evidence exists of a small number of coed shows produced in the 1890s, but in proportion to single-sex productions they remain insignificant. Continual coed casting did not begin until the advent of the Workshop 47 in 1912. See the Papers of Workshop 47, Records of Student Activities, RCA, and the Papers of George Pierce Baker, Theatre Collection.
29. Le Baron R. Briggs to Lucia R. Briggs, Nov. 8, 1912, Papers of the President of Radcliffe, vol. II, RCA. Although Briggs and Baker encode their preference for women in women's roles in a desire for the best aesthetic, they most likely feared the emasculation of men through cross-dressing. See Townsend's *Manhood at Harvard*, 146-47, for a further explanation of developing ideas on homosexuality at Harvard during the late nineteenth century.
30. "Clothes Make the Man: The Amazons," *Radcliffe Quarterly* 15 (July 1931): 108-9.
31. "School Girl" fashion plate, *Vanity Fair* 1 (1913): 12.

III.

VARIETIES OF
INEQUALITY
1900–2001

FAIR HARVARD?

Labor, Law, and Gender in the Harvard Scrubwomen Case

Linzy Brekke

On December 21, 1929, Harvard University fired 20 women employed as office and building cleaners in Widener Library, the nation's second largest library. In the wake of their unexpected termination, several of the women turned to community leaders for help. The Reverend William Duvall of Trinity Community Episcopal Church in East Cambridge wrote to Harvard president A. Lawrence Lowell, inquiring on behalf of one of the discharged women who lived in a tenement house operated by his diocese. Lowell responded to the minister with a terse letter maintaining that the woman and her coworkers had been dismissed because "the Minimum Wage Board has been complaining of our employing women for these purposes [cleaning] at less than 37 cents an hour, and hence the University felt constrained to replace them with men. Their replacement by men was prompted by the fact that men were not protected by the law that prescribed minimum wages for scrubwomen."[1] The men who assumed the work of cleaning Widener were fewer in number and were paid 32 cents an hour, instead of the 35 cents the women had received, a savings of $650 a year to the university.[2] Surprised at Lowell's callousness and outraged over his glib defiance of state labor laws, Duvall made a copy of Lowell's letter and sent it off to the press.

By the end of January, the story of "twenty poor scrubwomen fired four days before Christmas over a two-cent wage increase by the wealthiest university in the nation" was put on the Associated Press wire. Within days it was featured on the front pages of dozens of newspapers from Portland, Maine, to Portland, Oregon.[3] The ruthless attitude of the Harvard Corporation toward its female workers became common editorial fodder; as *Labor* magazine put it, "Harvard was cartooned, lampooned, and lambasted from end to end of the country."[4] What at first seemed like a local management issue became a national cause célèbre.[5]

Clashes between labor and management were hardly unfamiliar to Americans in 1929. For over a decade, organized labor had been battered by open-shop drives and intense anti-unionism, yet strikes, walkouts, and other manifestations of workplace conflict persisted.[6] Three central issues differentiated the Harvard case from other industry clashes of the era: first, Harvard's prestige, wealth, and international renown made it a powerful symbol for a diverse cross-section of the population as well as an easy target for social and class antagonisms. Second, as a university, Harvard was a tax-exempt, not-for-profit institution. As such, it occupied an ambiguous position between public and private, where moral and ethical ideals, not only laws and economics, held sway. Tensions over the proper behavior of a university that was also a corporation animated the debates over Harvard's treatment of its women workers. Third, Harvard stood accused of knowingly and willfully violating the Massachusetts minimum wage law, a law that was designed and enacted to protect just such unorganized and unskilled workers as Harvard's scrubwomen.

The premise behind "protecting" women and not men lay in the inequality of their bargaining power in the labor market. Women were one-fourth of the work force in the early twentieth century, yet they were concentrated in the poorest paid and least skilled jobs and industries and rarely had access to unions through which they could organize for better working conditions or wages. Protective legislation was intended to compensate for these disparities as well as to ameliorate the social costs of capitalism for women. The workers' gender in this case stirred up the public's paternalism and generated a virulent backlash against Harvard for turning the "mothers of the race" out onto the streets.[7]

For all these reasons the case attracted a diverse constituency of participants and passionate observers with differing agendas: prominent alumni and elite students sought to restore Harvard's "honor" and symbolically to usurp Lowell's power to represent the university; leftist political organizations like the Harvard Student Socialists and the Liberal Club publicized the scrubwomen scandal in order to garner support for socialist reforms; middle-class women reformers and protective legislation lobbyists like the Consumer's League, the Women's Bureau of the Department of Labor, and the Women's Trade Union League dissected the implications of the Harvard case for the future of protective legislation for women; members of the press who followed the story and refused to let it die did so because they had political grudges against President Lowell for his involvement in anti-unionism and his role in the infamous Sacco and Vanzetti case earlier in the decade.[8] Others saw a human interest story that offered them the chance to revive the muckraking tradition of the Progressive Era and to expose abuses of power and greed at the nation's highest levels.[9] When *The Nation* alleged in 1930 that the Massachusetts Minimum Wage Commission (MWC), the bureau charged with enforcing labor laws, had brokered a "gentlemen's agreement" to turn a blind eye to Harvard's labor practices for nine years, the media found its muckraking angle.[10] The combined effect of a multimillion-dollar university colluding with a government agency to evade a law protecting vulnerable working-class women heightened the scandal's legal, political, and social significance.[11] Walter Lippmann likened the scandal to "a chapter from Dickens."[12]

Even before the exigencies of strikes and massive public unrest in the early 1930s, respondents to the Harvard case began calling for changes in the way business and the state treated workers. The press saw in Harvard a frightening embodiment of the nation writ small: "labor ground under the heel of Higher Education, which, when you snap off its false whiskers, is no less than Capitalism," opined the *New Yorker*.[13] In the liminal period between the fragmented, anti-union era of the 1920s and the New Deal, an unlikely cross-class coalition emerged of elite alumni and students, leftists, middle-class reformers, government bureaucrats, and the reading public, all clamoring for justice from the nation's wealthiest university.

The incident the press dubbed "The Harvard Scrubwomen Scandal" reveals the disregard with which Harvard treated its women workers—and how they got away with it. As the case evolved, however, so did the politics of the participants. They launched a protest movement, turning a seemingly narrow demand of group interests into a critique of corporate capitalism.[14]

FACTS IN THE HARVARD CASE: 1921-1929

The peace and prosperity of the 1920s ushered in a new era for American business characterized by "welfare capitalism" where, as one historian has written, "the enlightened corporation, not the labor union or the state, would spearhead the creation of a more benign industrial society."[15] Harvard, however, remained in its own time zone. Hostile to unions, the university was run "on a thorough-going open shop basis," journalist Gardner Jackson wrote in *The Nation,* and it paid wages "lower all across the board than those paid on the outside."[16] Under Lowell's administration, Harvard had abolished the few fledgling unions that existed, refusing to employ even as temporary workers craftsmen who were affiliated with the American Federation of Labor.[17] In terms of wages for cleaning employees alone, Harvard's rate of 35 cents an hour stood in stark contrast to that of the Massachusetts Institute of Technology, which paid its workers 47 cents an hour, and the State House, which paid 60. Few of Harvard's unskilled and semiskilled workers were eligible for pensions, worker's compensation, or health insurance.[18] The Widener women complained of management tactics at Harvard that included speed-ups, intimidation, and job threats that prevented workers from climbing the chain of command to seek higher wages or from speaking to state inspectors.[19] Such practices had been condemned in business and labor circles for over a decade. But as late as 1937, Harvard officials lobbied the federal government to exempt universities from the Workmen's Compensation Act and the National Recovery Act.[20] The Harvard Business School may have taught its students the new code of welfare capitalism, but it remained an intellectual exercise so far as its own employees were concerned.

The man most singularly responsible for Harvard's retrograde business practices was university president A. Lawrence Lowell. By 1929, Harvard was well established as a prestigious and elitist institution. As such, it was also an inviting target for criticism, and Lowell was probably the most inviting target in Harvard's 300-year history. A popular Boston ditty satirized the Back Bay Brahmin society of his birth as a place "where Lowells speak only to Cabots and Cabots speak only to God." He was autocratic and an impetuous critic of liberalism; he later became a strident opponent of the New Deal. He personally recruited 200 undergraduates as scabs to break the Boston policeman's strike in 1919, and under his direction Harvard instituted quotas limiting the admission of Jews and African Americans. His leadership on the steering committee that sustained the death sentence for Nicola Sacco and Bartolomeo Vanzetti earned him lifelong animosity from liberals and the press. In short, Lowell embodied elitism and political conservatism.[21]

So it came as little surprise when, in December 1920, C. A. Martin, the forewoman of the Widener Library workers, acting as Harvard's representative, testified in the Massachusetts State House *against* a proposed increase in the minimum wage for office and building cleaners. She assured the board that Harvard had met the minimum wage requirements in the past but that the university's budget for the fiscal year had already been established. Forcing the university to meet the state's new rate increase, she claimed, would force her to fire her female workers. The Minimum Wage Commission suggested she cut the women's hours. Martin responded, speaking "on behalf of my women," that they "would rather . . . leave things as they are." The MWC reminded Martin that laws were not tailor-made for Harvard but applied to the entire state.[22] The university would have to pay the new minimum wage.

The minimum wage increase had been proposed after a 1920 investigation of working conditions for building and office cleaners across Massachusetts revealed that most cleaning women were widows with dependent children. They worked long hours and received among the lowest wages in the state, lower even than housecleaners or laundresses.[23] Harvard's cleaning women fit the state's demographic portrait of working women: they were predominantly Irish Catholic, widowed or unmarried, with dependent children. They worked several jobs and still relied on local relief agencies to get by. Several had worked at Harvard for over 25 years. The scrubwomen were precisely the kind of workers the legislation sought to protect.[24]

Both employers and the MWC, however, found room for interpretation between the letter of the law and its spirit, especially when the law carried no penalties except public exposure in newspapers. Copies of the new state law were sent to Harvard in the spring of 1921 and posted in Widener. At various inspections throughout the decade, the MWC accepted Harvard's vague and plaintive verbal assurances of compliance without checking the payroll. In 1925 a member of the Harvard Corporation, Thomas Nelson Perkins, established "an understanding" with the MWC that women's wages at Harvard were "all right."[25] That same year, four scrubwomen appeared before the commission complaining of the low wages they were receiving at Harvard. It took the MWC a year to follow up on their charges. In 1926 the university's comptroller, Arthur Endicott, met with the MWC and admitted that the women were not technically receiving the state minimum, but they were given benefits such as daily 20-minute rest periods, sick pay, and one week's paid vacation, which, when assigned monetary value, brought their wages to the state minimum. When interviewed, however, the scrubwomen had no knowledge of such benefits and had never availed themselves of them. Harvard even claimed that its "prestige" compensated for lower wages by making it more socially attractive than other employers.[26] Throughout the decade, the MWC consistently accepted the university's word without holding a hearing, interviewing workers, or requiring Harvard to file a formal statement on wages as the law required. The commission appointed to investigate noncomplying employers failed to perform even routine verification of the labor situation at Harvard. As the Women's Trade Union League later charged, the commission had utterly failed to "administer the law with sympathy and understanding of its purpose."[27]

The situation came to a head when Ethel Johnson was appointed assistant commissioner to the MWC in 1929. She warned the university that the commission would publicize it for noncompliance unless she had proof by the end of the year that Harvard wages conformed to the state's decrees. Not party to any gentlemen's agreement, Johnson was prepared to force Harvard to obey the law. Harvard comptroller Charles Apsted responded by firing the Widener women on December 21, 1929. Apsted thought that by simply dismissing the women he would circumvent the problem of the minimum wage law and avoid further confrontations with the MWC. He would come to rue his decision as the weight of angry public opinion fell upon Harvard in the ensuing year.

"LIKE A CHAPTER OUT OF DICKENS": THE PUBLIC RESPONDS

Why did Harvard fire the women workers and why, in the face of intense public pressure, did the university refuse to reinstate them or change its wage policy? Harvard's gendered and formalistic defense of the firing of the Widener women on January 30, 1930, revealed the ultimate perils of protective legislation. "We have not at any time attempted to violate the Minimum wage law," Arthur Endicott asserted, "but in replacing these women whose labor was not efficient with men, we have done exactly what the law intended to effect . . . the law does not intend to force the employment of labor inefficient for its cost but to insure that the labor which is employed shall be paid the wages its efficiency deserves."[28] Widener would be cleaned "by a high-speed crew of men cleaners, which the university found more efficient than the women," he stated.[29] Linking efficiency with men and inefficiency with women cut moral arguments to the quick by privileging capitalist arguments. By emphasizing women's physical difference—here construed as weakness—business could legitimate replacing women workers with men.

The same maternalist images of women as poor, weak, and dependent that Progressive activists used to garner support for protective legislation were wielded like a club against the Widener women. Harvard officials portrayed them as labor pariahs; exaggerating the women's ages, they claimed that the women were notoriously inefficient and costly. None of their employment records bore out such claims. The public, however, recast "weakness" and upheld Harvard's obligation of paternalistic protection. The *New York Telegram*, reporting Harvard's rumors that the women had grown "too old" and "too feeble" to do their work with competence, dryly concluded, "One never does grow younger scrubbing under bookshelves for 33 years." Editorials pushed Harvard to assume its manly duty and shield the women as the law had intended. "What is the matter with Harvard students?" one column shrilled; "are the young men all cowards, incapable of indignation and a desire to aid those who are in distress?"[30] Another editorial chastised Harvard "to be fair" to its "poor old scrubwomen," who had given long tenure of service. "Put these poor women back to work," it cajoled, "and pay them the two cents more."[31]

These editorials carried the kind of playful, indulgent tone a parent would take toward a child. Such reporting revealed fissures in cross-class coalitions. The press reported the intricacies of the women's personal lives in sensationalistic detail. "One widow, a mother of five children, was struggling to pay an undertaker's bill when she received her dismissal from the cleaning force at the library. She is Catherine Donlon of Laurel St. who lost her little girl, aged seven nearly a year ago. Another child is not so strong."[32] These were the war-horse stories that female Progressive lobbyists had been trotting out since the 1890s when the first protective measures were initiated. Whereas Harvard used the women's weakness and physical debility against them as lawful grounds for dismissal, the public reinterpreted such features as legitimate grounds for protection.

But there were dissenters. Protectionism's practical failure in the Harvard case pushed new voices into the debate. Women's organizations had argued over the implications of protective legislation before and after suffrage.[33] The National Woman's Party, led by Alice Paul, strongly opposed protective laws on the ground that their definition of women's "difference" endorsed and sustained female inequality. Many readers concluded from the mistreatment experienced by supposedly "protected" women at Harvard that all workers were at risk. Alma Lutz, treasurer for the Massachusetts branch of the National Woman's Party, submitted an editorial to *The Nation*, which had featured the Harvard controversy on the cover of its January 1930 issue. Lutz reminded readers that the Harvard incident "was not the first time in Massachusetts or in other States that the minimum wage law, which was designed to protect women, has interfered with their means of livelihood." If

"Fair Harvard?" Harvard Student
Socialists pamphlet cover, 1930
(Radcliffe College Archives).

the state sought to regulate minimum wage laws, Lutz argued, they must apply to both men and women.[34] Other voices began to echo Lutz's in support of extending wage legislation to include men. "To all who believe in a fair deal for the worker," an editorialist from the *Salt Lake City Tribune* wrote, the Harvard case provided a lesson. "Why were the women fired? Partly because of wages but also because men's wages are not protected by law in Massachusetts."[35] These editorials sought to shift labor legislation's emphasis away from gender to labor. Wage earners, in this discussion, faced employment obstacles as workers first and as men and women second.

Leftist groups drew on the case's relevance to class relations directly. The Student Socialists Club at Harvard published a pamphlet in response to the controversy: "This leaflet is not written by indignant citizens but by Socialists," it read, "and to us this scandal . . . is like the cough of the tubercular—not a disease but the sign of a disease. . . . it was outrageous not because of what was done to these particular women but because it shows the ruthless attitude of . . . great business men towards those who work." Harvard socialists saw structural problems in American capitalism, rather than flaws with protective legislation or even with the university itself, as the root cause of workplace conflicts. They emphasized the need for state unemployment insurance and the unionization of university workers.[36]

Harvard students who supported the university's decision were incensed at their peers for airing private laundry in public and felt embarrassed over the barrage of negative publicity the scandal generated. They heckled the Widener women at the public benefits held in their honor and brutally satirized their class, gender, and ethnicity in the *Harvard Lampoon.* Another group, donning blackface and dressing in drag, mock-scrubbed the steps of Widener.[37] Such antics were intended to cast humor on the situation, but they also revealed the prejudices of elite students toward the immigrant underclass who were uncomfortable fixtures in the university's public spaces.

The Harvard case exposed many of the fault lines in regional class and ethnic antagonisms. Harvard's endowment in 1929 was conservatively estimated by the *New York World* at $81 million.[38] "The battalions of books" in Widener Library "reached from floor to ceiling," wrote Heywood Broun, a leading organizer of the Newspaper Guild, in the *New York Telegram;* "in them was the stuff to make one free. But they were not for the likes of her [a scrubwoman]. This was fodder for the Lowells and the Cabots." The specter of a university with a "treasury that grows from year to year like the Manhattan skyline," as the *Telegram* described it, withholding two cents an hour from its workers rankled many.[39]

Harvard drew particular fire because it occupied an ambiguous position between public and private. Would the university's actions have aroused such ire if it were a private company? The *Weekly Standard,* in New Bedford, Massachusetts, thought not. "Because Harvard is a college, not an industrial or business enterprise, its failure to pay its scrubwomen the minimum wage was broadcast the country over."[40] Columnists criticized Harvard for ignoring what they considered its "moral" responsibilities. "Harvard, as a tax-exempt

Illustration from *The Survey,* March 15, 1930, during scrubwomen controversy.
Drawing by Helen B. Phelps (Radcliffe College Archives).

educational institution, has considerable responsibility in the community and to the community, and no such thing as hair-splitting technicalities to avoid the honest application of the law should be resorted to by it."[41] The *New York Telegram* argued that an educational institution "ought to be better than the average employer."[42] *The Survey* reiterated the *Telegram*'s message: "As an employer of labor, a university is expected to live up to a standard well above that of a sweatshop boss."[43] The Reverend Duvall, the man who had leaked the scandal to the press in the first place, issued a poignant plea: "Plenty of colleges may find help to do their work at a low wage; but are these institutions going to pay wages forever according to the law of supply and demand? Are educators justified as heads of concerns in accepting salaries from five to ten times as large as those who work for them? The way to give truth is to live truth."[44] His words were calculated to sting the institution that boasted *veritas* as its motto. Duvall made a moral argument of mutual obligation that true welfare capitalists would have understood. A university was *not* a business enterprise, yet many writers also claimed that Harvard had failed even to live up to the era's standards for private corporations.

Public anger over Harvard's behavior reached a crescendo in the spring of 1930. Editorials became personal and biting. The *New Republic* increasingly blamed Lowell: "the fact remains that President Lowell, in the present instance as so often in the past, has shown a conspicuous disregard for public opinion. He likes to think of Harvard as a national university, and yet he speaks in the public-be-damned voice that one expects from the manager of a grasping and selfish corporation."[45] Students and alumni, moved by both a sense of social justice and a desire to end the bad publicity for Harvard, issued a call for action to resolve the scandal. Since the Lowell administration adamantly refused to acknowledge any wrongdoing, a famous alumnus, Corliss Lamont, stepped forward to lead an alumni fund-raising drive to pay the Widener women a decade of earnings lost as a result of Harvard's failure to pay the minimum wage.

Lamont was the socialist son of billionaire Thomas Lamont, head of J. P. Morgan Investment Bank; an author and philosopher, he devoted his life to fighting for radical causes. In 1930 he launched a letter-writing campaign asking alumni and students for financial contributions to raise the scrub-women's back wages and to sign a petition expressing "moral outrage" at Harvard. Telegrams and letters pledging support poured into his New York apartment. "The institution is not only stingy and apparently callous and lacking in human sympathy but is not even living up to the standard of the ordinary decent citizen," wrote Herbert Ehrmann, an alumnus attorney.[46] Alumni sought to restore Harvard's honor and appealed to fellow students to "take a stand not only as Harvard men, but as men who insist on just and humane action in every sphere of life."[47] Alumni would demonstrate that they, and not Lowell, spoke for the "real Harvard."[48]

Alumni, students, leftists, labor leaders, and the public had expressed a consensus that employers had responsibilities toward labor that went beyond merely what statutory law enforced. Universities, they concluded, had even greater obligations. If Harvard had simply acknowledged its mistake, repaid the back wages, or reinstated the women workers, the controversy would have been resolved, and Harvard would have redeemed its public image. Furthermore, such a gesture would have indicated that Harvard was respon-sive to public opinion and prepared to make changes in its labor relations. As it turned out, "it remained for a generous alumnus," the *Raleigh N.C. News Observer* reported, "to see that the worker's rights were vindicated."[49] Elite paternalism, not university responsibility, won the day. With financial donations from 281 alumni, Corliss Lamont raised nine years of back wages due the Widener women. The "scrubwomen's Santa" divided $3,880 among them on December 25, 1931, two years after their ordeal began.[50] Alumni and the press congratulated each other that justice had been served in this case. As the *Labor Herald* proclaimed, "If the searchlight of publicity had not been turned on the niggardly policy of the Harvard authorities, it is doubtful if anything would have been done for the scrubwomen."[51] Private charity may have put an end to the scrubwomen controversy, but Harvard had remained recalcitrant to the end. And charity alone could not perpetually resolve labor disputes.

EATING PRESTIGE

When the Fair Labor Standards Act was passed in 1938 as part of the New Deal, federal legislation established minimum wages, maximum hours, and overtime pay rules for men as well as women. But that did not mean that the law no longer discriminated between male and female workers. On the contrary, most of the occupations *not* covered by New Deal legislation, including domestic service, were filled by women, and the National Recovery Act exempted universities from its provisions. Harvard had told cleaning women in 1929 that "prestige" could make up for low wages; 50 years later, in 1987, the Harvard Union of Clerical and Technical Workers' "We Can't Eat Prestige" slogan revealed how little things had changed. Indeed, Harvard's prestige and status as the nation's premiere university still make it a target for criticism and negative publicity, which, if history shows us anything, is far more expensive than the cost of labor.

Notes

1. A. Lawrence Lowell to Rev. William Duvall, Jan. 14, 1930, Corliss Lamont Collection, Schlesinger Library, Radcliffe Institute of Advanced Study, Cambridge, Mass. [hereafter, CLC/SL].
2. Arthur Endicott, *Alumni Bulletin*, March 12, 1930; A. Lawrence Lowell to Thomas Nelson Perkins, Oct. 20, 1930, Papers of A. Lawrence Lowell, 1929-1931, Harvard University Archives [hereafter, ALL/HUA].
3. *Portland Evening Herald*, "20 Harvard Scrubwomen Fired," Jan. 30, 1930; *Portland Oregon Telegram*, "Fair Harvard?" Jan. 19, 1930; *Boston Evening American*, "Indignation Over Discharge of Harvard Scrubwomen," Jan. 16, 1930; *New York World*, "Fair Harvard," Jan. 30, 1930; *New York Telegram*, "Scrubbers Discharged When State Ordered Minimum Wage Enforced," Jan. 29, 1930; *Baltimore Sun*, "Harvard Discharges 20 Scrubwomen Over Two Cent Issue," Jan. 17, 1930; *Philadelphia Record*, "Harvard Scrubwomen Fired—Two Cent Pay Raise Is Cause," Jan. 19, 1930; *Columbia State Sentinel*, "The Scrubwomen of Harvard," Jan. 19, 1930; *Raleigh News Observer*, "Harvard Female Employees Were Fired to Make Way for Cheaper Male Workers," Feb. 1, 1930; *South Bend Times*, "Millionaire School Fires Charwomen," Jan. 24, 1930.
4. *Labor*, "The End of the Harvard Scrubwomen Affair," Dec. 30, 1931.
5. *Boston Transcript*, Sept. 16, 1931; House Report No. 1225, *Report of the Special Commission Established to Investigate the Operation of the Minimum Wage Law* (Boston: Wright and Potter, 1932).

6. Irving Bernstein, *The Lean Years: A History of the American Worker, 1920-1933* (Baltimore, Md.: Penguin, 1960); Lizabeth Cohen, *Making a New Deal: Industrial Workers in Chicago, 1919-1939* (New York: Cambridge University Press, 1990).
7. Theda Skocpol, *Protecting Soldiers and Mothers* (Cambridge, Mass.: Harvard University Press, 1992); Diane Kirby, "The Wage-Earning Woman and the State: The National Women's Trade Union League and Protective Labor Legislation, 1903-1923," *Labor History* 28, no. 1 (1987): 54-74; Gwendolyn Mink, *The Wages of Motherhood: Inequality in the Welfare State* (Ithaca, N.Y.: Cornell University Press, 1995), 14-15.
8. Gardner Jackson, "Editorial," *The Nation* (Feb. 12, 1930); Jackson, "Harvard Explains," *The Nation* (Feb. 19, 1930); Richard Norton Smith, *The Harvard Century: The Making of a University to a Nation* (New York: Simon and Schuster, 1986), 89, 99; Gardner Jackson to Corliss Lamont, undated, CLC/SL.
9. Mary Anderson to Massachusetts Minimum Wage Commission, March 20, 1930; *Life and Labor Bulletin* [organ of the National Women's Trade Union League of America], March 1930, CLC/SL.
10. Gardner Jackson, "Harvard—School for Scrubwomen," *The Nation* (Jan. 29, 1930).
11. I am drawing here on Paula Baker's broad definition of politics as "any action, formal or informal, taken to affect the course or behavior of government or the community." See Paula Baker, "The Domestication of Politics: Women and American Political Society, 1780-1920," *American Historical Review* 89 (June 1984): 620-47.
12. Walter Lippmann, "Fair Harvard," *New York World*, Jan. 30, 1930.
13. "The Harvard Scrub Team," *New Yorker* (Jan. 23, 1930).
14. Commonwealth of Massachusetts Minimum Wage Commission, *Wages of Women Employed as Office and Other Building Cleaners in Massachusetts* (Boston: Wright and Potter, 1918); transcript, "Hearing in the Matter of a Minimum Wage for Office and Other Building Cleaners," Dec. 29, 1920, CLC/SL.
15. Cohen, *Making a New Deal*, 161.
16. Jackson to Lamont, Feb. 23, 1930, CLC/SL.
17. See Seymour Martin Lipset and David Riesman, *Education and Politics at Harvard* (New York: McGraw Hill, 1975), 133-55; Smith, *The Harvard Century*, 62-100.
18. Lowell to Thomas Perkins, Oct. 31, 1930; Jackson, "School for Scrubwomen," *The Nation* (Jan. 29, 1930); Gardner Jackson to Corliss Lamont, Feb. 28, 1930, CLC/SL.
19. Margaret Weisman, "Interviews," CLC/SL; see also John Trumpbour, ed., *How Harvard Rules: Reason in the Service of Empire* (Boston: South End Press, 1989), 202.
20. Lipset and Reisman, *Education and Politics at Harvard*, 159; Arthur Endicott to Lowell, Sept. 9, 1933; Lowell to Arthur Young, March 1, 1937, ALL/HUA.
21. Charles H. Trout, *Boston, the Great Depression, and the New Deal* (New York: Oxford University Press, 1977), 15; Smith, *The Harvard Century*, 62-100.
22. Transcript of the State House "Hearing," CLC/SL.
23. Massachusetts Minimum Wage Commission, *Wages of Women Employed as Office and Other Building Cleaners*, 11.
24. Margaret Weisman to Corliss Lamont, May 28, 1930, and undated transcripts of interviews with workers, CLC/SL.
25. Jackson, "Harvard Explains."
26. Ibid.
27. *Life and Labor Bulletin*, March 1930.
28. Statement published in the *Harvard Bulletin*, Jan. 30, 1930.
29. *Boston Post*, Jan. 18, 1930.
30. *New York Telegram*, Feb. 1, 1930.
31. Paul Cifrino, *Boston Post*, Jan. 26, 1930.
32. *Boston Post*, Jan. 19, 1930; see also *The Nation*, Jan. 29, 1930.
33. See Nancy Cott, *The Grounding of Modern Feminism* (New Haven, Conn.: Yale University Press, 1987).
34. *The Nation*, March 12, 1930.

35. *Salt Lake City* [Utah] *Tribune*, "A Fair Deal for the Worker," Jan. 30, 1930.
36. *New York Times*, May 27, 1930; "Harvard—School for Scrubwomen" pamphlet, "Scrubwomen"/HUA.
37. Harvard Square Deal Association, pamphlets, placards, 1930, "Scrubwomen"/HUA; *Harvard Lampoon*, Jan.8, 1931; *Time*, Jan. 15, 1931; *Buffalo, N.Y. News*, March 18, 1929.
38. *New York World*, Jan. 30, 1930, "Fair Harvard?"
39. Heywood Broun, *New York Telegram*, Jan. 20, 1930.
40. New Bedford *Weekly Standard*, Jan. 16, 1931.
41. *Boston Post*, Feb. 2, 1930.
42. *New York Telegram*, Feb. 3, 1930.
43. *The Survey*, March 15, 1930.
44. William Duvall to Corliss Lamont, undated, CLC/SL.
45. *New Republic*, Feb. 12, 1930.
46. Herbert Ehrmann to Corliss Lamont, March 8, 1930, CLC/SL.
47. Christopher Shreve to Corliss Lamont, April 4, 1930, CLC/SL.
48. Lamont, "Open Letter," May 5, 1930, CLC/SL.
49. *Raleigh N.C. News Observer*, Dec. 26, 1931.
50. Ibid.
51. *Labor Herald*, Wilmington, Delaware, Dec.12, 1931.

NEGOTIATING WORK AND FAMILY

Aspirations of Early Radcliffe Graduates

Jo Anne Preston

In 1928 Radcliffe president Ada Comstock announced, "We have come to see, I believe, that marriage is essentially far more compatible with continuation of a woman's career than has been assumed."[1] The inspiration for Comstock's remark was the surprising affirmation by five decades of former students that women could indeed successfully combine a career with marriage. To commemorate 50 years of offering higher education to women, the Radcliffe College Alumnae Association had just completed a thorough and far-reaching survey of all living graduates, nongraduates, and graduate students. The survey was unusual in two respects: first, it polled women both on information about their lives and on their opinions concerning a number of personal and social issues; second, it received an unusually high response rate of 56 percent of those polled, or 3,567 questionnaires completed and returned. Another noteworthy contribution, and one that caught Comstock's attention, was Radcliffe women's response to the question, "Can a woman successfully carry on a career and marriage simultaneously?" In an era of considerable disapproval of working wives and substantial barriers to women progressing in careers, an astonishingly high percentage of those who answered the question responded positively: 73 percent thought women could successfully combine marriage and a career. That question was followed by, "Can she, if she has children?" In response to the second question, Radcliffe graduates were less encouraging; still, 49 percent thought or wished it would be possible.[2]

Barbara Solomon and Patricia Nolan in their analysis of the 1928 survey concluded that the conviction among a significant number of early Radcliffe graduates that women could combine careers, marriage, and children was especially impressive given prevailing practices and attitudes. Solomon and Nolan noted that the married women in the survey were more positive about combining career and marriage than the single women, but they also noted that most of these married women had not achieved the goal they described.[3] Detailed employment and family histories reveal that Radcliffe women, like other college-educated women, faced formidable obstacles. Claudia Goldin, in her study of women college graduates in the twentieth century, concluded that those who graduated between 1900 and 1920 were required to choose between marriage and a career.[4] Few were able to achieve the integration of marriage and career that Harvard women seek today.

If the actual life histories of Radcliffe graduates show that their predictions were too hopeful, what then accounted for their initial optimism? An explanation cannot be found in the prevailing social norms or opportunity structures. Women entering Radcliffe in the first three decades of the twentieth century encountered frustrating and conflicting messages: strive for equality in educational opportunities but not in career opportunities; put your education to good use but not in the most prestigious and powerful professions; be independent but expect to be financially supported by your prospective husband. Their optimism might be better explained by considering the kinds of women who chose to attend Radcliffe College. They were women who yearned for the opportunity to obtain an education that would not just be the rough equivalent of those offered to Harvard men but would in fact comprise lectures given by the very same professors. One respondent replied that she would attend Radcliffe again "for the instruction by Harvard professors." In comparison to the other Seven Sisters, Radcliffe College drew the student body most interested in academic pursuits and least interested in social activities.[5] The alumnae responses on the 1928 questionnaire confirm the intellectual focus of the college. One answered the question concerning whether she would choose Radcliffe again with "Yes, I should say that the education at Radcliffe is taken more seriously than at many other colleges." Yet another answered in the affirmative and characterized the student body as "[having] a greater interest and success in intellectual pursuits than in others."[6]

Over the course of their Radcliffe education, women grew more indepen-dent and challenged the beliefs and practices that restricted their progress. In reunion books and surveys, many graduates testified to the transformative power of attending Radcliffe College. A 1910 graduate conveyed the following to her fiftieth reunion classmates: "To quote Stevenson, 'Radcliffe stabbed me broad awake'." By invoking this phrase from Robert Louis Stevenson, she endeavored to show how Radcliffe woke her up, apparently somewhat painfully, to worlds of which she had been previously unaware, worlds in which new modes of living could be forged. As a result of her awakening to new possibilities for women, she later became the president of the Lowell (Massachusetts) Equal Suffrage League.[7]

In spite of rising expectations, a deeply gendered labor market, one in which gender operated at different levels and in different ways, proved a formidable obstacle to early Radcliffe graduates. Exclusionary policies in the most powerful and prestigious professions slowed their progress. In medicine, the turn-of-the-century efforts to upgrade and regularize medical education led to the closing of women's medical schools. By 1903 only three women's medical colleges remained. With women excluded from most others or admitted only in very small numbers, the number of female physicians dwindled. Women's opportunities in the legal profession were just as limited. Few law schools would admit women and before 1900 only 200 women in the nation had earned a law degree. In the greater Boston area, for instance, only Boston University Law School admitted women and then only a few of them over a decade.[8] Frustrated by their limited opportunities for obtaining a legal education, Radcliffe students in 1915 lobbied the Harvard Law School to admit women. One of the students, Elizabeth Chadwick Beale, whose father taught at the Law School, prevailed on him and his colleagues to found the Cambridge Law School for Women. Unfortunately, after Elizabeth's departure following the first year, the school survived only an additional year, as Professor Beale lost interest and withdrew his support. Women fared no better in the equally high status but much less lucrative profession of the ministry. At the turn of the century, as a result of discriminatory practices in both professional education and in ordination, less than 4 percent of all ordained ministers were women.[9]

Because of the limited opportunities in law, medicine, and the ministry, Radcliffe graduates in the first three decades of the century sought careers in the traditional women's professions. The prospect of continuing their academic pursuits made teaching a more attractive option to many than social work, librarianship, or nursing. For those who graduated from 1900 to

1920, over 40 percent taught at some time in their lives. In the class of 1900, 49 women, or 78 percent of the class, became teachers. In the next two decades a smaller but still significant percentage of graduates taught for some portion of their lives: 62 percent of the class of 1910 spent part of their postgraduate lives teaching, while only 41 percent of the class of 1920 taught. For the small number of African American graduates of Radcliffe College, whose career choices were even more constricted, 52 percent of the 21 who attended Radcliffe College from 1900 to 1920 became teachers.[10]

Recognizing that educated women aspired to become teachers and that schools constituted a primary employer of college-educated women, Radcliffe College sought to increase its students' opportunities by offering education courses and negotiating with some cities and towns to place Radcliffe students in city schools to learn new methods of teaching. Education courses were offered as early as 1895, including courses on the history and current status of educational theory, and, for graduates exclusively, a seminar on pedagogy. The offerings in education grew so that by 1920 the college sponsored three courses for undergraduates and graduates and three restricted to graduate students. When, in the second decade of the twentieth century, public school boards began to require that prospective teachers complete a year of formal teaching under the supervision of the public schools before appointment, Radcliffe College made an arrangement with area public schools for its students to teach in these schools. Radcliffe repaid the towns by allowing a certain number of public school teachers to be admitted to Radcliffe without charge. Moreover, Radcliffe extended to other teachers a special rate or "teachers' fee" for courses offered at Radcliffe, which strengthened the connection between the college and the teaching profession.[11] Radcliffe voted to institute all of these measures, not so much to encourage women to enter teaching as to accommodate the need for employment of college-educated women.

Other forces were at work, however. When in 1900 the proportion of women teachers in New England schools grew to over 80 percent, school boards began to pass local ordinances banning the employment of married women or the retention of female teachers who married. Nor was the opposition to women teachers limited to local school officials. Even those in prominent positions supported the campaign against the employment of married female teachers. In 1904, A. E. Winship, the editor of the *Boston Globe,* argued that marriage should be a factor in the selection of female teachers. By 1913 public commentary over the hiring of married women rose to such a level that Charles William Eliot, the former president of Harvard, felt compelled to contribute to the debate. Married women, he pronounced, should not be employed in the schools, and furthermore, no woman, single or married, should be employed in teaching for more than five years. But at the time of his remarks, Radcliffe graduates were entering teaching in large numbers with the aspirations of combining a career with marriage, and Radcliffe College administrators, by securing connections with local schools and by offering courses in education, attempted to support their graduates' choices.[12]

A concerted and widespread ideological campaign accompanied the marriage ban. Public officials at the turn of the century began to speak out against female teachers' predominance in the schools—a phenomenon they termed overfeminization. A specific target of this campaign was the removal of all married female teachers from the schools, justified by two arguments: first, that married women teachers had an adverse effect upon students, and second, that married women teachers neglected their duties at home and thus weakened the social and economic fabric of society. The second view gained force with the growing apprehension concerning the employment of married women in any occupation.[13]

Radcliffe College graduates who sought teaching careers were gravely affected by the campaign against married women teachers. Those who chose to marry were forced out of their teaching positions. Of those graduates who entered teaching from 1900 to 1930, half of the women ended their teaching careers when they married. Few women continued teaching in the public schools after marriage.[14]

RADCLIFFE COLLEGE GRADUATES' RECOMMENDATIONS

What were the strategies that respondents to the 1928 survey proposed that would enable a woman to pursue a career while married or while raising children? Since the questionnaire allowed for open-ended responses, many volunteered their advice on how this goal could be achieved. Their responses were thoughtful and pragmatic, showing a realistic sense of the challenges they faced. For all their optimism, these women understood the world in which they lived, and they mobilized the resources at their disposal in order to overcome obstacles. One sometimes reads in what they wrote the blunt terseness of a seasoned veteran: "As one who has tried, I don't see why not." Others contributed their own thoughtful observations of women who successfully combined a career and marriage: "I know many who do"; "Yes—so far as I have observed it from friends and relatives"; "A large number of women have proven this"; and "Yes, my mother proved it."

Many who registered positive responses prefaced them with the word "depends." What successfully combining marriage and a career depended on varied. A careful choice of a husband was a frequent recommendation. It is possible to interpret these responses as qualifications—a woman can have a career only so long as her husband will tolerate it. But it is equally plausible to see these responses as pragmatic and positive, requiring women who would combine marriage and career to bear that ambition in mind when they weighed potential husbands. As one former Radcliffe student stated decisively: "Yes, if she has the right husband." She did not specify what she meant by "right," but others made some proposals. One respondent cautioned that the goal could be achieved if the woman "has the cooperation physical and spiritual of her husband." Another wrote: "it depends on the husband's character among other factors." None went so far as to prescribe husbands' sharing of domestic tasks, but many felt that it would not be impossible to find a husband who would approve of their career ambitions.

A second ingredient for successfully combining marriage and career was a strong constitution, which suggests that women would still be responsible for all domestic work. Respondents felt strongly that the double burden of a career and homemaking would require an enormous amount of physical stamina. One respondent enumerated a number of qualities: "It depends on the woman, her health and disposition, as well as her training." Mental as well as physical abilities—not just a woman's intelligence and education but also her insight and common sense—could be needed. One respondent agreed that a woman could combine marriage and career "if she has brains and strength sufficient."

Although good health and husbands' cooperation were important, former Radcliffe students recognized that they were not enough. Changes in conditions at home and at work were essential to combine marriage and career successfully. As one wrote: "That depends so largely on conditions that it can not be answered in one word." Some located the difficulty in the home. One believed a woman could achieve both "for a while if she had help in the house." Others understood that the careful choice of career would facilitate combining it with a marriage. One elaborated on this condition by suggesting that combining career with marriage would not be feasible "unless the woman can control hours of work." Choice of career, of course, was only one factor. As one graduate responded, "It depends on the woman, the husband, the pocketbook, and <u>what</u> career."

Although they considered it a more difficult achievement, the respondents cited conditions under which the integration of raising children and managing a career would be possible. As one respondent wrote: "It depends on her job. I think a woman could paint or write as these things can be set aside or done at her convenience. She might attend to real estate or advertising, [not] to be tied to hours." Another offered: "Yes, if she chooses occupations which can be adjusted to the demands of childbearing and homemaking." More hesitant in her support, one graduate replied, "I think she can with changes of hours and curriculum when the children are very young." A small minority advised that careers should be subordinated to child rearing. One 1910 graduate wrote, "Only if career is very flexible in its demands and is admittedly of secondary importance." In addition to a career with flexible hours, respondents recommended employing other women for child care when economically practical. One graduate approved combining a career with raising children "if she could afford expert outside care for children," though the graduates anticipated that women would still need to supervise the child care. Thus a successful women would need to be a "skillful manager and a good instructor of assistants," stressed a 1908 graduate.

In addition, respondents regarded the timing and location of a mother's work as crucial to success in combining child rearing and a career. A 1920 graduate tartly and forthrightly replied to the question concerning combining children and careers: "Not very successfully unless her work be done at home"; and another: "If the career allows her to remain at home, yes, otherwise no." The timing of childbearing needed to be coordinated with career development, according to some respondents. A 1910 graduate recommended that a woman could successfully combine a career and child rearing if "before she has [children] she has progressed sufficiently in her career to be able to leave it temporarily to be independent." Conversely, the timing of combining career and child rearing could depend on the age of the children. Many respondents felt that women could not engage in careers when their children were young. The suggestions varied as to the appropriate age of the children, but most respondents thought that women could have careers once their children entered school.

Though practical suggestions predominated, some women indicated that social conditions could affect a woman's success. A 1915 graduate thought women could combine marriage, children, and career if "she is in a community where other women are trying it." Another respondent perceived that women could do it but that it would be "Difficult because of society and the interruption during childbearing." A few even speculated on the positive outcomes for others if a woman could combine career, marriage, and child rearing. One graduate concluded from her observations of relatives that, when mothers have careers, "children seem to have more respect for the abilities of the mother."

CAREER AND MARRIAGE IN THE LIVES
OF THREE RADCLIFFE CLASSES

Were Radcliffe graduates able to employ these strategies to achieve their goals of combining a career with marriage, or even career, marriage, and children? By establishing timelines for three Radcliffe College classes—1900, 1910, and 1920—we can determine when women married, when they entered careers, and whether they were able to manage both simultaneously. By drawing on a variety of sources located in the Radcliffe College Archives—reunion books, survey responses, and correspondence—we can analyze the employment and family histories for all of these graduates. The reunion books offered what Robert Zussman calls an autobiographical occasion, in which one reports and synthesizes all aspects of one's life up to that moment.[15] Because class members reflected on their lives as well as reported on critical events, we can also examine how Radcliffe graduates interpreted these life events.

Radcliffe graduates in the three classes examined were far more likely to be gainfully employed than to be married. Whereas 94 percent of members of the class of 1900 were employed at some point in their lives, only 41 percent were ever married. For the class of 1910, the percent who had worked remained relatively high, at 88 percent, but the marriage rate had risen only slightly, to 49 percent. The trend continued for the class of 1920, with 82 percent employed at some time, and the marriage rate finally surpassing 50 percent. The explanations for the low marriage rate range from proposals that college education made women more discerning in their life choices to discussions about men's presumed dislike for intellectual women.[16] Whatever the reason, the low marriage rate would allow only a small number of women to combine marriage with a career.

Predictably, few women in any of the three classes successfully carried on a career and marriage simultaneously. In the 1900 class, only 11 percent, or 7 out of 63, were able to be employed and married at the same time. Over the next 20 years the rate rose to 27 percent, still astonishingly low in light of Radcliffe graduates' responses on the 1928 questionnaire. Nor, at least initially, did women combine marriage and careers for very long. Graduates of the 1900 class who combined their careers with marriage did so for an average of 4.5 years. Those graduating 20 years later, however, managed to combine marriage with a career for an average of approximately 13 years. Even more puzzling, the life-course data show that most of the women who were able to combine marriage and a career achieved that goal later in life. For those who graduated in the 1900 class, women who combined marriage and career took an average of 27 years after graduation to accomplish their goal. The average time dropped to 13 years for the class of 1920, which is still a considerable delay.

Why did women wait so long to begin dual commitments to marriage and family? Did they, as the respondents to the 1928 questionnaire suggest, wait until their children entered school or left home? For the class of 1900, three of the seven bore no children, yet waited for an average of ten years after marriage to enter or resume a career. One of these graduates left or was forced out of her teaching position when she married and then waited 19 years before entering another vocation. Those who had children did not enter the paid labor force again, on average, until the last child was 19. Graduates of the classes of 1910 and 1920 had similar patterns, but they entered the labor force sooner—on average, approximately nine years after the birth of their last child. The differences between the earlier and later graduates might reflect a greater determination on the part of later graduates to implement various personal strategies to cope with the demands of husbands and child care, or alternatively, changes in the social climate, perhaps in response to women's activism emanating from the suffrage campaign, that eased the employment of married women and mothers.

Changes in the social climate did not include those in school systems, the largest employer of graduates in all three classes. The marriage ban was adopted by more and more communities during the 1920s and 1930s, making employment in any public school after marriage almost impossible. Many graduates entered teaching upon graduation, only to have their positions terminated when they married. In the class of 1900, for instance, 19 women left teaching at the time of marriage, and in the 1910 class 44 stopped teaching when they married. Not all, of course, were terminated by the school system, but the prevailing campaign against married female teachers undoubtedly made it difficult to remain employed. In their reunion books, Radcliffe graduates lamented the interruption of their careers. One member of the class of 1920 reported the following to her classmates: "The years are divided into two parts: work following my A.B. and work following my MRS. Fortified by the former, I taught in the junior high school in Lexington. . . . In those days, a MRS marked finis to a public school career, so late in 1939 I took the present job of wife and mother."[17] Some women in the class of 1920 found an opportunity to return to teaching during World War II when male teachers entered the armed services. One such woman informed her reunion class: "I taught until 1936 when married women could no longer teach. From 1943 to 1945, I have been a Military Substitute in the Math Department of the Malden schools."[18]

The ban against married women created special hardships for African American graduates, for whom career and marriage was an important goal but whose career alternatives were more limited, leading a greater proportion of them toward teaching. Such was the story of Nadine Wright, a 1917 graduate of Radcliffe College. Nadine Wright's African American parents taught in racially segregated schools in Oklahoma where they were harassed by the Ku Klux Klan. To ensure her safety, they sent Nadine to Cambridge to live with an aunt; she was admitted to Radcliffe College in 1913. After Radcliffe, she overcame racial barriers when she was hired to teach in the predominantly white Cambridge schools, only to face discrimination later as a married woman. In 1938, after 16 years of service, the Cambridge school committee dismissed Nadine Wright because she married. She was unable to find employment until the Second World War, when she was hired by the Navy. Released from the Navy after the war, Nadine, still unable to regain her regular teaching position, elected to teach students with cerebral palsy, for which she received numerous awards for excellence.[19]

Well aware of the social constraints that prevented Radcliffe graduates from achieving their life goals, early Radcliffe graduates participated in various social movements to increase women's options, including the option to combine careers and marriage. Some graduates reported participating in organized political activity to rescind the marriage bans (as well as the discriminatory double salary scales that prescribed that male teachers would receive higher salaries than female teachers). For example, a member of the class of 1910 wrote to her reunion class that she worked with the American Federation of Teachers to initiate legislative bills for equal pay and the right of teachers to marry. Others found alternative employment in teaching by founding their own schools.[20]

These efforts marked only a beginning for Radcliffe women in their long struggle to achieve the dual goals of family and career. Despite their positive views concerning married women's careers, few early Radcliffe women were able to "successfully carry on a career and marriage simultaneously." Even fewer could marry, have children, and continue careers. The difficulties faced by graduates in attempting marriage and schoolteaching careers illuminate the interplay between exclusion and inclusion. Once formally excluded from higher education, women flourished at Radcliffe. Equal opportunities after college, however, remained elusive. By the early twentieth century when women were hired to teach in greater numbers, the conditions of inclusion formally demanded that women forgo marriage and family. In more subtle forms, but by no means less problematic, other professions that later became open to women excluded married women because they did not "adjust to the demands of childbearing and homemaking." The integration of marriage, children, and career could have been achieved, as another graduate predicted, "with all conditions favorable." The favorable conditions, for the most part, were not achieved, leaving this important task undone.

Notes

1. Ada Comstock, "The Fourth R for Women," *Century Magazine* 117 (1929): 413.
2. These percentages are from Barbara Solomon and Patricia Nolan, "Education, Work, Family, and Public Commitment in the Lives of Radcliffe Alumnae, 1883-1928," in *Changing Education: Women as Radicals and Conservatives*, ed. Joyce Antler and Sari Biklin (New York: State University of New York Press, 1990), 139-55.
3. Solomon and Nolan, "Education, Work, Family, and Public Commitment," 147-49.
4. Claudia Goldin, "The Meaning of College in the Lives of American Women: The Past One-Hundred Years," NBER Working Paper no. w4099 (June 1992), 2, 6-15.
5. See Helen Lefkowitz Horowitz, *Alma Mater: Design and Experience in the Women's Colleges from Their Nineteenth-Century Beginnings to the 1930s* (New York: Alfred A. Knopf, 1984), 240-41, for a comparison of Radcliffe with the other Seven Sisters.
6. The quotations are from responses to the 1928 Radcliffe College Alumnae Association Survey, Radcliffe College Archives, Schlesinger Library, Harvard University [hereafter, RCA]. Respondents were given the assurance of confidentiality so no identifying characteristics of the respondents will be disclosed. Subsequent quotations from Radcliffe graduates are from this survey unless otherwise noted.
7. Class of 1910 Fiftieth Reunion Book, RCA.
8. Paul Starr, *The Transformation of American Medicine: The Rise of a Sovereign Profession and the Making of a Vast Industry* (New York: Basic Books, 1982), 120-22; Thomas Woody, *A History of Women's Education in the United States,* 2 vols. (New York: Science Press, 1929), 2: 377-82.
9. Karen Berger Morello, *The Invisible Bar: The Woman Lawyer in America 1638 to the Present* (New York: Random House, 1985), 68-70; Paula Nesbitt, *Feminization of the Clergy in America: Occupational and Organizational Perspectives* (New York: Oxford University Press, 1997), 23-24; see Barbara Solomon, *In the Company of Educated Women: A History of Woman and Higher Education in America* (New Haven, Conn.: Yale University Press, 1985), chap. 8, for a discussion of career opportunities for college-educated women in the early twentieth century.
10. Solomon, *In the Company of Educated Women,* 76; data for calculations on the percentages of graduates of 1900, 1910, and 1920 was compiled from reunion books, individual files, undergraduate records, correspondence, and the 1928 Radcliffe College Alumnae Association Survey; "Black Alumnae of Radcliffe College through 1950," typescript, RCA.
11. *Course Schedule for the Society for the Collegiate Instruction of Women 1895* (Cambridge, Mass.: W. H. Wheeler Printer, 1895), 9; *Radcliffe College Course Schedule, 1920*

(Cambridge, Mass.: W. H. Wheeler Printer, 1920), 30. For a discussion of these arrangements with public schools, see *Radcliffe College Annual Reports, 1916-1917,* 55-56.

12. A. E. Winship, "Should Married Women Teach?" *Journal of Education* 64, no. 21 (Nov. 29, 1906): 581, reprinted from the *Boston Globe* editorial page, Nov. 11, 1906; Duane Moury, "Married Teachers in the Schools," in *Journal of Education* (Aug. 28, 1913): 176-77.

13. Claudia Goldin, in her book *Understanding the Gender Gap: An Economic History of American Women* (New York: Oxford University Press, 1990), discusses the scope and rationale for marriage bars in the first half of the twentieth century. See pp. 160-79.

14. These estimates were made from life-course data on graduates from the classes of 1910, 1920, and 1930.

15. Robert Zussman, in his essay "Autobiographical Occasions," *Contemporary Sociology* 25, no. 2 (1996), argues that one must recognize the social structuring of occasions that allow for biographical accounts. Vered Vinitzky-Seroussi employs this approach in her book analyzing high school reunions as autobiographical occasions. See Vered Vinitzky-Seroussi, *After Pomp and Circumstance* (Chicago: University of Chicago Press, 1998).

16. For a discussion of these proposals, see Goldin, "The Meaning of College," 7-12.

17. Radcliffe Class of 1920 Fiftieth Reunion book, RCA.

18. Radcliffe Class of 1920 Reunion Book, RCA.

19. Radcliffe Class of 1917 Fiftieth Reunion Book, RCA; Obituaries, *Boston Globe,* Aug. 1, 1994.

20. Class of 1910 Twenty-Fifth Reunion Book.

Woman Working At Harvard

HARVARD'S INVISIBLE FACULTY

Four Portraits

Jane Knowles

A poster from 1922 shows a Radcliffe student in academic robes passing through the gate of opportunity to serve the world. But this was not an "equal opportunity" gate, and women did not pass through it to take up teaching and research posts at universities such as Harvard. Three academic women who managed to enter a side door served as invisible faculty at Harvard. They were marginal figures, did not appear in catalogs, and have received little recognition in the histories of Harvard. The first is Susanne Knauth Langer, philosopher, Radcliffe A.B. 1920, Ph.D. 1926. She was appointed tutor at Radcliffe in philosophy in 1927. For men a tutorship was the lowest rung in the ladder to tenure; for women it was often a lifetime position. Langer stayed in that post until 1942, without tenure, research leave, or interaction with Harvard colleagues. Her work was largely ignored by Harvard, but she was not discouraged. She wrote three important books, including the best-selling *Philosophy in a New Key*, published by the Harvard University Press in 1942. Translated into 20 languages, it became one of the most influential books in the field of aesthetics. Her reputation blossomed. After her marriage to historian William Langer ended in divorce, she left Harvard to become professor and chair of the Philosophy Department at Connecticut College.

Mary Peters Fieser, a chemist, was able to sidestep the barriers to an academic position through her marriage to Louis Fieser in 1932. She met her future husband at Bryn Mawr, where she was a chemistry major and he a

Susanne Knauth Langer, A.B, 1920, Ph.D., 1926;
tutor in Philosophy at Radcliffe, 1927-1942
(Radcliffe College Archives).

lecturer in chemistry. He came to Harvard to teach and she followed to Radcliffe to do a master's degree in 1931, but she found a chilly climate for women in chemistry and decided to marry rather than to pursue a Ph.D. "I could see I was not going to get along well on my own. Louis wanted to get married and it seemed like a nice opportunity. . . . I liked the man. I could do as much chemistry as I wanted, and it didn't matter what the other professors thought of me." Mary was ultimately appointed a research associate, but she could not apply for research grants in her own name, was not eligible for tenure, and her contributions were overshadowed by, and her status dependent on, her husband. Nevertheless, she had a "creative and enterprising career." She was a gifted experimentalist and an influential part of the research group. "One day," she recalled, "when I came into the lab, Louis had cleared everything away from my bench so that I wouldn't be tempted to do more experimental work."[1] He had decided that she should concentrate on writing. She worked loyally on their joint projects, coauthored two textbooks, and for nearly 30 years edited a reference series that is still the bible for

Mary Peters Fieser, A.M., 1931, research associate in Chemistry (Radclife College Archives).

chemists. Her bright red Corvette convertible was a symbol of independence and a gesture of defiance.

Some women were faculty in everything but name. A photograph from the 1920s shows a group of extraordinary women astrophysicists at the Harvard College Observatory.[2] Cecilia Payne-Gaposchkin, an Englishwoman from the other Cambridge, who was a member of the Observatory staff from 1926 to 1966, faced every kind of obstacle: She wrote a brilliant Ph.D. thesis (the first in astronomy at Harvard). She lectured in the Astronomy Department but was not listed in Harvard and Radcliffe catalogs. She directed graduate research without status, had no research leaves, and was paid less after seven years than a beginning male lecturer. Her salary was listed under "equipment." Indeed, president A. Lawrence Lowell said that "Miss Payne should never have a position in the University while he was alive." Nevertheless, she was able to survive and flourish. "It has been a case," she said, "of survival not of the fittest, but of the most doggedly persistent." In 1938, under a new president, James Bryant Conant, she was appointed Phillips Astronomer, became professor in 1956, and eventually chair of the department. She was never bitter about her Harvard experience: "[We] could meet on equal terms with any astronomer in the world. Everyone who was

Right: Astronomer Cecilia Payne-Gaposchkin, Ph.D., 1925, portrait by Patricia Watwood (Harvard University Art Museums); left: Helen Maud Cam, first tenured woman professor in Harvard's Faculty of Arts and Sciences, 1948 (Radcliffe College Archives).

anybody . . . came through, and argued, and fraternized. Those were glorious days. . . . We met as equals; nobody condescended to me on account of sex or youth. . . . We were scientists, we were scholars ([and] neither of these words has a gender)."[3]

In 1948 Helen Maud Cam, a medieval historian and fellow of Girton College, became the first woman to receive tenure at Harvard. Under the leadership of Radcliffe College and the creative philanthropy of the Zemurray family, a chair was created for distinguished women in any field at Harvard, and Cam became its first incumbent. This unbarred the gates. Cam called herself the first swallow of summer and prophesied that soon a whole flock of swallows would follow. She was wrong. A number of women were appointed as lecturers, and some were even allowed to attend faculty meetings, but it took another 25 years and the revolution of affirmative action to bring a whole flock and to make women faculty visible at Harvard.

Notes

1. E. J. Corey with Mary P. Fieser, interview, Jan. of 1982.
2. See photograph of women staff at the Harvard College Observatory, p. 4.
3. Cecilia Payne-Gaposchkin, *An Autobiography and Other Recollections* (New York: Cambridge University Press, 1984), 26, 221-27.

WOMEN WITH HIGH INFLUENCE, LOW VISIBILITY

Phyllis Keller

I first came to work at Harvard in 1951, armed with a Barnard College B.A., a Columbia University M.A., and a crash course in shorthand and typing from the Delehanty Secretarial School. My particular corner was the Graduate School of Education, then in its Lawrence Hall quarters. I was one of many graduate student spouses who took an entry-level secretarial job to help meet expenses.

We were much in demand: we were educated (if inexperienced), eager to be part of the university, and bargain-priced.

Another category of employee then was (usually unmarried) older women who had gradually climbed up the secretarial ladder to positions of considerable administrative responsibility. They had long been essential to the smooth functioning of Harvard.

One such was Anne MacDonald, executive secretary of the Harvard College Admissions Office for four decades after 1900. When James Bryant Conant became president in 1933, she instructed him in the admissions process. The real work of the Admissions Office was in the hands of Miss MacDonald and her staff. She and her opposite numbers at Yale (a Miss Elliot), at Princeton (a Miss Williams), and the College Entrance Examination Board (a Miss McLaughlin) met yearly "to compare notes on all matters pertaining to admission."

This essay first appeared in the *Harvard University Community Resource*, Dec. 2001, 3.

Women with high influence and low visibility continued to flourish at Harvard. President Nathan Marsh Pusey proposed in 1955 that the status and perks (though not the salary and benefits) of Harvard Corporation appointments be given to "a small group of women in administrative positions whose responsibilities included confidential participation in the implementation of University policy at a relatively high level." He had in mind a half dozen or so movers and shakers. But new names came rolling in from the Law and Medical Schools and other venues, suggesting that Harvard's invisible government was larger than anyone thought.

When I came back to Harvard in 1973, there still were some "executive secretaries" whose titles belied their influence and managerial roles. One such was Verna Johnson, who rose through the ranks from the early 1940s to become the enormously influential secretary to the dean of the Faculty of Arts and Sciences by the time she retired in 1984. She knew everything there was to know about administrative practices, was keeper of the Faculty's institutional memory, and authoritatively instructed deans, faculty, and younger staff members like me.

These women were mainly in the offices of the deans and the president, no longer in the other administrative units. But clearly they too were a vanishing breed. In many cases the earlier generation of women had been replaced by "old boys"—Harvard College graduates or graduate students who were tapped for entry-level posts on administrative ladders.

From the 1970s on, professionally trained women (and men) began to compete for the specialized jobs (and attractive salaries) available in the burgeoning middle management ranks of large institutions such as Harvard. They came armed with Ph.D.s, M.B.A.s, LL.D.s, or equivalent work experience.

In the year 2000, as I look back over this major demographic and organizational shift, I am struck by the far higher proportion of women in key managerial and professional posts. Competition for attractive jobs is more open to all comers; the pool of qualified candidates for a wide range of positions continues to grow.

Women at Harvard have benefited greatly from these changes. What has been lost, however, is the sense of being part of an extended family, the continuity of lifetime employment, the preservation of institutional memory. The unresolved question is not whether growth, centralization, and specialization are good, but how much is too much.

HUCTW rally, Old Cambridge Baptist Church, Feb. 1988 (Marilyn Humphries).

FEMINIST LABOR ORGANIZING

Images from the HUCTW Campaigns

Several attempts at organizing Harvard's clerical staff having failed, Kristine Rondeau and a small band of Harvard workers and union organizers established a new group, the Harvard Union of Clerical and Technical Workers, or HUCTW, in 1985. After several years of effort, the union won certification in a very close election in May 1988. The campaign and subsequent contract negotiations have been widely discussed as a "feminine model" of union organizing. Words and images from the union archives suggest the sophisticated understanding of the Harvard work environment and workers' goals.

> From our first step in organizing Harvard back in the seventies . . . our union's goal has been to get our members on the other side of Harvard's doors into the rooms where decisions affecting workers' lives are made.
> —Kris Rondeau, HUCTW lead organizer

> You have to strengthen people as individuals, and you have to find a way for them to develop their own self-confidence. You have to find a way for them to express anger at being powerless yet somehow represent themselves in a positive way that works for them.
> —Kris Rondeau

Right: HUCTW rally and bake sale (Ellen de Genova); left: HUCTW rally for day care (Sue Leavitt).

A pat on the head can be quite condescending
But unions are a girl's best friend.

—HUCTW organizing song,
to the tune of "Diamonds Are a Girl's Best Friend"

Responsible, self-respecting adults should represent themselves in important matters, affecting their lives. We have until now allowed Harvard to decide everything to do with our work lives. Now we are ready to participate as equals in making those decisions.

—HUCTW open letter to the Harvard Community, Dec. 1987

It is our common purpose . . . to work together to advance the long-term role of Harvard University as a premiere center of learning. . . . We have learned that we share a commitment to the processes of reasoned discourse in resolving problems and issues that may arise. . . . We are optimistic about [the] future.

—Preamble, HUCTW-Harvard contract, 1989

. . . organizing isn't about the boss, it's about workers. It's about their need for some power or influence over their jobs and their lives. So it doesn't matter if the boss is kind or moderate, benevolent, or vicious. It just doesn't matter. Workers need their own voice. . . . This isn't about them; it's about us.

—Kris Rondeau, Oct. 1993

THE CHANGING "HARVARD STUDENT"

Ethnicity, Race, and Gender

Marcia G. Synnott

Harvard's stated admissions policies have had a notable consistency in language. What the university said in the mid-1940s was not too different from what it said in its 1977 brief to the Supreme Court in *Regents of the University of California v. Allan Bakke* or from what President Neil Rudenstine wrote on "Diversity and Learning" in *The President's Report 1993-1995*. In various statements about its admissions policies, Harvard has often emphasized "a broadly balanced and representative student body."[1] For much of the twentieth century, however, its admissions practices favored native-born, white, middle- or upper-class Protestant men over Catholics, Jews, racial minorities, and women.[2]

Comparing the history of religious, ethnic, and racial discrimination with the history of gender discrimination at Harvard shows both parallels and differences and demonstrates the university's ability to diversify and change in response to both national trends and institutional interests.

HARVARD AND RADCLIFFE IN THE AGE
OF ETHNIC AND RELIGIOUS QUOTAS

Today Harvard admits less than 11 percent of applicants and enjoys an acceptance yield of almost 80 percent.[3] By contrast, in July 1940, the Harvard

Committee on Admission acknowledged to president James Bryant Conant that it had "reached the bottom of the rope" in trying to fill 1,100 seats in the freshman class. To bring in enough paying customers in a still-depressed economy, Conant authorized Richard M. Gummere, chairman of the Committee on Admission, to admit an additional 100 students. Reluctant "to lower unduly the standards of admission," Conant wrote that "no one should be admitted to Harvard College who has not at least a fifty-fifty chance of being promoted to the Sophomore class." If 75 of the last 100 students "flunked," he "should feel that we had taken money under false pretenses." At that time, Harvard had a well-documented 15 to 16 percent Jewish quota, achieved largely through its "selective" admissions policy.[4]

Although a majority of Harvard faculty were probably not anti-Semitic, there were several who, sharing the opinions of former president A. Lawrence Lowell, made their views well known. In May 1939, a few months before the outbreak of World War II in Europe, Julian Lowell Coolidge, master of Lowell House (1930-September 1940), complained to President Conant about "the vexing question of the number of Jews in Harvard College," who continued to be too numerous for his taste. Coolidge was distressed that figures on house membership, compiled by the Dean's Office in the spring of 1939, indicated that the houses averaged 17 percent Jewish students, instead of the 10 percent agreed on by the masters in 1932. Jewish students were more likely to survive academically than non-Jewish students and hence remained eligible for House membership. Coolidge also emphasized that "the commuters were notoriously largely Semitic." After 164 Jewish freshmen were admitted in fall 1938, Coolidge urged the Admission Committee "to be even more vigilant in controlling Jewish admission to Harvard College."[5]

Harvard may have exercised an informal Jewish quota until the 1950s, even after Jewish students had gained the social acceptance that led to having a Jew as captain of the 1947 football team and another as the first marshal of the class of 1948. Replying to a Jewish alumnus who declined to contribute to the Class of 1901 Fund, Gummere wrote that

> we have no quotas of any sort,—religious, racial, or geographical. We are, in line with President Conant's policy, of course interested in a national spread from all parts of the country; and we are desirous of having a balanced freshman class each year. By 'balanced,' I mean, a fair representation of all groups, playing no favorites and with no prejudices.

Admissions decisions, Gummere insisted, were "all on an individual basis, taking into account scholarship, leadership and character."[6] Yet, as late as 1958, Harvard had to defend its requirement that an applicant submit a photograph, despite the possibility of "a formal complaint" by the State Commission against Discrimination. Admissions officers in the College and the Law School even maintained "that the photograph works to the advantage of Negro students," but at the time Harvard made limited efforts to recruit African Americans.[7]

Undoubtedly aware of Harvard's quota on male Jewish students and limited by a quota on women undergraduates, Radcliffe College too may have restricted its Jewish admissions from the late 1930s into the early 1950s. Jewish students were numerous enough to form a Menorah Society by the 1920s, the Zionist Avukah by the 1930s, and Hillel by the 1940s.[8] Although Radcliffe's total enrollment of Jewish students in 1936-37 was 24.8 percent, higher than Harvard's and more than double that of Smith's 10 percent, the next highest among the Seven Sisters, it sharply declined the following year to 16.5 percent while Smith's rose to 12.9 percent.[9] Though there were few letters alleging anti-Semitism at Radcliffe, in 1948 a Chicago alumnus complained to the Radcliffe Dean of Admissions about the rejection of his daughter, who was admitted to sophomore standing at Stanford University: "She was invited to one of those 'snooty' teas of local Radcliffe graduates where she was given the distinct understanding by alumni present that as a girl of the Jewish faith she might get in if there were not too many Jewish girls applying. In other words, very distinctly told that there was a non-official Jewish quota."[10] As Radcliffe moved from attracting a student body largely from Massachusetts to becoming a leading national college, it may have sought to recruit, as Harvard did, in euphemistic terms, "a national spread" and "a balanced freshman class."[11]

As academic standards rose at Harvard, the percentage of Jewish students climbed back to 21 percent, its level in 1922 before President Lowell began his campaign to limit their numbers. According to a 1961 tabulation on "Jewish Enrollment in Ivy League Colleges" compiled at Yale University, which then had 11.8 percent, Harvard's Jewish enrollment was ahead of Brown's 18 percent and Princeton's and Dartmouth's at 15 percent each. However, Harvard had fewer Jewish students than Columbia (45 percent), Cornell (26 percent), and the University of Pennsylvania (25 percent).[12]

Despite the fact that antidiscrimination laws prohibited Harvard from inquiring into student religious affiliation or preference, the university continued to exclude non-Christian private religious services from Memorial Church until 1958. In the eyes of Willard L. Sperry, dean of the Divinity

School and former chairman of the Board of Preachers, Memorial Church was "a Protestant institution," even though it had been built in memory of all Harvard graduates who died in the nation's twentieth-century wars.[13] When the policy of religious exclusion became public, many within the Harvard community protested verbally and in writing, prompting the Corporation on April 21, 1958, "to modify its policy governing Memorial Church to permit its use on certain occasions for private non-Christian ceremonies conducted by officials of other religions." While maintaining the "essentially Christian character" of Memorial Church, the university pledged "to try to honor the convictions of each member of the Harvard community."[14]

In contrast to Jews, Catholic students—and faculty—had generally found a degree of acceptance at Harvard since the nineteenth century, although the university was sometimes patronizing toward Catholic colleges. The attendance of Catholic students may also have been discouraged both by the prejudices of some Harvard students and by the extreme sensitivity of Catholic leaders at Boston College to the real and imagined anti-Catholicism at Protestant institutions. Numbering about 300 in 1894, Catholic students organized a St. Paul's Catholic Club at Harvard; in 1906 women formed a Catholic Club at Radcliffe. Acceptance of Catholics at Harvard, probably not unrelated to their growing political power, was conspicuously demonstrated, moreover, when James Byrne, class of 1877, became the first Catholic (1920-1926) on the seven-member Harvard Corporation. At the 1937 commencement, Harvard conferred an honorary LL.D. degree on Cardinal William Henry O'Connell, which an alumnus of the class of 1912, a former student president of the St. Paul's Catholic Club, felt "could not have happened twenty-five years before when I was a senior." In 1958 the Charles Chauncey Stillman Guest Professorship of Roman Catholic Studies was endowed in the Divinity School. Two years later, the election of John F. Kennedy, class of 1940, as the first Catholic president stifled those still harboring prejudice.[15]

THE RADCLIFFE QUOTA: A SEPARATE AND UNEQUAL STATUS

Harvard's delay in adopting full coeducation can be attributed both to its reluctance to commit substantial resources on behalf of women students and to Radcliffe's deference, despite its pioneering role in forging a coordinate relationship with a prestigious male university. Indeed, for decades Radcliffe had often been on the defensive in dealing with such Harvard presidents as Lowell, who viewed it as an encumbrance and its president, at most, no more important than a Harvard dean. Professor Le Baron Russell Briggs, who served as a part-time president of Radcliffe from 1903 to 1923, recognized that the possibility of Radcliffe's becoming a college within the university was dependent on a larger endowment and the mellowing of attitudes over time.[16] When Ada Louise Comstock left the deanship of Smith College to become Radcliffe's first full-time president (1923-1943), the Radcliffe trustees had to agree to limit undergraduate enrollment to 750 and graduate students to 250. The April 16, 1943, Harvard-Radcliffe Agreement significantly changed the relationship between the two institutions by allowing Radcliffe students above the freshman year to enter university lecture halls and Harvard students to follow their professors to Radcliffe classrooms.[17] Provost and history professor Paul H. Buck, who engineered the measure largely because of World War II's demands on Harvard faculty, persuaded them "to adopt" an "ingenious device," in Conant's words. In exchange for most of Radcliffe's tuition receipts, Harvard agreed to provide all instruction to undergraduate women; and to forestall complaints by faculty who lost the extra compensation for teaching at Radcliffe while gaining a heavier student load, Harvard raised its own faculty salaries by about 20 percent. Once an opponent of coeducational classes, Conant "became slowly convinced that administrative awkwardness was too high a price to pay for the continuation of the prejudices of those who, like myself, wished Harvard to remain strictly a man's college." The formalization of "joint instruction" occurred in 1947; freshman classes merged three years later.[18]

Coeducational classes with Harvard enhanced Radcliffe's desirability as a college for women. Administering its own admissions policies until 1975, Radcliffe was even more selective than Harvard, because of the limited number of places for undergraduate women, determined by the 4:1 male-female ratio that existed until President Derek Bok raised it in 1972 to 2.5:1 (from 300 to 450 women). For example, Radcliffe admitted only about 18 percent of applicants between 1964 and 1974; Harvard's acceptance rate gradually declined, between 1956 and 1973, from 43 to 19 percent. During the same period, the active recruitment of students from a wider geographic area gradually transformed Radcliffe from a heavily commuter college into a more expensive residential one.[19] Opening an academic and residential Graduate Center in 1956, Radcliffe added two dormitories, Holmes Hall (1952) and Comstock Hall (1958), to Moors Hall (1949). In 1961 cooperative houses, named for president Wilbur Kitchener Jordan, opened. With housing available for most students, only about 100 students commuted. By 1958-1959, total undergraduate enrollment reached 5,587—1,105 at Radcliffe and 4,482 at Harvard; Radcliffe graduate students numbered 513 of the total graduate enrollment of 6,669. Growing cooperation with Harvard resulted in contributions from Radcliffe of $250,000 to each of two construction projects of the Program for Harvard College: the Loeb Drama Center and the new University Health Center.[20]

Nevertheless, both institutions viewed a closer relationship with some suspicion. Nathan Marsh Pusey, A.B. 1928, the first Harvard president (1952-1971) to have a daughter since Radcliffe's founding in 1879, indicated on several occasions that Radcliffe was of secondary importance to his obligations to Harvard and its alumni. For example, he declined the invitation to attend the November 3, 1956, dedication of the new Graduate Center at Radcliffe, which was then third, behind Columbia and Chicago, in conferring Ph.D.s on women. In his place, Pusey sent dean McGeorge Bundy. Since the date and time—3:00 P.M.—were circled on the letter of invitation with a notation, "Sat–U of Penna. Game!" it may be assumed that Pusey instead attended the football game across the river (which Harvard lost to Penn, 14 to 28). Joining dean Bernice Cronkhite at the dedication of the center which would later be named in her honor was astronomer Cecilia Payne-Gaposchkin, Ph.D. 1925, whom Harvard appointed a tenured full professor in 1956, the first woman to rise through faculty ranks.[21]

Within Harvard University, women, like Jews, were a noticeable minority and did not enjoy full religious and social inclusion in an educational institution still perceived as predominantly for white Christian men. In the 1950s, Radcliffe students charged Harvard "with being anti-feminist, unchristian and behind the times in denying them admission" to morning prayers in Memorial Church's Appleton Chapel. In response, Dean Sperry of the Divinity School cited "the opinion of members of the Board and senior Faculty who come to Prayers [that] the presence of these girls would subtly alter the nature of the service." Into the "very masculine" service, then usually attended by only 50 male students and faculty, "the girls would tend to introduce a Christian Endeavor or Epworth League tone to the occasion and it would undoubtedly be used for social purposes." In the front pews of the church, however, a group of women formed "a kind of 'court of the women,'" where they could "overhear the service through the screen." Women could also enter an outside door to a lounge and rest room in the church basement. Vigorously insisting that Harvard was not "now fully coeducational," Sperry thought any decision to admit women to morning prayers should be made by a special vote of the Harvard Corporation.[22]

Not to be deterred from participating in morning prayers was Helen Maud Cam, Girton College, Litt.D., Cambridge University 1936, who taught English constitutional history from 1948 to 1954 as a tenured professor and first holder of the Samuel Zemurray Jr. and Doris Zemurray Stone–Radcliffe Professorship. She had, "qua professor at Harvard, . . . always exercised her right to pass within the grill," noted Mason Hammond, Pope Professor of the Latin Language and Literature and master of Kirkland House (1945-1955). "The present system smacks of the existence of matroneia in early Christian churches; screened galleries for the ladies," Hammond wrote President Pusey. "If we have joint education in the classrooms, how much more should there be joint worship in the House of God, which should know neither slave nor free, male nor female." On September 26, 1955, the Reverend George Buttrick agreed that "none should be barred from services in a Christian church because of sex, rank or race." And three years later, almost all approved the harmonious music when women joined the choir of Memorial Church for the first time.[23]

OVERCOMING THE COLOR LINE AT HARVARD AND RADCLIFFE

Race and gender, once rather separate categories, became linked by the late 1960s and 1970s with the growing debate on student diversity. Neither Harvard nor Radcliffe made racial diversity a priority admissions goal in the aftermath of *Brown v. Board of Education of Topeka, Kansas* (1954). Instead, both colleges sought to recruit more of the under-represented groups—white ethnic and religious minorities like Catholics and Jews; public, rather than private school graduates; and those from disadvantaged socioeconomic backgrounds. When Frank S. Jones entered in 1950, he was one of just four African American freshmen in "the largest [class] in the history of the College," numbering 1,645, including 896 veterans. The first black manager of the almost all-white football team, Jones was also selected second class marshal. Then averaging less than a dozen per class, African Americans were usually assigned other blacks as roommates. Meanwhile, Harvard had appointed to the Faculty of Arts and Sciences its first African American, Ralph Bunche, who later served as the first black Overseer (1959-1965).[24]

Radcliffe students also welcomed the few African American women who enrolled. For example, the senior class of 1948 chose Elizabeth Fitzgerald Howard as president and class marshal. Because the Admissions Office evidently did very little to identify the private and public secondary schools that academically prepared them, most black students came to Radcliffe because of family connections, the influence of a particular teacher, or residential proximity to the college.[25] Despite the absence of a recruitment policy, Radcliffe was, according to Linda Perkins, "by far the leader in the number of Black women graduates among the Seven Sisters colleges." Between Alberta Scott, A.B. 1898, and the 1950 commencement, Radcliffe graduated 92 African Americans, 56 undergraduates and 36 graduate students.[26] Yet, there were probably not more than two, possibly three, blacks in any of the ten classes from 1955 through 1964.[27]

Harvard's commitment to recruiting racial minorities and more international students, many from Africa and the West Indies, came with Fred Glimp's tenure as dean of Admissions and Financial Aid (1960-1967). By 1964, about 25 blacks entered each Harvard freshman class.[28] Progress did not come fast enough for Harvard and Radcliffe students energized by the civil rights movement.[29]

Radcliffe students were among those questioning college admissions policies and supporting demands by Harvard's African American students, on April 10, 1968, for the proportional recruitment of black students and the establishment of an Afro-American Studies program. On November 26, 1968, the Radcliffe Ad Hoc Committee of Black Students met with the Radcliffe Policy Committee on Admissions and Financial Aid to insist on "much more active recruiting" of black students. The college affirmed its commitment "to seek more black and 'disadvantaged' students," including "some rethinking of past criteria for admission." On December 10 a small group of black women students sat-in at Fay House to emphasize the seriousness of their demands. Meeting that afternoon with the black students, Radcliffe president Mary Ingraham Bunting agreed with "a minimum target of 30 black students for the Class of 1973" but would not establish a quota. New Radcliffe recruitment initiatives involved visiting city schools in Boston, Philadelphia, and Brooklyn and sending letters to all National Achievement Scholarship Program semifinalists and to historically black Southern high schools. Radcliffe also sought to hire a black admissions officer the next year, following Harvard's 1968 hiring of its first black financial aid and admissions officer. Such recruitment efforts became essential to ensure Radcliffe's leadership in attracting the best women after Princeton and Yale became coeducational.[30]

On April 9, 1969, Harvard and Radcliffe students, led by the campus chapter of Students for a Democratic Society, took over University Hall; among their demands were the abolition of the Reserve Officer Training Corps (ROTC) on campus and student participation in recruiting faculty for Afro-American Studies. To settle the two-week strike that resulted when President Pusey ordered in the police, the Harvard faculty agreed, on April 22, to establish an Afro-American Studies program and to terminate ROTC. Under admissions director Chase Peterson 1952 (1967-1972), Harvard recruited over 100 blacks for the class of 1973. Between the classes of 1972 and 1975, the percentage of black students at Harvard doubled, from 4.24 to 8.68 percent.[31]

During the same period, the views of women students dramatically changed, leading to demands for the admission of more women, the hiring of more women faculty, and a closer relationship between Radcliffe and Harvard.

TO MERGE OR NOT TO MERGE RADCLIFFE COLLEGE WITH HARVARD: THE 1950S TO 2000

Because each college was independently managed by its own officers and trustees, an assistant to President Pusey reassured a member of the Corporation in May 1959, it was "absolutely untrue to say that the education of women at Radcliffe involves the misappropriation of Harvard funds." Moreover, women had proven their merit academically and also discredited "the Radcliffe myth" of "unattractive and unmarriageable" students, "since more than sixty per cent of the Radcliffe girls who marry choose Harvard men as their husbands."[32]

The image of Radcliffe College in the late 1950s suggested that it had achieved the best of both worlds as a coordinate college with Harvard. It seemed to be maintaining a unique identity as a separate college for women while providing entrée for its students into Harvard classrooms and most libraries. Radcliffe began to undermine its own identity, however, beginning in November 1957, when it formed more than half a dozen joint extracurricular activities with Harvard. The result of the *Harvard Crimson*'s inclusion of women staff members was the deterioration, if not the demise, of such publications as the weekly *Radcliffe News*. In addition, both the *Radcliffe Freshman Register* and the *Radcliffe Yearbook* were taken over by Harvard Yearbook Publications, which included women staff members. By 1960 only the Athletic Association and the Christian Fellowship survived among Radcliffe's original group of independent extracurricular activities. By 1968-1969, only the Choral Society remained a Radcliffe organization.[33]

In an essay entitled "Decline and Fall?" the *1960 Radcliffe Yearbook* recognized the cost of collaboration: "Old activities are either dying out, merging or fighting for existence while, paradoxically, new groups are formed in their stead." The college, "undeniably, at a turning point," had two choices: either "become an actual part of Harvard University," with "the absorption of its characteristics" being "inevitable if it is to conform to a university idea"; or developing "its 'identity'" within Radcliffe.[34]

President Bunting, who became Radcliffe's fifth president—and its first woman president with a Ph.D.—in February 1960, began to revive Radcliffe as a collegiate experience for women while pursuing even closer cooperation with Harvard. Nationally recognized for her research in microbial genetics, she also brought to her presidency experiences as dean of Douglass College (1955-1960), Rutgers University, and as a widowed mother of four children.[35] "Harvard Faculty meetings *are* different—more absurd and more wonderful than I ever anticipated," President Bunting said after receiving an honorary master's degree, making her a member of the Harvard alumni. She cultivated a cordial relationship with President Pusey, although, as in the past, he continued to send Harvard professors to represent him at Radcliffe commencements.[36]

President Bunting launched a personal "campaign against apathy" among Radcliffe students. In "The Decline and Fall of Radcliffe Apathy," the *1961 Radcliffe Yearbook* described her initiatives. To exchange information on undergraduate views and opinions, she formed the President's Advisory Board of five undergraduates and all the deans. Bunting's President's Fund provided financial support for new activities in each dormitory. Believing "that one must gain invaluable experience in college in order to organize one's life in a healthy integration of family and community," she promoted activities in the residential Radcliffe Quadrangle: thesis readings followed by discussions led by Harvard professors; "Living Room Talks" on students' future roles as wives and mothers; weekly seminars with Harvard faculty. Though "one cannot say Radcliffe has gone from apathy to booming activity," the yearbook concluded, "the Radcliffe spirit, long swamped in Harvard activity, has again begun to be heard." An incentive to extracurricular participation in college was the Admissions Office's decision to consider, in addition to grades, an applicant's high school activities. Another sign of involvement was the 1961 Student Government Association's debate over more frequent "open-open house" parietal hours (allowing male guests upstairs); each dorm then decided for itself. Parietal rules continued until the 1970s and the inauguration of coresidency.[37]

In 1961 Bunting established the Radcliffe Institute for Independent Study and introduced the Radcliffe House system. The three units—South House, North House, and East House—were later combined into two Houses. Currier House (1970), the first to be constructed on the House plan, consisted of four halls—Bingham, Daniels, Gilbert, and Tuchman. Expanding and improving

Radcliffe's physical plant was essential to a future merger with Harvard, much as a bride's dowry was to a marriage.[38]

In the 327th year of Harvard College and the 84th year of Radcliffe College, the first Radcliffe seniors received degrees, in English, from Harvard University; the class of 1963 would subsequently publish the first coeducational twenty-fifth anniversary report. Not until 1970, however, did Radcliffe seniors gain the right to join the commencement procession in Tercentenary Theatre. After the ceremony, women and men seniors received individual diplomas in, respectively, the Radcliffe Quadrangle and the ten Harvard Houses. In 1963 the Harvard Business School opened all programs to women, and the Harvard Corporation and the Radcliffe Council of its Board of Trustees agreed to merge their respective graduate schools. In 1966 Hilles Library opened to both women and men at the Radcliffe Quadrangle; Lamont Library (completed in 1949) finally opened to women in 1967.[39]

Despite Bunting's and Pusey's mutual commitment to the development of a closer relationship between Radcliffe and Harvard, they had first to overcome alumnae/i opposition and to weather the student protests and strikes from 1968 to 1970.[40] Some alumnae, encouraged over the decades to give money to Radcliffe because of its uniqueness, raised the question of why a merger with Harvard was needed. But the step promised greater educational gains and avoided continuing financial shortfalls. In spring 1970 "an experimental change in residence" began when 150 men from Adams, Winthrop, and Lowell Houses exchanged with 150 women from Smith, North, and East Houses. Further coresidency depended on the joint administration implemented by Radcliffe and Harvard's 1971 "nonmerger merger." Harvard became financially responsible for most of Radcliffe's daily operations in exchange for all of Radcliffe's undergraduate tuition fees and endowment income and gifts for current projects. Radcliffe still controlled its endowment, capital, and buildings and was responsible for administering and supporting the Radcliffe Institute, the Schlesinger Library on the History of Women in America (founded in 1943, it moved in 1965 to the former Radcliffe College Library), the Alumnae Association, and the Office of Alumnae Career Services. In 1971, after the Harvard Corporation voted Harvard degrees retroactively to all Radcliffe degree holders, alumnae from earlier classes became members of the Harvard Alumni Association. Indeed, the progress of women from the 1943 Harvard-Radcliffe Agreement to 1971's "nonmerger merger" might best be described as "coeducation 'by degrees'."[41]

After reviewing the 1971 Harvard-Radcliffe "nonmerger merger," a joint committee of faculty, administrators, alumni/ae, and members of the Governing Boards appointed by Radcliffe's sixth president, Matina Horner (1972-1989), and Harvard's twenty-fifth president, Derek Bok, concluded unequivocally in 1975 that

> any kind of quota, and in particular quotas based on race, religion or sex, are inconsistent with the role of an institution serving the public in a free society. Once it has accepted the task of educating both men and women, a university, dedicated as it is to intellectual freedom and dispassionate analysis, must provide equality of opportunity in admissions and intellectual development for both sexes.

Because "a sex quota" was no more "acceptable" than "other quotas," the committee recommended "a policy of equal access" for women undergraduates, a principle already endorsed by both Princeton and Yale, which began admitting women undergraduates in 1969. A new Harvard-Radcliffe Office of Admissions and Financial Aid would seek to recruit the best men and women applicants and bring their numbers toward parity.[42]

Within two years after a revised ratio of 2.5 men to 1 woman went into effect for the class of 1976, Radcliffe substantially diversified its applicant pool. To the class of 1978, it admitted 60 (9.3 percent) African American women and 18 (2.8 percent) Spanish-speaking women, which exceeded Harvard's admission percentages of the same groups: 97 (6.7 percent) African American and 37 (2.6 percent) Spanish-speaking men. Thus, the 567 women (a 1.8:1 ratio) admitted to the class of 1980 by the joint Office of Admissions and Financial Aid, the first year of equal access, promised to increase ethnic and racial diversity. Indeed, "equal access" for women combined with the aggressive recruitment served the overall goal of expanding diversity within Harvard.[43]

The next major step affecting undergraduate women occurred on May 11, 1977, when presidents Horner and Bok signed an agreement reaffirming Radcliffe's separate corporate status and defining their individual and mutual educational responsibilities. Radcliffe delegated to Harvard not only responsibility for undergraduate instruction but also management of the House system, with the Radcliffe president retaining a right of consultation. In 1977-1978 Radcliffe paid to Harvard all tuition money and almost one million dollars in endowment income and unrestricted financial aid funds. This agreement fell far short, however, of the complete "marriage" that Bunting, and probably first president Elizabeth Cary Agassiz, had hoped for by Radcliffe's hundredth anniversary.[44]

The long-anticipated marriage was finally consummated on October 1, 1999, under the Harvard-Radcliffe Merger Agreement signed by President Neil Rudenstine and Nancy-Beth Gordon Sheerr, chair of the Radcliffe Board of Trustees. The corporate demise of Radcliffe College and the merging of its assets with Harvard's had momentous consequences for alumnae and women undergraduates. In place of the college, a nationally important Radcliffe Institute for Advanced Study was to emerge, sustained by $300 million jointly contributed by both institutions; the remaining $50 million of Radcliffe's endowment would go toward undergraduate financial aid. The Institute's goals included supporting academic research and artistic endeavors and maintaining "Radcliffe's commitment to women, gender and society." On January 1, 2001, Drew Gilpin Faust, former University of Pennsylvania Annenberg Professor of History, took office as the new dean of the Radcliffe Institute for Advanced Study with tenure as a full professor of history in the Faculty of Arts and Sciences.[45]

Dropping "Radcliffe" from the title of the Harvard College Office of Admissions meant that beginning with the Class of 2004 only Harvard is directly involved in undergraduate education. As women undergraduates approach 50 percent of incoming classes, it will be a challenge for the dean of Harvard College—and the new university president, Lawrence H. Summers—to ensure that they experience the same opportunities as those enjoyed by men.[46] Throughout Radcliffe's history, many championed its separate identity, just as others applauded every step leading toward complete merger with Harvard. The ultimate success of total merger awaits judgments from another generation, which might well consider Paul Buck's observations on Harvard's history:

> At any fixed point of time something is being born while something is dying and something else is reaching full maturity. . . . Each generation has its own assignment to work out in terms of the forces, pressures, trends, factors, circumstances, resources, liabilities, legacies from the past, and horizons for the future . . . and the only judgment history can properly make is to measure the achievement in terms of the accompanying circumstances.[47]

Notes

1. U.S. Supreme Court Justice Lewis F. Powell, Jr., citing the Harvard College Admissions Program, 352-55, *Brief of Columbia University, Harvard University, Stanford University*

and the University of Pennsylvania as Amici Curiae, June 7, 1977 (in the Supreme Court of the United States, October Term, 1976, no. 76-811, *Regents of the University of California, Petitioner, v. Allan Bakke,* Respondent). President Neil Rudenstine, "Diversity and Learning," *The President's Report 1993-1995* (1996): "the 'measure of a class' consists largely in 'how much its members are likely to learn from each other—the real beginning of learning, both intellectually and emotionally.' The range of undergraduate 'interests, talents, backgrounds and career goals affects importantly the educational experience of our students,' because 'a diverse student body is an educational resource of coordinate importance with our faculty and our library, laboratory and housing arrangements'" (32-33, quoted from Harvard Admission Committee Reports 1963-64, p. 92, and 1964-1965, pp. 100-101).

2. James M. Landis to A. Calvert Smith, March 13, 1945, enclosing "a redraft" on Harvard admissions, Papers of President James Bryant Conant [hereafter, JBC Papers], file "As-Alk," Harvard University Archives [hereafter, HUA]. See a defense of affirmative action by former Harvard and Princeton presidents Derek Bok and William G. Bowen, *The Shape of the River: Long-Term Consequences of Considering Race in College and University Admissions* (Princeton, N.J.: Princeton University Press, 1998).

3. "It's another record breaker: class of 2005 chosen from a record pool of 19,009," April 5, 2001; and "FAS admissions yield is close to 80 percent," May 17, 2001, *Harvard University Gazette Online* at www.news.harvard.edu/gazette/2001. Since early action cases totaled 53.4 percent of those admitted, the acceptance rate for regular decision was 10.6 percent (Nicole B. Usher, "Acceptance Rate For Class of 2005 Hits All-Time Low," April 4, 2001, *Harvard Crimson Online* at www.thecrimson.com/news/article.asp? ref = 11685.

4. Richard M. Gummere to James B. Conant, July 22, 1940, and Conant to Gummere, July 1, 1940, JBC Papers, file "Admission, Committee on."

5. Julian L. Coolidge to James B. Conant, May 9, 1939, JBC Papers, file "Lowell House 1938-39."

6. Richard M. Gummere to Marcus I. Goldman, Feb. 5, 1948, JBC Papers, file "Aa-Alk."

7. McGeorge Bundy to President Nathan M. Pusey, May 29, 1958, Papers of President Nathan Marsh Pusey [hereafter, NMP Papers], file "Admissions & Financial Aids," HUA.

8. Dorothy Elia Howells, *A Century to Celebrate: Radcliffe College, 1879-1979* (Cambridge, Mass.: Radcliffe College, 1978), 89. Harvard Jewish students had organized a Menorah Society in 1906.

9. Barbara Miller Solomon, *In the Company of Educated Women: A History of Women and Higher Education in America* (New Haven, Conn.: Yale University Press, 1985), 143-45, Table 7A, Percentages of Jewish Students Enrolled at Five Eastern Women's Colleges, 1936-38, and Table 7B Radcliffe Freshman Admissions, 1934-37, based on a chart in file, "Admissions, the Jewish Problem," Nov. 1, 1937, in the Ada L. Comstock Papers, Radcliffe College Archives.

10. Maxwell Abbell to Dean of Admissions, Radcliffe College, Jan. 23, 1948, enclosing copy of a similar letter to David McCord, executive secretary of the Harvard Fund, JBC Papers, file "Radcliffe 1947-1948."

11. Richard M. Gummere to Marcus I. Goldman, Feb. 5, 1948.

12. Marcia Graham Synnott, *The Half-Opened Door: Discrimination and Admissions at Harvard, Yale, and Princeton, 1900-1970* (Westport, Conn.: Greenwood Press, 1979), chap. 3, "Harvard: Debate on Restriction, 1922." Rabbi Richard J. Israel, director of B'nai B'rith Hillel Foundation at Yale University, "Jewish Enrollment in Ivy League Colleges," Nov. 27, 1961, sent by Sidney Lovett to President A. Whitney Griswold, Dec. 11, 1961, Records of Alfred Whitney Griswold. President of Yale University (RU 22), box 6, folder 41, Manuscripts and Archives, Yale University Library, New Haven, Conn.

13. W. L. Sperry, Memorandum for the Chairman of the Board of Preachers, NMP Papers, file "Memorial Church 1953-1954."

14. Jerome D. Greene to Nathan M. Pusey, April 15, 1958; and Jerome D. Greene, letter, "Right of Rite," to the *Harvard Crimson,* April 12, 1958; news release, Wednesday, April 23, 1958; and News About Harvard [press clippings], April 19-May 2, 1958, NMP Papers, file

"Memorial Church, 1957-1958." Among the Harvard seniors signing a letter of protest to President Pusey were the first marshal of the class, the Student Council president, the *Crimson* president, the varsity track captain, the presidents of Signet and Spee clubs, Phi Beta Kappa members, both Henry Fellows, the Paine Traveling Fellow, a class agent, and the conductor of the Bach Society Orchestra: Adam Clymer, et al., to Nathan M. Pusey, April 14, 1958, NMP Papers, file "Memorial Church 1957-1958."

15. Hugh Hawkins, *Between Harvard and America: The Educational Leadership of Charles W. Eliot* (New York: Oxford University Press, 1972), 184-90; Howells, *A Century to Celebrate,* 89; George H. McCaffrey to James B. Conant, Aug. 11, 1937, JBC Papers, file "59 McA McD"; News About Harvard, April 2-19, 1958 [press clippings], NMP Papers, file "Memorial Church, 1957-1958." Charles Joseph Bonaparte, class of 1871, was Harvard's first Roman Catholic Overseer (1891). The same year, Harvard awarded an LL.D. to Bishop John Joseph Keane, first rector of Catholic University.

16. Howells, *A Century to Celebrate,* 20-22, 44, 37.

17. Ibid., 20-26.

18. James B. Conant, *My Several Lives: Memoirs of a Social Inventor* (New York: Harper & Row, 1970), chap. 28, "Coeducation in Fact If Not in Theory," 374, 377-80, 374-83; Howells, *A Century to Celebrate,* 26-29, 54.

19. Howells, *A Century to Celebrate,* 27, 29, 37. Harvard University, *Report of the Committee to Consider Aspects of the Harvard-Radcliffe Relationship that Affect Administrative Arrangements, Admissions, Financial Aid and Educational Policy* (Cambridge, Mass.: [Harvard University], Feb. 26, 1975), 5, HUA.

20. "Working List of Capital Needs," Sept. 1956, file "Radcliffe 1956-1957"; William Bentinck-Smith to Thomas S. Lamont, May 13, 1959, both in NMP Papers, file "Radcliffe 1958-59"; Howells, *A Century to Celebrate,* 27, 33, 86-88, 92.

21. Howells, *A Century to Celebrate,* 55, 62; W. K. Jordan to Nathan M. Pusey, Sept. [12], 1956, and Pusey to Jordan, Sept. 13, 1956, NMP Papers, file "Radcliffe 1956-57."

22. Sperry, Memorandum for the Chairman of the Board of Preachers, 1954.

23. Mason Hammond to Nathan M. Pusey, Feb. 22, 1954, NMP Papers, file "Memorial Church 1953-1954"; Harvard University News release to the Sunday Papers of Oct. 2, 1955, NMP Papers, file "Memorial Church 1955-1956."

24. Frank S. Jones, "A Half-Century of Change: Race, Admissions, and the Harvard Community," in *Yesterday, Today, and Tomorrow: The Harvard Class of 1950 Reflects on the Past and Looks to the Future,* ed. George S. Mumford (privately published by the Harvard Class of 1950 at the time of their fiftieth reunion: Travers Press, 2000), 135, 126-48. One of the other three black freshmen was Oscar DePriest III, who graduated *summa cum laude* and earned an M.D. from Harvard. All four African Americans were veterans. A son of David D. Jones, president of Bennett College in Greensboro, North Carolina, Frank Jones had attended Phillips Academy, Andover, for three years and then followed his brother David to Harvard. Frank Jones retired from MIT as Ford Professor of Urban Affairs. Ralph Bunche, a 1927 *summa cum laude* graduate of UCLA and a basketball player, earned a Harvard A.M. (1928), Ph.D. (1934), and LL.D. (1949). He was the first black to win the Nobel Peace Prize (1950). In 1952 he resigned his Harvard professorship in government without having taught.

25. "Elizabeth Fitzgerald Howard, 'Miss Radcliffe'," *Newsweek* (1948) and "Three Generations of a Black Radcliffe and Harvard Family," *Radcliffe Quarterly* (1984), in *Blacks at Harvard: A Documentary History of the African-American Experience at Harvard and Radcliffe,* ed. Werner Sollors, Caldwell Titcomb, and Thomas Underwood (New York: New York University Press, 1993), 301-9.

26. Linda Perkins, "The African American Female Elite: The Early History of African American Women in the Seven Sister Colleges, 1880-1960," *Harvard Educational Review* (Symposium: The History of Women in Education) 67, no. 4 (Winter 1997): 729; 726-29. Black women found it difficult to receive scholarships and were denied dormitory accommodations until the mid-1920s.

27. See the *Freshman Register, Radcliffe College Yearbook,* and *Harvard and Radcliffe Yearbook* for the appropriate years, from the class of 1955 to the class of 1969, Radcliffe Archives; Howells, *A Century to Celebrate,* 89.

28. Jones, "A Half-Century of Change," 141, 142, 135-42. From the admission of Richard Theodore Greener (A.B. 1870) in 1865 through the class of 1986, some 2,600 black men and women had enrolled as Harvard and Radcliffe undergraduates; see Caldwell Titcomb 1947, A.M. 1949, Ph.D. 1952, "A Note on the Black Presence at Harvard," Harvard University's 350th Celebration (1986), Harvard University News Office.

29. "The Color of Protest," *The Radcliffe Yearbook 1964* (Cambridge, Mass.: Harvard Yearbook Publications Inc., 1964), 167; 166-73.

30. The April 10, 1968, assassination of the Rev. Martin Luther King, Jr., sparked African American students to publish "Four Demands to '*Fair* Harvard'" in the *Crimson:* establishment of an endowed chair for a black professor; scheduling of "courses relevant to Blacks at Harvard"; the hiring of more black faculty in the tenure-ladder ranks; and the admission of black students in proportion to their percentage in the national population (Jones, "A Half-Century of Change," 144). Agreement resulting from the meeting on Nov. 26, 1968, between the Radcliffe Ad Hoc Committee of Black Students and the Radcliffe Policy Committee on Admissions and Financial Aid, Dec. 5, 1968; Mary I. Bunting, statement on the recruitment of black students, Dec. 10, 1968; and WB-S [William Bentinck-Smith] to NMP, Radcliffe Sit-In, Dec. 11, 1968, all in NMP Papers, file "Radcliffe 1968-69."

31. Jones, "A Half-Century of Change," 142-48. Harvard established the W. E. B. Du Bois Institute in 1975, and Radcliffe launched its Black Women Oral History project in 1976. See Richard M. Freeland, *Academia's Golden Age: Universities in Massachusetts* (New York: Oxford University Press, 1992), 173-76.

32. William Bentinck-Smith to Thomas S. Lamont, May 13, 1959, NMP Papers, file "Radcliffe 1958-59"; Howells, *A Century to Celebrate,* 27, 54.

33. *1960 Radcliffe Yearbook* (Cambridge, Mass.: Harvard Yearbook Publications, 1960), 40-41; Howells, *A Century to Celebrate,* 27, 29, 71-92. In 1977 Gay Seidman, 1978, became the first woman president of the *Harvard Crimson.*

34. *1960 Radcliffe Yearbook,* "Activities," "Decline and Fall?" 41; 40-41. News Release, Nov. 21, 1957, NMP Papers, file "Radcliffe 1957-1958." Some new groups were the Radcliffe Debate Council; the Radcliffe Shield, an honorary group formed by deans to serve as guides; the Radcliffe Forum; and the Radcliffe Union of Students; see Howells, *A Century to Celebrate,* 87, 89.

35. Radcliffe College News Release, June 1959, NMP Papers, file "Radcliffe 1959-1960." A Phi Beta Kappa physics major at Vassar College (1931), Bunting completed her master's and doctoral degrees at the University of Wisconsin (1934).

36. [Mary I. Bunting], handwritten note to Nathan M. Pusey, March 1, 1960, NMP Papers, file "Radcliffe 1959-1960."

37. *1961 Radcliffe Yearbook* (Cambridge, Mass.: Harvard Yearbook Publications, 1961), "Activities," "The Decline and Fall of Radcliffe Apathy," 43, 44, 45; 42-46, 49, 50-51; Howells, *A Century to Celebrate,* 89, 92, 115.

38. Howells, *A Century to Celebrate,* 29, 32-34, 54, 83, 133.

39. Ibid., 32-33, 54; Proposed Release: Morning Papers of Monday, Jan. 5, 1970, NMP Papers, file "Radcliffe 1969-1970." Prior to 1970, it did "not seem to the Corporation that it would be appropriate to have alumnae who have just received their degrees from the University marching in the Commencement procession with those about to receive their degrees." Instead, Pusey suggested that Radcliffe seniors ask to join the afternoon alumni procession in Harvard Yard. See Nathan M. Pusey to Roberta C. Mowry, March 30, 1966, NMP Papers, File "Radcliffe 1965-66."

40. In 1966 Harvard and Radcliffe students protested a campus visit by Defense Secretary Robert McNamara; in 1967, they protested a recruiter from Dow Chemical Corporation (Freeland, *Academia's Golden Age,* 173-76). On Dec. 12, 1968, Radcliffe women also sat-

in at Paine Hall in protest against the Vietnam War and the campus ROTC. The probation given to 17 Radcliffe students led to an April 28, 1969, "invasion of President Bunting's office" (Howells, *A Century to Celebrate,* 115-17). See also Morton Keller and Phyllis Keller, *Making Harvard Modern: The Rise of America's University* (New York: Oxford University Press, 2001), chap. 13, "The College," and chap. 14, "Crisis and Recovery," 290-338.

41. Proposed Release: Morning Papers of Monday, Jan. 5, 1970. See drafts and redrafts of reports of the Committee on Harvard-Radcliffe Relationships in NMP Papers, file "Radcliffe 1970-1971" and file "Radcliffe Merger 1970-71." Mrs. Carl J. Gilbert to Hugh Calkins, Aug. 14, 1970; Revised Report of Committee on Harvard-Radcliffe Relationships, Jan. 25, 1971; News Release, March 8, 1971; and 1971 Amendment to Agreement Between President and Fellows of Harvard College and Trustees of Radcliffe College, June 2, 1971, NMP Papers, file "Radcliffe Merger 1970-71"; Howells, *A Century to Celebrate,* 33-34, 30, 82, 115, 123, 125, 133. Helen Homans Gilbert 1936 chaired the Radcliffe Board of Trustees (1955-1972) and was acting president of Radcliffe (1964-65). The first woman Overseer from 1970 to 1976, she also chaired its board.

42. *Report of the Committee to Consider Aspects of the Harvard-Radcliffe Relationship that Affect Administrative Arrangements, Admissions, Financial Aid and Educational Policy,* 8, 9, 10, 19. See also "Equal Access Admissions," in *Harvard Almanac 1975: A Report to Alumni and Friends of Harvard and Radcliffe* 1, no. 1 (Cambridge, Mass.: Harvard University, Dec. 1975), 11, 13-14.

43. *Report of the Committee to Consider Aspects of the Harvard-Radcliffe Relationship that Affect Administrative Arrangements, Admissions, Financial Aid and Educational Policy,* Appendix 2, Harvard Admissions, pp. A2-1-A2-4; Appendix 3, Radcliffe Admissions, pp. A3-1-A3-7; Ethnic Diversity, pp. A4-5-A4-6; Economic Diversity, p. A4-6. Radcliffe's pool of applicants had 203 (6.8 percent) African American and 62 (1.8 percent) Spanish-speaking women. Harvard's pool included 293 (3.8 percent) African American and 159 (2.0 percent) Spanish-speaking men. Howells, *A Century to Celebrate,* 37.

44. Howells, *A Century to Celebrate,* 36-38, 121. Mary I. Bunting to Nathan M. Pusey, Dinner Meeting of the Radcliffe Board of Trustees, Nov. 16, 1966, NMP Papers, file "Radcliffe 1966-1967."

45. Under Linda Wilson, Radcliffe's seventh and last president (1989-1999), the college succeeded in raising $85 million of a $100 million capital campaign. Rosalind S. Helderman and Adam A. Sofen, "With Merger Sealed, Task Turns to Dean Search," Monday, Oct. 1, 1999; Joyce K. McIntyre, "Committee Creates Shortlist for Radcliffe Dean," Monday, Feb. 7, 2000; and McIntyre, "Dean Faces Myriad Challenges," Monday, April 3, 2000, all at *Harvard Crimson Online* at www.thecrimson.com/news/article.asp?ref=6692. Since the 1970s, affirmative action significantly increased the number of tenured women professors, from three in 1968-1969 to thirteen in October 1977 (about 3 percent) (Howells, *A Century to Celebrate,* 55, 57). Today, the number of tenured women had risen to almost 16 percent in the Faculty of Arts and Sciences.

46. Based on the 2,041 acceptance letters mailed in April 2001, "Women will comprise nearly 49 percent of the class, an unprecedented proportion" ("It's another record breaker: class of 2005 chosen from a record pool of 19,009," *Harvard University Gazette,* Thursday, April 5, 2001, at www.news.harvard.edu/gazette/2001). Even at 48.5 percent of the incoming freshman class, women still do not enjoy the same social opportunities as the men: they are not admitted to Harvard's independent social clubs (called "final clubs"), which the university considers to be "private." Nor will Harvard build them an all-women's center, a function once served by Radcliffe College, because doing so could be seen as discriminating against men. See *The Women's Guide to Harvard,* ed. Peggy Lim (published by the Harvard-Radcliffe Women's Leadership Project, 2002).

47. Paul H. Buck to James B. Conant, Nov. 20, 1952, JBC Papers, file "Administrative V.P. to Annual Report."

V.

COEDUCATION BY DEGREES
1941–2001

FEMINISM AND FEMININITY IN ALMOST EQUAL BALANCE

Andrew K. Mandel

At century's midpoint, Radcliffe College's leaders faced a dilemma of institutional proportions. Harvard, compelled by wartime necessity to mix women into its classrooms in 1943, soon found the arrangement efficient and surprisingly without objection among its notoriously stodgy alumni. Harvard's subsequent offer of permanent "joint instruction" in 1947 was at once joyous—gaining women access inside Harvard's gates had been Radcliffe's purpose since its inception in the 1870s—and frightening. Radcliffe officials worried that such an arrangement would eliminate Radcliffe's individuality, and ultimately its entire raison d'être. But by 1950 Radcliffe's leaders had refashioned their conception of the school's role. Radcliffe as an institution was more necessary than ever, its leaders argued, because it provided a space for women to nurture their separate identity within a mixed-sex environment. With this new theory in place—with coeducation not an admission of obsolescence but rather a new reason for Radcliffe to exist—the full merger of classes could move forward.

This equal-but-separate system, in which women would attend rigorous classes with the men at Harvard but be content with different social opportunities at Radcliffe, was unrealistic. Radcliffe's model of separatism bred latent resentment. Many female students found less and less reason to be cloistered at Radcliffe when increased excitement and opportunity, as well as the college's own educational and social directives, pointed toward further union with men at Harvard.[1] Some Radcliffe students began to abandon their alma mater and make their way into previously all-male sanctums. But in their quest for an integrated community, they had to learn new rules to gain entry; they had to balance their infamous intellectualism and self-described "feminism" with femininity in order to become, quite literally, "part of the club." The story of social integration and extracurricular merger at Harvard and Radcliffe shows how women tried to erase their in-between status as not-quite equals, and how they ended up erasing women's distinct voices in the process. Despite popular belief about total complacency during the 1950s, the silencing of Radcliffe students did not escape the notice and outrage of some campus watchers, but it was not until the 1960s that compromise bloomed into consciousness-raising.

SECOND-CLASS CITIZENS

Throughout its early history, Radcliffe was Harvard's neglected, precocious, younger sister—mocked in the pages of the *Crimson* and the *Lampoon* for unsightliness and mannishness. When joint instruction emerged after a series of negotiations in the 1940s, the Radcliffe administration was excited about finally gaining the stability of a contractually guaranteed professoriat, but its students were wary of integration into the traditionally off-putting Harvard community. In fact, the student-run weekly, the *Radcliffe News*, reported soon after the deal was struck that if it had not been for the war, the student body would have protested the move, citing a desire to maintain a realm for educated women unfettered by men. "Under ordinary conditions, most Radcliffe students are opposed to coeducation, not only because it would necessitate a long walk to Harvard, time-consuming and unpleasant during most of the Cambridge winter; but also because it tends to limit the freedom and spontaneity of classroom and round-table discussions."[2]

Three years later, the discomfort led to an assertion of women's rights. "Morale does not stay high nor enthusiasm for a given system of education strong when instructors always address their remarks solely to the men present and refer to themselves as 'Harvard instructors'—never as 'Harvard and Radcliffe'," student editorialists opined in a *Radcliffe News* piece titled "Radcliffe Is Annoyed."[3] In 1947, as more female students poured into Harvard lecture halls thanks to increased "joint instruction," assigned seating arrangements for men prevented women from sitting just anywhere—and, as the *Radcliffe News* noted, "acoustics become notably bad when one is squatting on the floor behind the last row of seats."[4] Female students were "embittered and frustrated" by the situation, noting that "no matter how fast they run between classes, they arrive to find the few seats that are theirs taken by the auditors. They pay their tuition, read their assignments and seldom cut lectures, but Harvard gets the seat." Even if Harvard was, as one dean put it, only "slightly coeducational," female students felt entitled to basic rights.[5]

LEARNING THE RULES

Though they clamored for seats in the classrooms, Radcliffe students knew that access to Harvard Yard did not connote equal opportunity. Some women called themselves "intruders" and "invaders," and they were known as such.[6] The first tenured female professor in Harvard's Faculty of Arts and Sciences, Helen Maud Cam, joined the History Department in 1948. Her appointment, the Zemurray-Stone chair, was financed by a grant to Radcliffe, not to Harvard. When Harvard officials refused to open the new Lamont Library to women in 1949, Radcliffe president Wilbur K. Jordan was satisfied that at least the larger Widener Library would be lifting all restrictions to Radcliffe students.[7] Asking for full and equal access to traditionally all-male institutions felt like a labor in vain. "The . . . habits and ways of thinking of centuries, which all involve a distrust in woman's thinking apparatus, are not easily broken down," the *Radcliffe News* explained. "Once women realize the futility of it all this clamoring for instruction will cease."[8]

Marriage loomed large in American society in the postwar era; spinsters and homosexuals both were scorned.[9] Each engaged senior at Radcliffe was presented with a ring of pink rosebuds at a June luncheon ceremony, and the first graduate to become a bride received a set of Radcliffe china. The first baby girl born to a member of the graduating class received a silver spoon and became the mascot of her mother's class. The class of 1948's ten-year anniversary survey showed that 93 percent of the class was married, averaged 2.3 children, and three out of four were "busy housewives."[10] Radcliffe students were not thinking about the years after graduation, adopting a "cross that bridge when we come to it" stance. The Radcliffe yearbook from 1953 explains this day-by-day mentality: "The Korean war has had a decided effect on us—not only in that many of us are getting married early because of the menace of the draft, but also in our general attitude of dealing with things as they arise, with little real planning for the future."[11] As Elaine Tyler May shows in a larger study of the period, marriage and domesticity became safe options in an unstable world.[12]

Student tea at Radcliffe, 1950, Whitman Hall (Radcliffe College Archives).

Radcliffe College officials encouraged their students to pursue the marriage route. In fact, in their ten-year anniversary survey, the class of 1948's greatest complaint was the lack of counseling, both vocational and personal.[13] The Harvard House system boasted faculty affiliates; Radcliffe dormitories were run by "house mothers," retired women unconnected with the networks that linked Harvard's seniors with their postgraduation employers. There was no official career advising at Radcliffe except for one interview during the last months of the senior year; the Appointment Bureau dealt largely with placements for summer jobs or temporary posts right after college. Those Radcliffe deans who did encourage academic pursuits were oriented toward Ph.D. work, which for women was stigmatized as producing loneliness and frigidity.[14] And though he told his students to finish college first, President Jordan's prescriptive messages regarding marriage were clear: "I should like to see you all married on the day after graduation."[15]

To be sure, with articles in the *Radcliffe News* every year featuring graduating seniors' vocational plans, students did not abandon the notion that any future was possible: "Some of us consider ourselves tomorrow's hope. Others just hope to be tomorrow's housewives," the yearbook editors wrote.[16] And, though officials clearly had their preferences about a woman's future, the college promoted the idea that every door was at least theoretically open. The Appointment Bureau frequently reported the various jobs secured by recent graduates—but the bureau collected most of its data only six months after graduation, before women generally had children, or when they were working to help put a husband through graduate school. The Radcliffe Appointment Bureau's director also recognized the serious costs of marrying: "employers seem to be more selective and, because they are more cost-conscious, are less willing to undertake the expense of training an employee who does not give some promise of continued success."[17] Since marriage connoted giving up full-time employment, all graduates could do was to find "the best solution within a rigid framework."[18]

"STRATEGIC POINTERS"

Radcliffe students may have complained about seating arrangements, but they also began to cast themselves as helpless, seductive, and unconcerned with schoolwork. When Harvard announced that women would not be permitted to enter the newly built Lamont Library, the *Radcliffe News* did not fail to notice the restriction. But a winning song in a college contest, to the tune of *South Pacific*'s "I'm in Love With a Wonderful Guy," illustrates the new Radcliffe shrug: "Tech men take us dancing in Boston / Dartmouth takes us to ski in Vermont / Yalies will wine us and Princeton men dine us / So who wants to get into Lamont?"[19] The *Radcliffe News* batted its eyes when Theodore Ropp, a visiting lecturer from Duke, offered the first few rows of his classroom to the "fairest flowers," his Radcliffe students. "Southern chivalry has become an exciting novelty in cold New England halls," the *News* wrote.[20]

It is hard to tell whether the women genuinely giggled and blushed at a professor's patronizing comments, or whether they grinned and bore the leers for the sake of a seat in lecture. Implying that the library was merely a venue to meet men—or, as the 1947 freshman issue of the *Radcliffe News* suggests, that classes were merely "date bureaus"—could have been a coping mechanism for discrimination.[21] Barnard sociologist Mirra Komarovsky's research in the 1940s and early 1950s showed that half of her surveyed pool of female undergraduates purposefully hid their intellectualism on dates and in school so men would like them.[22] Perhaps Radcliffe students were following the advice of elders like Barnard dean Millicent McIntosh, a guest on the NBC Lecture Hall on November 14, 1953: "I think one of the mistakes that young women who have been to college make is to expect to change their environment immediately to suit their own needs. . . . she can gradually win over her husband to giving her more freedom and more opportunity to pursue her own interests if she is sympathetic and tactful and does it gradually."[23] Rather than challenging an entire paradigm of gender roles, women searched vigorously for that "best solution within a rigid framework."

This search led Radcliffe students to pound home the importance of conspicuous femininity. In 1947 the *Radcliffe News,* "as a result of many requests," began a column to announce student engagements."[24] The 1950 Radcliffe handbook warned against wearing slacks, shorts, or blue jeans. "We know that beauty is only skin deep, but you don't have to look as though you lived only for things of the mind," the student handbook counseled. "Radcliffe girls ought to look like ladies; it is imperative that they be recognized as girls."[25] When students competed in the *Crimson*'s annual "Miss Radcliffe" contest, the goal seemed to be to change Radcliffe's image: "Socially, the 'did she go to Radcliffe or did a horse step on her face' is old hat, and 'why I would have guessed Wellesley' is the Harvard man's left handed compliment which we have learned to accept with good grace," the 1953 yearbook cheered.[26] Hyperfemininity was a way to attract attention and to gain acceptance and importance in the social community.

Indeed, the approach granted "feminine" women access to a previously all-male world and integrated them into the social world of Harvard. Suddenly, after "years of sneers," Harvard men were finding Radcliffe women attractive. "Former Aesthetic Nonentities Now Charm Harvard Eyes" read the headline of the full-page *Crimson* story on Radcliffe beauty in 1951.[27] Harvard men also found it easier to scoff at women's academic success, claiming that they were intellectual lightweights; women feverishly and blindly copied down every single word a professor uttered, Harvard men claimed, implying that women lacked the acute analysis necessary to discern truly important information. In a 1960 *Harvard Alumni Bulletin* story, Mark H. Alcott 1961 wrote a wry column about "galloping feminism" at Radcliffe, suggesting how women sneakily "infiltrated" their way into clubhouses without the men realizing it.[28] Men felt less threatened by "feminine" women in their midst—a crucial ingredient to the later merger of extracurricular activities.

A DELICATE BALANCE

But Radcliffe students, with their tradition of intellectualism, tried to maintain a balance between books and boys. In 1952, the college yearbook said that Radcliffe represented a perfect blend of the two.[29] The 1954 edition explained, "This more than slight bluestocking interest in the intellectual is ridiculed . . . but it is this interest that brought us here, and we intend to get our stockingsfull."[30] Indeed, there were some Radcliffe students who attempted to maintain their individuality and spurned affectations with their "green book bags, uncombed tresses [and] lipstick-less faces," though these "grinds" were often mocked.[31] More often, female students dressed with care and tried not to let fashion consume their lives. The 1954 yearbook pointed out, "Where else but Radcliffe would a girl in high heels, hat and fur coat be seen on a bicycle?"[32] This double identity led one Harvard professor to tell *Mademoiselle* magazine: "The Radcliffe girl carries feminism and femininity in almost equal balance. It's enough to upset anybody."[33]

Radcliffe students were in a double bind: they would betray their intellectual tradition if they did not get their "stockingsfull" of education, but both men and women measured the success of female students within a domestic context.[34] When author Rona Jaffe wrote her first successful book, *The Best of Everything,* the Radcliffe newspaper called the unmarried author "Miss Lonelyheart" and suggested that her smash hit had reaped the greatest reward, a slew of potential fiancés: "Big brown eyes, a Radcliffe degree, and a novel worth a speculated $150,000 have succeeded in projecting this self-styled 'bachelor girl' into a land of leisurely success and a daily tide of marriage proposals."[35] A headline in the *Crimson,* "'Cliffe-dweller Dwelling at Kirkland House Shatters Precedent with Dean's Approval," sounds like glass-ceiling breaking rhetoric but actually accompanies a story about Dorothea Hanson, an undergraduate who married a House administrator. "'I was going to teach when I got out of college,' the pretty Radcliffe girl said yesterday. 'But now I guess I'll just be a Kirkland House housewife'."[36] The Harvard administration also emphasized the degree to which women were "taking over" the campus. "I have been told that three out of every four Radcliffe graduates marry Harvard men," Harvard president Nathan M. Pusey 1928 said in 1953. "If this continues it is clear that it is only a question of time until Radcliffe takes over Harvard. Here is infiltration indeed."[37] The community conflated "infiltration," or social integration, with equality, and such eliding allowed women to see themselves "on solid middle ground."

In 1957 Harvard and Radcliffe agreed to allow joint extracurricular activities, a move previously stalled by Radcliffe administrators who feared that women would lose their sense of Radcliffe identity without separate activities. But many students were pulled toward Harvard; men's activities were more exciting, representing more opportunity and freedom. Why work for the *Radcliffe News* when you could write for the better funded, better respected, and more widely distributed *Harvard Crimson*? "If you were any good at all, then you didn't work for the *Radcliffe News,* you worked for the *Crimson,*" recalled Caroline G. Darst 1960.[38] With restrictions lifted, the *Radcliffe Yearbook* folded, and its staff joined the men at the *Harvard Yearbook.* The newly merged activities were proclaimed as entirely progressive: when WHRB allowed a female announcer on the air for the first time, *Harvard Alumni Bulletin* undergraduate columnist Mark Alcott proclaimed that man's "will to resist has gone." He concluded his article with the cheeky, if prophetic, "one can only hope that when the millenium [*sic*] comes and the two noble institutions become one, they will let us call it Harvard, rather than Radcliffe, University."[39] A *Crimson* photo feature similarly tried to suggest that, although women are "usually denied equality," the "'Cliffe girls play significant roles in College clubs." The page pictures two Radcliffe students playing with children, two students portraying brides in *Trial by Jury,* and two others singing and dancing; a final picture shows that "a few work for us" at the *Crimson.*[40] What a perfect encapsulation of "integration" in the 1950s: describing social "merger" in terms of women in sex-segregated functions—and calling *that* equality.

ROWBOATS AND BATTLESHIPS

These contradictions did not elude some Radcliffe observers, including students who felt there was greater strength in separatism. Throughout the 1950s, some students saw value in single-sex activities. The *Crimson* and the *Radcliffe News,* for example, discussed merger in 1952. "A battleship has a large deck, and there may be room yet. Besides, while one can always be the captain of an independent rowboat, there always will be storms, and the bigger the ship, the more comfortable the going," *Crimson* president Philip Cronin 1953 offered.[41] But *News* editor Patricia Arens ultimately declined the union after her demands for significant editorial control were denied. Recognizing the inferior status available for women in a Harvard organization, Arens planned to retort to Cronin that "an independent row boat is better than the lower deck of a battleship."[42] The leaders of Radio Radcliffe grappled over whether to merge with WHRB, which had recently moved to the FM dial and offered more reliable broadcasting. "To merge would probably mean the end of any individuality . . . maybe I'm just biased, but it really would take the spirit out of R2 if it became only part of WHRB," one student wrote to the Radio Radcliffe president in 1957.[43] "Unless a miracle does occur before I graduate next year, one of Radcliffe's few remaining claims to identity has vanished," wrote another in the club comment book.[44] Although they were never specific about the value of separatism, students articulated a concern about an intangible "spirit" or "identity" placed in jeopardy by the mergers.

Once groups did begin to unite, *News* writers wondered where that independent spirit, once associated with the entire college, had gone. "Perhaps the pride went with the struggle," lamented one columnist, noting that the student body no longer knew the words to Radcliffe songs but sang Harvard tunes with "great gusto." "Did the fall come with complacency?"[45] The editors of the *Radcliffe News*, witnessing club after Radcliffe club fold as its members joined with Harvard, asked former Radcliffe president Ada Comstock her thoughts on the developments. "Fortunate insofar as it gives our students the opportunity of working on projects of greater magnitude . . . unfortunate if it makes it less easy for Radcliffe students to show initiative and carry responsibility," Comstock replied in comments reprinted by the newspaper. "I should be sorry if the characteristic post for a Radcliffe woman in a Harvard-Radcliffe organization was that of assistant secretary."[46] But indeed that is what happened. Some boasted that the *Harvard Yearbook* in 1958 became the first Harvard publication to elect a woman to its executive board, but the two female officers of 1959 held glorified secretarial positions: head of publicity and clerk to the corporation.[47] *News* writers recognized the false sense of equality achieved by Radcliffe students.[48] The *News* editor wrote a column for the *Radcliffe Quarterly* about the change: "Harvard has no place in its social system for women except as the invited guests of its men. . . . Moreover, the overpowering discrepancy in numbers places a Radcliffe candidate for office or simply for membership in a merged club at a decided disadvantage."[49] This private and public outrage at the status of the integrated, inferior Radcliffe woman represents a protofeminist impulse in the late 1950s, but it was not enough to keep the newspaper alive. The student body voted to make subscriptions no longer compulsory, cutting into the *News*'s budget. Its editors tried to sustain the operation under a new name, the *Percussion*, and aimed to "engender a spirit of liveliness and interest and to counteract the current Radcliffe apathy."[50] But the *Percussion* too folded, in 1959.

Being a student at Radcliffe after 1943 meant negotiating two impulses: the feminist and the feminine. "Feminism," as a term, was fairly out of vogue by World War II, reserved for old-fashioned suffragists. Yet there was a separatist sentiment, to have "a room of one's own" to develop and grow, that grew out of the ghettoized nature of Eastern women's colleges. When Harvard-Radcliffe transformed into a largely coeducational community after a series of politically slippery negotiations, students struggled to maintain a balance between their bookish, independent roots and the new hyperfemininity sweeping American teenage-dom in the late 1940s and early 1950s. To maintain a strict separatist community would have been too frigid during this period of "togetherness." At the same time, women actively recognized the futility of attempting to secure an equal place at the table. Instead, with cultural directives guiding the way toward domesticity, they schooled themselves in femininity. The subsequent transformation of the Annex bluestocking into the Radcliffe girlfriend disarmed masculine insecurities and ended up providing women access to a once-exclusive community, though the question of status within that community created a rift between separatists and integrationists. The integrationists prevailed at Radcliffe—until the rise of activism reminded women that they were being treated as inferiors and convinced them that things did not need to stay that way.

Notes

1. It is, of course, tricky to recreate a social landscape. As Helen Lefkowitz Horowitz discusses in *Campus Life*, there are many different kinds of students: grinds, rebels, extracurricular queens. Every student has a different story, and interviewing alumnae about four-decade-old events is not always effective, especially since hindsight often clouds memory. My conclusions stem from an extensive examination of period printed materials; I have focused on public expressions of social attitudes through newspaper and yearbook articles. When I refer to "Radcliffe students," then, I am often allowing newspaper writers to speak for their classmates. Given that my argument discusses women who integrated into Harvard's social sphere, the *Radcliffe News* writers who pursued a separatist activity were even less influenced by these forces, but enough to prove my points amply. My sense of the era has been enriched by limited recollections of alumnae who wrote their memories in reunion books and other published sources. As Alison Lurie's chapter in *My Harvard, My Yale* demonstrates, diaries may unlock extensive private articulation of frustration during this period. See Helen Lefkowitz Horowitz, *Campus Life: Undergraduate Cultures from the End of the Eighteenth Century to the Present*

(New York: Alfred A. Knopf, 1987); Alison Lurie, "Their Harvard" in *My Harvard, My Yale,* ed. Diana Dubois (New York: Random House, 1982).

2. Anne Chisholm, "The Annex and Coeducation," *Radcliffe News,* April 23, 1943, 2.
3. "Radcliffe Is Annoyed," *Radcliffe News,* April 20, 1946, 2.
4. "Radcliffites Become Harvard D.P.'s," *Radcliffe News,* Oct. 31, 1947, 1.
5. "Does Joint Instruction Mean No Seats?" ibid., 2.
6. "Women Invade Hallowed Territory Via Thorny Path of Coeducation," *Radcliffe News,* Freshman Issue, 1947, 3; "Joint Instruction Flourishes in First Year: Begun During Wartime, Female Invasion Is Here to Stay," *Harvard Crimson,* May 6, 1948, 3.
7. Radcliffe College Council, Minutes, 2 May 1949, Radcliffe College Archives [hereafter, RCA].
8. Ann Ginsburgh, "Law School Advances Traditional Arguments for Refusal of Women," *Radcliffe News,* Nov. 2, 1945, 1.
9. For a period polemic against spinsters, see Ferdinand Lundberg and Marynia F. Farnham, *Modern Woman: The Lost Sex* (New York: Harper & Brothers, 1947); for commentary, see Elaine Tyler May, *Homeward Bound: American Families During the Cold War Era* (New York: Basic Books, 1988), 94-95.
10. "Ten Years Later: A Statistical Report on the Class of 1948," *Radcliffe Quarterly* 42, no. 3 (Aug. 1958): 22.
11. *Radcliffe Yearbook, 1953,* 75.
12. May, *Homeward Bound,* 107.
13. "Ten Years Later," 23.
14. Jean Darling Peale, "Carving a Niche," *Harvard Crimson,* June 5, 1984, 13.
15. Wilbur K. Jordan, Opening of college speech, Sept. 28, 1949, WKJ Papers, RCA.
16. *Radcliffe Yearbook, 1955,* 75.
17. Wilbur K. Jordan, *Reports of Officers Issue, 1957-58,* 73.
18. Wilbur K. Jordan, *Reports of Officers Issue, 1959-60,* 64.
19. "We're the Girls," *Radcliffe Student Handbook, 1952-53,* 108.
20. "Radcliffites Become Harvard D.P.'s," 1.
21. "Women Invade Hallowed Territory," 3.
22. Mirra Komarovsky, "Cultural Contradictions and Sex Roles," *American Journal of Sociology* 52 (Nov. 1946): 184-89.
23. Millicent Carey McIntosh, Transcript of NBC Lecture Hall (1953), Millicent McIntosh Papers, Barnard College Archives, New York City.
24. "Column To Announce Radcliffe Engagements Inaugurated by News," *Radcliffe News,* Feb. 28, 1947, 3.
25. *Radcliffe Student Handbook, 1950-51,* 100.
26. *Radcliffe Yearbook, 1953,* 65.
27. Stephen O. Saxe, "Radcliffe Survives Years of Sneers," *Harvard Crimson,* June 20, 1951, 3.
28. Mark H. Alcott, "The Challenges and Rewards of Galloping Feminism," *Harvard Alumni Bulletin* (March 5, 1960), "Gender at the Gates" Display files, HUA.
29. *Radcliffe Yearbook, 1952,* 7.
30. *Radcliffe Yearbook, 1954,* 23.
31. Janet Ross and Hope Mourousas, "Fadcliffe," *Radcliffe News,* Oct. 5, 1957, 2.
32. *Radcliffe Yearbook, 1954,* 18.
33. Nancy Lynch, "Radcliffe College," *Mademoiselle* (Oct. 1951), 6, "History (1950-59)" file, RCA.
34. Wini Breines discusses the sociological perspective of the double bind: "boys and girls were formally treated as equals in the midst of a tendency toward increased differentiation of their future roles." Winifred Breines, *Young, White and Miserable* (Boston: Beacon Press, 1992), 34-36.
35. "Miss Lonelyheart," *Percussion* [Radcliffe student publication] (Feb. 6, 1959), 3.
36. "'Cliffedweller Dwelling at Kirkland House Shatters Precedent with Dean's Approval," *Harvard Crimson,* Sept. 29, 1950, 1.

37. "Eight Honored by Radcliffe," *Boston Herald,* Dec. 4, 1954, 3.

38. Shari Rudavsky, "Struggling with the Dilemmas of Inequality and Feminism," *Harvard Crimson,* June 3, 1985, 11.

39. Alcott, "Challenges and Rewards."

40. Photo feature, *Harvard Crimson,* Jan. 17, 1958, 3.

41. Philip M. Cronin to Patsy Arens, Nov. 6, 1952, *Radcliffe News* Records, RCA.

42. The "lower deck" quote appears in an apparent draft of the letter. Arens ended up being less saucy, but still firm: "I am sure now that we both understand that neither ship needs a lifeboat." Patricia Arens to Philip Cronin, Nov. 8, 1952, *Radcliffe News* Records.

43. Sally Boyle to Stephanie Walser, Aug. 25, 1957, Radio Radcliffe Records, RCA.

44. Radio Radcliffe Comment Book, March 30, year unspecified, Radio Radcliffe Records.

45. "Happy Birthday Alma Mater," *Percussion* (Feb. 20, 1959), 1.

46. Vyola Papps, "Comstock Urges Girls to Assume Leadership," *Percussion* (Nov. 14, 1958), 1. Comstock's full response appears in her personal papers. See Ada Louise Comstock to *Radcliffe News,* undated correspondence, Ada Louise Comstock Papers (81-M287), RCA.

47. "Radcliffe Helps on Harvard Yearbook," *Percussion* (April 10, 1959), 4.

48. Ross and Mourousas, "Fadcliffe."

49. Vyola Papps, "Have We Reached the End of This Road?" *Radcliffe Quarterly* 42, no. 4 (Nov. 1958): 15.

50. "Percussion Elects New Editors," *Percussion* (Feb. 6, 1959), 1.

Midcentury Memories

MEMORIES OF LIFE AT RADCLIFFE

Ruth Hubbard

I came to Radcliffe in September 1941, three months before Pearl Harbor. That year and the next were the last gasp of the old Radcliffe, at which Harvard and Radcliffe classes were entirely separate but taught by the same and, of course, entirely male Harvard faculty.

Try to imagine: Harvard professors would give their lectures to a large class of Harvard "men" and then come and repeat the same lecture to a much smaller class of Radcliffe "girls." Radcliffe, at that point, was about one-quarter the size of Harvard. Especially in the sciences (I majored in biochemical sciences), Radcliffe classes were much smaller than the same classes were at Harvard.

The senior professors—Harvard's "great men"—were less than thrilled to have to repeat their lectures at Radcliffe. The lower-rank faculty members who sometimes were detailed off to teach the introductory science courses at Radcliffe instead of teaching Harvard students, felt even more déclassé.

Let me say at once that I think Radcliffe's pride in the fact that we were taught entirely by Harvard faculty was ill conceived. The fact that Radcliffe never developed a faculty of its own, as did Barnard, was a terrible mistake. We were second-class, or indeed nth-class, citizens from day one. And this certainly affected our day-to-day experience as students—and especially in the sciences, where myth still has it that women are "by nature" less adept than men.

For example, in my freshman year I took introductory chemistry. The class was taught by a young man who felt he was being exiled to the boondocks. Fresh from Dartmouth, he always wore his green blazer and dripped disdain. Our lab instructor was a woman graduate student. She was nice enough, but soon married a fellow graduate student and decided there were better things to do with her life than study chemistry at a place where her husband might some day get a job but she never would.

During the summer following my freshman year, I went to summer school. This was the beginning of the three-term, year-round schedule that operated throughout the war so as to give the men a chance to get their undergraduate degrees before being drafted into the armed services. But that summer, it was still also summer school and therefore coed.

I took introductory biology. The zoology part was taught by Professor Frederick Hisaw, one of the elder statesmen in the Biology Department, whose research focused on the hormones of the female reproductive system. Soon news trickled down to us (I don't remember by what route) that he resented having to teach a coed class because it forced him to clean up the humor in his lectures. His teaching fellows included women as well as men. So, it isn't that there weren't any women around. Just that they were second-class citizens, clearly not even to be considered for a faculty post.

Sometimes it was worse than that. Some 50 years later, the woman graduate student who mentored me during my undergraduate research project told me that one of the younger biology professors had refused to let her enroll in his course. She could audit it but could not take part in class discussions or take the exam and, therefore, could not get credit. And, since the subject matter was close to her thesis research, she did exactly that. Why didn't she report it to the Radcliffe graduate school? All she could say, all those years later, was that she just accepted the situation; but that very fact is an indication of the prevailing atmosphere.

A final story. That summer—still 1941—I also took the first semester of introductory physics in summer school. It was a large class, taught in the largest lecture hall in the physics building, and somehow not until the semester was almost over did I wake up to the fact that I and another woman were the only two females in the course, and she didn't go to Radcliffe. Of course, that meant that the second semester of Physics 1 would not be given at Radcliffe but only at Harvard that fall.

I presented my problem to the professor who taught the course and asked whether I couldn't just continue with the other (male) students and take the second semester at Harvard. He didn't see why not but suggested I talk to the chairman of the Physics Department. He, too, saw no reason why that shouldn't work but felt we needed to get approval from the Governing Boards of Harvard and Radcliffe, so that I could get credit for the course. We petitioned, and both Harvard and Radcliffe refused. (A year later classes were merged, but that fall it was impossible for one lone Radcliffe student to attend a class at Harvard.) At this point the Physics Department came up with the idea that if I could persuade three Radcliffe students to take the second semester of Introductory Physics before they had had the first semester, the department would send us an instructor to give the lectures and another to teach the lab, and that's what we did. It was extremely nice of them, but turned out to be a not very adequate course—nothing like the course the men had that fall at Harvard.

And that's the point. My undergraduate science experience was not anything like the experience the men had—at least not until after my second year, when our classes were merged. That is why I was not the least surprised at a table in Margaret Rossiter's *Women Scientists in America,* in which she arranges, in order, the colleges and universities at which the women scientists listed in the 1938 edition of *American Men of Science* (the annual compendium of distinguished American scientists) had received their undergraduate degrees.[1]

At the top of the list stands Mount Holyoke, with 99 entries in *American Men of Science.* Next in order come Barnard (87), Smith (79), Vassar (73), and Wellesley (70); then four large coed universities; then Bryn Mawr (44) and Goucher (42); then six coed state universities; and finally, at number 18, Radcliffe with 27 entries, barely over a quarter as many as Mount Holyoke. In fact, Mount Holyoke had nearly as many distinguished chemists to its credit as Radcliffe had scientists in all fields.

From the beginning, Radcliffe apparently failed to recognize that, by proudly offering its students the privilege to sit at the feet of Harvard's Great Men, it lost the opportunity to awaken in us the expectation that we might some day become Great Women.

Toward the end of my last semester, I got into a conversation with my physical chemistry professor. The Great Man in the field had gone off to the war, as had many Harvard professors, and this was a younger man from a state university in the Midwest. He asked what my plans were and I told him I was going to take a war-related research job and, after the war, go to graduate school or medical school. "If you go to graduate school," he said, "don't go to Radcliffe. You should not go to a school where you have no chance to become a faculty member." I must admit, I was too unaware to understand what he was telling me and, in the end, did come back to Radcliffe. But, that's another story.

It is worth remembering that, during the debate that preceded the decision to admit the first six women to the class that entered Harvard Medical School in the fall of 1945, the opponents of this radical plan—physicians all—argued that to admit women was to go against "the fundamental biological law that the primary function of women is to bear and raise children."[2]

Times have changed. But we need to recognize that such nonsensical claims about "woman's nature" get revived again and again. And also, that women and men will not truly be equal at Harvard until students are as likely to encounter women as men at all levels of the faculty and administration and until the images that look down upon us from Harvard's hallowed walls include many more women than they do now.

Notes

1. Margaret Rossiter, *Women Scientists in America: Struggles and Strategies to 1940* (Baltimore, Md.: Johns Hopkins University Press, 1982).
2. Mary Roth Walsh, *Doctors Wanted: No Women Need Apply* (New Haven, Conn.: Yale University Press, 1972).

Nostalgia and Promise

Ann Karnovsky

When I was a student at Radcliffe in the late 1940s, early 1950s, there was a rumor that president James Bryant Conant, on his visits to Harvard clubs around the country, would declare that "Radcliffe may be coed, but Harvard isn't." We met the remark with amusement rather than resentment.

My freshman year at Radcliffe was the last time professors left the Yard to teach the same course at Radcliffe at 11:00 A.M. that they had taught at Harvard at 9. History I was my only experience with the system, and it was an unhappy episode for me in several ways. It was, in fact, the first and last time I found myself in a single-sex class. I had been at coeducational schools all my life, and what I perceived as factual nit-picking seemed a speciality of some women in the class. Those who had been at traditional women's schools took excellent notes but seemed focused on minutiae and grades. Of course, it was the nature of the first-year survey courses, not the single-sex aspect, that was so galling. I was at a complete loss when asked to draw a freehand map of the route of the Visigoths across northern Europe; and to find that the hour exam counted for a considerable portion of course credit came as a shocking surprise. But another survey course, this time at the Fogg, and coeducational, also dwelt on detail. Did a given slide depict the east pediment of the Parthenon, or the west? It became clear that the surest way to differentiate the interiors of various cathedrals was to make note of which way the chairs were facing.

When one made it past the surveys to electives, the academic world brightened. There were of course "gut courses." I remember a senior in Briggs

Hall jealously guarding entry into Roman Law, a course with famously little reading material. In my chosen field of Social Relations, it was a golden age of Henry Murray, Robert White, Robert Sears, and B. F. Skinner. The latter, in line with his theory of behavior modification, also gave a course containing only a brief mimeographed syllabus. A reunion classmate has reminded me that Clyde Kluckhohn did not want women in his anthropology classes because he would be unable to tell dirty jokes. I did take a class with him and was shocked to hear a risqué joke. Needless to say, I still remember it while the Navaho kinship system is long forgotten.

I had been drawn to Radcliffe in part after reading an article by Talcott Parsons on the role of women. I must admit that another draw was a memorable luncheon I shared with a member of the class of 1949, when I was trying to finalize my college decision. We sat at a long table at Le Petit Gourmet in Chicago, and Marian regaled me with tales of dates with everyone from the cox of the Harvard crew to first-year law students. As we got up to leave, one of the middle-aged women who had shared our table said, "Girls, we could not help overhearing your conversation. Tell us, do you need college boards to get into Radcliffe?" In the Midwest Radcliffe had not yet made it onto the map of prestige colleges, and now, 50 years later, it has vanished from the map again.

There were a few advantages Radcliffe had over Harvard. The most highly regarded was the honor system as it pertained to examinations. The story of a woman graduate student who was allowed to take an examination with Harvard men if she promised not to go to the bathroom is no myth. The reason behind this ridiculous-sounding demand was that at Harvard proctors routinely followed the men to the toilet, whereas at Radcliffe we were free to leave the examination room at will and alone, leaving our blue books temporarily in official hands.

No description of the 1950s at Radcliffe would be complete without mentioning the concept of "gracious living." It was a prescription for behavior appropriate to females: no smoking on the street; no shorts to be worn in the dining rooms—not just in the service of modesty but because bare legs might ruin the finish on the wooden chairs. In the dorms we were sometimes invited to 10:00 P.M. chats in the House mother's quarters, where crackers and guava jelly were staples. Coffee was served in demitasses in the living room, an elegant touch but frustrating to those who needed a caffeine jolt for a late night of studying. Many of us smoked then. I for one took it up to look more sophisticated. There was a "smoker," a room on each floor of the dormitory, but we usually sat on the threshold of our rooms with our cigarettes extended into the corridor. Thirty years ago I was having dinner at Eliot House and explained our smoking behavior to a student. "Oh, that's why they're called 'smokers'!" she said.

Undergraduates today say that the Health Service is not always responsive to student needs. In the 1950s the Radcliffe Infirmary was notoriously inadequate. I knew a very unhappy student who went to the infirmary and was asked what was wrong. She answered through her tears that she didn't know. "Well, come back when you do," she was told. A good friend reminded me of a week she was forced to spend in the infirmary because, when seeking some relief from a headache, she mentioned that the children where she had her room-and-board job had measles. Although my friend had had measles and was now immune, the nurse insisted that she stay in quarantine, not even allowed to send for library books lest they become contaminated. Needless to say, she never went near the infirmary again. No wonder that my kit of medical samples, packed by my physician father when I went off to college, was popular. Emperin #2 was especially helpful for cramps.

In the early 1950s Radcliffe was indeed separate but unequal, and it sometimes bothered us, especially in small ways. Harvard Houses served ice cream every day; we had it only on Sundays. Harvard still had "biddies" to clean the rooms and staff to serve. Of course, tie and jacket were mandatory in the Houses at meals. Meanwhile, back at the Quad, Radcliffe women worked "bells" (the switchboard), washed dishes, set the tables, and served in the dining rooms. Harvard men, because of postwar space shortages, were "crowded" four to a suite, sharing two bedrooms, a living room that often had a fireplace, and a bathroom. In the Quad, many so-called emergency doubles originally meant for one person now accommodated two. A whole floor of perhaps 20 women shared one bathroom, with two toilets, four washstands, and two baths or showers. It certainly was an unequal situation, but resentment of our lack of privacy did not include resentment of Harvard. We just wished that Radcliffe would improve conditions. (Guess what? Conditions were not improved until men moved into the Quad, and even then, not immediately.)

Parietal rules also differentiated Radcliffe and Harvard. If we left after dinner, we had to sign out saying where we would be, and we had to return by 1:00 A.M. Freshman year we were allowed only 15 "one o'clocks." I still regret being unwilling to spend one of those precious one o'clocks with my parents and, of course, ending the semester with several to spare. Arriving even a few minutes late brought down the wrath of the House Committee. In those days the college took its role *in loco parentis* very seriously, and so did our parents. While we chafed against the rules and found them extremely annoying and inconvenient, they also served to bolster our superegos. They could be a soft way to end a date with someone overbearing or boring, and they could also strengthen our resolve not to give way to temptation. When Mary Bunting abolished the one o'clock sign-in, she made it clear that it was unfair that women could not spend the night at the lab if an experiment warranted. I do not think she realized what confusion she was creating for women who had no intention of spending the night at the lab.

Radcliffe women all rode bicycles to classes in the Yard, or to the library, which is now the Schlesinger. Neither rain, nor snow, nor dark of night could keep these hardy souls from their appointed rounds. It was only with the advent of the stronger sex in the Radcliffe Quad that the shuttle bus made its appearance. But to be honest, we rather liked riding our bicycles or walking briskly with our green bookbags. We made fun of the Jolly-Ups, when women could invite men to dances at the Quad, but we understood the truth of the Radcliffe song: "Wellesley has a muddy lake, muddy lake,/But Radcliffe has its weekends all week long." We were airily dismissive when young men told us they could be taking out Wellesley girls if only they had a car.

There were certainly inequities, and petty annoyances did weigh on us, but when it came to the really nasty inequalities, we were amazingly nonconfrontational. Being banned from the newly built Lamont Library, specifically meant for undergraduate use, was a true slap at Radcliffe, but it never occurred to us to protest. Harvard Law School and Harvard Medical School had just opened to women but, when making career plans, we were cautioned to perfect our typing skills. One classmate wrote in our 35th reunion book: "It is astonishing how accepting we were."

Since the days of the Annex, Radcliffe women wanted to be accepted into Harvard College on an equal footing with men, soaking up the vaunted intellectual atmosphere, sharing in the richness of extracurricular life, and being part of a long and illustrious tradition. That was the dream, but it took more than a century to become reality. Those of us who graduated in 1952 found ourselves midway on the path from a separate college, and a separate identity, to full integration.

Throughout life we gain new identities, often at the expense of losing old ones. In our day, when a woman married, she changed her maiden name.

There were other crises of identity when we became mothers, or divorcées, or widows. At our fiftieth reunion, some feared that we had lost our identity as Radcliffe women. If our collective dream, set forth so long ago, was to be an integral part of Harvard at last, then what we wished for has been achieved. We may want to cling to our old identity, especially since the new one is so vague, but we will surely adjust in time. Perhaps we will hyphenate our names, Radcliffe-Harvard, or more likely, Harvard-Radcliffe; perhaps eventually we will identify with the Radcliffe Institute. It is important to realize that whatever the future brings, our memories are valid and comforting, and we should accept our nostalgia as an appropriate response to change.

10,000 MEN OF HARVARD

Eva S. Moseley

Ten thousand men of Harvard
Want vict'ry today,
For they know that o'er old Eli
Fair Harvard holds sway;
So then we'll conquer old Eli's men,
And when the game ends we'll sing again,
Ten thousand men of Harvard
Gain'd vict'ry today.
                    —Harvard football fight-song

There were no men, except some professors, at Mount Holyoke, so after four years of famine, I looked forward to a relative feast at Harvard when I began graduate study there in 1953. Was the ratio 10:1, 20:1, 100:1? It was, at any rate, a lot of men per woman, especially in the Graduate School of Arts and Sciences, where I had come to earn a degree in Sanskrit and Indian Studies. In those days I wasn't thinking in feminist terms about why there were so few women, but in female terms about possible friends, admirers, lovers. Sometimes there was a steady stream—literally, when one admirer came in the door of my rooming house, 52 Irving Street, as another was leaving. But so many men meant what it always tends to mean: some friendships, some less-than-wonderful sex, being pursued by those I didn't care for, longing for those who didn't care for me—or who did but were committed to other women.

I was not a self-defined feminist till the early 1970s. My aim while in graduate school was to learn Sanskrit so as to read the *Upanishads* and other texts in the original, but for personal, "spiritual" reasons more than scholarly, professional ones; when I thought of working, I imagined being someone's assistant, a man's, perhaps my (eventual) husband's. I wanted marriage and children and probably did not long for a solo, stellar career because of the situation I had grown up with: my mother had a career (as a couturier—she was more than a dressmaker) and to a large extent neglected her children, and my parents were divorced when I was 14. My father worked too, but my mother was the one with the vocation. So I was evidently looking for the opposite of what I had known, and surely Harvard, with its 10,000 men, was a likely place to find one essential ingredient.

There were many places to look for men while learning Sanskrit grammar and its wonderful script—a syllabary rather than an alphabet, called *Devanagari* (City of the Gods). Because the Sanskrit library, in room A on the top floor of Widener Library (where it still is and where Professor Daniel H. H. Ingalls taught elementary Sanskrit) was too small and quiet, and the Widener reading room too big and distracting (with a constant shuffle and buzz of chairs, whispers, footsteps), I came to frequent the Harvard-Yenching Library, then in Boylston Hall, which also held some of the books I needed: on Buddhism, on Chinese poetry. There I met Peter and other budding scholars of East Asia.

Peter became a friend, a sort of little brother. In his family in Taiwan he was the first-born son and so a little big shot, but here the arrogance to which he was trained mingled uncomfortably with a wistful sense of inferiority. He was not going to marry a Chinese woman, he told me repeatedly, but he worried about his ability to satisfy a Caucasian wife. Unable either to agree or reassuringly disagree, I just listened with interest and sympathy to such endearing and repellent frankness. From Peter I first heard of ginseng; he told me with great relish that it not only is used to restore women's health after childbirth but also is considered to be a potent aphrodisiac.

Peter shared an apartment at 367 Harvard Street. The building, with its bow windows, is still there, probably still full of students. He invited me for supper and I watched him stir-fry Chinese cabbage in a cast-iron frying pan: some oil, soy sauce, a pinch of sugar, a few moments with a spatula and it was done. It was a revelation. I'm not sure I had ever eaten Chinese food before and certainly had never seen it prepared. The term "stir-fry" was then unheard of and most American cooks boiled cabbage.

Peter's family was among those Chinese who had migrated to Taiwan from Fukien Province late in the Ming Dynasty. Sandwiched between the indigenous Taiwanese, whom he looked down on, and the recently arrived Kuomintang (who came over with Chiang Kai-shek in 1949, when the Communists won the civil war), whom he hated, Peter was full of bitter thoughts and doubts about his future. He hated the Japanese too, as these "ocean dwarfs" had occupied his homeland before and during World War II. Yet his dissertation was about the creation of the Japanese Imperial Army, so he likely had the same sort of love-hate connection to things Japanese as I do to the German language, having been thrown out of Austria by the Nazis for being Jewish. (My parents and brother and I arrived in New York early in 1939; we were among the relatively few lucky ones.) In 1957-1958, I sweated over the tortured English of Peter's first draft, spending many hours editing and still others trying to get him to clarify what he meant to convey.

In the introduction to his dissertation, he thanks two professors especially, Edwin O. Reischauer and Benjamin I. Schwartz. About Reischauer particularly he can hardly say enough: "He permitted me to intrude upon him in his office, to seek his advice or have him listen to my views. . . . he always bore with my brashiness [*sic*] and listened patiently to my ideas." These effusive thanks were surely deserved, for it took great patience to deal with Peter, brash and humble, superior and needy as he was. He gave me my due very briefly, listing me among the three friends who "helped me to express my thoughts in English more effectively."

For me, Peter didn't figure as a man, and there were others like that as well. Though I cooked in my room quite often, sometimes I'd go to Harkness Commons, the graduate dining hall renowned for its Bauhaus architecture and its terrible, but cheap, food. There I met various chaps while lining up for supper, among them a classics student named Marc.

Along with elementary Sanskrit and other courses on India, I was trying to keep up my Greek with a course on *The Republic*. When Marc found out that I was having trouble with Plato, he invited me to his rooms on Farrar Street so he could help me with the Greek. He was probably in his thirties but already an old fussbudget. As I held his copy of the book, one of my sweaty fingers left a smudge in the margin. Clucking accusingly, he hurried to find an eraser and made the page pristine again. Why were we using his *Republic* rather than mine? I don't know, but the fact that he couldn't wait to clean up the book till I'd left made him as distasteful to me as the smudge was to him. By mutual if silent consent there were no more Greek lessons, but he did take me to lunch at Henri IV (pronounced *à la française*), an elegant and very French restaurant in a wood-frame house in Harvard Square. He was a regular there and was known as Monsieur Marc.

But there were other chaps who did figure as *men,* or who I thought might, or who thought they might. The International Student Center was on Garden Street, in a building later devoted to Transcendental Meditation and now part of the Longy School of Music. My housemate Sylvia Slotnick, then called Pinky, and I went to a mixer there and got mixed up with three charming gents from the British Commonwealth: John from England, Neville from Australia, and Ken from Canada. Neville was the best looking of the three and as I recall a rather simple, direct sort, a scientist. Going home on a bitter cold night once, I met him near Oxford Street coming from the lab. He wore no coat, only a tweed jacket, and when I remarked on his meager dress, he showed me between shirt buttons that he wasn't wearing an undershirt. He was warmer than I with all my warm layers. Neville and I must have dated a bit because I recall his saying goodnight at the foot of the stairs at 52 Irving Street. I was wearing my new red leather jacket from Ohrbach's, so new that it creaked as he embraced me. "Get rid of the jacket," said Neville with a last friendly peck, but I didn't, and it was my son who wore it to tatters three decades later.

But Ken was the one who appealed to me the most, and I more or less threw myself at him. He was, I think, flattered but full of doubt. We did some necking once in his room in one of the older graduate dorms on Oxford Street—till his roommate appeared, to Ken's embarrassment and relief. He made sure it didn't happen again. There was perhaps a little regret—after all, I was there and willing—but he didn't like being unfaithful to his fiancée, who was not there.

My international brigade also included an Egyptian whom I found baffling, a world-weary philosopher from El Salvador, one or two fellow refugees, and a barrel-chested European gent who invited me to his room on Broadway, put on a record, and got me to dance with him. It felt artificial, awkward, annoying. He evidently expected the rest to follow and was amazed and contemptuous when, instead of succumbing, I extricated myself and escaped. My heart was pounding with (as I interpret it now) both fear of someone strong enough to pursue and subdue me if he chose and anxiety caused by my own hubris at saying no to a man. His attitude seemed to be: How can you be so stupid as to turn down such an offer from *me?*

I was heartbroken for a while over Robert, a freshman who lived in the garret of one of the big houses on upper Irving Street. His older brother, Paul, had a room in number 50, Pinky's side of our double rooming house. He and

Pinky were an item for a time, while I hankered after Bobby, who had just graduated from High Mowing School in New Hampshire and was blond, guitar-playing, not exactly handsome but somehow romantic. Bobby was unsure of what he wanted to do with his life—appropriate enough for a freshman—but he was quite sure that he did not want to be romantically involved with me. I consoled myself, sort of, with Guido, a law student who lived down the hall. There was no real feeling on either side, though.

So I was ready for the would-be major romance of my two years at GSAS, which began one warm spring evening as Pinky and I were wandering about the Old Yard. We sometimes fed the squirrels there, and once, when I was wearing a dress mother had made of denim striped black, brown, and gray, a squirrel jumped up on my skirt for a moment, evidently mistaking me for a tree trunk. This evening, though, we paused near Hollis Hall, one of the (then all-male) freshman dorms. Someone called down from an upper window and he soon appeared, an excruciatingly hand-some—or so I thought then—young man, John. He was from Kansas City and, like Bobby, four years younger than I.

He was evidently attracted; I was smitten. But there wasn't much to it, partly because he had a serious girlfriend at Radcliffe. John later sent me a photo of himself with an older man, whom I take to be his father, striding down what is presumably a Kansas City street, both looking quite at home and entitled. Perhaps it was this quality, along with his triple-barreled name—in those days Jews, at least those I knew, tended to make do with just two names—and, of course, the golden hair and good build and handsome face that captivated me, though I wasn't conscious of it then: that air, and indeed fact, of belonging to a dominant class, which, like most Jews almost anywhere then and as refugees here, my family and I had to do without.

There were only a few encounters, but I continued to carry something of a torch for him, and we carried on some sort of a correspondence, probably a sporadic and lopsided one. There was even talk of going to Ireland together one summer; I recall shopping for a drip-dry blouse at Macy's, one that would go with everything. I had the blouse for years and a recipe for Irish soda bread that John gave me, but nothing came of the trip.

Then in 1957, when he was still an undergraduate, I visited Cambridge and we spent part of an afternoon together, walking around Harvard and down by the river. There we encountered John Finley, whose course on *Oedipus Rex* I had taken in the spring of 1954. John knew him too. Finley was walking his dog, just then running free, and as we chatted, he twirled the leash and hit himself in the face with it. It made me wonder whether it is typical of performers—and Professor Finley was definitely a performer—to be quite self-possessed, in control, in front of an audience but awkward in an individual encounter.

Even more than Professor Finley's leash, what made the afternoon memorable was that John told me—and he was as kind about it as he could manage—that he was about to marry his Radcliffe fiancée. This goodbye was devastating, even though I had thought that I neither expected nor even imagined any sort of life together for John and me. A friend was doing research at Houghton Library, and I was due to meet her at 5:00 when it closed. This was lucky, as she held me together. We went to see the movie *Giant,* and I found it soothingly distracting for most of its long length, till there was a wedding and my own pathetic reality came flooding back. But I got over John soon enough and, except for the continuing friendship with Peter and despite my many years of working at the university later on, that was pretty much the end of my flirtation with Harvard men.

How typical were my views and expectations of men at Harvard? They were to some extent typical of the 1950s. Much as I detested the political timidity and general conformity of that decade, I was typical in my assumption that *la difference* is of ultimate significance in relations between the sexes, division of labor, and everything else. Even Betty Friedan did not yet subscribe to the feminism she revealed a decade later. In my honors thesis at Mount Holyoke I had explored relations between men and women in the *Laws of Manu,* the Hindu social code, and found ample support for my views: *la difference* with a vengeance, one might say. So I was not ready to learn much from the evidence my male acquaintances presented me with.

Did it matter that these were Harvard men? I could have gone to Johns Hopkins, which also taught Sanskrit and also had admitted me. Would my experience with men there have been any different? I doubt it. I would have brought with me the same memories and desires, and the elite and male sense of entitlement of most academic men was surely the same at Hopkins. It took the salutary upheaval of the women's liberation movement to shift my point of view, like that of so many others, toward the conviction that the common humanity of the sexes counts for much more than the differences.

INTEGRATING WOMEN AT OXFORD AND HARVARD 1964–1977

Marie Hicks

In February 1969 an article in an Oxford undergraduate magazine proclaimed: "No more hungry stares across the Bodleian."[1] For years Oxford's women and men undergraduates had studied together in this central university library during the day before returning to their single-sex colleges at night.

In the same month, in the same year, in the same situation, but in a different country, dozens of Harvard and Radcliffe undergraduates were writing to Mary Bunting, president of Radcliffe College, to lobby for coresidence in the Harvard and Radcliffe Houses, residential units modeled on the Oxford colleges. "For the sake of the Radcliffe girl caught in between the Harvard and Radcliffe communities but part of neither," wrote one Radcliffe undergraduate, "I urge you to support the proposed merger with Harvard and plans for coed living."[2]

In 1969 coeducational housing was not a new issue in either England or America. The newer "redbrick universities" and the University of London had opened many of their colleges to women during the 1960s, and coresidence had come to many private institutions in the United States by the 1960s. But Oxford and Harvard joined the coresidential trend hesitantly, after all of their peers had done so. Oxford established coed colleges in 1974, three years later than its traditional rival, the University of Cambridge. Harvard went partly coresidential in fall 1971, a crucial, tumultuous two years after Yale and Princeton, and even then integrated only in stages, completing plans for coed living in 1972. Not until the late 1970s did Oxford and Harvard begin to admit women according to the same criteria as men, abolish quotas, and award similar scholarships.

Ironically, the sharpest criticism of coresidence came from the women of Oxford and Harvard universities. By the time coresidence was being seriously considered in each institution, the five women's colleges of Oxford were significantly opposed to immediate coresidence, and Radcliffe College, the coordinate women's college of Harvard University, also had substantial factions who feared that the benefits women could accrue from coresidence and closer integration with Harvard would not outweigh the negatives attendant on the change.

Though far from homogeneous in position or outlook, the women's colleges displayed a hesitancy and fear that reveal important aspects of the crucial period of transition for women in elite institutions. Their dissension makes clear that many important changes for women had more to do with institutional concerns than with higher ideals of women's rights. Studying the women's colleges' widespread, vocal, and organized dissent permits a greater understanding of why and how Harvard and Oxford went coed when they did and of what the change implied for women at different levels in each institution.

WORLDS UNTO THEMSELVES: THE OXFORD WOMEN'S COLLEGES

In the University of Oxford, the presence of women was a comparatively new development. Whereas men had studied at Oxford since the Middle Ages, women had been allowed in—and then only within limits—when pioneers gained access to some Oxford lectures in the late nineteenth century and residential halls opened for women students in 1878. Gradually gaining access to parts of the university after that point, women students and teachers nonetheless had to wait until 1920 before they were granted degrees for their work and study. And the petitions of the women's societies for the abolition of strict limits on the number of women in the university succeeded only in the 1950s. Though possessing highly qualified faculty, and students who on average were even more successful in university examinations than the men students, the women's societies were not finally recognized as real colleges of the university until late 1959. After their quotas were lifted and their status assured, the women's colleges took loans and embarked on a series of building projects and a period of expansion in order to bring more women to Oxford.[3]

Remarkably, as the five women's colleges were finally coming into their own, less than four years later a men's college began seriously talking about going coed. In 1964 a notoriously conservative member of one of the oldest men's colleges initiated the first discussion of accepting some women along with men. He felt that women students should be given the chance to benefit from male tutors, though his college, of course, should not open its faculty positions to women by the same reasoning.[4] Thus New College, founded in 1379 by William of Wykeham, broached a desire to allow a quota of women students into the college with letters to the university vice chancellor and to all the colleges, and with a long article in the university magazine expounding the virtues of the plan for women.[5]

The five women's colleges were taken aback. In the same year that New College proposed coresidence, a major university commission made up of five men and two female dons and chaired by Sir Oliver (later Lord) Franks began investigating questions about the future size and shape of the university. Though the commission declined to make plans for coresidential Oxford colleges, it took extensive written and oral evidence from all the colleges touching on the subject of women's future place in the university.[6] Three of the heads of the five women's colleges spoke to the commission. The least averse to New College's plan, the principal of Somerville College, Dame Janet Vaughn, wrote to the Franks Commission saying, "I do not attach much importance to the value of shared residence. . . . [but] The quickest and cheapest method [to increase the number of women] would be for some of the men's colleges to take some women and reduce the number of men." She added, however, that such coed colleges must be open to women on the faculty and administrative levels as well or else be "unbalanced communities." She concluded by stressing that coresidence was only an expedient: if money could be secured to expand the existing women's colleges or even to found an entirely new coed college, those would be better options.[7]

Lady Mary Ogilvie, the principal of St. Anne's College, disagreed. In speaking to the Franks Commission she restated and reinforced her opposition to integrating the Oxford men's colleges:

> I am not against mixed halls of residence. What I am against is a men's college taking even a fairly large handful of women and then grafting it onto

what is essentially a male society. . . . they would remain an appendage to the college. There are centuries of tradition at the men's colleges of an all-male community. There would also be a predominance of men dons and I think it would be exceedingly unlikely there would ever be a woman warden [the top administrator in a British men's college]. This would be a case of women implanted into a men's society.[8]

In the statements of the women's colleges against coresidence, no aversion to the idea of coed living emerged, but a fear predominated that coresidence and its attendant closer integration of women would be detrimental to the gains women had made and might yet make in Oxford. Principal Ogilvie synthesized a main concern of the women's colleges by pointing out that women's concerns in a men's college could not be as accepted or as important as they had been in all-women's colleges, whose raison d'être was to improve opportunities for women. "Grafting" women onto centuries-old, consciously masculine traditions would put the women in a minority position in colleges where members were not as attuned to or concerned with issues of gender discrimination as the women's colleges were. She also highlighted the concern that women academics and administrators would not be accepted into men's colleges as easily as students and would not be on an equal footing with men once there. Because the predominantly female-staffed women's colleges had deliberately served as niches for women to enter into the Oxford faculty, this was extremely significant. By preferring qualified women candidates to men, they allowed women university teachers to constitute a higher percentage in Oxford than they did nationally, even though on the student level the situation was the reverse.

The third woman principal who gave evidence, Lucy Sutherland of Lady Margaret Hall, also pointed out the problems of making a coresidential college by simply adding a quota of women to a men's college: if coed colleges were to be, they should be so from their founding, with the number of men and women "roughly equal" and "women playing a full part rather than forming a small appendage to an essentially male institution."[9]

The Franks Commission agreed that if a few colleges went mixed, the other men's colleges, in an effort to compete, would also rush to go coed, robbing the women's colleges of their applicant pool. For this reason, the Franks Commission recommended a different course of action for increasing women's numbers: the women's colleges should endeavor and be helped to expand further, creating between them the equivalent of a student body of a sixth women's college.[10]

The organ for university opinion, the *Oxford Magazine,* lamented the failure of the New College plan and, ignoring the concerns of the women's colleges, stubbornly claimed that they had "put the interests of the women's colleges *before* the interests of the girls."[11] Some glibly accused the women's colleges of willfully hindering women's interests in Oxford after furthering them for almost a hundred years. Most also ignored the fact that the New College plan had floundered due to lack of support within New College's governing body, not because of the women's colleges.[12]

After New College dropped the idea of going mixed, the topic of coresidence lay relatively dormant for five more years. Ominous rumblings began as the University of Cambridge began to discuss coresidence. In 1970 when several Cambridge men's colleges announced that they would admit women within two years, one Oxford men's college quietly formed a committee of men's colleges interested in becoming coresidential. In early 1971 this group remained underground, refusing to bring up their interest at the Conference of Oxford Colleges so that the issue could be discussed. Fearful that the inclusion of the women's colleges in the debate would shape or hinder their plans, the 16 interested men's colleges resolved to keep quiet until they had come up with a definite plan for gradual implementation that would abide by the university's belief, which came mainly from the recommendations of the Franks Commission, that change had to be gradual so as not to hurt the women's colleges and thus the university.[13]

When the women's colleges were notified about the committee and its mission, the interested men's colleges assured them that any change would be orchestrated so as not to demolish the women's colleges by taking away their best applicants and forcing them immediately into competition with wealthier, more prestigious men's colleges. Tiring of such limitations, however, one or two men's colleges made national headlines by considering going coresidential independently of the committee's plans.[14]

Immediately the women's colleges expressed alarm that the plans would simultaneously fail to protect the interests of women in the university and also run the women's colleges into the ground, depriving Oxford women, and especially Oxford women faculty, of their traditional advocates and sanctums.[15] Because of their lower prestige and income, the women's colleges would not be able to compete for good men applicants, who expected larger scholarships as students and higher salaries as faculty. As the principal of St. Hilda's, the largest women's college, pointed out when asked about finances by the vice chancellor, "If academic quality, actual or expected, attracts hard cash, hard cash is a considerable help in building up academic quality. . . . Our yearly budgeting remains a sustained feat of tightrope walking. . . ."[16] Because of the youth of the women's colleges and their beginnings as women's societies that became real colleges only in the late 1950s, they were in no position to compete with the men's colleges. "In my experience," she told the vice chancellor, "the main—almost the only—reason that women undergraduates give for thinking that the colleges should go mixed is that the men's colleges are so much richer and can provide so many more amenities in consequence."[17]

The women's colleges also had little reason to want to take in men students: on average, women's degree examination results were higher than those of most of the men's. The Norrington Table, which ranked the Oxford colleges in order of the performances of their students, consistently counted the five highly selective women's colleges near the top. It was generally assumed that in the event of coresidence, all of the best women students would choose to go to former men's colleges, and therefore the men's colleges that went mixed would be doubly blessed: they would get the best women applicants as well as the best men applicants, who would presumably be more attracted to a coed college. Meanwhile, the women's colleges would get the dregs.[18]

From the first serious talk of coresidence in 1965 to the actual planning stages in 1971, the five women's colleges of Oxford generally remained strongly against the idea. Though some in their ranks offered qualified support to the idea of men's colleges taking in women, their principals almost unanimously agreed that coresidence would have a negative effect on the faculties, staffs, and even students of the women's colleges. One woman don wrote in the university magazine that if one looked beyond the boundaries of women as undergraduates and thought "instead about women in general, and their place in society as a whole, and above all their career opportunities, then it seems to me we should be far less sanguine about the prospect of mixed colleges."[19] However, the formation of committees of the numerous men's colleges interested in coresidence reduced the women's colleges to a small protest group. Comprising only a fifth of the 25 Oxford undergraduate colleges, and an even smaller fraction of the 39 colleges in the university, the women's colleges lacked sufficient representation in the university's structure to be able to deal with the men's college committees on equal terms.

A COLLEGE WITHOUT A FACULTY: THE TROUBLE WITH RADCLIFFE

At Radcliffe the issue of coed living for students was inextricably tied to the issue of a Harvard-Radcliffe merger. Women's closer integration into the older, predominantly male Harvard college and university structure became, as at Oxford, a more contentious issue than coresidence alone. Unlike the Oxford women's colleges, however, Radcliffe was handicapped by a lack of autonomy: it had always hired Harvard faculty to teach its classes.

Radcliffe women had been, by degrees, allowed into classes with men since 1943. A wartime agreement let Radcliffe women fill the empty spaces in the men's classrooms in order to conserve university resources. However, strict quotas limited Radcliffe admissions. In the late 1960s, the median Scholastic Aptitude Test scores on both the math and verbal sections were higher for accepted Radcliffe applicants than for Harvard's applicants.[20] It was widely acknowledged in the university that the much larger Harvard classes accepted men students who would not have passed the rigorous standards the university imposed on Radcliffe's admissions, but the university justified the practice with the argument that educating a greater number of men was more socially and economically desirable than educating equal numbers of men and women.

When Mary Ingraham Bunting became the president of Radcliffe College in 1960, she devoted herself to bettering the position of women at Radcliffe and Harvard. She launched the Radcliffe Institute in 1960 to aid women who sought to fulfill high aims in the academic and professional sphere, remodeled the Radcliffe dormitories on Harvard's collegial House system, and built a new library for undergraduate women.[21] But as early as 1965, President Bunting ran into the problem that Radcliffe's student body was not allowed to expand to meet the growing demand of qualified women for a Radcliffe education. The dean of Harvard College told her that further increases in Radcliffe's student body could not be justified unless Harvard's also grew; otherwise, the women would drain away university resources intended for men. Bunting was instructed to freeze current admission rates at one Radcliffe student to every four Harvard undergraduates until Radcliffe's agreement with the university was renegotiated. She therefore began to believe that the best way to increase women's opportunities in the university was to try to make women more a part of Harvard.[22]

In a letter to Harvard's president Nathan Pusey, Bunting stated that she "had begun to wonder whether Radcliffe would not now be able to work more effectively for women's education if it were a unit within the University," and that she now believed "that the discussion will not be as disturbing as I, and various [Radcliffe] trustees, at first, feared." Bunting asked that a committee be set up to report on merger within the next few months. She noted, however, that "Women's education can not be properly managed without concern for its special features. There is ample evidence that it is not always sufficient to open existing educational opportunities to women. . . . For this fact to be recognized by Harvard would carry far more weight than for it to be argued by Radcliffe."[23]

Advancing the concerns of women required bringing them into the power structures of already well-established and respected institutions. Mary Bunting ardently desired a merger that others feared would "submerge" Radcliffe and hurt women's interests in the university because she believed that women would actually wield more influence if they were more integrated and not in an isolated stronghold at Radcliffe. She felt that the condition of Radcliffe women not really being "full members of Harvard" could be rectified only by making Radcliffe students *into* Harvard students. Merger, she claimed, would give women "a legitimate voice in Harvard policies and procedures in a way that has never been true before."[24] By integrating Radcliffe into Harvard's structure on all levels—administrative, faculty, and student—Bunting thought women would be able to set their own educational goals and make changes from within the university.

Not surprisingly, Bunting earnestly declared her view of merger "as fulfillment for Radcliffe."[25] As she would frequently tell newspapers and conferences, "I believe our society will never be truly open to women until our top universities are, and I would not want to see Radcliffe stand in the way of this."[26] Bunting's strong conviction that merger was beneficial influenced her stance on coresidence. Amid growing student unrest and demands for reform, President Pusey stated staunchly in December 1968 that there could be no coresidence until all undergraduates were under one administration.[27] Mary Bunting's views on coresidence after Pusey's announcement worked in tandem with her strong desire to effect a merger.

She later explained to a parent, "My first reaction to the idea of coeducational Houses was quite negative but I've been convinced partly by the arguments and by our students and partly by the experiences of other colleges that the step is *probably* a good one."[28] When addressing a group of alumnae in 1969, the year coresidence and merger were seriously considered, Bunting told them, only half-jokingly, "for this awkwardness, I blame Yale! . . . had the word not gotten all the way from New Haven to Cambridge that they were planning, at Yale, to let women live right in the Yale colleges," Harvard might not have felt it necessary to go coresidential at that time.[29]

After Pusey insisted on the connection between merger and coresidence, Radcliffe found itself under student pressure to merge so that coresidence could occur. Pleased by the attention merger was now getting, albeit for somewhat disconnected reasons, Mary Bunting gladly responded to overtures from the university that the administration and Faculty of Arts and Sciences would now welcome a proposal of merger, though they would not initiate one. At a meeting of the Radcliffe Trustees in February 1969, she proposed that the Radcliffe Council initiate discussion with the President and Fellows of Harvard College, "with a view to merging the two institutions," as Pusey had asked. He wanted Radcliffe to initiate any discussions to show that it desired merger as a whole.[30]

All but one of the Radcliffe Trustees assented to initiating discussions, but that lone trustee came down firmly against even entering into discussions, saying, "it would be an irreversible error to remove the potential that Radcliffe offers. . . . I think coeducational housing should be added to the already available options. Coeducational instruction has worked without administrative merger. I hope that we can have a merger of interests and not a dissolution."[31] The trustee was concerned that Radcliffe was already committing itself to a merger just by entering into discussions, and she noted that she had received calls from alumnae who strongly agreed with her view. Soon after, she joined the committee formed by the Radcliffe Alumnae Association to investigate the idea of merger and the full extent of its implications for Radcliffe—the Committee to Study the Merger, which became the voice of the many Radcliffe women who believed their college could better serve women if it remained autonomous.

The dissent of the well-organized Radcliffe Alumnae Association was comparable to that of the Oxford women's colleges in several important respects. The governing bodies of Oxford women's colleges and the Radcliffe Alumnae Association both represented mature women with close ties to their universities. Members of these groups remembered how each university's commitment to the education of women had been firmly isolated in its colleges for women. Both the women's colleges and the Radcliffe alumnae were also very interested in changing the treatment of women throughout the course of their lives, not just when women were younger and their life-patterns more easily mirrored those of men students. Both groups concerned themselves more with women's treatment in a society where academic and professional achievement were male oriented, and they felt that assenting to the students' and the universities' ideas of progress would result in women being forced to live even more by rules set by and for men. Neither group hoped to stave off integration or merger forever, nor did they have objections to coresidence in principle, but both believed that closer integration at that moment—after the women's institutions had firmly established themselves but before they had changed the way women were treated outside their walls—would not be good for women. Women's colleges, they felt, had not yet achieved their full purpose.

The Alumnae Association formed its Committee to Study the Merger in January 1969, before it was even clear to the larger community that merger would, in fact, be discussed. Over the course of several months they met, compiled information, and tried to decide whether merger was the best route to follow, and by June 1970 they issued a research portfolio containing ideas on a merger they believed was still indefinite. In reality, however, by then the merger negotiations were nearly finished.

Aware that decisions on merger might be made in private, the committee had also sought to define the optimum administrative arrangements for women in the Harvard community and how the "Radcliffe entity" could best serve women's needs after a merger. They nevertheless remained strongly against merger in their recommendations portfolio, a lucid and convincing document outlining the serious Radcliffe doubts about the value of a merger.

They began with the charged assertion that:

> While coeducation has been available in some colleges for a century, we observe that it has not succeeded in releasing many women (or men) from the traditional expectation that the primary role of women is to be wives and mothers. Presumably women have been more interesting wives and more inspiring mothers by virtue of their education, but hard is the path of the woman who tries to step out of the traditional mold to "use" her education. She encounters a society that signals "no" with criticisms, lower pay, and lower status jobs than those available to men who have the same training. Our concept is that women should have opportunities to choose a combination of roles according to their individual abilities and desires.[32]

The first proposition of the alumnae committee was to challenge the assumption that further coeducation was indeed beneficial to women. They noted that traditional expectations of women's roles had not changed much despite closer integration into many men's institutions, and they implied that such institutions had often stifled rather than liberated women. Second, they argued that women's willingness to integrate into an unequal situation, and thus to help perpetuate it, was directly linked to society's different and unequal treatment of women. In a society that already closed doors to women, they contended, integrating women into an elite university on an unequal basis would pose even more problems in the long term than remaining separate from their powerful neighbor.

President Bunting hoped that further coeducation and coresidence would lead to women being more accepted and she aimed at diversifying women's image in the university and beyond. She saw the solution very differently from the alumnae, however—she felt that a literal "equalization" of women's opportunities and treatment would lead women out of traditional, gendered roles and ease discrimination. The alumnae committee strongly opposed this view because they believed that Harvard was a "predominantly masculine institution" that was likely to treat women as "little men." For them, Radcliffe needed to play a central role for women, both before graduation and after, through aid in career planning and by providing opportunities for women with families, to counteract the structure of the university and society.

By 1970 the draft report of the university-appointed Committee on Harvard-Radcliffe Relations shared misgivings about total corporate merger and advised that steps "short of merger" be taken.[33] In fact, however, the text of the agreement proposed a merger in all but three respects. Radcliffe would keep its corporate identity, land, and endowment, but would turn over all income from tuition, endowment, fund-raising, and other sources to Harvard and give Harvard responsibility over Radcliffe's budget, students, and day-to-day administration. Barbara Voss, the president of the Alumnae Association, continued to dispute the assumption that equal opportunity for women required the dismantling of Radcliffe and its absorption into Harvard. Chief among her concerns was that funding for Radcliffe programs for women would be reduced once Harvard controlled all the finances.[34] In response to Mary Bunting's contention and the belief of some of the other trustees that merger would legitimate Radcliffe's influence in the university and make it more far-reaching to include all women, the alumnae committee argued that "control over all women in the university is in effect no control at all."[35] This statement addressed the key issue that if Radcliffe were not promised actual administrative positions in exchange for merging, then its role as caretaker of women's interests would be nominal at best, having no place in the power structure of the university or any definite way to effect change. The alumnae committee repeatedly asserted that Radcliffe's ability to effect policy at high levels needed to be more concretely addressed in the merger agreement.

In trying to draw attention to why women would be better served in the long run by Radcliffe's autonomy, the alumnae committee looked at the reasons why many Radcliffe students so eagerly desired coresidence and integration. The students said that their primary concern was to be allowed to live in the Harvard Houses. For the most part, they did not want coresidence as an end in itself, but rather desired access to the more centrally located, better-staffed and well-appointed Harvard dormitories. Much like the women undergraduates at Oxford who wanted to become members of the richer, more prestigious, and better-equipped men's colleges, Radcliffe students held ideas about coresidence that were largely influenced by the poorer state of the women's college. Mary Bunting sympathized with their desire to belong to the older, richer, more prestigious institution, feeling that the students understood what they wanted. The alumnae, however, once Radcliffe students themselves, were convinced that the undergraduates' coveting of Harvard's perquisites and privileges lacked foresight.

Many administrators and faculty at the women's colleges of Oxford staunchly stood against coresidence, as did some administrators and many vocal alumnae at Radcliffe. Though the protests of the two groups took different forms, in each case their dissent revolved around the common theme that coresidence and further integration of women into the most elite male universities at that precise moment would be more detrimental than helpful to women's advancement. After fighting so long to help women gain access to Oxford and Harvard, the Oxford women's colleges and Radcliffe had entered an uncertain period where the direction of further progress became unclear. The condemnation of mixed men's colleges by many of the most influential women scholars in Oxford and the schisms of opinion at Radcliffe on the subject of closer integration into Harvard University betray mixed feelings and hesitancy about further integration and reveal a profound change in direction of privileged Anglo-American women's aspirations, which until that point had been enthusiastically integrationist and had identified with masculine privilege.

Despite contemporaries' charges that women who stood against closer integration at this time were selfishly motivated or reactionary, analysis of the evidence presents the opposite view: these individuals fully believed that longer-term concerns about women's place in society necessitated forgoing such immediately gratifying social advances as coed colleges. Far from being reactionary or conservative, the opponents shared a prescient, and perhaps vaguely radical, viewpoint that dictated the further strengthening of separate women's institutions and a delay of integration in order to achieve more successful integration down the line.

FACULTY, STUDENTS, AND ALUMNI:
TACIT ASSUMPTIONS AND WIDE-RANGING OPINIONS

Throughout the coresidence experiments, students, faculty, and alumni registered their opinions with their university administrations as well as with university and national news publications, which anxiously reported on any development, however small, at Oxford and Harvard. Coresidence inflamed deeply held convictions about social mores, gender roles, and, most important, heterosexual interaction, as well as feelings of anger and impatience that these top universities had so long remained unchanged. Women's rights continued to be overshadowed, however, by other social and political concerns.

When faculty spoke out against the administration's view in matters of coresidence, they usually confined themselves to criticizing specific plans for coresidence rather than the principles behind the plans. By contrast, students remained extremely critical of the late moves to coresidence, and they tended to view the universities' actions as too limited. Indirectly, majority student opinion held great sway, but the frantic editorializing of the students and their direct appeals to the administration seldom if ever produced concrete results. The universities, concerned with where future students would enroll rather than with what current students thought, often made plans that were immensely frustrating to most men students and uninformed by women students' opinions. Alumni response also showed divisions along lines of gender—vocal alumnae, the Radcliffe association's committee notwithstanding, largely being in favor of coresidence and vocal alumni most often being against it. The notable exceptions came up not in discussions of coresidence *per se* but in discussions of whether coresidence and integration would promote more equitable treatment for women.

At Oxford, an apparent minority of faculty seemed to believe that coresidence would be a positive thing in itself, irrespective of its attractiveness to applicants or the places it would open up for women. A modern history tutor in a women's college, going against the general opinion in her college, repeatedly asserted that the separate "intellectual and social lives" of "girls" needed to be integrated. Much like Mary Bunting at Radcliffe, she felt that "it is easier for men and women to get to know each other as working partners and equals if they are not separated by college."[36] These remarks, from an interview given to an undergraduate magazine at a time when undergraduates were loudly campaigning for the university to admit that coresidence had some intrinsic merit, were likely genuine, but other dons privately remarked that the "starry-eyed" accounts of the "moral benefits" of coresidence that other universities gave to the press were "not worth the paper they are written on."[37] Despite some dons' attempts to bolster coresidence with the idea that adding a scant few women to men's colleges would create a "more natural" environment where "emotional and sexual tension is likely to decrease" with the aid of casual intergender contact, most focused on the institutional results coresidence would bring.[38]

While these arguments over integration raged, women continued to be excluded from the premier, all-research-fellows' college in Oxford, All Souls. One don quipped that "a college of All Hearts, a wholly female research institution is too much to expect."[39] Even after coresidence ended the blockade on women faculty in men's colleges, women were elected to fellowships in the newly mixed colleges at an alarmingly low rate.[40] Worse yet, they saw their previous faculty strongholds in the women's colleges being whittled away as women's colleges went coed and bulked up on male faculty so as to compete and to be taken seriously by applicants.[41] Not until 1980, after all but one of the men's colleges had gone coresidential, were fellowships at All Souls opened to women.[42]

At Harvard, one of the more outspoken professors came out against the entire idea of lifting quotas for women, arguing that it was inappropriate to institute such a "fundamental change on the basis of an abstraction, namely the equality of women."[43] His argument turned mainly on the specific impact more women would have on Harvard and on Harvard men. The faculty considered his arguments but ultimately rejected them and endorsed the committee report that advocated lifting the quotas and publicizing the move to entice more women applicants. Nonetheless, women remained in a confining and somewhat unwelcome position in the university.[44] In 1970 there were no tenured female professors among nearly 400 of that rank in the Faculty of Arts and Sciences.[45] By 1998 the number of tenured women had risen to 58 out of 433, or just over 11 percent.[46]

A key aspect of Harvard opinion toward women students emerged in the Kagan Report on coresidence. Led by prominent Harvard professor of child psychology Jerome Kagan, the committee assumed no increase in the numbers of female students in the near future but supported coresidence, with a higher ratio of women to men than was possible in 1970, for its "psychological" benefits—namely, the way it would "allow each student to gain a finer appreciation of the subtle differences in motives, strains, and style of living that characterize American men and women."[47] The report revolved around the comforts of heterosexual men students, dwelling on how "the traditional living arrangement" made it difficult for "some young men who just want to talk to a Radcliffe woman in a common room to gain this goal in any way except by asking her for a date." One of the report's main points was that coresidence would allow "the man who is temperamentally hesitant with women . . . to establish an easier relationship in the context of the House without the extra burdens attached to the dating ritual."[48] Male-initiated heterosexual interaction preoccupied the committee just as much as it preoccupied male students at the time.

When it came to addressing Radcliffe women's fears of being in Houses where they would be greatly outnumbered by men, the report barely shifted focus: "The Radcliffe woman in a coeducational house should develop an understanding of the young man that is a more accurate reflection of the complex mosaic of motivations and anxieties that he carries."[49] In another attempt to address "women's issues," the report explains, "women, in and outside of the university, are becoming increasingly preoccupied with their role in our society. Coresidential living, by allowing more frequent discussion of this theme, should help to broaden the male's appreciation of this experiential issue."[50] Not only did the report center around "the male's appreciation" even when discussing women's issues, but in passages like this it betrayed an unconsciously pejorative attitude toward women. The term "preoccupied" implied that women were too focused on their own current position in society, while "experiential" suggested that their concerns were ephemeral and primarily personal.

Several of the prominent male faculty members on the Kagan committee were openly antifeminist. One member, dean of freshmen and master of the newest Harvard House, F. Skiddy von Stade, wrote a long letter in 1969 to the Radcliffe dean of admissions. "I do not see highly educated women making startling strides in contributing to our society in the foreseeable future," he stated. "They are not, in my opinion, going to stop getting married and/or having children. They will fail in their present roles as women if they do."[51] Furthermore, in reasoning against the merger he noted, "when I see the bright, well-educated, but relatively dull housewives who attended the 'Seven Sisters,' I honestly shudder at changing the balance of males vs. females at Harvard." As women became more integrated into the atmosphere of male educational privilege, they continued to be subject to labeling devices that would perpetuate their status as intrinsically less important and essentially outsiders.

An outraged Radcliffe student living in Dunster House at the time wrote to Mary Bunting, saying, "although I was amazed at the explicitness of his [Von Stade's] male chauvinist remarks, I realize that his sentiments must indeed be similar to those held by the rest of the administration. Obviously, if this University did not want to discriminate against women, it would not maintain its blatantly discriminatory practices on every level. . . ."[52] Bunting gave a commiserative reply, saying she was aware of the dean's views, but claimed that such sentiments were not represented in the soon-to-be-instituted merger agreement.[53]

Yet, a meeting of faculty and deans to consider merger in the same year, 1969, still debated whether it was to Harvard's benefit to make closer ties with Radcliffe, even though the consensus of the meeting was that Radcliffe "girls" did not get the same advantages as Harvard students. One faculty member maintained that they were "obligated to right a situation in which the girls are in an intrinsically inferior position," but most discussed the costs of any such moves. As one future Harvard dean noted with foresight, the savings that would come from closer Radcliffe integration could not be overlooked either.[54] Even though some faculty viewed the inequitable arrangements for women as a reason to integrate, the emphasis remained on the advantages Radcliffe could bring to Harvard through merger and coresidence.

In 1971, when women took up residence in all of the Harvard Houses (but not in the freshman housing in picturesque Harvard Yard), they were outnumbered in some Houses seven to one. Meanwhile, Harvard, much like Oxford, feared that an increase of women would hurt their science departments and swell their liberal arts fields while decreasing future alumni contributions. In the course of the year, Harvard extensively lobbied lawmakers on the national level to defeat a bill requiring that all universities receiving government funds abolish undergraduate sex quotas immediately. Citing "educational and financial risks" to the university in the event of their abolition, Harvard and several other elite private institutions suc-ceeded in destroying the first bill that would have mandated women's academic equality.[55]

The outsider status of women at Oxford and Harvard contributed to great divides of student opinion along gendered lines. For the most part, students of both genders favored coresidence in principle, but the nuances of men and women students' opinions, and the reasons they gave for holding similar views, often varied greatly. Additionally, students' attitudes changed signifi-cantly over time, especially after coresidence was enacted. The trajectories of these changes help reveal complexities that administrators often ignored or of which they were unaware.

At Oxford, the key argument of male students initially hinged on the need to get more women to Oxford but gradually transformed into the argument that coresidence would create a more "natural," less stressful environment with more chance for interaction with the opposite sex on a casual basis. Women undergraduates saw the general crux of the issue quite differently, supporting coresidence mainly because they wanted finally to become members of the most prestigious and well-equipped Oxford colleges, and also because they wanted more places for women applicants. Often women made plain their resentment that coresidence might find more support on the basis of social instead of purely academic and ethical arguments. Student editorials reflected this division subtly, but unmistakably. In one, a male undergraduate begins, "social life in Oxford is very much affected by the fact that the population is divided into twenty-three men's colleges and five women's colleges"; a woman writing in the next issue leads with, "the women's colleges at the periphery of the town [are] condemn[ed] to being the poorest and worst equipped," as well as being vastly outnumbered in students.[56] While her male counterpart talked about the social benefits of a mixed college, she angrily claimed that this type of irrelevant "social argument" gave segregationists their best ammunition by painting women students as an "other," an opposite-sex distraction.

Illustrative of this division is the 1969 report, "Towards Co-education: The Case for Exeter College Becoming Co-residential," written by John Gray, a second-year Politics, Philosophy, and Economics undergraduate who later went on to become a professor of political theory at the London School of Economics. The report comprises more than 30 pages of meticulous, single-spaced type, by far the longest report on coresidence produced by any single university member, faculty included. Largely because of its length and because the Student Union published copies for circulation, Gray's report became one of the focal points of the debate and the exemplar of the "sensitive" male undergraduate's view of the issue. Gray's point, to which he was doggedly devoted, was twofold: Oxford needed more women on ethical grounds, and, *"even if it were possible to set up new women's or mixed colleges, coresidence would be a desirable end in itself,* and that in practice the only viable solution . . . is for several of the men's colleges to become co-residential and admit women in the near future."[57] Over 20 percent of the report was devoted exclusively to a discussion of the salutary effects women would have on men's social, psychological, and sexual lives, including, but not limited to, alleviating loneliness, discouraging rowdiness and abusiveness, and affording men a womanly perspective. Gray also followed the usual line of men who harangued the women's colleges for their desire to preserve themselves, and used the royal "we" to proclaim, "if and when the women's colleges were ever in a position where becoming mixed was a necessary expedient, we would not find anything wrong in this."[58]

Gray's pamphlet was lauded by many for its lucidity but also was attacked by women students who saw its emphasis on men's social, psychological, and sexual comfort as highly problematic. One woman undergraduate editor, Gillian Rose, described the tone of the debate as "Men will take our bodies but not our minds," and she pointed out that Gray vacillated between advocating coresidence on the grounds that it would make more places for women and on the grounds that it would somehow help solve "the sexual maladjustment of this unbalanced, segregated community of scholars," and end the "hungry stares across the Bodleian," the main library where students did much of their studying and eyeing of the opposite sex.[59] Though Rose did not disagree with the idea that coresidence might have favorable social effects, she took issue with the fact that Gray and others used this idea as a main, and often the most important, support of their arguments. Rose promoted women's inherent right to have access to places that excluded them on the grounds of gender alone and noted that Gray's argument smacked too much of allowing women into men's colleges for the sake of men, not for the sake of the traditionally marginalized and outnumbered population of Oxford women.

In an era when the student newspaper still ran weekly contests for photographs of the prettiest undergraduates and managed to slip in more images of bikini-clad women than could generally be considered newsworthy, most male editors denigrated the academic, social, or psychological arguments for all-women's colleges while focusing on their own desires.[60] One extremely unusual editorial in the undergraduate newspaper painted a positively bleak picture of Oxford society, but rather than calling for the addition of women to remedy the situation, it called for a greater sensitivity from men: "while we in our arguments are making them into everything from political machines to sex-symbols, the real flesh-and-blood women of Oxford are suffering gross misunderstanding and neglect. We are giving them a pretty rotten deal, and it's time we did something about it."[61] But, unlike this writer, few mentioned the "petty injustices and cruel degradation" women had to put up with to hold their own at Oxford, and women students angrily pointed out the hypocrisies of the coresidence debates, even as they allied with male undergraduates to support coresidence. By 1975, a year after limited coresidence had come to Oxford, male editors became much more quiescent, but women redoubled their efforts, creating women's action groups and an explicitly all-women protest group against Oxford's quotas.[62]

Only a late shift in opinion by male editors and the male-run union of students changed the model of consistently blaming the women's colleges for hurting coresidence and women through an "irrational" fear that there were not enough good women applicants. In 1979 the effects of coresidence began to show the prescience of the women's colleges' fears, and student newspapers reported on the close to 25 percent drops in the number of applications to the women's colleges as the rest of the men's colleges went coresidential in a group.[63] But old stereotypes still died hard, and the "ladies colleges" continued to be dismissed as "slow as ever to adapt to new trends."[64]

At Harvard, remarkably similar gendered trends in undergraduate opinion prevailed. Radcliffe students, like their Oxford counterparts, desired access to the more prestigious and better equipped men's Houses and wanted the quota on women at Harvard lifted, whereas male undergraduates favored coresidence for the supposed social and sexual improvements it would bring.[65] The rigid parietal rules governing the scant few hours when women could come into certain parts of men's colleges or Houses were not effectively abolished until coresidence was about to begin in each university. Students went from sharply restricted contact with the opposite sex to theoretically unlimited contact nearly overnight.

Some of the most interesting expressions of students' views are found in letters to Radcliffe's President Bunting. Many Radcliffe and Harvard students wrote to her about coresidence after the university had made clear that not until Radcliffe merged could coresidence be considered. None of the letters were against coresidence, but the motives and reasons for favoring coresidence varied greatly. One Harvard freshman wrote to express his desire for coresidence, claiming, "Enforced separation between the sexes is unnatural at this stage of life when nearly all of us will spend the rest of our lives with our wife."[66] This writer universalized a heterosexual masculine perspective and repeated many of his classmates by labeling dining hall restrictions the greatest impediment to socializing. Right up until women moved into men's Houses, they were not allowed in men's dining halls except on certain nights, and then only if they were the "date" of a House member who would accompany and pay for them.[67] Given the responses of men and women in House polls on coresidence and inter-House dining, it seems clear that if dining restrictions had been relaxed earlier, the demand for coresidence would have been substantially reduced.

The real imbalance of the two colleges' resources and student body sizes greatly contributed to lowering enthusiasm for coresidence. Most men in the Harvard Houses, while favoring coresidence in principle, did not want to participate in the coresidential plans because they feared they would be forced to leave their nicer, more centrally located Houses to move to the distant and austere Radcliffe Quadrangle. When Lowell House planned its experimental 1970 exchange with one of the Radcliffe Houses, 75 percent of the men responded in favor of the exchange, but fewer than one-quarter wanted to participate because it would entail moving to inferior living quarters.[68] Responses on the Lowell questionnaire ranged from "need stronger incentive to move to the 'Cliffe" to "Move to Cabot? Are you kidding?"[69] For other Lowell respondents, the disadvantages of moving to Radcliffe were clearly outweighed by social considerations. Said one, "I'd love to have the Cliffies next door," while another simply wrote, "Want to go! (pant)." A few men took the opportunity to critique the habits of their housemates, as did one who claimed, "[Lowell] is nothing but a god-damned glorified whorehouse and friendships here are few between the sexes. Males bring girls in here—pay for their meals and movies and then take them back to their room for—. . . . Changes are needed and I think coed housing is a good start."[70] Indeed, the fact that the student House Committee voted to put *Playboy* magazine back on the shelves of the House library the same spring that 50 women moved in for the experimental exchange shows the lack of concern most Harvard men had for the comfort of their Radcliffe classmates.[71] The male-headed student newspaper also displayed similar crassness in reporting the Radcliffe merger, jibing on the front page of a special extra edition that, with men allowed in Radcliffe, the innovative new Hilles Library would now be turned to a more useful function: a motel.[72]

Radcliffe students also had strong and conflicted feelings about coresidence. In response to an inquiry from President Bunting, several Radcliffe dorms held meetings to decide their collective views on coresidence and, implicitly, merger. One dormitory proclaimed, "We want to retain the name of Radcliffe, we can't be Harvard women; we're Cliffies."[73] They favored coresidence but did not like the idea of merging "under the Harvard Faculty," and they wanted female counselors and tutors provided in the event of merger. Another dorm agreed that coresidence would be best if a ratio of two to one, or one to one if possible, were enforced, rejecting the idea that women be required to move into all of the men's dorms and thus be outnumbered by four to one. They strongly favored the men's system of House tutors, instead of their resident assistants, but felt that it was crucial that some dorms remain all-women. They worried about women's position in the university, especially on the faculty level. Highly ambivalent about the merger, these students concluded that perhaps they should forgo coresidence if merger was inextricably linked: "Maybe after careful consideration, we don't want to join them, after all. . . ."[74] However, they felt that coed dining was "a necessity" and posited the idea of Harvard-Radcliffe House alliances, as well as demanding much-needed renovations for the Radcliffe dorms.

One of the Radcliffe students who wrote personally to President Bunting supporting the merger gave a thoughtful critique of women undergraduates' position in the university. "Radcliffe is a paradox," she wrote. "It calls itself a college, and yet does not educate its student body. Instead, it collects tuition, provides a place of residence, and sends its students to another college for classes," resulting in a total loss of a feeling of college community. Meanwhile, Radcliffe students remained outsiders to Harvard, feeling like "guests" and "exceptions" and being seen as "curve-wreckers" and "untouchables" by Harvard students. Radcliffe students were torn, having no home community in the university, plagued by what this writer termed a "feeling of universal loneliness."[75] Many other women clearly agreed with her, as their refusal to be isolated in the men's Houses with low numbers of women shows.

The Harvard dean's office set up a committee in 1974 to investigate the effects of coresidence on students. Both men and women students rated the Radcliffe Quadrangle's coed atmosphere, with equal numbers of men and women, very positively and claimed this was the most positive aspect of their House environments. However, according to a "happiness index," men and women rated the Radcliffe Houses with their lesser amenities lower than those Harvard Houses that had a "high" ratio of women to men (one woman to every 2.5 men). Women stuck in the Harvard Houses where the ratio of women to men was "low" (one woman to every five men), rated their atmospheres lowest and also gave the lowest happiness index ratings.[76]

CONCLUSION

Men at Oxford and Harvard both tended to view coresidence in terms of the benefits of increased social and sexual interaction, though with notable public exceptions. Women, on the other hand, focused in their writings and correspondence on the urgent need for equality of treatment and greater opportunity for women; they were concerned first and foremost with ending their obvious second-class status at Oxford and Harvard. The cautious and complex feelings Radcliffe students had about coresidence and the merger it necessitated were similar to, though less vehemently against merger than, the ideas of the Radcliffe Alumnae Association and the many alumnae who took the time to write long letters to President Bunting. Women at Radcliffe and at Oxford both saw the limits of coresidence as a strategy for advancing the status of women.

In 1964 a principal of one of the Oxford women's colleges told the Franks Commission that more creative thinking on women's issues was needed if women were really to advance in all levels of higher education. "The Americans are doing it—notably at Harvard," she said, in what was certainly a scathing jab for Oxford, which tended to regard itself as superior to any American university.[77] Though Oxford undoubtedly needed to consider more creative solutions to the problems of women in higher education, this principal's faith in Harvard proved misplaced. In 1972, the year Mary Bunting left Radcliffe, murmurs of dissatisfaction with the merger agreement from the year before had already surfaced in the Radcliffe administration. Indeed, by 1977 a new Radcliffe president renegotiated the terms of the 1971 Radcliffe merger to symbolically, if not truly, return more control to Radcliffe's administration, which had come to feel that its interests had not been adequately served after it integrated with the university.

Notes

1. Gillian Rose, "Coeducation," *Isis* [Oxford student magazine] (Feb. 12, 1969): 8.
2. Christine P. Almy, letter to Mary Bunting, Feb. 19, 1969, folder 656, Papers of Mary Ingraham Bunting [hereafter, PMB], Radcliffe College Archives [hereafter, RCA].
3. L. Grier and Lucy S. Sutherland, "Women's Education at Oxford," in *The Oxford University Handbook* (Oxford : Clarendon Press of Oxford University Press, 1965), 305-11; Lucy Sutherland, "Women in Oxford since 1945," typescript of Seminar at Nuffield College, Oxford, on March 11, 1986, Bodleian Library [hereafter, BOD].
4. Sir William Hayter, "How It All Began," *Ten Years of Women in New College* (Oxford: New College, 1990), 15-16. The tutor in question, Harry Bell, had noticed the favorable effect of male tutorship on his college-age daughter at the coed Trinity College, Dublin.
5. G. E. M. de Ste. Croix, Fellow of New College, "The Admission of Women to New College," *The Oxford Magazine* [hereafter, OM] (Oct. 15, 1964): 4-7.
6. Agenda, "[For the Hebdomadal Council only] Admission of Women to New College: Memorandum by Mr. Vice Chancellor," Nov. 9, 1964, W/12 file 1, Oxford University Archives [hereafter, OUA]. Don is the term used to refer to a teaching member of the university. Franks, who formerly taught philosophy at Oxford, had also served as British ambassador to the United States, 1948-1952.
7. Dame Janet Vaughn, "The Higher Education of Women," OM (Oct. 22, 1964): 24-25. Also see "The Number of Women at Oxford," OM (May 6, 1965): 312-13, and "Women at Oxford," OM (Oct. 1966): 405-6.

8. Lady Mary Ogilvie, principal of St. Anne's College, Franks Commission Oral Evidence, Nov. 24, 1964, typescript, BOD.

9. Dr. Lucy Sutherland, principal of Lady Margaret Hall, ibid.

10. University of Oxford, *Report of Commission of Inquiry* vol. 1 (Oxford: Clarendon Press of Oxford University Press, 1966), para. 102.

11. Editor, "Women," *OM* (May 13, 1965): 1.

12. Vice-chancellor, Note for the W/12 registry file, June 24, 1965, W/12 file 1, OUA: "A motion put to the Stated General Meeting of the Warden and Fellows of New College on the 24 June to amend the Statutes to permit the admission of women did not achieve the necessary two-third's majority. The voting was 17 in favour and 14 against, with 4 absent."

13. Letter to University Registrar, Feb. 22, 1971, W/12 file 1, OUA.

14. "Oxford [Lincoln] College may take women," *The Oxford Mail* (May 7, 1971), clipping, W/12 file 1, OUA.

15. Lucy Sutherland, letter to vice chancellor, May 25, 1971, W/12 file 1, OUA; Mary Trenamen, principal of St. Anne's, letter to all the women's colleges, Nov. 16, 1971, Coresidence file, Somerville College Archives [hereafter, SCA].

16. Mary Bennett, letter to Vice-chancellor Alan Bullock, Feb. 3, 1972, W/12 file 2, OUA.

17. Ibid.

18. Pauline Adams, *Somerville for Women, 1879-1993* (Oxford: Oxford University Press, 1996), 277. Adams suggests that the rising scores of the women's colleges directly affected the desire of some men's colleges to go coresidential. Based on the available evidence, however, it seems clear that the men's colleges were more concerned with being able to attract better men undergraduates by admitting women.

19. Mary Warnock, "Coresidence at Oxford?" *OM* (May 26, 1972): 6.

20. Notes from Meeting of the Departments of Administration, April 21, 1967, folder 21, Radcliffe Deans of Residence Papers, RG VII Series 6, RCA.

21. The Harvard House system, established in the 1930s, is modeled on the Oxford system of Colleges. Each House provides its member students not only with a place to live, but also with academic and personal guidance through tutors, professors, and university officials resident in the House. The Houses, like the Oxford Colleges, have individual dining halls and Junior and Senior Common Room memberships for recreation, meetings, and functions. The Houses are also responsible for disciplining students in many instances.

22. Dean [Franklin] Ford, letter to Mary Bunting, Sept. 22, 1965, folder 473, RGII Series 4, PMB.

23. Mary Bunting, letter to Nathan Pusey, Nov. 29, 1965, folder 473, PMB.

24. Mary Bunting, letter to an Alumna, April 7, 1969, folder 656, PMB.

25. Mary Bunting, letter to director of Continuing Education at Claremont College, Feb. 21, 1969, folder 656, PMB.

26. Mary Bunting, speech at alumnae conference, June 1969, folder 618, PMB.

27. As the chairman of the Radcliffe Alumnae Committee on Merger noted, this "was taken to imply that Radcliffe would vote itself out of existence." Alice Blackmer Skinner, "Association News: against and for merger," *Radcliffe Quarterly* (March 1970), 21.

28. Mary Bunting, letter to a parent, Dec. 18, 1969, folder 687, PMB.

29. "Women and the University" Conference, March 1, 1969, Coresidence file, Radcliffe Vertical Files [hereafter, RVF], RCA.

30. Mary Bunting, letter to Nathan Pusey, Feb. 22, 1969, History-Harvard-Radcliffe Merger Discussions file, RVF, RCA.

31. "Mrs. Crevoshay's Statement," Feb. 22, 1969, Radcliffe College Alumnae Association's *Portfolio of the Study Committee on Merger*, RVF, RCA.

32. "Report to the Overarching Committee," 1969, History-1970-Merger file, RVF, RCA.

33. Committee on Harvard-Radcliffe Relations, "Second Draft," Sept. 30, 1970, folder 775, PMB.

34. Barbara Voss, letter to Hugh Calkins, Nov. 11, 1970, folder 775, PMB.

35. Deborah Batis, "Response to the draft of the merger," History-1970-Merger file, RVF, RCA.
36. Jenifer Hart, interview with Sally Emerson, *Isis* no. 1650 (1973): 14. See Jenifer Hart, *Ask Me No More* (London: Peter Halban, 1998), 142-43.
37. Lady Margaret Hall Admissions Tutor, letter to Warden of Wadham, Feb. 2, 1972, "Coresidence, 1968-73" file 2B/I, WCA.
38. Ste. Croix, "The Admission of Women to New College," 6.
39. A correspondent, letter to Editor, *OM* (Feb. 7, 1957): 250.
40. Six years after Brasenose College went coresidential it had no women faculty on a staff of close to 80; Jesus College represented the best men's college in this respect, with five women on a staff of a similar size. *Oxford University Calendar 1980-1981* (Oxford: Clarendon Press of Oxford University Press, 1980), 300-04, 342-45.
41. By contrast, only one year after they allowed in men, the women's college Lady Margaret Hall had 17 men faculty on a staff of about 40, St. Anne's had 16 men on a staff of the same size, and St. Hugh's had 12 men on their staff of 40. Ibid., 355-58, 424-26, 454-57.
42. *Oxford University Calendar 1998-99* (Oxford: Clarendon Press of Oxford University Press, 1998), 190-95.
43. Professor Harvey Mansfield, as quoted in Calvin Mosley, "The Impact of the Merger of the Offices of Admissions and Financial Aids at Harvard and Radcliffe Colleges," Harvard School of Education, Analytic Paper, 1981, Gutman Library, 75-76.
44. Ibid., 76-77.
45. Liva Baker, *I'm Radcliffe, Fly Me* (New York: Macmillan, 1976), 50. Helen Maud Cam had died in 1968; Ceclilia Payne-Gaposchkin was *emerita*.
46. Harvard University News Office, June 30, 1971, 1969-1970 press release file, Harvard University Archives [hereafter, HUA], and Communications Office of the Faculty of Arts and Sciences, inquiry, March 2000.
47. Kagan Committee Report [1969?], folder 687, PMB, 4.
48. Ibid., 3-4.
49. Ibid., 5.
50. Ibid., 6.
51. Dean F. Skiddy von Stade, letter to David K. Smith, Radcliffe Dean of Admissions, Aug. 25, 1969, reprinted in "Von Stade Wrote Letter Against Merger, Saw No Benefit in Educating More Women," *Harvard Crimson*, Nov. 6, 1970, 1.
52. Katherine Fletcher, letter to *Harvard Crimson* and Mary Bunting, Nov. 6, 1970, folder 776, PMB.
53. Mary Bunting, Nov. [?], 1970, reply to Fletcher, folder 776, PMB.
54. Notes of Meeting, Aug. 6, 1969, folder 716, PMB.
55. Peter Shapiro and Susan F. Kinsley, "The No Sex Quota Provision: Harvard Lobbies for Time," *Harvard Crimson*, Nov. 9, 1971, 1.
56. Anthony Slade, "Is the College System an Anachronism?" *Isis* (Jan. 30, 1965): 13, and Sally Hunt, "Monasticism—or Mixed Colleges?" *Isis* (Feb. 13, 1965): 13.
57. John Gray, "Towards Co-residence: The Case for Exeter College Becoming Co-residential" (Oxford: Oxford University Student Council, 1969), preface, emphasis added.
58. Ibid., para. 162.
59. Gillian Rose, "Coeducation," *Isis* (Feb. 12, 1969): 8.
60. See *Cherwell* [Oxford student newspaper], 1963-1975.
61. Simon Thrush, "It's Not a World for Women at Oxford," *Cherwell*, Nov. 10, 1962.
62. Jackie Ashley, "Women in Oxford," *Isis* (Oct. 10, 1975): 6.
63. Tony Carritt, "Sex-Change Revelation," *Cherwell*, Nov. 24, 1978.
64. Editor, "Coresidence," *Cherwell*, June 8, 1979.
65. Kagan Report, folder 687, PMB, 3.
66. Harvard student, letter to Mary Bunting, Feb. 20, 1969, folder 656, PMB.
67. Minutes of House Committee, March 19, 1969, Lowell House Office Files [hereafter, LHOF], general records, 1968-1972, HUA.
68. Lowell Questionnaire Results Poster, 1969, ibid.

69. Collected comments, Lowell House Questionnaire, 1969, ibid.

70. Ibid.

71. Lowell House Committee Minutes, April 21, 1970, LHOF, general records 1968-1972, HUA.

72. Photo caption, *Harvard Crimson Sunday Extra,* Feb. 23, 1969, folder 655, PMB.

73. Notes from Daniels Hall meeting, March 11, 1969, folder 655, PMB.

74. Notes from Briggs Hall meeting, March 11, 1969, ibid.

75. Christine P. Almy, letter to Mary Bunting, Feb. 19, 1969, folder 656, PMB.

76. Dean K. Whitla and Dan C. Pinck, *Perspectives on the Houses at Harvard and Radcliffe* (Cambridge, Mass.: Harvard, 1974), 80-82.

77. Lady Ogilvie, Franks Commission Oral Evidence, Nov. 24, 1964.

FROM SYMPATHIZERS TO ORGANIZERS

Jennifer J. Stetzer

The April 1969 Harvard-Radcliffe Student Strike marked a turning point in Radcliffe women's involvement in student activism on campus. Radcliffe women had participated in student politics throughout the 1960s, often playing important but unheralded roles in Students for a Democratic Society (SDS), the center of the radical student movement.

The strike drew scores of students, many of whom had not been involved before, into radical politics. This participation in student activism was a source of empowerment and education, especially for many of the women, in that they gained experience organizing social movements and acquired intellectual frameworks for defining and critiquing oppression; women would later apply those skills and ideology in the independent women's movement.[1]

The 1969 student strike at Harvard-Radcliffe mirrored trends nationwide, as more than 300 colleges and universities erupted in student demonstrations in the spring of 1969. Nonetheless, protest, violence, and bloodshed at "fair Harvard" were unsettling, given the popular belief that "it couldn't happen here." As a result, the 1969 strike received widespread media attention and analysis in secondary sources. Reporters covered the 1969 strike extensively, students wrote memoirs reflecting on the event, and historians have studied it repeatedly; but in all of these sources women's contributions to the movement have gone unnoticed and the gender dynamics of that movement have gone unexplored.[2] Scholarship of radical politics on a national level parallels this trend; as the editors of an anthology on women in social protest explain, "interested readers are hard-pressed to find the *mention* of women, let alone comparative analysis of men and women's roles, attitudes, and feelings as social protesters."[3] Only by asking new questions of the traditional sources and by looking to new sources such as interviews with participants can these formerly untold stories now come to the forefront.

SDS came to Harvard-Radcliffe in 1964 as a liberal reform organization focused on community organizing and political activism. Within two years it had become the largest chapter in the country, with over 200 members.[4] Widely publicized demonstrations, such as a confrontation with Secretary of Defense Robert McNamara in 1966, a sit-in prompted by Dow Chemical's recruiting efforts on campus in 1967, and a demonstration against the presence of the Reserve Officers Training Corps (ROTC) in 1968, drew more and more students into the ranks of SDS. Although the leadership of SDS tended to be mostly male during this period, SDS members did elect several women to top positions in the organization, such as Amy Delson (treasurer, 1964), Barbara Easton (secretary, 1965), Ellen Klein (steering committee, 1967), and Beth Harvey (steering committee, 1969).[5]

When Radcliffe students joined forces with their Harvard peers, men stood out as the leaders and decision makers. When fighting for their own interests at Radcliffe, however, women organized themselves very effectively, and the women themselves were vocal and visible. For example, the 1968 demonstration against ROTC (known as the Paine Hall demonstration for its location) comprised both men and women, and Harvard and Radcliffe punished the participants separately, with each institution deciding on the consequences for its students. This opened the door for Radcliffe students, who had not previously targeted their college for protest, to mobilize against the administration.[6] The 26 Radcliffe students who had been involved refused to meet individually with their deans, announcing that they would instead go as a group, since, they said, "We acted as a group and we have decided to confront the Administration in the same way."[7] The students accepted full responsibility for their actions but stood behind their political principles, saying, "We are participating in the fight to abolish ROTC at Harvard because we protest the American policy of counter-revolution in Vietnam and elsewhere in the world."[8] After student-administration negotiations on appropriate punishments failed, several dozen women stormed Radcliffe president Mary Bunting's office, demanding amnesty for the demonstrators. Led by student Naomi Schapiro, this activism by and for women provided important experience for those involved.

Though factions within SDS differed on tactics, by April 1969 the group was eager to launch a massive campaign against university policy, especially the presence of ROTC on campus and Harvard's expansion into low-income Boston and Cambridge neighborhoods. Early in the morning of April 9 the more militant faction decided to take over University Hall, the main administration building, later that day.[9] By noon several hundred male and female students had gathered in front of University Hall. Many were SDS members or supporters; others had heard rumors of a possible building takeover and were curious onlookers. SDS co-chairman Norm Daniels climbed to the top of the stairs and proclaimed, "There is only one enemy here, the Harvard Corporation. It's time for us to tell the Corporation now by action what we've been telling them all fall by words." Once inside, SDSers rounded up the deans and workers in the building and escorted them out. The students met resistance from several deans, whose refusal to leave prompted the students to use physical force.[10] Meanwhile, Lowry Hemphill and Ellen Messing, two long-time SDS members, reportedly stood together inside the building debating whether it was ladylike to throw out the deans.[11] This conversation indicated the opposing forces pulling women activists in two directions; in their minds, traditional femininity and political activism did not mix.

For 17 hours the 250 students inside University Hall discussed strategy and plans, they "liberated" confidential administrative documents, they sang, they slept, and they made their demands heard.[12] Nicholas Gagarin, a student who later wrote about his University Hall experience for the student newspaper, the *Harvard Crimson*, described the mood inside the building as one of euphoria: the students had successfully taken a building from the most prestigious university in the world. Moreover, Gagarin wrote, "For those few hours we *were* brothers and sisters. We did reach out and hold onto each other. . . . We were very beautiful in University Hall, we were very human, and we were very together."[13] In addition to taking a political stand, many radical students discovered in their "liberated area" a sense of community and solidarity with their peers.

Women participated in the takeover in disproportionate numbers. Though women constituted about 20 percent of the undergraduate student body, 32 of the 118 (or roughly 27 percent) of the students indicted for trespassing in University Hall were Radcliffe women.[14] Photographs from inside the building that night show men and women with arms linked as they waited for the police bust.[15] As one reporter declared,

Harvard Strike, "The Bust": police expel students from University Hall, April 9, 1969 (Dorothy Darrah, *Harvard Crimson*, Radcliffe College Archives).

> The seizure of Harvard's University Hall this week was an imposing show of male-female solidarity. Radcliffe women were out in force, distributing leaflets, demonstrating, getting arrested, and getting injured right along with the Harvard men. It was the first major demonstration of inter-campus unity since the recently-proposed merger between administrations of the two schools.[16]

Although this statement glosses over some of the gender dynamics among the student activists, it does point to the significant role that Radcliffe women played in the occupation of University Hall.

A bloody police bust at dawn on April 10 evicted the student protesters by clubbing them and pushing them toward the doors. The police did not discriminate in their violence; they went after anyone in the way, men or women.[17] As Radcliffe student Carol Sternhell, who covered the event for the *Crimson*, later recalled,

> There were tons of police in baby-blue helmets. I was standing on the steps nearest the chapel when they came at us. The demonstrators' arms were

linked, and the police charged. Up to then, it had all been pretend. Then the police grabbed people off the top steps and threw them down. People were screaming. It was a madhouse. I saw them beat up a guy in a wheelchair. I was so terrified. I ran and kept running.[18]

This violence cracked open some of the veneer of genteel hostility between men and women activists. Though the draft resistance movement, the main thrust of student activism at the time, had pushed women to the periphery—since their lives would not be on the line in the war—women in the University Hall bust put their bodies on the line and demonstrated the strength of their commitment to the movement. Perhaps seeing Radcliffe women dragged out of the building, beaten, and loaded into paddy wagons helped men and women imagine new possibilities for women's participation in the movement.

But these changes did not come without taking a toll; the bust was emotional and traumatic for many of the students involved. One woman jumped out of a window to escape arrest, found two friends and quickly left the Yard. She later wrote, "The three of us clung to each other and wept and shivered and cursed all at once. . . . I felt a fear that turned to fury and a fury that turned to sorrow and a sorrow that turned to tears, and I started to cry, and cried and cried until I thought I would never stop."[19]

The majority of undergraduates held moderate political views and disagreed with the militancy of SDS's action. Yet when students watched anonymous police officers violently beating their classmates, mainstream opinion shifted dramatically; suddenly the administration seemed every bit the powerful, malevolent enemy SDS had depicted, for they had brought in outsiders to do their dirty work. Within a few hours more than 2,000 moderate students squeezed into Memorial Church and overwhelmingly voted to boycott classes for at least three days.[20] For eleven days the students executed their strike successfully. Many professors continued to hold classes, but attendance was less than 25 percent, and those classes that did meet mainly discussed the political issues immobilizing the campus.[21] Instead of attending classes, most students spent their time engaged in discussions, strategy sessions, or demonstrations.

As with the University Hall takeover, women were heavily involved in the strike. When it came to demonstrating, leafletting, and other rank-and-file activities, women at Radcliffe participated in the strike in proportionally greater numbers than Harvard men.[22] Women walked the picket lines and political brigades, attended meetings, colloquia, and rallies in large numbers.

While the exact numbers of Harvard and Radcliffe students participating went unrecorded, several strike participants remembered that about half the strikers were female.[23] Even women who had not previously been involved in SDS or radical campus politics joined in, arguing that a boycott of classes was the only way to pressure the administration to heed the student demands. For example, Laurent Delli-Bovi had not been an active SDS member and had never participated in a demonstration before. "I never really thought I would be in a demonstration," she told a reporter.

> I hadn't really talked to anybody about going into the building when I went in. I just sort of made the decision on the spot that it was time I did something to back up what I'd been talking about. I've been anti-war and anti-ROTC all along. I'd been helping circulate petitions to put ROTC off campus. But the petitions were submitted months ago, and it finally seemed that there were no other channels except to take an action like this.[24]

Delli-Bovi's statement indicates how the strike broadened the base of SDS support and drew many new women into radical politics. The strike afforded women the opportunity to stand behind their objections to the war and to Harvard's role in it.

The Radcliffe Union of Students (RUS), the representative student government, had difficulty taking decisive action during the strike for fear of marginalizing certain viewpoints and sparking dissension. At an April 11 meeting, the group called for a campaign to solicit a diversity of student opinions. They proposed a referendum or a questionnaire to discover what Radcliffe students thought about the issues, specifically their attitudes toward ROTC and a possible restructuring of the university. Because so many women were, in RUS members' opinion, "uninformed and confused" about the strike, the group decided to serve as a clearinghouse of information. They considered sponsoring meetings and colloquia to discuss the strike, but rather than meeting separately, they decided instead that they should include Radcliffe in Harvard colloquia by sending qualified speakers to the Harvard Houses.[25] This attempt to bridge the gap between the two colleges and to increase women's presence in the heart of the strike actually made it more difficult to draw new women in, since few of the meetings or debates were held in the women's dormitories. Also, because RUS wavered between endorsing the radical and the more moderate factions—offering and then withdrawing support as the tides of opinion changed—it did not take one strong position and defend it, thereby minimizing the weight of the group's decisions.

Woman protester during 1969 student strike
(Radcliffe College Archives).

The Harvard strike, which began with a dramatic and definitive event, had a much more unspecified end. For African American students, the strike ended on April 22, with the endorsement by the Faculty of Arts and Sciences of their black studies proposal. By then, most white students had already abandoned the strike. Many had drifted back to classes as the constant political activity began to take its toll and as final exams loomed nearer. The strike had been gradually losing support as a result of faculty responsiveness as well; the faculty toughened its stance on the status of ROTC, which satisfied many moderate students. Though SDS members vowed to maintain their boycott until all demands were met, those who continued striking were overwhelmingly in the minority, and the strike fizzled to an end.[26]

Radcliffe students confront John Harvard over equal access, Commencement, 1971 (Radcliffe College Archives).

Though student activism at Harvard-Radcliffe would continue, the 1968-69 academic year witnessed the most turmoil, uprisings, and changes in university policy. The 1969 strike is widely considered a turning point in the university's history.[27] Together, thousands of students succeeded in shutting down the university and in making their demands heard. Aided by the faculty's efforts to resolve the crisis, the students' demands were met on almost all counts. The protesters led the way toward creating important and enduring changes in the institution, most notably in reducing the status of ROTC, increasing Harvard's efforts to help its low-income neighbors, giving students a voice in the creation of an Afro-American Studies program, and adding students to several faculty and administrative committees. It was the only time that SDS succeeded in rallying campus-wide support to launch a mass movement.

The strike is less commonly associated with changes in women's status and experiences at Harvard-Radcliffe. As a key event with profound impact on both the university and its students, the strike provided women with important political experience. Many were drawn into campus protest for the first time and discovered new possibilities for themselves as political activists. Particularly for moderate students, the 1969 strike provided a political baptism. Twenty years later, many women who had participated in the strike looked back to it as a defining moment of their lives; Marjorie Starkman called the strike the most important part of her education at Harvard-Radcliffe, commenting that the events of that spring "marked the beginning of my political awareness, and are therefore largely responsible for the person I am now."[28] Marcia Livingston noted, on the twentieth reunion of the strike, that political activity was "the best part" of her experience at Radcliffe; she called the Progressive Labor Party study groups and the SDS conferences, demonstrations, and protests the "classes" that really mattered to her, for they gave her "an understanding of world events and inspired me to act."[29] Thus, the radical student movement at Harvard-Radcliffe was an exciting and eye-opening environment for many young women. It provided women with important political experience, knowledge, networks, connections, role models, and revolutionary ideology. In doing so, the New Left gave a hands-on course in social movements.

By providing opportunities not available to women elsewhere—to be social critics and to stand up to the power structure—radical student politics empowered many women. By espousing the goals of equality and participatory democracy, the New Left sought to provide a welcoming forum for women's activism. In the movement, these women discovered new found strength, self-respect, purpose, and ability to effect change.

Notes

1. The Radcliffe students who joined SDS were overwhelmingly white and upper middle class. As was true of the majority of Radcliffe students at the time, they generally came from cities in the eastern United States and had attended private high schools.-
2. The most comprehensive work on the 1969 strike was written by four Harvard students who covered the events as reporters for the campus radio station. It provides valuable day-to-day accounts of the major events leading to the University Hall takeover, the police bust, and the subsequent strike. See Lawrence E. Eichel et al., *The Harvard Strike* (Boston: Houghton Mifflin, 1970). Several memoirs also document these events, including Steven Kelman, *Push Comes to Shove: The Escalation of Student Protest* (Boston: Houghton Mifflin, 1970); Richard Zorza, *The Right to Say We: The Adventures of a Young Englishman*

at Harvard and in the Youth Movement (New York: Praeger, 1970); Roger Rosenblatt, *Coming Apart: A Memoir of the Harvard Wars of 1969* (Boston: Little, Brown, 1997).

3. Guida West and Rhoda Lois Blumber, eds., *Women and Social Protest* (New York: Oxford University Press, 1990), 5.

4. Eichel et al., *The Harvard Strike*, 30. "Harvard-Radcliffe SDS Chapter Registration," SDS Papers, 1958-70 (Microform Corporation of America).

5. While the exact sex ratios among SDS members are unavailable, the student group registration forms that SDS filed with the Radcliffe Government Association indicate that in both the 1964-65 and the 1965-66 academic years one of the four leadership positions was held by a woman. "Harvard-Radcliffe SDS Student Group Registration," Radcliffe Government Association Records, 1962-67, Radcliffe College Archives [hereafter, RCA].

6. The smaller, more intimate environment of the women's college may have helped it escape previous student protest. Radcliffe president Mary Bunting took pride in her school's attention and responsiveness to student demands and the peaceful manner in which the administration and students settled most complaints. Because it offered student participation in administrative and judicial committees, Radcliffe may have provided better channels of communication with its students than did Harvard. One student leader praised Radcliffe for dealing with student activism positively and for attentively listening to student demands. In a 1968 Radcliffe newsletter, senior Deborah Batts commends the women students themselves for not "losing their heads" and called for a "quiet revolution as a continuing process which functions as a fundamental tool of progress." "A New President Speaks of the Quiet Revolution," *Radcliffe: News From the College* (Autumn 1968), 1. Another likely explanation for why students generally targeted Harvard, not Radcliffe, for their protests was Radcliffe's secondary status. The women's college was seen as an auxiliary, unconnected to the center of decision making by the Corporation and by Harvard's president, Nathan Pusey.

7. Marjorie Angell, quoted in "Anti-ROTC Demonstrators Collect Signatures for Ad," *Harvard Crimson*, Jan. 7, 1969, 1.

8. "Statement of Participants in the Faculty Meeting Demonstration to the Judicial Board of Radcliffe College," Dec. 17, 1968, Dean of Residence Office, Genevieve Austin Papers, RCA.

9. William R. Galeota, "300 Storm Pusey's House After Anti-ROTC Meeting," *Harvard Crimson*, April 9, 1969, 1. The article notes that approximately 450 students attended a meeting in Lowell Lecture Hall on April 8, where students argued over strategy and demands.

10. Eichel et al., *The Harvard Strike*, 85-86.

11. Carl Offner, interview with author, Cambridge, Oct. 23, 1998.

12. E. J. Kahn, *Harvard Through Change and Through Storm* (New York: W. W. Norton, 1969), 21. The "Eight Demands" were the rallying cry of the student protesters. When SDS took over University Hall, they made only the first three demands, but the number later grew to these eight: 1)Abolition of ROTC; 2) Replace ROTC scholarships with the equivalent Harvard scholarships; 3) Restore scholarships to Paine Hall demonstrators; 4) Rent rises in university-owned apartments be rolled back to the level of January 1, 1968; 5) University Road apartments not be torn down to make way for the Kennedy complex; 6) One hundred and eighty-two black workers' homes in Roxbury not be torn down to make room for Harvard Medical School expansion; 7) No punishment of any kind for those who sat in at University Hall; no legal or academic action. 8) Establish a meaningful black studies program with curriculum and requirements for tenure to be determined by the chairman of the department and by the students. "A Reply to Pusey," SDS position paper, April 11, 1969, SDS General Folder, Harvard-Radcliffe Chapter, 1965-73, Harvard University Archives [hereafter, HUA].

13. Nicholas Gagarin, "Non-Politics on the Battlefront," *Harvard Crimson*, April 12, 1969, 3.

14. Scott W. Jacobs, "Who Are Those Kids in University Hall?" *Harvard Crimson Commencement Issue*, June 1970. This data comes from a *Crimson* survey of 118 undergraduates who

were indicted. Of these 118, the majority lived in the eastern part of the country and had attended private school. Illustrating the class component of student protest, the survey found that only 24 percent of the Harvard students and 19 percent of the Radcliffe students held scholarships. The most popular majors among those arrested were English and Social Relations. Only one of the 118 students polled was black.

15. "Photographs of the Harvard Strike," Materials Related to Eichel et al., *The Harvard Strike,* HUA.

16. Janet Riddell, "Fourth of Demonstrators Radcliffe, B.U., MIT Women," *Boston Globe,* April 11, 1969, 25.

17. Marianne DeKoven, correspondence with the author, Oct. 13, 1998.

18. Quoted in Rosenblatt, *Coming Apart,* 38.

19. Jody Adams, "Inside, With Arms Linked, the Kids Awaited the End," *Harvard Crimson,* April 12, 1969, 4.

20. Samuel Goldhaber, "Moderates Set Up Mass Meeting, Issue Statement on Police Action," *Harvard Crimson,* April 10, 1969, 1.

21. Kahn, *Harvard Through Change,* 27.

22. Naomi Schapiro, correspondence with author, Dec. 8, 1997.

23. "To All Sisters," *Old Mole Strike Special: The Sixth Day,* April 15, 1969; Naomi Schapiro, correspondence with author, Dec. 8, 1997; Deborah Hurst, interview with author, Oct. 11, 1998, Cambridge, Mass.; Marianne DeKoven, correspondence with author, Oct. 13, 1998; Henry Sommer, interview with author, Nov. 29, 1997, Philadelphia, Pa.

24. Quoted in Riddell, "Fourth of Demonstrators Radcliffe, B.U., MIT Women."

25. "Minutes of Radcliffe Union of Students Meeting," April 11, 1969; "Minutes of the Meeting of the Radcliffe Union of Students Legislature," April 14, 1969, RUS President's File, Dean of Residence Office Records, RCA.

26. Eichel et al., *The Harvard Strike;* "Chronology of the Harvard Strike," *Boston Globe,* April 20, 1969, 17.

27. See, for example, Eichel et al., *The Harvard Strike,* 346; Rosenblatt, *Coming Apart,* 215.

28. Marjorie Starkman, "Personal Statement," *The Twentieth Reunion of the Harvard-Radcliffe Strike,* 98; Susan Neiman Offner, "Personal Statement," ibid., 88.

29. Marcia Livingston, "Personal Statement," ibid., 79.

Memories of Change

Integrating Lamont: men only (Harvard University Archives).

INTEGRATING LAMONT

JANUARY 1949.
Lamont Library opens to Harvard's all-male undergraduates.

Experience here and elsewhere has shown that a library for men only or for women only can be administered with almost no supervision in the reading rooms, but that a coeducational library requires supervision if reasonable quiet is to be preserved. In order to achieve most efficiently its primary aims, Lamont has been designed in such a way that the staff would have to be doubled if adequate reading room supervision were to be provided on a coeducational basis.

—Keyes D. Metcalf, *Harvard Library Bulletin* 3 (Winter 1949)

"We're the Girls" (Sung to the tune of: "I'm in Love with a Wonderful Guy"); words by Holly Butler 1953 and Barbara Williams 1955:

> We're the girls who have classes at Harvard,
> We're the students whom none can excel,

Adapted from *Women in Lamont,* a brochure prepared for the May 1999 celebration of Lamont Library's fiftieth anniversary.

Integrating Lamont: women reach the front desk (Harvard University Archives).

Very well read and though not quite co-ed,
We think joint education is swell.

Tech men take us dancing in Boston,
Dartmouth takes us to ski in Vermont.
Yalies will wine us and Princeton men dine us
So who wants to get into Lamont?

As you can guess, we lay plenty of stress,
On Epicure and Freud.
We find their theories a logical series
And not only learn but enjoy.

Helen of Troy can be seen in our faces,
Venus de Milo gave all of us charms.
But you can see, we're much better than she,
We have not only faces but arms.

When we are gone they'll be others to follow,
Radcliffe girls are blue stockings no more,
Our stockings are sheerer, our minds are much clearer.
We're better, we're better, much better, lots better
Better than ever before!

OCTOBER 1964.
Radcliffe students gain use of a sixth-floor classroom in Lamont but are required to get to it via a side entrance and staircase.

As every good Frenchman knows, it was when the *women and children* of Paris rushed into the streets that the Bastille fell. . . .
So be it. The women and children of Harvard University have at last stormed the final symbol, have brought about, as if accidentally, the first blushing dawn of the new regime. Lamont has been penetrated.
—"Battle of the Books," *Harvard Crimson,* Oct. 1964

"The Radcliffe Revolution" (Sung to the tune of "Battle Hymn of the Republic"); words by Residents of Cabot House:

We'll put Dean Kerby-Miller down in Massachusetts Hall.
CHORUS:
Harvard then will be the Annex (3 times)
When the Radcliffe Revolution comes.

We'll put the Crime out weekly and the NEWS out every day.
We'll serve Scotch and sodas at President's teas.
We'll all queue up for open house instead of closed reserve.
We'll all have Crimson garters to keep blue stockings up.
We'll have a ladies restroom in the basement of Lamont.

JANUARY 1966.
Harvard Undergraduate Council votes against permitting women broader access to Lamont.

3. Girls in Lamont would inevitably be a distraction. Though the atmosphere of Lamont is subject to much derision, over 1,200 Harvard students find it the best place to work. Study dates and other social phenomena would certainly endanger the present solitude.
—Letter from Harvard Undergraduate Council
to Merle Fainsod, director of the University Library, Jan. 3, 1966

SEPTEMBER 1966.
Radcliffe women are allowed to use all facilities of Lamont because of a delay in the completion of Hilles Library.

They've been letting Cliffies into Lamont for close to two weeks now and lo!

Integrating Lamont: together at last (Harvard University Archives).

The hallowed walls have not fallen. In fact, the short tenure of emergency coeducation in Lamont has accomplished what years of verbiage could not— proven, once and for all, that people can study for Harvard degrees in a heterosexual library.

—*Harvard Crimson*, Oct. 6, 1966

OCTOBER 1966.
On the opening of Hilles Library at Radcliffe, female students are again denied access to reserve materials and study areas in Lamont.

They're gonna throw us out of Lamont today.
After two weeks of coeducational study, Harvard has refused to integrate permanently its last bastion of monasticism.

—Nancy H. Davis, "Lamont Banishes All Cliffies to Hilles,"
Harvard Crimson, Oct. 10, 1966

DECEMBER 1966.
Library Committee of the Faculty of Arts and Science recommends that Lamont be open to all Harvard and Radcliffe undergraduates on an experimental basis.

A Harvard man commented, "I'd rather take a break looking at a girl's legs than smelling some guy's sweaty socks." Girls have heard about the smell at Lamont, but one Cliffie predicted confidently that "the stronger Cliffies can take it."

—*Harvard Crimson*, Dec. 16, 1966

FEBRUARY 1967.
Radcliffe students are allowed permanent access to all areas of Lamont.

THE LOST GENERATION

Linda Greenhouse

Although I graduated in 1968, my undergraduate experience was not really all that different from Ann Karnovsky's, who was in the class of 1952, 16 years earlier. So not a whole lot had changed. Recently I got in the mail from Harvard a very glossy—I'm sure very expensive—little booklet celebrating the integration of Lamont Library, which happened at the beginning of my junior year. I read this, needless to say, with some interest. It gives the various reasons why women had not been allowed in Lamont—admitting women would have made it too crowded, or women might have been a distraction to the young men. But this booklet doesn't really convey the reason given at the time, which was—smelly socks! What they said at the time was that Harvard men liked to study with their shoes off and that the smelly socks would create an atmosphere in which the young women of Radcliffe would certainly not be happy studying. We were kept out Lamont for our own good!

The 1960s was the decade of the mixed message, the really mixed message: on the one hand, the dominating fact about undergraduate life for Radcliffe students was numbers—there were four Harvard men to every one of us. So we were told that we really were quite special, that it was much harder to get into Radcliffe than into Harvard, and that consequently we were smarter and better prepared and so on. Yet, on the other hand, not one of the postgraduate fellowships was open to us: the Rhodes, the Marshall, the Sheldon. It wasn't even a question of competing; they just simply would not have accepted an application from a woman. On the *Harvard Crimson,* I was essentially fungible with all of the guys that I worked with, yet after graduation they had these fellowships and marched off to various interesting destinations.

I didn't expect a Rhodes scholarship, but I would have been very happy to accept membership into the Signet, a literary society that all the guys belonged to. Once in a while the *Crimson* would have functions there, and I thought this was really cool because in those days I had literary pretensions beyond mere journalism. Every time they had a Signet election, I would ask male friends at the *Crimson* to put me up for election—just to do it kind of symbolically. And they always promised that they would and they never did. When I was back for my twentieth reunion, almost 15 years ago, one of those guys—whom I hadn't seen for a couple of decades—showed up to participate and essentially took one look at me and said, "Linda, I apologize. I'm sorry I never put you up for the Signet Society."

I concentrated in government, which was a heavily male concentration. I will never forget the first class day of my freshman year, section meeting in Gov. 1A. I got there early (Radcliffe women were always on time), took my seat, and watched as the room filled up with 25 or 30 of the other members of the section, and it dawned on me that I was the only female in the room. It also dawned on me that this should be a thrilling experience. This was wonderful, me surrounded by 29 Harvard guys! But it didn't feel so good; it just felt strange. I had only one female professor during my entire undergraduate tenure at Harvard. She was a junior faculty member in the Government Department who did not get tenure there but went on to have an extremely distinguished career at the University of Virginia.

The Radcliffe students had work assignments in the dorms—waiting on tables and so on—that Harvard students didn't have. This was all under the rubric of "gracious living." Gracious living in the late 1960s was becoming darned inconvenient, because in order to have dinner you had to dress, you had to wear a skirt, you had to come back from whatever your activity was in the Square and get dressed and take your seat. To be on the first floor of a dorm on a Sunday to read the paper or just hang out you had to wear a skirt. It came to mean that I was almost never able to *have* dinner back at the dorm because of my work on the *Crimson.* The *Crimson* had an arrangement with Adams House, which is right next door to the *Crimson* offices, so that the guys could eat in Adams House every night, but of course women could not eat in Adams House. So all the Harvard students would go off to Adams House, leaving me alone in the newsroom without so much as a goodbye, and

I would go get a 50-cent hamburger at Tommy's Lunch. That was my dinner night after night after night.

I think the basic fact of our existence was that Radcliffe students were not the norm. We were the deviation from the norm. Yet, we didn't have the language, we didn't have the concept to formulate our situation in political or systemic terms. We thought it was a problem with us. I thought, "I'm a *Crimson* editor. They are *Crimson* editors. They're eating at Adams House. Why can't I eat at Adams House?" I didn't have the conceptual framework to think, "I'm a woman, I'm paying the same tuition, I'm paying the same room and board, what gives here?"

There's only one respect in which we had the last laugh: we did have separate commencement ceremonies, and on my commencement day, which was a rainy Thursday in Radcliffe Yard, as I recall, the commencement speaker, the father of a classmate, was the mayor of Washington, D.C. Perhaps no big deal, but the Harvard men had as their commencement speaker the shah of Iran. Need I say more?

REMEMBERING RADCLIFFE

Katharine Park

My class—the class of 1972—was one of the last to graduate before many of the important changes that marked the relationship between Harvard and Radcliffe in that decade, including the abolition of the famous four-to-one ratio of male to female undergraduates and the Agreement of 1977. What was Radcliffe before that year? Working from hindsight, including 17 years spent teaching at Wellesley, I can most easily characterize what it was not. It was not a women's college, in any sense that alumnae of Wellesley, Smith, Bryn Mawr, or Mount Holyoke would understand. It was not a community of women. In fact, as I remember it, it was not a community at all. I had no sense of being a member of a college; my community was, most immediately and strongly, the inhabitants of my dorm, Comstock, and then, more dilutely, of my House, North House (now Pforzheimer). I doubt if I was friends with more than a handful of women from other Radcliffe Houses; I believe I once set foot in one of the dorms in South House. I am quite sure I never entered any of the Cabot dorms at all. I could not then have named any but the dorms in my own House, though by the time I graduated I knew (and had spent time in) every Harvard House and could describe in detail their particular characters and reputations. Radcliffe, in contrast, had for me no identity of its own and no sense of unity that such an identity might anchor. It was in every sense, as it had begun, the Annex—a place to eat, to study (it had a lovely library), to hang out with my dorm mates, and to sleep, but not a focus of what I then viewed as important: political activism, cultural events, intellectual life, social and sexual exploration, the last of which I saw in completely heterosexual terms. All of those were located at Harvard, in the Yard, the Houses, and the Square.

The reasons for Radcliffe's invisibility to me were, I think, partly internal and partly institutional. Internal in that, like most of the women I knew, I came from a public high school that sent students to Radcliffe with great infrequency, so I didn't arrive knowing other students in the college; I constructed my own community out of my dorm mates, the women I saw every day. More than that, however, I was completely male-identified. I think this was fairly common for a girl of my race (white) and class (upper middle/ professional), growing up in the late 1950s and 1960s, before second-wave feminism had made appreciable inroads into American culture. My father was a high-achieving physicist, my mother (class of 1944), a highly gifted and profoundly dissatisfied caretaker of four children who taught part-time at a local community college—no role model for the shape of a female life there. Virtually all of my high school teachers were male. Though my best friends were all girls, real social life in my high school was by definition heterosexual. So I wasn't prepared to appreciate, or even to see, a community of women, particularly one so dilute and ambiguously constituted as Radcliffe, devoid of a curriculum or a faculty, and overshadowed in every respect by its bigger, richer, more fascinating brother.

There were many institutional factors that played into my own insensitivity to the possibilities of female community at Radcliffe. The focus on heterosocial and heterosexual interaction was reinforced by numerous Radcliffe practices, in which we were all complicit. Take, for example, the tradition of Saturday night milk and cookies dished out by Mrs. Perry (wife of the North House master) in the Comstock living room. The message was clear: if you didn't have a date on Saturday, you stayed in, and this was a consolation prize. The message was made even clearer by the fact that we were encouraged to come down in our pajamas and bathrobes to hear Master Perry read a bedtime story. (I don't think any of us thought that dateless Harvard men were spending Saturday evening in the same way.) Aside from Mrs. Perry, I do not remember meeting a single adult woman associated with Radcliffe—by adult I mean a woman who was not some kind of student— except for the food service workers in the dining room and kitchen. I have no idea what Mrs. Perry did with the rest of her time; she may have been a remarkable woman, of great energy and accomplishment. But, except for one or two ceremonial occasions, I do not believe I ever saw her (or any other female adult at Radcliffe) doing anything but serving food. I don't remember if my House had faculty associates; in any case, none were likely to have been women, given the constitution of the faculty at that time. I do not remember meeting a Radcliffe administrator of any description, which now strikes me as remarkable. This remarkable dearth of any women who might have served as plausible role models for an intellectually and professionally ambitious woman—and I was both—may explain the enormous impact on me of my only two female professors in 12 years of higher education, Joan Cadden and Caroline Walker Bynum (assistant professors in the History of Science and History Departments, respectively, without any prospect of tenure), whose fields of medieval intellectual and religious history ultimately became my own. But they belonged to Harvard, not to Radcliffe.

Unlike the students I later taught at Wellesley, I do not remember having any sense of pride in Radcliffe as a college. Indeed, as I have already indicated, I didn't really think of it as a college at all. I remember being proud of having been admitted to Radcliffe when I was still in high school, but it was hard to retain that sense of pride in the face of what I can only describe as an unrelenting rain of contemptuous messages from Harvard faculty, administrators, and students about those they called Cliffies. I still can't hear that word without flinching; it was inevitably part of some piece of mindless vituperation. Whenever my Fine Arts 13 professor put up a slide of a painting that showed a particularly ugly woman, he would say, "There's another Cliffie." I remember Skiddy von Stade, the dean of freshmen, protesting any change in the four-to-one male to female undergraduate ratio on the grounds that the education of women, who couldn't be expected to use it, was basically thrown away. My tutors used the phrase "like most Cliffies" a fair amount. I was told that, "like most Cliffies," my work was highly competent but not creative. My senior year, after I had won a Marshall Scholarship for graduate study in England, the head tutor of my concentration, History and Literature, called me in for a special meeting to warn me against delusions of grandeur—in this case, planning on a graduate education. Like most Cliffies, he said, you're still riding on your laurels from high school.

Being hit on by tutors and teaching fellows—we had no word, or even a mental category, for what later came to be called sexual harassment—was an ongoing fact of life. Comments about "Cliffie bitches" were too numerous even to notice—fallout in part from that dreadful four-to-one ratio and from the general stigma attached in that period to smart, intellectual women. I don't think any of us really believed the awful things Harvard men said about us, but it made it hard for me to take much joy in the abstract fact of being a Radcliffe student. In this connection, I remember the utter shock of seeing

Love Story, released in 1970, which portrayed a Radcliffe student as a romantic heroine (even if she did die in the end).

The spring of 1970 brought changes far more significant than the release of *Love Story*, however: the bombing of Cambodia, the cancellation of classes and finals in the wake of protests, riots, and tear gas in the Square. A quieter revolution was happening at Radcliffe with the beginning of coresidence, when 40 women from the three Radcliffe Houses moved into three of the Harvard Houses (Winthrop, Adams, and Lowell), and 40 men from those Harvard Houses moved up Garden Street to take their places. For me, things got worse rather than better because I chose to be one of the first 40 North House students to move into Winthrop. Wasn't Harvard where the action was? This turned out to be a mistake. Other Radcliffe students had better experiences, and the situation in Adams was reportedly very good. For me, however, Winthrop was a nightmare. Many of its students had opposed coresidence—some had even been moved out of their suites to accommodate the arriving Radcliffe students—and the hostility was particularly palpable in my entry, where our entry mates used to urinate against our door.

I won't dwell on this unhappy experience because I want to emphasize instead the effects of coresidence at Radcliffe, which—when I returned the next fall—had undergone what I remember as a remarkable transformation. Arriving back at North House was in some respects disconcerting. Even to my less than embryonic feminist consciousness, it was surprising to find that students of the House, still overwhelmingly female, had elected an all-male slate of student officers, from the president right down to the fire marshal. But House officers were seen as pretty much a joke anyway, particularly in the context of the national political firestorm of spring and summer 1970. The most amazing long-term change in my House—and I'm sure each House differed—was a dramatic sense of relaxation. We (the women residents) worked less, stressed less over our courses, and had more fun. A lot of really weird behaviors around food and eating—lining up in front of the dining room door at 4:45 P.M., eating only a mini-can of tuna fish at dinner and then gorging on a dozen doughnuts—mostly either stopped or went underground.

I'm still not quite sure why the presence of men made such a difference. Partly, I think I was very lucky; I was by then living in Wolbach, and the men and women there got along extremely well. The bonding took place both around forms of mild social rowdiness and around more serious, political things as well; most of the men in my dorm were seniors and many faced the draft in a war that virtually all of us abhorred. Partly it was because their presence validated Radcliffe; amazingly, a small number of men considered the place interesting enough to move there voluntarily. This made it seem less of a ghetto, despite its pitifully inadequate housing and its distance from the Square. Mostly, however, I think it was the particular men who had initially chosen to come to Radcliffe. They were, on the whole, men who actually *liked* women, who enjoyed our company, appreciated our intelligence, and found us interesting and funny (which we were). This was presumably why they decided to join us in the first place. I'm sure there were lots of men who liked women both on the faculty and among Harvard students in 1970, but I doubt if they were in the majority, and their voices were in any case lost in the much louder cacophony of generalized institutional and personal misogyny.

For me, at least—and this is not something I'm particularly proud of—the fact that these men liked me and my dorm mates made me begin to realize how much I liked us as well. So much so, in fact, that at the end of my junior year, in the summer of 1971, I moved down Walker Street into 60 Walker, a small frame building that was still part of North House, and its last remaining all-female dorm. Thus, I spent much of 1971-72 as part of a surrogate family of irreverent Radcliffe women, presided over by a marvelous dorm resident (a graduate student), whom we called Mothah and who was about as different from Mrs. Perry as it was possible to be. That was, I think, my first conscious appreciation of the joys of female community—an appreciation that truly flowered only much later, during my years teaching at Wellesley. That, then, was *my* Radcliffe in the early 1970s: no Adamless Eden, to be sure, but at least no longer a no-man's land, in a larger institution where man was still without question the measure of all things.

FOUNDING THE COMMITTEE
FOR WOMEN'S STUDIES

1970s.
Students establish an ad hoc Committee for Women's Studies
to lobby for a concentration in the field.

By the mid-1970s, as the Boston area women's movement fragmented, Radcliffe student activists—liberal feminists, radical feminists, socialist feminists, Third World feminists, and Marxist-Leninists—joined together to fight for women's studies at Harvard. Part of the forgotten story of the student movement of the 1970s, the Committee for Women's Studies aimed to create a Women's Studies Department along the lines of the embattled Afro-American Studies Department and to infuse women's scholarship and experience into the entire Harvard curriculum. The egregious exclusion of all but a few distinguished women from Harvard's faculty and the invisibility of women in our studies kept us focused on the task at hand. We had a multi-pronged strategy, from educational forums to leaflets and petitions to negotiating with the administration. At the time, as an art student, I saw my main contribution to the Committee for Women's Studies as designing educational and polemical materials. As a historian today looking back, I can discern in my participation in the Committee for Women's Studies the beginnings of my longstanding research interests in feminism, gender, and race. I still carry with me lessons learned about respecting the political, social, and cultural differences among us, the painful personal costs of racism and homophobia, and the importance of taking a stand in the supposed ivory tower of academia.

—Yaël Simpson Fletcher

Poster advocating a concentration in Women's Studies, 1970s
(Yaël Simpson Fletcher).

1978.
Faculty Council establishes a Committee on Women's Studies to encourage the development of departmental courses in the field.

The Faculty Committee will not recommend establishing a department or a concentration in women's studies, Edward L. Keenan '57, dean of the Graduate School of Arts and Sciences and chairman of the Faculty Committee, said yesterday. The standing committee that would be created would primarily concern itself with encouraging departments to offer courses in women's studies, and would probably not offer courses on its own, Keenan said.

—*Harvard Crimson*, May 24, 1978

A graduate student said she thought it was unfortunate that someone could go through Harvard and "not know a single thing about one woman in the world."

—*Harvard Crimson*, Feb. 9, 1979

1986.
Harvard faculty debates Women's Studies.

A month after a leading British historian [Olwen Hufton] accepted the University's first joint tenured position in Women's Studies, the field is on the verge of becoming an official Harvard concentration. . . . As the vote approaches, however, the idea that was first advanced more than eight years ago remains a subject of disagreement among professors.

"Courses taught by women under Women's Studies have been a vehicle for feminist propaganda," Harvey C. Mansfield, Jr., Professor of Government, said yesterday.

"People want Women's Studies as a political symbol, but you'll find that no one will concentrate in it," said David Riesman '31, Henry Ford II Professor of Social Sciences *Emeritus*.

It may disrupt the process of integration of Women's Studies courses with other disciplines," said Steven E. Ozment, professor or history and associate dean for undergraduate education. "It's like trying to bottle sunlight," said Ozment. "The experience of women is so broad that it may be impossible for a set core of courses to define it."

"I think Women's Studies would be the best 350th gift that Harvard would get," said Assistant Professor of History, Catherine Clinton.

—All from the *Harvard Crimson*, Oct. 23, 1986

With only one dissenting voice, the Faculty of Arts and Sciences voted yesterday to create an undergraduate degree-granting program in Women's Studies. . . . "I am delighted," said Women's Studies Committee Chairman Susan R. Suleiman, professor of Romantic and comparative literature. "This is a really important and historic day for Harvard and I am gratified by the reaction of my colleagues who have shown they are not unresponsive to the needs of students."

—*Harvard Crimson*, Nov. 19, 1986

Harvard is the latest of some 450 schools, including the seven other Ivy League colleges, to adopt women's studies, a field first recognized in the late 1960s and now considered at the cutting edge of many scholarly disciplines.

. . . The approval yesterday followed several years of work by a faculty committee and a petition signed last spring by 2,104 students, nearly one-third of Harvard's undergraduates.

—*Boston Globe*, November 19, 1986

A Radcliffe Girl at Harvard

or Why Members of the Class of 1958 Staged a Revolution in 1993

Ann R. Shapiro

I left New York for Cambridge with my classmate, Dinah, on a sunny spring morning in early June 1993. The thirty-fifth reunion promised to be fun—three days to be college "girls." The painful events from those college days were now just a part of one chapter in a long personal history, no different from most in its combination of joy and sorrow. I was now divorced, but even though the marriage ended, I was not bitter or even unhappy about it. I had three grown children, one of whom had graduated from Harvard with a Phi Beta Kappa key, and I no longer had to please anyone but myself. My career had been far from brilliant, but it was good enough. I was a tenured professor of English at Farmingdale State University of New York's, a second-tier college in New York state's enormous archipelago. I was earning a decent, if modest, living and had two books and many articles in women's studies to my credit. What if I had been a man? Who knows? I had little cause for complaint.

When we pulled into Radcliffe Yard in a much smaller car than the one that had deposited me there 35 years earlier, the building facades looked much the same, and yet much was different. The dormitories were no longer called dormitories but Houses, like the Harvard Houses, whose towers poked up along the banks of the Charles River on the other side of Harvard Square. Harvard now owned the Radcliffe buildings, and when the College was in session, the dormitories were occupied by both men and women. Radcliffe girls had become Harvard women, and students of both genders were much in evidence, lounging on the Quad, packing gooseneck lamps and computers into waiting vans, or toting suitcases for the returning alumnae settling in for the upcoming festivities. No one was wearing a raincoat to cover her shorts, and there were no House mothers pouring tea. Hilles Library loomed over the smallish Houses in the Quad. Built as a new Radcliffe undergraduate library, it now opened its doors to all students.

I was shown to my room in North House by a smiling student, who chatted amiably about meal tickets, buses to the Square (for us aging alumnae), and other essentials. The fourth-floor room to which I had been assigned looked exactly like the one I had vacated 35 years before—the same thin striped mattress and wooden chest, the same dimly lit mirror. The communal bathroom was down the hall. Radcliffe's benefactors had clearly not been the CEOs or family scions who had endowed Harvard's more gracious accommodations. My helpful companion wished me a pleasant stay as she hurried off to help another alumna find her way in the new Harvard House, which was, after all, indistinguishable from the old Radcliffe dorm.

Alone now in my tiny cubicle, I began to wonder exactly how different things really were after all these years, but I was interrupted by Dinah, who wanted to go over the long list of events to which we had been invited. We would go to the Pops Concert with our Harvard classmates, but mostly we would socialize with Radcliffe women in Radcliffe Yard or Radcliffe Quad. Our class had graduated well before the merger with Harvard in 1977. Therefore, the reunion organizers had decided that our real ties were with Radcliffe, which was still soliciting our money for its ever-growing endowment. In the next three days, we would be with women—a radical departure from our undergraduate years, when most of our time had actually been spent in the company of men—male undergraduates who dominated the classrooms and social activities; male Harvard professors who taught our classes.

The dinner that night at Radcliffe Yard under the tent was without incident. President Linda Wilson looked elegant and presidential in her summer suit as she welcomed us back to our college. What college? I had graduated from a male-dominated institution called Harvard and was being welcomed back to a woman's college called Radcliffe. Thank God everyone was wearing a large name tag hanging from an elasticized string around the neck. These were my classmates but, except for those who had lived in my own dormitory, both names and faces were unfamiliar. We had been lost to one another in Harvard's male world. I was greeted several times by one or another vaguely recognizable woman, who invariably cooed, "You look exactly the same." It is a lovely lie that we all tell each other at reunions. There was little resemblance between the aging faces around me and the young women I had seen that morning bustling around Radcliffe Quad. Many of my classmates were attractive, some even distinguished, but we all wore reading glasses, and most of those I recognized were noticeably thicker around the middle.

I felt increasingly disconnected from the lectures, meetings, and meals on the following day. Something was wrong, and I couldn't put my finger on it. That evening I would understand. Having already grown weary of reunion activities by midafternoon, I met an old friend and shared a glass of wine at her house in Cambridge. It was a pleasant break in the tightly scheduled activities, and I was not at all sure that I wanted to attend the Class of 1958 dinner that evening. But I had promised Dinah that I would be there, and besides, I had paid for the meal. And so I wearily made my way back to Radcliffe Yard to rejoin my classmates. The fruit cup on the tables was past its prime and there was bad news from the speaker's platform. Jane O'Reilly, who had written all those irreverent articles in *New York Magazine* about her sex life and other unspeakable matters (while I was changing diapers, as forecast by both my mother and the *Radcliffe Yearbook*); was to be the speaker. We were told that Jane's mother had died that morning, so Jane would be unable to attend. Someone suggested that since there was no speaker, we might use the opportunity to talk about our Radcliffe experience.

I was already bored and in no mood to pretend that I had shared all those happy times with this group of mostly strangers, but by now I was hungry, and even the aging fruit cup was beginning to look palatable. Eyeing the fruit and planning my escape, I was listening only intermittently to the speaker who had just finished apologizing for Jane's absence. But then I was stunned. The speaker was saying something that I had never expected to hear amidst the reunion banalities. She had just declared that she had hated Radcliffe— that she believed that the Admissions Office had made a mistake when they admitted her. I had barely assimilated her words when someone else grabbed the microphone and announced, "If there ever had been a Mother Radcliffe, she had clearly deserted us; we were made to feel second class." Another voice reminded us of the professors who clearly preferred our male class-mates and ignored us. Someone remembered the classmate who had been raped and was afraid to tell. "And what about our male classmates? Most of them are now earning six-figure salaries, while we are earning roughly half or less—good for women, but . . . ," the voice trailed off.

The comments kept coming. Each of us during our undergraduate years had apparently considered herself the misfit or malcontent—the one person who had failed to fulfill the promise. We were finally admitting that we had been short-changed at Harvard. It was exhilarating to realize, however belatedly, that no one was alone in feeling cheated. But at the same time I was getting more and more depressed that all this truth was coming up too late in a game that was already lost—at least for us.

Feeling empowered by the wine that had now begun to take effect, I stood up and delivered a short speech that went something like this:

> We cannot change what happened to us, but if sexual discrimination still exists at Harvard, we must change things for the young women who are there now—those women students who may still feel the sting of unequal treatment. If today's students are like we were, they may be like the proverbial fish who do not see the ocean; they may not see the sexism that surrounds them and instead blame themselves. As alumnae, we may be uniquely qualified to understand what may be wrong, and we are free to insist on reform. After all, what can they do to us now?

My comments were greeted with applause. I therefore suggested that we write to President Wilson and ask that Radcliffe take a leadership position in ensuring equality for women at Harvard. I added, "If Radcliffe would not take such leadership, then perhaps it was time for Radcliffe to go out of business altogether." There was only one vocal dissenter. Peggy Groome, our class secretary, replied that we needed Radcliffe to protect women because Harvard could surely not be trusted. "It was," she added, "like asking the fox to guard the chicken coop."

I did not want to argue. I responded, "Anyone who wants to discuss how we follow up can meet with me at our hospitality suite after dinner." It was an amazing catharsis. I finally put into words what I had been thinking for 35 years but had not dared to say, even to myself.

By the time I reached the hospitality suite back at the Quad, the room was jammed. People were sitting on the arms of sofas and standing in every vacant corner, apparently indifferent to the lack of air conditioning. I offered to write a letter to President Wilson stating the problem and asking for redress. I would circulate the letter for corrections and additions to anyone who would give me her name and address. Someone passed a legal pad around the room, and the pages soon filled up. We tried to outline the content of the letter, and I scribbled furiously as people stated their thoughts. But I was getting too tired to focus clearly and suggested that people contact me by mail or phone during the next month. I walked back to my room that night feeling something that I had never felt before at Radcliffe—I was part of a community of women.

The next day there was an urgent phone message from my classmate, Gabriela Schlesinger. Gaby had been eating lunch in Harvard Square when she overheard the conversation of a group of women from the class of 1953, who were talking about the very concerns that had galvanized us the previous night. Gaby soon joined the conversation and learned that they had already organized an action committee. When I completed the letter, I was to send a copy to Peggy Schmertzler, chairman of that committee.

That July I wrote the letter. Not only did classmates write and phone, but Joan Baer visited me in the summer house I was renting in Vermont. Something had happened that seemed very important, at least to some of us. If we could change Harvard, the most powerful institution of higher education in America and maybe the world, we might be able to move a giant step closer to attaining equality for women. It was an idea almost too marvelous to contemplate.

We did not see each other again until the following December. On a snowy morning, 15 women from the classes of 1953 and 1958 met for breakfast at the Copley Plaza Hotel in Boston to strategize for a meeting with Radcliffe's President Wilson the following day. We came mainly from New York and Boston, but also from Chicago and Maryland. The Committee for the Equality of Women at Harvard was founded that morning and incorporated shortly thereafter.

The next day five of us congregated at 8:30 A.M. in the president's conference room at Radcliffe to meet with President Wilson. We had masses of data, and everyone was impeccably polite as we systematically went through the evidence of a century of discrimination against women. Linda Wilson praised us and we, in turn, lauded her efforts and good intentions. Although she proved to be both competent and intelligent, Wilson made it clear that she had no power at Harvard. That afternoon we resolved that not only would we pursue our cause with Radcliffe, but we would also have to meet with members of the Harvard administration. Over the next several years we talked to Harvard and Radcliffe deans, faculty, students, and Overseers. We solicited Radcliffe alumnae and soon had a group of almost

2,000 supporters. While there were many issues on our agenda, we agreed that the central concern was the paucity of tenured women on Harvard's faculty. We created a junior faculty fellowship for a nontenured woman on the Harvard faculty and attempted to draw attention to our goals through seminars, mailings, and an occasional *Crimson* article, but we needed to do something more dramatic. With the help of a wealthy Radcliffe alumna, we therefore set up an escrow account and asked all Radcliffe alumnae and targeted Harvard alumni to contribute their gifts to the account rather than to the Harvard Campaign. The money would be distributed to Harvard when some specified changes had occurred.

The escrow account was dynamite. The response to our press release exceeded our expectations. Articles soon appeared in *Newsweek,* the *Chronicle of Higher Education, Women in Higher Education,* and the *Boston Globe, Washington Post, New York Times,* and *San Juan Star.* We were even featured on CBS television news in Boston. Harvard and Radcliffe finally took notice. Whether they approved of our actions or not, at least they knew we existed, and over time we were invited to meetings, lunches, and dinners with administrators and donors.

In the next few years, we expanded our activities. With grants from two foundations and a supportive Harvard alumnus, we held a national invitational academic conference, the proceedings of which were published in a book. Although we were pleased with our accomplishments, change at Harvard was glacial. More women were being tenured, but Harvard still lagged behind most other universities.

Then one day everything changed. Provost Harvey Fineberg called to announce that Radcliffe College was about to become the Radcliffe Institute of Advanced Study. While the new Radcliffe Institute would have a "commitment to women, gender, and society," it was unclear what that meant. We were uncertain whether women would now play a greater role at Harvard or whether they would be marginalized as in the past.

When Radcliffe acting dean Mary Dunn suggested that we might give our escrow account to the Institute, we refused because we were told that the Institute would have no professors tenured at Harvard. The turning point came one afternoon when I was startled by a phone call from Mary Dunn. She wanted me to speak to incoming dean Drew Faust, and she had alerted Drew that I would probably call in the next few days. I spoke to her that evening and by the end of our conversation, I was won over. She saw the crucial need to increase Harvard's women faculty and had negotiated that there would be some joint tenured appointments at Harvard and the Radcliffe

Institute. She further assured me that she shared our goals of advancing women's equality in the Harvard community. A few months later she convinced the rest of the committee, and we unanimously voted to give the Radcliffe Institute the escrow money.

I was immediately put in touch with Ellen LaFolette; 1954, who had raised money from two alumnae groups in California, and together we launched a campaign for the Radcliffe Alumnae Professorship, a joint professorship between the Radcliffe Institute and the Harvard Faculty of Arts and Sciences. With the help of alumna Carol Pforzheimer, Mary Dunn, and the Radcliffe Development Office and a matching grant from Harvard, we not only endowed the professorship but we have also provided substantial seed money to endow a new junior faculty fellowship.

A few weeks ago, I resigned as cochair of the Committee for the Equality of Women at Harvard. I am content that I found the community of women that eluded me in my undergraduate years at Radcliffe, and with them I may have moved Harvard a few steps along the road to women's equality. Gloria Steinem once wrote, "One day, an army of gray-haired women may quietly take over the earth." Perhaps she is right, but I believe that it is now up to younger women to complete the revolution.

UPS AND DOWNS
WITH HARVARD

Affection, Justice, and Reciprocity
in the University Community

Helen Vendler

Although we are all assembled at this gathering because we have been 25 years at Harvard, today I am privately celebrating 53 years of attachment to Harvard, to which I first came when I was 15. (If I were to take this account back all the way, I would have to say that I am celebrating 68 years at Harvard, since my parents brought me to the Arnold Arboretum from the time I was an infant.)

When I was a girl in Jamaica Plain, I used to go every Saturday to Copley Square to get books from the Boston Public Library. I learned, by bitter experience, to submit whole packets of request slips, because at least half always came back saying "Lost," "Not on Shelf," "At the Bindery," or "Out to Another Borrower." One dismal Saturday I put in 24 slips and got no books. Dismayed at having no mental food in the cupboard for a week, I denounced the inadequacy of the library at the family dinner table. "What you need," said my father reminiscently, "is Widener." It turned out that he had had a

---

This speech, given at a 25-year recognition ceremony for faculty and staff, was originally published in *Harvard Magazine,* Nov.-Dec. 2001.

Harvard Library card when he was studying for the Ph.D. at Boston University (a study eventually abandoned in the wake of three children). "Maybe," he continued, "Harvard would give me a card again." He wrote a letter asking for a card, and since he was a Boston high school teacher, Keyes Metcalf, then librarian of Widener, gave him a card for a year. As my father's surrogate, I used the card every Saturday so religiously that eventually, tired of getting me piles of books, the circulation staff sent me off with a stack pass to gather them in the future for myself.

That year was the happiest of my youth. In the best of all possible worlds, the Widener stacks would be given to every voracious 15-year-old reader. When the card ran out, I was grief-stricken. But the bulletin boards I had seen showed me that there was more to Harvard than Widener, and I began to come frequently to concerts and lectures and poetry readings: I caught pneumonia at age 17 in November 1950, sitting on the unheated floor of Memorial Hall while T. S. Eliot lectured in Sanders Theatre. I wanted desperately to enter Radcliffe, but it was the era of the Cold War, and the cardinal of the Boston archdiocese was informing Roman Catholic parents that it was a mortal sin to send one's children to godless secular universities. My parents believed him and sent me to Emmanuel College, where I was not happy. I vowed to return to Harvard some day.

My next attachment to Harvard was as a member of the office staff. When I was admitted to graduate school here, my parents were still opposed to my coming, and so I had to support myself. As soon as I had my spring admission letter, I went to Fay House, the administrative center of Radcliffe, and said, "You've let me in; now you have to give me a job so that I can afford to come." The dean of the graduate school was flabbergasted enough by this direct demand to provide me a job, and more. I was the floating substitute for anyone on vacation; I ran the switchboard; I typed academic transcripts; I entertained aspiring freshmen and their parents; I transcribed admissions interviews. I answered the phone, and, after learning to use the adding machine, made up, in double-entry form, the entire budget of Radcliffe College. I proctored exams and delivered blue books to professors in their studies and suites, being warned before delivering blue books to Professor Arthur Darby Nock that he sometimes answered the door naked. A bit taken aback, I nonetheless went to his Eliot House suite, but saw nothing more shocking than a floor covered feet-thick with files.

My principal employer—during that first summer and the four years to follow (because I worked during term-time whenever a Fay House office needed me)—was Ruth Davenport, the registrar. She was the ideal supervisor.

"This is the work that needs to be done every day; when you've finished, aside from answering the phone and attending to anyone who comes in, you may read," she said. I was very fond of Miss Davenport; when I was leaving, she gave me a book we had discussed, Adrienne Rich's first book of poetry, *A Change of World*, inscribed to me by Adrienne, whom I hadn't yet met. During my years at Fay House, I learned a great deal about good supervisors and bad, snobbish ones and democratic ones, and the experience made me sympathetic to staff and their difficulties. I literally would not be here today had I not been given a job at Harvard; and I passed the graduate Latin exam on the reading time Miss Davenport allowed me.

At some time or another, I expect, many of us have felt unwanted by Harvard. When, in my first week of graduate study, I entered the office of the chair of the English Department to have my program card signed, he said, without preamble, "You know, we don't want you here, Miss Hennessy: we don't want any women here." I left trembling. (He apologized, 13 years later.) But I soon found other teachers—John Kelleher, Douglas Bush, and Reuben Brower—who sponsored me as generously as they sponsored their male students. It was, however, a strange existence I had during the four years of graduate school: because women could not live in the Harvard graduate dormitories, could not be resident tutors in the Houses, and could not apply for Harvard fellowships, we lived a relatively impoverished and isolated life. Most of the women left. But I was happy: I had Widener again—and I still went to the lectures and concerts and plays and poetry readings. And, once I was a tutor, I had students, wonderful ones, as I still do. I met my husband at Harvard, and we went off to teach at Cornell in 1960.

By 1966 I was back in Boston, divorced and teaching at Boston University. Eventually, I was offered a professorship at Harvard—not so much because the English Department wanted to change its habit of appointing only male professors, but because, so I was told, the Department of Health, Education, and Welfare was threatening to withhold money from Harvard unless a good-faith effort to appoint women was put in place. But times were changing, and I was made to feel welcome when I came back. I was very happy to have Widener once more—and everything that went with it except half of my after-tax salary, which I was handing over to Harvard for my son's tuition, room, and board. A good bargain, in the end.

Most of us here, I expect, have had some of the same ups and downs with Harvard that I have had—good and bad supervisors (or chairs, or deans); good and bad working environments (my Barker Center office, with its heating and cooling controls, has made me, for the first time in my working life, comfortable). Many of us remember fraught moments here during protests of one sort or another. I recall the minuet that went on when the students, one May, erected shanties on campus to protest apartheid. When the administration courteously asked whether the students would take them down for commencement, the students replied, equally politely, that one of the points of the shanties was to let commencement visitors see them. The administration, with perfect good sense and continued courtesy, thereupon rerouted the commencement procession around the shanties. I was the escort, that day, of the South African novelist Nadine Gordimer, who was being awarded an honorary degree; she greeted the students in the shanties warmly and wore one of their ribbons on her gown. The glorious later moment of Nelson Mandela's release, and his visit to receive an honorary degree, made me glad to remember that the administration and the students had acted intelligently, both of them, on that commencement day. Later protests, too, have been finally courteously resolved since a mutual respect has prevailed.

One of the aspects of Harvard we all profit from is its invigorating and changing beauty. I am grateful to have my half-century of memories of the Yard at all seasons—especially during those early years when Dutch elm disease had not yet felled the elms. There is nothing like looking up, after spending the afternoon deep in a book in the Widener reading room, and finding that snow has fallen, and dusk has come—that the spire of Memorial Church presides over a transformed scene. And there is nothing like seeing old engravings of the first College buildings and recognizing that the fine brick presence of Massachusetts Hall is still here. When I first saw the Yard in the 1940s, I was touched by the uniform handsomeness of the young men stepping quickly across the Yard in their wool jackets and silk ties. Now the young come in both sexes and wear many costumes—and the sight is more amusing and more democratically reassuring, if not so beautiful.

Even in the 1950s, Harvard was more diverse than, say, Princeton—but now we have truly made an effort, ably defended by president Neil Rudenstine, toward economic and racial diversity. I was touched to hear one student say to his friend, as they walked ahead of me down the stairs of Harvard Hall, "And of course I send my mother $50 every month." Prejudice never disappears entirely; but I don't think anyone would dare now tell a student openly that he isn't wanted, as I was told 45 years ago. Some things do get better. And that includes the students: our current ones are astounding. Give them anything to do, intellectually, and they will do it. And they will do it while putting out the *Crimson* or working as part of dorm crew or getting up at unholy hours to row. They are runners and wrestlers, mail assistants and research helpers, singers and artists; and their energy makes the whole place hum. The older I get, the gladder I am to be in their vivid company.

A sociologist seeing us all here together—librarians, secretaries, locksmiths, administrators, teachers, chefs, police, lawyers—would reflect on the variety of talents it takes to keep a university running. What would be hidden from the bird's-eye view of the spectator would be the private lives that we juggle in tandem with our Harvard work—our lives as children of our parents, parents of our children, lovers, friends, volunteers, grandparents. We couldn't do our daily work here if we weren't ourselves kept afloat by our affections. If we are lucky, two or three of our fellow workers know and sympathize with us when trouble comes, and we discover that the workplace, too, can be a place to find affection.

It should also be a place to find justice. A university ought to be a small model of a just community. When the administration keeps its word to its students and to us, it is part of that model; when we keep our word in return, we affirm the model. We want the students to leave here not only with some knowledge and a résumé, but also with the memory of the society that they have seen here. They will remember us as welcoming or hostile, just or unjust. In recognizing our years of service today, Harvard harks back to the old tradition of the feudal lord's ring giving to his faithful retainers. The university, in the idealization common to all such rituals, presumes that the society we make together today, and have made together for the past quarter-century, is a just one; in accepting the honor Harvard pays us, we signify our faith in the worth of our common work. We must go back tomorrow to the unidealized ordinary circumstances of daily life, but something of today's recognition will linger as an aftershine. Most of us, I think, will feel, as Harvard expresses its gratitude to us, our gratitude to it.

Mingling Promiscuously

A History of Women and Men at Harvard

Drew Gilpin Faust

I am Drew Faust, dean of the Radcliffe Institute for Advanced Study and professor of history in the Faculty of Arts and Sciences.[1] I am here because in October 1999 Radcliffe College merged with Harvard University. Radcliffe, which was founded in the late nineteenth century to give women access to a Harvard education, has now evolved into an Institute for Advanced Study, and Harvard College has fully integrated women and men within its undergraduate body. Unlike women students accepted before 1999, none of you was admitted to Harvard-Radcliffe; unlike women who graduated before 1999, none of you will have the signature of a Radcliffe president on your diplomas. You all, women and men alike, will receive the same piece of paper when you graduate on June 9, 2005.

You are enacting a new twenty-first-century chapter in the long and complicated history of women and men at Harvard University. But you are also the heirs of a past that has profoundly shaped this university and that will, inevitably, have an influence on your experience here. I am by training and temperament a historian, so I tend always to see the past as prologue. I arrived here only last January after 25 years of teaching at the University of

This essay derives from a lecture delivered in Fall 2001 to the Harvard Class of 2005 at the invitation of the Ann Radcliffe Trust, Harvard College, printed in the Radcliffe Quarterly (Winter 2002).

Pennsylvania to become the first dean of the newly reconfigured Radcliffe—no longer an independent college but now one of Harvard's ten schools. In the months since, I have been repeatedly struck by the relevance of Radcliffe and Harvard's past to where we find ourselves today. I want to share a little of that past with you—so you see not just the Harvard of 2001 as you wander its paths and corridors and sit in its classrooms. I hope that history will bring another dimension to your understanding of your environment, a dimension that will enable you not only to appreciate the lives of those who preceded you, but more fully to understand your own role as pioneers of a new order, of a new set of relationships between women and men at Harvard.

Harvard College's evolution into the coeducational undergraduate institution it is today is unique; it has followed a path unlike that of any other college or university in the United States. When it opened in 1636, it was, of course, designed exclusively for the education of men. But that did not mean that the Harvard community did not from the outset include women: women who swept the halls, cleaned the rooms, even women who offered the College support through donations and legacies. Harvard has never been a woman-less place—though for too long, as Laurel Ulrich of the History Department has noted, it has had a womanless history.

By the nineteenth century, women's rights and women's access to higher education had become significant social questions, and females began actively to seek admission as Harvard students. A woman applied to the Medical School in 1847. The dean assured Harvard's governing body, the Corporation, that she was old and unattractive enough not to disrupt the male students' concentration, but she was still denied a place. Just two years later, Sarah Pellet sought admission to the College. President Jared Sparks replied to her directly: "I should doubt," he wrote, "whether a solitary female, mingling as she must do promiscuously with so large a number of the other sex, would find her situation either agreeable or advantageous."

In the decades that followed Sarah Pellet's disappointment, the expansion of higher education for women in the United States was dramatic. Oberlin had been path-breaking in admitting women in 1837; Mount Holyoke Seminary was founded the same year; Vassar opened in 1865 as a college exclusively for women; Cornell accepted an endowment for a college for women in 1872; Smith and Wellesley opened for women students in 1875. These developments did not go unnoticed in Cambridge, where a group of women—wives, daughters, and sisters of its highly educated elite—became increasingly vocal about their desire to partake of Harvard's intellectual riches.

Harvard spoke and would continue to speak out firmly against coeducation. Charles W. Eliot, who became the university's president in 1869 and remained in office for 40 years, established his position in his inaugural address, declaring that the policing of hundreds of young men and women of marriageable age would be impossible. He had doubts, moreover, about what he called the "natural mental capacities" of the female sex. Harvard would not follow the coeducational example of Oberlin. But neither would the Cambridge supporters of women's education model their efforts on Wellesley or Smith. Their hopes for eventual integration with Harvard led them to invent a different structure.

Since early in the nineteenth century, individual women had, under a variety of informal arrangements, gained entrance to some lectures at Harvard College, and this may have fueled an appetite for greater access. In 1872 a group of Cambridge and Boston ladies formed the Woman's Education Association and invited President Eliot to a meeting to consider women's admission to Harvard.

Eliot's opposition to coeducation was unyielding, and he cited reasons that ranged from the already overcrowded state of the College to the violation of moral and religious tenets. The discussion about coeducation at Harvard during these years extended well beyond the president, as students and faculty articulated the principles of manliness that they regarded as the essence of the College's identity. Barrett Wendell, professor of English, proclaimed that there must be no deviation from the tenet that had ruled since the founding of the College in 1636: "that the influences amid which education should be obtained here must remain purely virile." Even more than an "institution of learning," Harvard was, he affirmed, "a traditional school of manly character." The *Crimson* described coeducation as "a dangerous tendency in American society," best left to the likes of Oberlin, Cornell, and Boston University, and resisted by elite schools like Yale and Harvard. The *Harvard Graduates Magazine* was gratified that the university was not being "incautious" by precipitously embracing women's education. It noted with approval that Harvard was in fact "behind most of the great colleges in the world" on the question, for "so much had been accomplished for women's education almost everywhere else." This tone of seeming wistfulness belied the pride in Harvard's judicious conservatism that infused the essay.

Under the leadership of Elizabeth Cary Agassiz, widow of the distinguished Harvard scientist Louis Agassiz, the women proposed a compromise, officially titled "Private Collegiate Instruction for Women" but popularly known as "the Annex." Women students would be taught by Harvard professors in classes and lectures given in addition to their regular obligations to the College. Opening in 1879, the Annex came to offer 20 or 30 courses a year, less than a quarter of the number at Harvard, to a population of young women drawn overwhelmingly from the local area. Elizabeth Agassiz regarded the arrangements as a temporary measure and continued to work for the full admission of women to Harvard, even raising funds to present as an endowment to cover costs associated with the adoption of coeducation. But Harvard remained resistant.

By 1890 the Annex had grown to more than 200 students, had acquired Fay House, the building in which my office is located, and required a more regularized structure. In 1893 the Annex offered Harvard its real estate and $150,000 as a lure to merge, but as a Harvard faculty member later wrote, this had small influence. The Annex, he explained, "had nothing to offer Harvard but girls, whom Harvard did not want."

Thus, in 1894, Radcliffe College was born—as a compromise between what women wanted and what Harvard would give them, as an alternative to the two prevailing models of coeducation and separate women's institutions. Radcliffe College would educate women by contracting with individual Harvard faculty to provide instruction, would offer its own diplomas, to be countersigned by Harvard's president, and would be subjected in academic matters to the supervision of "visitors" from Harvard. Elizabeth Agassiz was pleased with this outcome and became Radcliffe's first president, firmly believing that the College over which she presided was a temporary expedient and that women would soon be admitted as full students to Harvard. She would have more than a century to wait.

One of the peculiar results of the arrangements agreed upon in 1894 to establish Radcliffe was that the new college would never have a faculty. Radcliffe was structured as an administrative rather than an academic unit. This also meant that its students were not exposed to female instructors, for the Harvard faculty had no women at all before the arrival of Helen Maud Cam in 1948. By 1919, 100 percent of Barnard's faculty were women; 55 percent of Bryn Mawr's, 80 percent of Vassar's, 82 percent of Wellesley's, 30 percent at coed Swarthmore, and 29 percent at Oberlin. But all of the 185 Harvard instructors who offered courses at Radcliffe that year were male and crossed Garden Street to deliver their lectures in Radcliffe classrooms filled exclusively with women. Ruth Hubbard, an accomplished scientist who graduated from Radcliffe in 1944, remarked on the implications of this dependence upon Harvard faculty for instruction. "From the beginning," she mused, "Radcliffe apparently failed to recognize that, by proudly offering its students the privilege to sit at the feet of Harvard's Great Men, it lost the opportunity to awaken in us the expectation that we might someday be Great Women."

In fact, Ruth Hubbard did become a "Great Woman" and did witness at the end of her undergraduate life the beginnings of a revolution. The outbreak of World War II depleted the numbers of both Harvard students and faculty. To offer separate instruction for women and men seemed wasteful under such circumstances, and so in 1943 Harvard and Radcliffe signed an agreement that brought males and females together in all but a few freshman classes. Radcliffe also ceased making individual arrangements with dozens of Harvard professors, each paid individually for his time teaching women. Harvard's Faculty of Arts and Sciences undertook to supervise course offerings and assign instructors in exchange for approximately four-fifths of Radcliffe's tuition revenue. Originally cast as a war emergency measure, this arrangement was ratified as permanent in 1947. But Harvard was careful not to call this new departure coeducation. It was, instead, "joint instruction." One Harvard official celebrated this distinction in a 1949 interview, noting that the continuation of Harvard's and Radcliffe's separate extracurricular activities, separate living arrangements, and separate administrative structures meant that men and women would be spared, as he put it, "each other's oppressive continuous presence."

Nevertheless, the changes in the place of women during the war years at Harvard were profound, reflecting in part women's altered role in American society during a time of mass mobilization and world upheaval. But popular wisdom at Harvard offered a different explanation. In 1949, just a year after his graduation from the College, Anthony Lewis, whom you know as one of the *New York Times*'s most distinguished columnists, wrote a piece about women at Harvard. Change, he explained, had been aided by a transformation in the girls themselves. Before the war, he noted, one frequently heard the saying, "Is she a Radcliffe girl, or did a horse step on her face?" By the late 1940s, he observed, "everyone agrees that Radcliffe girls are prettier than they used to be. This has an effect on Harvard's attitude." Such perceptions were both widely shared and long-lived. In 1962, a Harvard faculty member remarked in similar terms upon the improvement at Radcliffe. "When I first came to Cambridge [as an undergraduate]," he remembered, "there were four certifiably good looking girls at Radcliffe. By the time I had graduated from College there were nine. By the time I had finished graduate school there were seventeen and the number had started to increase geometrically."

But Harvard remained averse to coeducation, even as more and more of student life became merged in the postwar years. While this opened many new opportunities for Radcliffe students, it also undermined many independent women's activities. As women joined the *Crimson* and the Harvard yearbook staff, Radcliffe's publications weakened or disappeared. And many central aspects of Harvard undergraduate life still remained closed to women. Radcliffe students were not part of the Harvard House system. They lived in dorms, without common rooms, without resident tutors, without faculty regularly present at meals. Unlike Harvard students, they were required to wait tables in the dining halls; they were governed by dress codes that mandated skirts for most of daily life. They were not permitted in morning chapel in Memorial Church; they could not study at [the undergraduate library] Lamont—because, the head librarian explained, echoing Charles W. Eliot's worries of the late nineteenth century, there were too many dark corridors and alcoves to police. Women would not be permitted in Lamont regularly until 1967.

A member of the Class of 1952 reflected on these postwar days at the time of her thirty-fifth reunion. "I am increasingly aware now of what we as women were deprived of then—of what we couldn't join or do or go to. We were intelligent, amusing, decorative second-class citizens, educated for lives as wives, teachers, and secretaries, but rarely for careers of our own choice. It is astonishing how accepting we were." It was much as Virginia Woolf had described the Oxbridge of a generation earlier: "Partridge for the men; prunes and custard for the women."

But the acceptance and complacency of the 1950s would prove short-lived. In 1960 a new president came to Radcliffe, the first woman president of the postwar era, Mary Bunting, a scientist and a former dean of Douglass College at Rutgers University. Bunting was filled with plans and energy, decrying in her first meeting with the Radcliffe board of trustees the waste of educated women in a society that did not honor and make use of their accomplishments. Bunting identified a "climate of unexpectation" for women that led her to found the Radcliffe Institute for Independent Study for postgraduate women—the real forerunner of the Institute that exists today. Throughout her tenure, she struggled as well for greater opportunities for women in undergraduate life. Bunting endeavored to establish a Radcliffe counterpart of the House system, though architectural realities and limited funds inhibited its emergence. Nevertheless, Currier House, the first structure erected specifically as a Radcliffe House, opened in 1970 as one outcome of her efforts.

Bunting's desire to ensure that Radcliffe's women had an educational experience equal to that of Harvard's men contributed to a number of significant changes during her term. Emerging consciousness about women's issues nationwide and growing pressure for coeducation at schools—such as Yale and Princeton—that Harvard did regard as its peers contributed to the power of demands for change. In 1963 women students for the first time received Harvard diplomas, and by 1970 Harvard and Radcliffe had joined their commencement ceremonies. The same year saw an experiment in coresidence with an exchange between the river Houses and the Quad; by 1972, living became completely integrated as women moved into the freshman dorms in the Yard. A Harvard alumnus of the class of 1933 greeted this innovation with the declaration that Harvard had torn "down the scheme set up by the civilized to govern the relations between the sexes. . . . Civilization is dead."

Despite vocal opposition from many Radcliffe as well as Harvard alums, by the late 1960s Bunting had come to feel that the merger of the two institutions should and could be accomplished. Bunting and Harvard president Nathan Pusey optimistically undertook a series of discussions, but she would not realize her goal. Radcliffe's trustees insisted upon a slowing of the movement toward consolidation of the two institutions, and Radcliffe's alumnae voiced their concern that an irrevocable merger might leave Radcliffe without the flexibility to respond to rapidly changing notions about the place of women in higher education. Was the sweeping national movement toward coeducation perhaps just a passing trend? In 1971 these reservations yielded the curious set of arrangements that came to be known as the "nonmerger merger," an agreement between Harvard and Radcliffe that placed women's residential life under Harvard's direction, Radcliffe's employees subject to Harvard's personnel administration, and most of Radcliffe's income under Harvard's control.

Significantly, the task force President Pusey had appointed to advise him about the merger also submitted recommendations that extended beyond the question of Radcliffe to address the larger place of women in the university. The report called for the "full and equal participation in the intellectual and social life of the University by women in roles other than as students—as faculty members, as alumnae, and as members of the Governing Boards." In 1970, there were no tenured women in the Faculty of Arts and Sciences; by 1975, there were nine. In 1971 the Faculty of Arts and Sciences created a committee to report on the status of women. The woman question at Harvard was becoming more than just about Radcliffe. Faculty hiring lay entirely outside Radcliffe's purview, as did curricular questions, which attracted increasing attention as other colleges and universities began to offer courses in women's studies. A 1974 survey of the Harvard course catalog revealed that only four courses in more than 650 pages of course offerings were described as relating to women. A 1975 poll of chairs of 14 departments about the possibility of including women's studies in their offerings prompted one faculty member to respond that his department did not offer any relevant courses—but also had no classes dedicated to the study of "cannibals, children, or veterans of foreign wars." Eleven years later, the faculty would at last establish the Committee on Degrees in Women's Studies, permitting students to select women's studies as a field of concentration.

Growing sentiment in favor of the equality of women had a direct impact on Harvard and Radcliffe throughout the 1970s. Some of these effects occurred in response to national imperatives such as the passage of Title IX and the consequent revolution in women's sports everywhere. For Radcliffe students, Title IX meant an almost complete transformation of athletic opportunities, including access to Harvard gyms and playing fields, professional coaching, and a far more competitive atmosphere for varsity sports. Equality had other implications as well. Radcliffe's size had been limited by an agreement between the two institutions, so that the ratio of undergraduates at the beginning of the 1970s was approximately four men for every woman student. This meant that it was in fact much more difficult to get into Radcliffe than into Harvard. In the late 1950s, Harvard was accepting more than 40 percent of its applicants, while Radcliffe took only 18 percent. The deans' lists reflected this differential, with the proportion of Radcliffe students qualifying in the early years of the 1960s nearly half again as large as the proportion of Harvard undergraduates. President Derek Bok, who replaced Nathan Pusey, and president Matina Horner, who succeeded Mary Bunting in the early 1970s, recognized that these quotas for women represented a form of discrimination and contributed to a student environment in which men predominated by sheer force of numbers. In 1972 Bok determined that the ratio should be changed to 2.5 men to each woman, and in 1975 Harvard and Radcliffe admissions merged and adopted an equal access policy for all applicants regardless of gender.

By the end of the 1970s, Radcliffe had ceded to Harvard every formal responsibility for undergraduate life. The Radcliffe name was still on the letter of admission for women students, and the president of Radcliffe countersigned women's diplomas. But most women undergraduates proudly described themselves as Harvard students—embracing the identity that

Elizabeth Agassiz, Mary Bunting, and many others had so long struggled to make possible.

Radcliffe College began to redirect its efforts toward postgraduate and research endeavors dealing with questions related to women. The Schlesinger Library, established in 1943, found new prominence as the growing field of women's history made its extraordinary manuscript and book collections a treasured resource. The Murray Research Center, an archive of longitudinal social science studies, was founded in 1976 and has also become a highly valued collection for students and scholars. The fellowship program Mary Bunting established in 1960 to fight the climate of "unexpectation" for women has produced an extraordinary array of scholars and artists— including poets Adrienne Rich and Anne Sexton, dramatist Anna Deavere Smith, novelist Alice Walker, and historians Linda Gordon and Caroline Bynum. But Radcliffe still called itself a college, and its administrators, trustees, and alumnae worried that, without Radcliffe's oversight and support, women students would not be adequately cared for at Harvard. Radcliffe thus continued to offer an array of services and programs for undergraduates. Students who gathered in Radcliffe's Lyman Common Room or who received summer traveling fellowships or joined together in the Science Alliance or drew strength from the Mentor Program or became advocates for women through involvement with the Radcliffe Union of Students developed deep loyalties to Radcliffe College. But many women undergraduates of the 1980s and early 1990s had no connection with Radcliffe at all, and even feared that such an identity would somehow brand them as second-class citizens.

By the late 1990s, however, the anomaly of a college that bore almost no responsibility for the day-to-day operations of undergraduate life led to another consideration of merger. This time, nearly 30 years after the "nonmerger merger," Harvard and Radcliffe would finally join, in many ways ratifying the *fait accompli* of integration of men and women in the student body and the emerging emphasis at Radcliffe on postdoctoral research. The merger agreement of 1999 ended Radcliffe's existence as a separate, independent corporation and established it as one of ten Harvard schools, led by a dean who participates fully with deans of the other faculties in the governance of the university. Radcliffe is now fully inside Harvard's gates. The merger agreement also specified that all responsibility for the lives of women undergraduates would now rest with Harvard College. Neil Rudenstine, the Harvard president who negotiated the merger with the Radcliffe board of trustees, proclaimed Harvard's "full commitment to women" and its dedication to "making sure undergraduate education is excellent both for women and men." Radcliffe, in turn, would become an Institute for Advanced Study, a place where individuals pursue learning at its outermost limits, creating new knowledge in every field from poetry to string physics. And the Institute, in recognition of Radcliffe's past, would maintain a special commitment to the study of women, gender, and society.

What does all this history that I have recounted mean for you as you set forth on your Harvard career? Why do I think it matters that you know about Radcliffe's past and about the history of women at Harvard? I want you to think of yourselves as pioneers, adventurers at the beginning of a time of transformation, members of just the second class in which women and men received the same letter of admission. You enter an institution that has made a commitment to the equality of all members of the community, regardless of gender; this is a university that has articulated its dedication to the success of every student, male or female. But I invoke the past today to remind you that such commitments are not deeply rooted in Harvard's history, that they require a transformation rather than an extension of tradition, and that such transformation requires work and attentiveness. An institution that less than a century ago defined itself as an incubator for virility is still working out how fully to incorporate women.

Linda Greenhouse, class of 1968, now the *New York Times*'s Supreme Court reporter, commented on women's experience at Harvard when she was a student here more than three decades ago. "The basic fact of our existence within the Harvard community was that we were not the norm. We were the deviation from the norm." In her day, with the 4:1 male to female ratio, that was literally as well as figuratively true. But I would suggest to you that Harvard is still in transition to a state in which men are not the norm, a norm that has been defined in no small part by the weight of Harvard tradition and expectation and culture as well as by the realities of Harvard life today. I am the only woman among Harvard's ten deans.[1] That certainly makes me some kind of deviation from the norm. Undergraduate women's numbers are at last almost equal to those of the men—women comprise 48 percent of this year's entering class. But the faculty that will teach you still has only 17 percent women among its tenured ranks. All of this is happily changing: 46 percent of new tenured appointments to the faculty in Arts and Sciences this year are women. And remember that as recently as 1970 women constituted zero percent of the tenured faculty. Both history and present-day reality define Harvard as a work in progress on the gender question.

This means we have extraordinary opportunities and responsibilities. As dean of Radcliffe, I can see myriad ways in which the Institute can make a difference for women and thus for all of us at Harvard. We can help increase the numbers of women faculty, the quality of their experience, the excellence and importance of gender studies at the university, and the richness of undergraduate intellectual life as well.

But you too must take advantage of this extraordinary moment at Harvard—must as both women and men affirm your equal right to be the norm, to define Harvard as being a woman's as much as a man's space. To do that, I believe you must understand not only the Harvard world you see most immediately before you but also the history that has produced it. When you hear—in this most wonderfully tradition-bound institution—that something is because it has always been that way, take a moment to ask which of the past's assumptions are embedded in that particular tradition. If men and women are to be truly equal at Harvard, all traditions cannot be viewed as equal.

Women and men have both been at this university from the time it was founded. As women and men together at last in a truly coeducational institution, you all reap the benefits of the struggles of those—from Sarah Pellet to Elizabeth Agassiz to Mary Bunting to Neil Rudenstine—who worked to make a Harvard education fully available to both sexes. Celebrate what they accomplished and fulfill their aspirations by claiming Harvard as at last truly the property of men and women alike.

Editor's note: Things sometimes change rapidly. Ellen Condliffe Lagemann became dean of the School of Education in 2002 and Elena Kagan became dean of the Harvard Law School in July 2003.

Notes on Contributors

LINZY BREKKE is a graduate student in history at Harvard University.

GLORIA BRUCE has an undergraduate degree in history from Harvard and is currently working at the World Resources Institute.

DREW GILPIN FAUST is dean of the Radcliffe Institute for Advanced Study.

YAËL SIMPSON FLETCHER is a visiting assistant professor at the University of the South.

LINDA GREENHOUSE, a graduate of Radcliffe College, is the Supreme Court correspondent for the *New York Times*.

MARIE HICKS is currently pursuing a Ph.D. in history at Duke University.

KRISTIN HOGANSON is an associate professor of history at the University of Illinois, Urbana-Champaign.

HELEN LEFKOWITZ HOROWITZ is Sylvia Dlugasch Bauman Professor in American Studies at Smith College.

RUTH HUBBARD is a professor *emerita* of biology at Harvard University, the first woman in that department to be awarded a professorship.

ANN KARNOVSKY, a Radcliffe alumna, is a child psychologist.

PHYLLIS KELLER was the associate dean for academic affairs of Harvard's Faculty of Arts and Sciences from the 1970s to the 1990s.

JANE KNOWLES is the archivist at the Schlesinger Library of the Radcliffe Institute for Advanced Study.

KAREN LEPRI is currently working toward a master's in education at the University of Massachusetts of Boston to become a high school history and creative writing teacher.

FRANCES HERMAN LORD received her Ph.D. from the University of New Hampshire and is an independent scholar.

ANDREW K. MANDEL is currently the director of curriculum development for Teach for America and is pursuing his master's degree at the Harvard Graduate School of Education.

ROBIN MCELHENY is associate archivist for programs at the Harvard University Archives.

MARGOT MINARDI is a graduate student in the Department of History at Harvard University.

EVA S. MOSELEY, a Radcliffe alumna, retired several years ago after 27 years as the Johanna-Maria Fraenkel Curator of Manuscripts at the Schlesinger Library.

BEVERLY WILSON PALMER is director of the Writing Center and editor of the Lucretia Coffin Mott Papers Project at Pomona College.

KATHARINE PARK is the Samuel Zemurray, Jr., and Doris Zemurray Stone-Radcliffe Professor of the History of Science and of Women's Studies.

JO ANNE PRESTON is assistant professor of sociology at Brandeis University.

SALLY SCHWAGER is lecturer on education at the Harvard Graduate School of Education.

ANN SHAPIRO is Distinguished Professor of English at the State University of New York at Farmingdale.

JENNIFER STETZER has an undergraduate degree in history from Harvard and currently teaches middle school history and English in New Haven, Conn.

BRIAN SULLIVAN is the senior reference archivist at the Harvard University Library.

MARCIA G. SYNNOTT is a professor of history at the University of South Carolina.

LAUREL THATCHER ULRICH is James Duncan Phillips Professor of Early American History at Harvard University.

HELEN VENDLER is A. Kingsley Porter University Professor of English at Harvard University.

CONRAD EDICK WRIGHT is Ford Editor of Publications at the Massachusetts Historical Society.

Index